BADAL SIRCAR

BADAL SIRCAR

TOWARDS A THEATRE OF CONSCIENCE

ANJUM
KATYAL

SAGE www.sagepublications.com
Los Angeles • London • New Delhi • Singapore • Washington DC

First published in 2015 by

SAGE Publications India Pvt Ltd
B1/I-1 Mohan Cooperative Industrial Area
Mathura Road, New Delhi 110 044, India
www.sagepub.in

SAGE Publications Inc
2455 Teller Road
Thousand Oaks, California 91320, USA

SAGE Publications Ltd
1 Oliver's Yard, 55 City Road
London EC1Y 1SP, United Kingdom

SAGE Publications Asia-Pacific Pte Ltd
3 Church Street
#10-04 Samsung Hub
Singapore 049483

Published by Vivek Mehra for SAGE Publications India Pvt Ltd, typeset in 11/13.5 pts Minion by Diligent Typesetter, Delhi, and printed at Sai Print-o-Pack, New Delhi.

Library of Congress Cataloging-in-Publication Data

Katyal, Anjum.
Badal Sircar : towards a theatre of conscience / by Anjum Katyal.
pages cm
Includes bibliographical references and index.
1. Sarkar, Badal—Criticism and interpretation. 2. Theatre—India. 3. Experimental theatre—India. I. Title.
PN2888.S197K38 891.4'4271—dc23 2015 2015026694

ISBN: 978-93-515-0370-5 (HB)

The SAGE Team: Shambhu Sahu, Sanghamitra Patowary, Nand Kumar Jha and Ritu Chopra

To my mother, Uma. For setting standards.
And for always being there.

CONTENTS

FOREWORD

A few days back, the author of this book, Anjum Katyal, asked me to write a few lines about her book on Badal-*da*. When I browsed through her rigorous effort in the form of *Towards a Theatre of Conscience*, my first reaction was, 'Badal-da deserved this during his lifetime!' Anjum's book is not only well researched in terms of immaculate footnotes and authentic chronology of events, but also has in-depth analyses of Badal-da's vital plays. She has also added varied quotes from almost all significant *natakwalla*s (theatrefolk), supporting her succinct observations. All this gives a holistic perspective of Indian theatre, and not just Bangla theatre, spread through four decades, from the 1960s to 1990s. The interjections from Badal-da's *Purano Kasundi*, his memoirs, made me feel as if Badal-da himself was conversing on that point. This book is going to be providential to the younger generations as it recreates the ambience of Badal-da's long creative journey. If not the man himself, who inspired me and my generation, this book will inspire the tenderfeet.

In the following paragraph, I wish to highlight Badal-da's stupendous contribution to the experimental Marathi theatre movement in the 1970s and 1980s, to which the world outside of Marathi theatre might be oblivious. We, the natakwallas of my generation, owe so much to Badal-da that I feel fulfilled to be a part of this splendid treatise.

In 1966, the Government of Maharashtra convened a committee to seek solutions to infrastructural and urban redevelopment issues of Bombay (as it was called then). The central government deputed Badal Sircar to this committee as a 'town planning expert'. The area of New Mumbai was developed as a result of this committee. During that time, Badal-da used to visit Mumbai very often. At the end of the day and of his official role, his feet automatically walked in the direction of natakawallas! On one such evening, Satyadev Dubey introduced me to Badal-da as the translator of his play *Ballabhpurer Rupkatha* into Marathi. I had co-directed the said play with Dubey. This was the very first production of a Marathi play by the Theatre Unit (a group headed by Dubey). I had also performed the lead role. Though at that time Badal-da was casual towards my triple role vis-à-vis *Vallabhpurchi Dantakatha*, later he developed a tremendous affection for and attachment to me.

Then Rajabhau Natu of Maharashtra Kalopasak (a leading Pune-based theatre group) invited Badal-da to meet theatre practitioners from Pune. I escorted Badal-da from Mumbai to Pune. This voyage, which started then with countless puffs of cigarettes, was to continue for the next 35 years, long after I quit smoking! Mumbai, Pune, Kolkata, Delhi—our meeting places kept on changing but our bond remained insoluble. People surrounding both of us went on changing, our lives also changed a lot, but our mutual love remained untouched. I kept on meeting him with or without any purpose!

After *Vallabhpur*, the Theatre Unit decided that I should translate Badal-da's new play *Pagla Ghora* and direct it in Hindi and Marathi simultaneously. I sought Badal-da's written permission and also expressed my desire to deviate from the realistic set design conceived by him while writing the play. Badal-da pounced on me saying, 'Why ask for my permission to alter anything in the play? Whatever you wish to change, please do so!' When I tried to convince him of my different interpretation, he added, 'Whatever I had to write, I've done so. Now you are free to murder my play!' He added, with a twinkle in his eyes, 'However I reserve my right to declare publicly that you've murdered my play.'

I directed *Pagla Ghora* in Hindi and Marathi in 1968, then again in Marathi in 1980, and once again in 2009 in Bengali. These three productions were completely different from each other. The play offered me immense scope for different interpretations, rare for most plays. Badal-da's writing was so powerful and layered that it had the strength to convey the theme even through different theatrical styles. Badal-da liked my interpretations, specially the one in which the central character of the girl was performed by six different actresses. He also commended my editing of his text, which brought down the performance time from two and a half hours to 90 minutes. While patting me on my shoulder, he said, 'A few years ago, I managed to cut it to 105 minutes. Further editing is an achievement on your part!' I haven't come across any other playwright who was so genuinely appreciative of the director's versions. Most hesitate to let the director change even punctuation, let alone appreciating different interpretations. Badal-da was one of a kind indeed!

> I want to write about people of this soil but I know nothing about the farmers. I have no clue about the pain of the fishermen and toilers. Besides, what kind of dramatic moments can possibly be offered in my middle class urban life? What can happen in my mundane routine that is new?

These questions were powerfully raised in his *Evam Indrajit*, written in the 1960s. Along with many of my contemporaries, I was truly motivated by this brilliant play. Ironically, someone who perceived life as never-crossing parallel railway tracks, drastically kept crossing the never-ending paths vanishing into the horizon! The poetics of his writing was so different and so lacking in his real life, that one always wondered how and from where he got such inspiration about rebellion and toil? His scripts offered a fresh impetus for contemplation every time one read them.

In the 1970s, Badal-da had quit the city-based theatre scenario of Kolkata and begun to explore avenues outside of the proscenium arch. During the Emergency, his theatre took a novel turn. A totally unconventional form was evolved through his *Juloos* and *Tisvi Shatabdi* which didn't necessitate sets, lights or a stage. His *Basi Khabar* and *Bhoma* highlighted his anti-establishment stand, though he was never active in party politics. The vivid memory of Badal-da himself performing with his Satabdi colleagues in Curzon Park on a Sunday morning during the early Emergency days is still etched in my memory. I was wondering at how the din of the trams and heavy vehicles had receded miraculously as the performance began, sans the glamour of costumes, lights and music; just then a posse of mounted policemen surrounded us on their tall horses. To my utter surprise, neither the performers nor anyone from the audience paid any attention to that force, and they left after a while. This stirring experience inspired me and the Mumbai-based troupe Bahuroopee to perform *Juloos* as our small protest against the Emergency. We performed the play over 200 times in every possible nook and corner of Mumbai as well as all over Maharashtra! Badal-da had started performing his plays in the rural areas of West Bengal. There was an underlying thematic similarity between his earlier plays and these low cost productions, that is, protest against the suffocation of the educated middle class, and his firm faith that 'surviving enables everything'. With his shift to the rural audience, Badal-da conceptualised and also realised his dream of the 'Third Theatre'. He believed that a distinct form should be created beyond the 'First Theatre' that was traditional folk art, and the 'Second Theatre' that represented urban theatre with a Western influence. In this journey, Badal-da got estranged from most of the mainstream theatre practitioners. The critics also distanced themselves from his complex plays. Despite this ostracism, Badal-da continued his search for a variant expression.

In 2004, I heard that Badal-da was admitted to a nursing home as he had met with an accident. When I called my local friends to verify the news, none of them knew about it. 'He has become a recluse', 'Now he is absent from the theatre world' and more such comments were forthcoming from the Bengali theatre fraternity. I must say that I felt disturbed by these insensitive remarks. Next day, I just landed up at Badal-da's house. His eyes welled up to learn that I had come to Kolkata for no other purpose than to be with him. He was bedridden; he admitted that he could not afford a round-the-clock nurse. In addition to his physical ailments, psychologically he was at his lowest. He felt neglected by his contemporaries. Though my body was with him that whole day, I was thinking of a solution to pull him back into life. How could I help him without hurting his esteem and pride? I thought of organising a Badal Sircar Festival in Pune as a retrospective of his stupendous contribution to Indian theatre. All the theatre stalwarts, such as Dubey, Shyamanand Jalan, Pratibha Agarwal, Vijay Tendulkar, Amrish Puri, Rajinder Nath, Kulbhushan Kharbanda, Naseeruddin and Ratna Pathak Shah, Mahesh Elkunchwar, Nilu Phule, Rohini and Jaidev Hattangadi, Nana Patekar and many others participated in the festival. On the concluding day, once again I did *Juloos* with newcomers from various colleges of Pune. Badal-da's interview for almost half a day proved to be the centre of attraction. On behalf of the entire theatre world, we handed over a significant amount to Badal-da as his 80th birthday gift, which he could not refuse.

Overwhelmed by the genuine love of the audience he experienced in Pune, Badal-da expressed his gratitude in one line: 'Your love is going to keep me alive for at least the next 20 years.' Though he didn't live for those many years, he certainly was rejuvenated. He translated a few books, he finished writing a play based on the sex workers of Sonagachi, he also thought of performing it with those workers themselves.

He is no more with us now, but his incessant quest for life will always inspire me; his magical words will continue to haunt me:

Though I don't see the end of this road,
Though Heaven is not assured at that end,
Nor a promise offered
To make me forget these aching feet,
Why does this voyage NOT seem without a purpose?

Amol Palekar
Pune, May 2015

ACKNOWLEDGEMENTS

This book has had many helping hands along the way. My gratitude is due to the following:

Bharati Chatterjee, Badal-da's daughter, for her quiet support and facilitation at several levels; photographer Avik Chatterjee, his grandson, for so generously permitting access to his photographs; Third Theatre veterans Sumit Biswas of Pathasena, Kalyan Ghosh and the Satabdi group for their time, cooperation and generosity with materials and photographs; Malini Mukherjee and Anshuman Das likewise; Bisakha (Meera) Ray for taking the time out of a busy schedule for an invaluable discussion.

Amol Palekar for so unhesitatingly agreeing to contribute the Foreword, in memory of the inspirational figure Badal-da was to his generation; Naveen Kishore and Seagull for replying promptly and helpfully to all requests; Sibaji Bandyopadhyay for his thought-provoking insights and for gifting me essential reading material; Pratibha Agarwal and Natya Shodh Sansthan for being the source of important research material and photographs; Shanta Gokhale, Rustom Bharucha, Sudhanva Deshpande, Sumanta Banerjee and Samik Bandyopadhyay for sharing their time and thoughts with me; similarly, theatre directors Probir Guha, Heisnam Kanhailal, Tripurari Sharma, Madeeha Gauhar, Mangai, Mohammed Waseem, Santanu Bose and Abanti Chakravarty; Lakshmi Subramanyam for sending me useful reference material; Bangladesh activists Nishat Jahan Rana and Mahmood Hasan for their warm and useful responses; Arundhati Ray for uncomplainingly sacrificing hours to help me with the translation; her parents Piyali and Arabinda Ray for contributing their expertise and knowledge; my friends Lali De and Kalyani Patranobis for being on call for urgent queries; Rajasri Mukhopadhyay for her help in deciphering a challenging text; Kavita Panjabi for patiently participating in endless discussions on the work in progress and her invariably helpful comments; Gulan Kripalani for her feedback; and Agniv Ghosh for his key research assistance.

And finally, I would like to thank my daughter Diya for putting up with the stress I had exuded as I struggled to find time to complete this book, with not much more than a frequent rolling of her eyes.

INTRODUCTION

Badal Sircar, playwright, actor and director, died at his north Calcutta residence on Friday evening. He was 86 and had been suffering from prostate cancer and chronic lung disease. He was awarded a Padma Shri in 1972 and offered a Padma Bhushan in 2010, which he declined. His body has been donated.

— *The Telegraph*, 14 May 2011

I remember staring at this brief notice tucked into a corner of a newspaper page that screamed momentous headlines at me.[1] Alongside was a thumbnail portrait of Badal-da (as he was widely known in the theatre world), the face deeply familiar. I remember thinking, 'So, he's gone.' To me, the notice was a masterpiece of terse understatement which nonetheless spoke volumes about the person he was. Someone who was offered one of the highest state honours in the land, the Padma Bhushan, which he refused because it would compromise his beliefs. Someone who chose to donate his body to scientific research. Remaining an iconoclast to the end, denying normative cultural and religious practice, quietly preferring to exercise a more scientific (and philanthropic) choice. That he chose to do this with his body seemed poignantly symbolic, given the significance of the body in his theatre.

This is someone who never sought the limelight, who turned his back on the mainstream theatre stage and who spent his last years far from the glitter of media attention; and yet ironically, Badal Sircar is, to my mind, the single most influential figure in the extensive and diverse field of contemporary Indian theatre. This may seem like a tall claim, but it is one I am prepared to uphold. Can one think of any other individual in the 1960s, 1970s and 1980s who had a more pervasive impact on theatre thinkers and

[1] This was also the date on which the West Bengal state election results were announced. After decades, the ensconced left front government lost massively to the rampant Trinamool. Much has been made of this serendipitous occurrence by various commentators.

workers—directors, playwrights, actors—across the Indian subcontinent? From Manipur to Kerala, Kashmir to Tamil Nadu, from Maharashtra to Pakistan and his native Bengal, there is scarcely a corner of theatre activity that has not been influenced by Badal-da one way or another. Some have been impacted by his workshop practice, others by his ideas of a free, non-proscenium theatre, yet others by his play scripts. This is not to claim a straightforward acceptance of his theory and practice in all instances, but to recognise that alongside critical appraisal there runs a widespread acknowledgement of this influence.

It is rare to find a single individual who is widely performed as a playwright; whose theories of form and approach still find their way into current practice; who as a pedagogue has influenced myriad theatre workers through his workshops. This volume sets out to study, analyse and document this unique legacy.

Badal-da first gained a reputation in the theatre fraternity as a playwright. His *Ebong Indrajit* (And Indrajit, 1963)[2] seemed to capture an existential angst, a quest for meaning, which spoke for an entire generation. Badal-da's other plays, such as *Baki Itihas* (The Other History, 1965) and *Pagla Ghora* (Wild Horse, 1967), also received critical appreciation and attention in theatre circles, and were produced by leading directors and theatre groups. He was considered one of the new 'modern' playwrights in the country to watch out for, experimental in terms of form, structure and registers of language, contemporary in subject matter.

However, by the early 1970s, he was already moving away from proscenium theatre and the entire economy on which this theatre was premised. He coined the term 'Third Theatre' to distinguish this form from both the traditional, popular, folk forms of theatre that he termed First Theatre, and the urban, Westernised proscenium model that he called Second Theatre. His Third Theatre was based on the centrality of the actor, and on the human connection both between actors and between them and the audience. He wrote several essays on his philosophy of the Third Theatre and lectured widely on the subject. He soon began to prefer the term 'Free Theatre' to describe it, explaining that it was free because the public has free access to

[2] First accessible to the public in 1965, published in the July 1965 issue of the journal *Bohurupee* and produced by theatre group Souvanik.

the performance; because productions can travel freely to the people, using any available venue and, thus, staking the claim that any space can be turned into a performance space; and because the actor is freed from certain restrictions inherent to proscenium theatre and can approach the audience freely.

Badal Sircar travelled across the subcontinent through the 1970s, 1980s and 1990s, holding workshops at different places, including Pakistan and Bangladesh. The outcome is a wide range of people in India who have been influenced to a greater or lesser extent into adopting the principles of his kind of theatre. His impact on the alternative, activist theatre circuit in neighbouring Pakistan and Bangladesh is also significant. No other Indian theatre personality has had quite the same effect.

His was theatre as anti-establishment counterculture, challenging normative middle-class mores and complacency, an attempt at conscientisation and awareness-raising, protest and political comment. It drew on the daily reality of the common man, the entire gamut of oppression, corruption, injustice, power politics, struggle, disillusionment, despairing hope, battered idealism and confused questioning that all of us experience as we grapple with the everyday. Badal-da used evocative motifs to communicate his ideas—the young man who gets killed over and over again in *Michhil* (Procession, 1974), the walking dead man in *Basi Khabar* (Stale News, 1978). Badal Sircar strove for the ideal of a truly democratic space for theatre—a non-commercial space where human beings could meet voluntarily as equals. He said,

> When afterwards we spread our cloth for contributions, they don't have to pay. If they do pay, it is neither a gift nor a price—it is participation, in some way. They are indicating that they liked what they saw, that they want this kind of theatre to go on. *That* is a human relationship.[3]

In the long decades between his embracing non-proscenium, non-commercial theatre and his death as an ailing 86-year-old, he never quite gave up his involvement with the theatre. Till the end, he remained curious, interested and open to learning. I remember meeting him in 2009. By then, his movements were restricted, and he was almost completely confined to his room in his house in north Kolkata. We spoke of several things, but what came through clearly was his deep passion for and commitment to the theatre path he had chosen to walk for the past 40 odd years.

[3] Quoted in Anjum Katyal, 'Distance, Access, Control: The Philosophy of Space in Badal Sircar' in Anmol Vellani (ed.), *Beyond the Proscenium: Reimagining the Space for Performance* (Bangalore: IFA Theatre Infrastructure Cell, 2010), pp. 139–50.

Badal-da has passed away, but his legacy lives on. The leading personalities of Indian theatre acknowledge their debt to him. Girish Karnad, playwright, director and actor, has said that Badal-da's path-breaking play *Ebong Indrajit* taught him about fluidity of structure. To veteran actor and director Amol Palekar, Badal-da was a great inspiration for his entire generation. For Manipuri director Heisnam Kanhailal, respected throughout the country for his distinctive dramaturgy, it was a workshop by Badal-da that set him on the path towards his own unique theatre style. Even someone like Naseeruddin Shah, who comes from an entirely different school of theatre, has said, 'My theatre is also moving towards Sircar's theatre.'[4]

Nor is it just his own contemporaries who found meaning in his plays. Interestingly, succeeding generations have continued to turn to Badal-da's texts. *Michhil* is a favourite with college and youth groups, *Pagla Ghora, Sara Rattir* (All Night Long, 1963) and *Baki Itihas* often appear on stage in different languages, while *Hattamalar Oparey* (Beyond the Land of Hattamala, 1977) is still popular fare, especially as children's theatre. A cursory search on the internet will yield some of Badal Sircar plays being performed somewhere in the country.

This study of Badal-da's theatre must be seen in context. Theatre studies in India, particularly of the twentieth century and after, have to grapple with certain challenges. First, documentation is inadequate, although this is changing as digital technology renders instant and ongoing recording, shooting and storage easy and, above all, affordable. The twentieth century and earlier, however, suffered from a paucity of documentation—visual, audiovisual or textual—for a variety of reasons, including financial ones. This is true of all the art forms in India and the performing arts, especially.

Moreover, like dance and music, since theatre happens in time and space, a production can never really be replicated. Documentation of a production is intrinsically a problematic proposition: how does one capture the totality of the experience even with the most expensive and elaborate camera set-ups? With a 'moving camera', one cannot avoid editing, which means that it is always somebody's version—a reading, an interpretation—that you receive.

[4] Deepika Arwind (22 May 2011) Tribute/A life on the Fringes, *The Hindu*. Retrieved from http://www.hindu.com/mag/2011/05/22/stories/2011052250130200.htm (accessed 18 April 2014).

So, one accepts that it cannot be 'objective' documentation. Still photographs can help string together sequences but cannot capture fluidity of movement or action. The script is just a skeleton; a production goes way beyond the playscript. So, where does one turn for 'authentic' documentation? To viewer accounts? Actor testimonies? Director's notes? Critics' reviews? I would say—one turns to all of these. And this is just for a conventional play, on a proscenium stage. If we consider site-specific work, or street theatre, or performance texts which communicate nonverbally, or plays that improvise rather than follow a script, it gets much more complicated.

Also, theatre is about more far more than the end result, a production. It is as much about process: rehearsal, actor preparation, dramaturgy, discussion, training and workshops. How does one document something as ongoing, multi-faceted and nuanced as that? Firsthand accounts? Observations and notes? Journals and diaries? Practitioners' notebooks and jottings? Photographs, video documentation? Again, I would say, all of these. To further problematise the issue, Rustom Bharucha notes:

> The life of any theatre extends beyond what one sees on stage. Social and personal relationships, economic problems, sexuality, politics, struggles within a group, dreams and disillusionment, all these factors (and many more) contribute to the making of theatre. Unfortunately, most writers never address this messy backstage of theatre life.[5]

And yet this 'messy backstage of theatre life' is not irrelevant or trivial; it has a major impact on the theatre that emerges from it.

So, for a scholar of theatre interested in doing a book on a theatre artist or movement, research methodology can quite justifiably be compared to detective work—piecing together clues, locating reliable sources, arranging fragments of information into coherent patterns, drawing conclusions based on a variety of data, reading between the lines and interpreting diverse voices, balancing different inputs in an attempt at impartiality.

Accordingly, this book too weaves together a broad spectrum of material: Badal-da's own writings, both autobiographical and theoretical; his play texts; a wide range of others' writings on him, from journalists to scholars to theatre critics; footage of productions; interviews and conversations with audience members, workshop participants and theatre persons. A conscious choice has been to substantially incorporate criticism which is

[5] Rustom Bharucha, *The Theatre of Kanhailal: Pebet and Memoirs of Africa* (Calcutta: Seagull Books, 1998), p. 11.

not easily accessible, for the benefit of future scholars. The aim is to create a comprehensive account of his theatre-making, tracing its trajectory with the major influences, shifts and changes of direction.

At different points of time, Badal-da has held different views. Even his formulation of Third Theatre altered over time. He began with theorising it as a synthesis of the rural and the urban, and then changed his mind about the synthesis aspect; the idea of it being a 'free' theatre also grew gradually—at first, this was not part of the philosophy. Again, some decades into his Third Theatre, he began to reintroduce the playwright's text which he had rejected in the first flush of his collective theatre-making phase. Towards the end of his life, he was enthused by the play reading or 'audio play' format, which seems to totally negate the actor's body on which he had premised his non-proscenium theatre, and returns once again to the written play text. This study tracks these developments and twists along the long road of his journey in theatre.

In terms of structure, the book follows a narrative of development from Badal-da's early years to the crystallisation of his Third Theatre. From his introduction to theatre, to major influences on his thinking, to milestones along the way including major plays, a chronological approach seeks to identify the various stages of his 'voyage in theatre'.[6] Chapters 1 to 11 deal with this trajectory, as well as the three major aspects of his oeuvre which are his playwriting, his philosophy and practice of the new theatre form commonly referred to as Third Theatre, and his training and empowerment workshops and outreach activity. Chapters 12 and 13 investigate two significant aspects of his theatre—politics and gender. Chapter 14 looks at the slow fade-out of his final decades and tries to understand it in light of his earlier work.

My conclusion at the end of this journey of exploration and documentation is that Badal-da's theatre began and ended as a theatre by, of and for the middle class—his own class. Although there was a strong interest in reaching an audience of the poor, the unlettered, the rural, the approach, finally was from a conscientised middle-class perspective. Even when rural content was used—Bhoma's story, for example, or the Santhal rebellion—it was essentially to educate, inform and politicise the urban educated middle class. Badal-da himself recognised the limitations of trying to create a theatre of the working class:

> The ultimate answer ... is not for a city group to prepare plays for and about the working people. The working people—factory workers, peasants, the

[6] 'Voyages in the Theatre' is a series of lectures, the Sriram Memorial Lectures, delivered by Badal Sircar in April 1992.

> landless labourers—will have to make and perform their own plays.... This process, of course, can become widespread only when the socio-economic emancipation of the working class has also spread widely.[7]

One could argue that it was this 'socio-economic emancipation' that he hoped to further by taking his plays to them, plays which challenged the status quo and presented an alternative, more equitable society; and also through his workshops with rural participants. Nishat Jahan of Bangladesh, for example, talks of his highly successful workshops with rural NGO groups doing rights awareness-building through theatre in the late 1990s. Without undervaluing this aspect of his work, however, it is still possible to conclude that the central concern of his plays remains to communicate with his peers; to shake them out of their comfortable convictions, to move them to some sort of action. In short, to conscientise them. To politicise them. Even the demographics of his theatre group bear this out. Satabdi members come from the urban middle–middle class. They always have.

But then it has frequently been members of the middle class, all over the world, who have acted as the vanguard of political and social change, of radical thinking. A middle-class theatre does not necessarily mean a non-political theatre. And political Badal-da's work definitely was. It was political in its choices—a free theatre which would travel to the people, which would remain flexible, portable and inexpensive in order to avail of available performance spaces, which would use the actor as the chief resource; it was political in its process—a gender-neutral democratic space where each participant was seen as equal, a collective and collaborative creative methodology (to a greater or lesser degree depending on the play); it was political in its aim, which was to be part of the process of effecting social change; it was political in content, by exposing and critiquing injustice and exploitation in society and history; it was political in form, eschewing heroes and heroines in favour of ensemble, group work, remaining in close communication and on the same level with the viewer; and it was political in impact, seeding much alternative, socially engaged theatre activity on the subcontinent and acting as a liberating choice for many theatre practitioners who were not part of the mainstream.

However, there was one interesting difference between most political theatre and Badal-da's approach. Anger, accusation, outrage, a clear identification of the enemy, polemics, propaganda and slogans are part and

[7] Quoted in Sadanand Menon, 'Badal Sircar (1925–2011): A Curtain Call for Political Theatre', *Economic and Political Weekly*, Vol. xlvi, No. 22, 28 May 2011, p. 20.

parcel of most political theatre, as is imparting information in order to shape points of view, and a sharp demarcation between 'us' and 'them'. Badal-da is less interested in allocating blame than in accepting blame. The deeply Christian emotions of guilt and responsibility are embedded in his theatre: the very same middle class to which he himself belongs is complicit in the problem if it does not stand up in protest. How exactly this protest is to happen is not explored in his theatre. Solidarity is sought, and that seems to be enough. In short, the project is one of conscientisation. By taking on the burden of injustice, by placing the middle class in the centre of the discourse, he shifts the focus from 'out there' to 'in here'. His is a theatre of conscience. Combined with a powerful physicality and evocative images he creates a theatrical expression that, at its best, is profoundly affective.

By way of a coda, I must add a recent experience of seeing Satabdi perform an old favourite of Badal-da's—*Hattamalar Oparey*[8]—as part of a regular bi-monthly outdoor performance schedule. This is on 20 July 2014. The venue is outside Nandan, now an established public space for cultural activity of various kinds. I join the ring of spectators, a motley gathering consisting of ageing middle-class men and women like me who have come specifically to catch the show, people of poorer backgrounds who seem to have stopped for a while out of curiosity and interest, and a smattering of children from different socio-economic backgrounds, including local street children. Different age groups are represented here, as are different social strata: typical of a street performance in Kolkata. The Satabdi actors range from young and lithe to middle-aged and measured. The well-known allegory, full of broad humour, picks up pace and energy as it proceeds. We see the familiar features of a Satabdi production: the actors' bodies forming trees, streams, buildings; the actors' voices producing bird call, chirrups and whistling breezes. The transitions are not as smooth and quick as they should be; the mimed actions not as crisp. But the two irrepressible thieves—Becha and Kena—grow into their roles, becoming characters as we watch. The younger apprentice is easily swayed by the charms of this topsy-turvy land where no one wants or takes more than he needs, and therefore theft is irrelevant. The older one, more set in his ways, is reluctant to forego a lifetime of training

[8] Badal Sircar, 'Hattamalar Oparey', Natak Samagra, Vol. 3 (Kolkata: Mitra and Ghosh, 2012); English translation published in *Beyond the Land of Hattamala and Scandal in Fairyland* (Calcutta: Seagull Books, 1992).

and pride in being a skilled thief. I watch the faces of the spectators. The children are delightedly laughing at the antics of the thieves, and several of the adults have an amused, indulgent smile on their faces. There is a sense of benign goodwill. Attention holds despite some unscheduled disruptions which rudely intrude into this little fantasy space of naive innocence. The play ends with the thieves being happily and productively subsumed into the barter economy of this fairytale land, and the actors enter as a human chain, singing a wishful song of hope:

Since we make all that we need
markets are a waste indeed
don't let money so enslave us
Add your voices to our chorus
Come on, let us share our food
Come on, let us share our food.[9]

It is a strange moment. A strong wave of nostalgia sweeps over me. For a younger self and a more idealistic time that is gone, it seems, forever. And yet, it is more confused than that. On the one hand, the sentiments of the closing song feed directly into the debates and controversies plaguing our economy—the farmer and the middleman, the food distribution system, hunger and unequal access to food. One cannot deny that they speak to the need of the hour. One cannot dismiss them as irrelevant. On the other, they appear as a simplistically Utopian or even Luddite approach to a vastly complex economic situation, and as such totally unrealistic. On the one hand, a part of me wistfully wishes that life could indeed be so simple and idealistic; on the other, it all seems hopelessly old-fashioned and childish in today's world. I realise that what I am feeling is a microcosm of the conflicting arguments over the political efficacy of Badal-da's theatre, which has been discussed in this book. I contribute my mite to the 'collection plate'[10] and slowly walk away, realising all over again how complicated this whole business of guilt, responsibility and conscience is. Does a theatre of conscience work today? And yet, without at least the vision of a more equitable society, however unrealistic it may seem, will there ever be a move towards a more just world?

[9] Sircar, 'Hattamalar Oparey', trans. Anjum Katyal, p. 406.

[10] Satabdi typically lays out a *gamchha* or cloth after the performance for voluntary donations.

CHAPTER ONE

BITTEN BY THE BUG

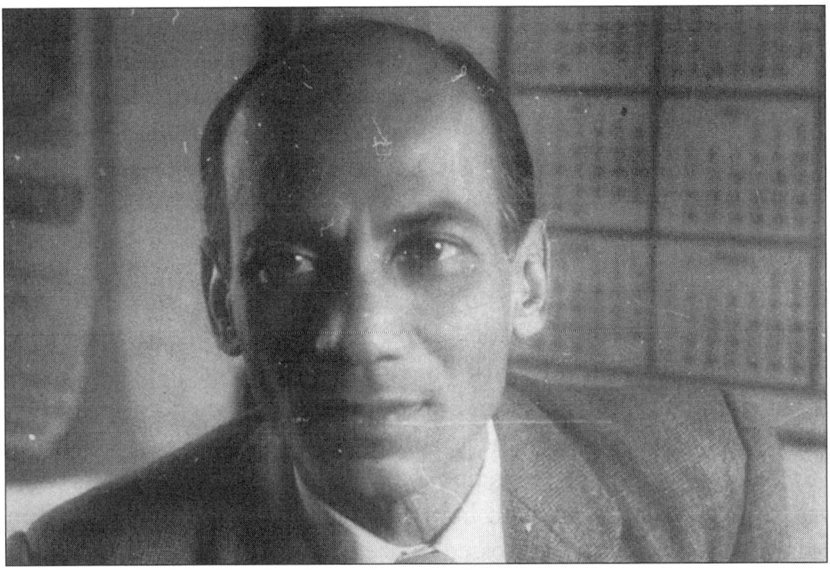

A young Badal Sircar
Courtesy: Satabdi

Born in Calcutta on 15 July 1925 into the 'middle–middle class', Badal Sircar was formally named Sudhindra—although Badal was the *daaknaam* or nickname that stuck. Sircar's family was emblematic of the urban educated *bhadralok* (gentlefolk) which came to be the focus, both as subject and target, of much of his theatre. Theirs was a Christian family. Badal's father, Mahendra Lal Sircar, taught History at Scottish Church College, Calcutta, and from childhood, Badal too was inducted into the cultural ethos of his class. He was an avid reader and read whatever he could lay his hands on:

> Studying in the Bengali medium Scottish Church Collegiate school, it was naturally Bengali compositions to begin with. But, as the family's stock of

> Bengali plays ran out, I thought of teaching myself a bit of English. I was delighted to be introduced by my mother (Sarala Mona Sircar) to grandmother's (Virgina Mary Nandy) collection of western literature. Grandma, incidentally, was amongst India's first lady physicians and very well read.[1]

He professed to an interest in play scripts from a young age. 'People normally read novels and short stories and watch plays. I relished reading dramas.'[2] He also recalled an interest in organising space:

> Right from my school days I enjoyed making plans of space—I remember once we went to a village where my father's ex-students made available a thatched house standing in a two acre garden, for a minimal rent. The garden was very interesting, the outhouse at a distance, paths winding through, a lotus pond. I made a kind of railway chart based on those paths, and worked out a timetable, with up trains and down trains! So long before I studied town planning or anything, I would play this kind of a game. It's probably in my blood.[3]

Theatre scholar Pabitra Sircar, in his introductory essay to Volume One of the *Complete Plays* of Badal Sircar in Bengali[4] has carefully culled references made by Badal-da to the world of theatre and drama from his autobiography, *Purano Kasundi* (Old Mustard).[5] In addition to his penchant for reading plays, he also loved acting them out. From the time when he was in class six or seven (that is, around the age of about 12 years), he gained access to a room on the top floor of his home at 1A Peary Row, the address which was to become identified with him. He would spend Sunday afternoons by himself in that room, engrossed in one Bangla play script after another, enacting all the parts in turn. There weren't too many play volumes at home, but he read Dwijendralal, Kshirodeprasad and Girishchandra.[6] He confessed to the comic roles being his favourites. Thus was planted the 'first seed' of his lifelong love of theatre.

[1] Quoted in 'Badal Sircar—Off Stage', http://www.indiaprofile.com/people/badalsircar.htm (accessed on 27 January 2015).

[2] Ibid.

[3] Interview with the author, 11 January 2009.

[4] Badal Sircar, *Natak Samagra*, Vol. 1 (Kolkata: Mitra and Ghosh, 2009).

[5] Badal Sircar, *Purano Kasundi*, Vol. 1 (Kolkata: Lekhani, 2006).

[6] Dwijendralal Ray (1863–1914), Bengali poet, playwright, and musician. Kshirodeprasad Bidyabinode (1863–1927), Bengali dramatist. Girish Chandra Ghosh (1844–1912), Bengali musician, poet, playwright, novelist, theatre director and actor.

The 'second seed' was his addiction to radio plays. One day a week, there was a broadcast of radio drama for three hours at a stretch. So keen was he to listen that his parents indulged him by excusing him from homework, and allowing him unfettered access to the radio, at the time a 'crystal state' machine, which could only be heard through headphones. He describes keenly listening to hours of drama through headphones, along with his sister—the uncomfortable ringing in his ears no deterrent to his enjoyment. Later, the advent of the valve radio meant he could free himself from the headphones. As a result, although there was no custom of theatre going in his family, and he says he has no memory of actually visiting the theatre as a child, he was nonetheless intimately familiar with the voices of all the popular radio thespians of the time. The only plays he saw performed were student productions, skits or Sunday school efforts. Parashuram's short pieces were popular fare, he recalls.[7] The cumulative effect of all this was to generate a deep desire in the child Badal to be a theatre actor.[8] He was well and truly bitten by the theatre bug. It is interesting, however, that theatre was initially, and for many formative years, primarily an aural and textual experience for him, rather than a visual one. It was the voice and dialogue that meant theatre to him: not difficult to trace a trajectory from here to playwriting.

His first foray into playwriting also occurred in his boyhood. He remembers Sarashi-babu, his class six Bengali teacher, who taught him two enduring lessons about writing, which remained useful all his life.

> One was—Go ahead, write, write, there's a reason why we say *lekhapora* (write–read) and not *poralekha* (read–write). The other was—when you write something, put it away for a month or so; thereafter if you still think it's good, you'll know that you've made no progress at all. If it seems flawed to you, then you'll know you've improved somewhat.[9]

Encouraged by this teacher, he dashed off a play on the Pindari Wars, part of his class seven history syllabus. This was his very first play, several pages long, which, he exclaims thankfully, was lost forever.[10]

[7] Parashuram was the pen name of Rajshekhar Basu (1880–1960), a Bengali writer, chemist and lexicographer known for his comic and satirical short stories.

[8] Sircar, *Purano Kasundi*, Vol. 1, pp. 27–30.

[9] Ibid., trans. Anjum Katyal, p. 39.

[10] Ibid., p. 39. See also Pabitra Sircar, Introduction to Sircar, *Natak Samagra*, Vol. 1, pp. iv–v (char-paanch).

His second attempt at playwriting was clearly a fond memory, since he refers to it jovially more than once. When he was in class 10, he wrote *Slippers of Cinderella.* By now he had read more plays. Saradindu Bandyopadhyay's[11] *Detective, Bondhu* and *Lalpanja* (the latter two volumes actually paid for out of his own precious and sparse resources) were particular favourites. 'These plays were imperfect in many ways, but there was such a shortage of Bengali comic plays that we loved them.'[12] The penchant for comic plays is stitched through the fabric of his growing up: from preferring comic characters to enjoying Parashuram skits to devouring these plays. No surprise, then, that his first few plays as a playwright are to be comedies. About *Slippers of Cinderella*, he says:

> The venue was this very [room].... During the holidays, in 1941, I had adapted *Cinderella* from my sister's textbook and enacted it, with cousins and friends, before a family gathering. Casting myself in the plum male role. Rarely can a theatre personality claim the distinction of beginning as playwright, director and principal actor.[13]

He expands on the memory later:

> A makeshift stage made up of two wooden *chowkis* covering two-thirds of the space in a 16 ft × 11 ft drawing room. Bedsheets, saris and dhotis serving as curtains, backdrops and wings. An audience of 15 or so composed of parents, aunts, uncles, grandfather, grandmother, a cast of brothers, sisters, cousins, some friends. A boy of 15 years and seven months begins his voyage in the theatre as director, principal actor, playwright; the play being an adaptation of an English play.[14]

That script too is lost, he says regretfully; he can't even recall the Bengali title.[15]

By now World War II had begun. Inevitably, the negative impact began to be felt on daily life. The cost of living rose steadily and he saw hunger and destitution in the streets. He says, 'I learnt two new words: hoarding and blackmarket.'[16] In the midst of this upheaval, many families left the

[11] Saradindu Bandyopadhyay (1899–1970), well-known literary figure of Bengal.

[12] Sircar, *Purano Kasundi*, Vol. 1, trans. Anjum Katyal, p. 40.

[13] See 'Badal Sircar—Off Stage' and Sircar, *Purano Kasundi*, Vol. 1, p. 47, quoted in Pabitra Sircar, Introduction to Badal Sircar, *Natak Samagra*, Vol. 1, p. v (paanch).

[14] Badal Sircar, 'Voyages in the Theatre', *On Theatre* (Kolkata: Seagull Books, 2009), pp. 94–95.

[15] Sircar, *Purano Kasundi*, Vol. 1, pp. 46–47.

[16] Ibid., trans. Anjum Katyal, p. 41.

city for the interiors, fearing an imminent invasion by the Japanese. His was one amongst them.

A house was hired in Tamluk, some distance from the city. Here, the thirst for theatre, which had been kindled by his experience with *Cinderella*, nagged him. He instigated some of the lads into mounting a play—his old favourite, Saradindu's *Detective*. Rehearsals began. His role was that of the stuttering Samaresh. Then the boys got to hear that two all-night theatre performances were being planned—of two plays, *Kedar Rai* and *Sirajuddaulah*. There was an outbreak of feverish activity all around them, with majestic props being assembled and prepared in every available space. Knowing that *Sirajuddaulah* was a short play which could not run all night, he conceived of an ambitious idea: why not stage their *Detective* before the main play? With this in mind, they did a run-through for the adults. The outcome was unexpected. Impressed, the grown-ups took over the proceedings. The hero was promptly borne off to play the heroine, and Badal himself was offered the role of the heroine's older sister, Surma. His misgivings over playing a woman were overcome, he recounts, by the lure of the stage. This was the first and last time he essayed a female role. He says that he has never forgotten the experience of those two nights—the huge crowd of about 3,000 people, every line of the text retained, songs and all, seeing so many actors together on stage—he loved every minute of it. It was truly a night to remember.[17]

During his time at Scottish Church College, he borrowed books from lending libraries and read insatiably, plays along with everything else. 'Went through all of Bernard Shaw, struggled with Shakespeare and Sheridan which I couldn't quite get my teeth into, Moliere I was familiar with'[18]—along with Galsworthy, Maeterlinck, D.H. Lawrence—'and discovered that Rabindranath had written not just poetry but drama, novels, stories as well'.[19] He mentions seeing the legendary Tagore on stage twice, and hearing him recite some of his poetry. He also saw a production of Tagore's *Shapmochan*. The third time he saw him was in his funeral procession, which he watched from the verandah of a friend's house near Jorasanko.[20]

Another play he adapted, produced, directed and acted in at home was based on Sibram Chakraborty's story about selling tickets for a charity show.[21] This script too is lost. His memories of it resound with laughter as

[17] Sircar, *Purano Kasundi*, Vol. 1, pp. 51–52.
[18] Sircar, *Purano Kasundi*, Vol. 1, trans. Anjum Katyal, p. 56.
[19] Ibid., trans. Anjum Katyal.
[20] Sircar, *Purano Kasundi*, Vol. 1, p. 60.
[21] Sibram Chakraborty (1902–80), Indian novelist.

one disaster after another rendered the show comical beyond intention. Clearly, comedy was a source of immense pleasure to this future playwright.[22]

During his four years at Shibpur engineering college, his interest in theatre remained restricted to viewing rather than acting, as the seniors offered him only female roles.[23] But this was a period of transformation in other ways. He began to distance himself from the conventions of middle class life. He rejected church-going and declared his lack of belief in religion,[24] and he began to develop his political beliefs. No guru or 'authority figure' influenced him; rather, he claims, he formed his own convictions. Reading Leontiev's *Political Economy*[25] helped him understand that the repressive society he saw around him was not cast in stone; rather, it was in a process of ongoing change. Bringing about this change was the most important task. As he continued to read, to discuss these issues, he felt that he had entered another world. The passion for theatre did not ebb, rather it lay buried within him, waiting to emerge some years later.[26] Not that there was no engagement with writing in these years—he went through a phase of poetry writing. 'I wrote a satirical poem mocking the modern style; it had everything in it from chlorine gas to dustbins'; he received some encouragement, and for some time, he continued to write poetry.[27]

His next foray into playwriting was when he took Galsworthy's *The Roof*, added characters and ideas from his own imagination and created a piece called 'Fire' (*Aagun*). 'On writing it I felt breathless with joy. I felt that I had written something really worthwhile. This was no weak prose poetry—this was "fire!"' He took it straight to Sukumari Bhattacharji,[28] his guide and mentor in matters of writing, and handed it over to her. 'The next day. I was convinced that Sukumari-*di* would say—I was wrong in encouraging you to write poetry; you should write only plays.' He emerged from the encounter totally demolished; she had read it with ruthless attention, catching every flaw, of which there were many. She criticised it so thoroughly that he came away feeling that it was no play at all, just flatulence. He gave up writing plays for 12 years. And when he did write again, he kept a strict inner eye on a

[22] Sircar, *Purano Kasundi*, Vol. 1, pp. 62–64.

[23] Ibid., p. 73.

[24] Ibid., pp. 71–72.

[25] A. Leontiev, *Political Economy, A Beginner's Course*, originally published in the Soviet Union in 1935; a popular textbook on Marxism and how it related to the problems of the day.

[26] Sircar, *Purano Kasundi*, Vol. 1, pp. 73–74.

[27] Ibid., trans. Anjum Katyal, p. 75.

[28] Sukumari Bhattacharji (1922–2014), Sanskrit scholar.

tendency to use words injudiciously. This, he says, was a lesson taught to him by Sukumari-di which, left to himself, it may have taken him years to realize.[29]

In September 1949, some months after he got married to his first wife, Putul, he joined Jadavpur University engineering college in the civil engineering department, as a lecturer. Here, theatre re-entered his life. At the convocation, the lecturer's association was slotted to perform, and he was allotted a part. He was delighted to accept. 'There had been such a long gap, I thought that phase was over, but I was to realize that this seed could not be killed.'[30] *Kedar Ray* was the chosen play, and he was to play Kilmak Khan. In addition, he found himself performing a series of impromptu appearances as sundry messengers, hilariously recounted in a manner worthy of his best comedies.[31] What comes through clearly is his unabashed pleasure in being part of the excitement of theatre again.

He describes his years away from theatre, thus:

> Several years of ... nothing to do with theatre. Well, not entirely correct. Reading plays and watching student-productions avidly—those were also voyages in the theatre. Only no attempt was made to do theatre, never thinking I had the knack for it. Also, other voyages demanded all my spare time. Those were the years of studies, of freedom movements, of examinations, of political upsurges, of hideous communal riots, of Independence, of Partition, of graduation, of refugee camps, of service in the day and classes in the evening, of marriage, of fatherhood. Those were years of great illusions followed by stupendous disillusionment and frustration.[32]

But now that the dormant seed had re-sprouted, theatre was to remain a part of his life.

At this time, he was living in a housing complex consisting of four blocks of flats around a central green. He and his neighbours soon began to plan a play for the *pujas*; in fact, this phase of his life was the fodder for his comedy, *Boro Pishima* (Eldest Aunt, 1956).[33] They first attempted to put up Parashuram's *Birinchi Baba*, but after the first and only rehearsal, the manuscript remained in storage, and the project was abandoned. Soon after, roping in a group of enthusiasts from the neighbourhood, they formed ENACA (Entally Novice Artiste's Cultural Association). They performed

[29] This incident is from Sircar, *Purano Kasundi*, Vol. 1, trans. Anjum Katyal, pp. 79–80.
[30] Sircar, *Purano Kasundi*, Vol. 1, trans. Anjum Katyal, p. 147.
[31] Sircar, *Purano Kasundi*, Vol. 1, pp. 147–51.
[32] Sircar, 'Voyages in the Theatre', p. 95.
[33] Sircar, *Purano Kasundi*, Vol. 1, p. 151.

Atithi by Subodh Basu at the small hall in the YMCA in College Street. 'I got a lot of joy out of everything to do with doing the play' but because his role as Monu babu went unnoticed 'I was convinced that theatre was not my line'.[34] His deep enjoyment of it, however, and the pleasure it gave him, led him to continue despite such self-deprecation. With ENACA, he also performed in Saradindu Bandhopadhyay's *Lalpanja* and *Bondhu*.

Life was hard and stressful at this time—long hours of work and commuting—so much so that he even thought of dropping the town planning diploma course he had signed up for. His first child, a son, was born in September 1951. The following October, his daughter arrived. His examinations were almost upon him, his wife and he were trying to manage the babies, the cooking, the household, alongside his studying for his examinations, when, as he says, 'ENACA suddenly woke up and decided to do *Chirakumar Sabha* by Tagore.'[35] They needed him to act; they couldn't do without him. He was being offered the role of Rasik: 'long, tough...and very very attractive. I was too greedy to refuse.'[36]

In March 1953, he applied for and was appointed to a position with the Damodar Valley Corporation, after an interview which, as he describes it, could be straight out of his own later play, *Ebong Indrajit*.[37] He was posted in Maithon.

Here, the hours hung heavy, and aside from the favourite mode of passing time—*adda*—and some badminton, there wasn't much scope for entertainment. So, he and Jyotsna babu, friend and colleague, started Rehearsal Club. The Rehearsal Club was begun on the condition that, 'There will be no theatre, only rehearsal.'[38] The next person going to Kolkata was given the task of procuring and bringing back several plays.

> The books arrived. *Baikunther Khata, Natun Yehudi, Detective, Bondhu, Manmoi Girls School, Atithi*, and more. Some plays lasted for just a few readings, some we continued with day after day. Even the wives participated, and a few audience members were always present. When we proposed the idea we never imagined that such enthusiasm could be sustained at a stretch for so long. Every day. At E-44, from around 5.30 to 9 or 10 pm, tel muri, pyazi, fried papad, and tea. And Capstan, Wills, beedi, whatever was going.[39]

[34] Sircar, *Purano Kasundi*, Vol. 1, trans. Anjum Katyal, p. 161.
[35] Ibid., trans. Anjum Katyal, p. 165.
[36] Ibid., trans. Anjum Katyal.
[37] Sircar, *Purano Kasundi*, Vol. 1, pp. 166–67.
[38] Sircar, *Purano Kasundi*, Vol. 1, trans. Anjum Katyal, p. 174.
[39] Ibid., trans. Anjum Katyal.

The heady atmosphere of friends relaxing together, absorbed in a common enterprise, is deftly conveyed in his crisp prose. He recalls:

> The play which underwent the most rehearsal was *Detective*. My part as Samaresh required me to stutter which I did to my heart's content, though there was little physical similarity between the character and myself. Santosh, in his school days, had played Pratihari and Sainik, here he was the perpetual hero. Ashu was very shy and had never dreamt that he could ever do theatre, but he played Bolai, a long part, with great enthusiasm.[40]

His dry comments and tongue-in-cheek tone cannot disguise the pure pleasure this activity obviously provided to someone who has at various times referred to his attraction for the theatre as *nasha* or intoxication, addiction. Things were rolling along smoothly, when to his secret delight, someone put a spanner in the works. How? By demanding that enough with all this rehearsing, let's just put up the play!

> Suchitra caused the problem—my colleague Ranjit's wife. One day she cornered Jyotsna and me: What's the use of all this endless rehearsing? Let's do the play! Everyone's ready with their roles, what's the point if we don't perform the play? Actually, this hidden desire had already sprouted in my mind, and Jyotsna and I had secretly discussed it.[41]

In his autobiography Badal-da spends quite some time on this initial foray into theatre at Maithon and claims several firsts in relation to it.[42] It is worth our while to dwell on this experience awhile, in order to understand why it remained so meaningful in his memory.

First, there was the whole middle-class taboo against women performing on stage, in public. He was determined that he was not going to allow males to dress up and act as women. If the ladies could not perform the female roles, he was not interested in mounting a performance. Here, he was amply supported by the various wives who asserted their interest in performing in public.

Second, there was the mathematical detail with which the engineers involved in the production measured and prepared diagrams to scale, to mark stage dimensions, props, movement of actors, entries and exits from various wings and so on. Scene changes were worked out with military precision so that they could be done within a minute.

[40] Sircar, *Purano Kasundi*, Vol. 1, trans. Anjum Katyal, pp. 174–75.

[41] Ibid., trans. Anjum Katyal, p. 175.

[42] Sircar, *Purano Kasundi*, Vol. 1, pp. 175–77.

Third, there was the teamwork, cooperation and enthusiasm which drew neighbours together in a common enterprise. This receives a warm acknowledgement from Badal-da. In many homes, he says, people slept on the floor as the beds were removed for the sets, or to form the stage. People eagerly contributed expensive items which they'd got as wedding gifts—saris, curtains, tablecloths, vases—and were disappointed if you didn't accept them.

He pinpoints these aspects—women acting as women, efficient and quick scene changes, no call for prompting, clockwork precision, error free performances—as records set in Maithon, and as firsts in his theatre experience.[43]

Another satisfaction shines through. The play was a popular success. People kept asking for a repeat show. Those who had missed it clamoured to know when they could see it: 'Whatever social reservations may have existed regarding theatre were vanquished with this one play.'[44] One can sense that this meant a lot to this particular theatre lover.

Soon two more plays, *Bondhu* and *Atithi*, were performed. Performances were held in other neighbourhoods outside the engineers' 'mohalla'. *Manmoi Girls' School* was staged at the Recreation Club. *Birinchi Baba* was taken out of cold storage and produced. Again, we see the quiet satisfaction of noting that with this first advent of theatre into their neighbourhood, people were very pleased and appreciative.[45]

However pleasurable and fulfilling it was in terms of his amateur theatre initiatives, the Maithon phase of his life was soon to be over. By January 1955, Badal-da had joined the Calcutta Municipality Survey department as Deputy Chief Valuer and Surveyor. After settling into his new office and home, he found the evenings a bit flat. Especially after the hectic activity of daily rehearsals he was now used to. He became part of Engineers' Circle. This group had an office on Ganesh Chandra Avenue where they would meet regularly. Badal-da suggested that they fix one day a week for a session in which the members in turn gave a talk on a subject of their choice. Tuesday was the day fixed upon.

Meanwhile, friends who dropped in for adda at home inevitably began to discuss doing theatre again. Rehearsals were to be held in a neighbour's place, and the shows at the YWCA hall. Light-hearted comedies were the staple fare. Then came Badal-da's adaptation of *Dena Paona*, culled from the novel by Saratchandra, *Saroshi*, about which he says, 'I adapted this

[43] Sircar, *Purano Kasundi*, Vol. 1, p. 177.

[44] Sircar, *Purano Kasundi*, Vol. 1, trans. Anjum Katyal, p. 177.

[45] Sircar, *Purano Kasundi*, Vol. 1, p. 176.

play from his novel.'[46] His friends in the Engineers' Circle also did a play in which, naturally, he acted: Rabindranath Tagore's comedy *Baikunther Khata*, which they staged at the IPS Pavilion.

Next, Badal-da flagposts his first proper effort as a playwright. After seeing a movie called *Monkey Business*,[47] of which he claims, 'I didn't really follow the dialogue well, I only got the gist of the story,'[48] he wrote *Solution X*. He states: 'This is really my first play. I'm not counting *Cinderella,* Sibram's stories, *Birinchi Baba, Aagun*. This was in 1956.'[49]

So, before he leaves for his first visit to London, he has already written what he considers his first proper play. The year is 1956. The play is a comedy, as are his next few works. He is to write his next play, *Boro Pishima*, in London.

This would be a good time to look back over what we have learned about Badal Sircar's formative years in connection with theatre. The first volume of his autobiography offers much food for thought in relation to his evolving theatre philosophy. One thing that leaps out at us is the importance to him of comedy, and the comic. Even the tone of the memoir is wry, humorous and self-deprecatory ('Autobiography, Life saga: these are heavy words, I have neither the ability nor the desire to write anything so weighty ... all life experiences cannot be taken lightly, but I've given the lighter moments importance here, not deliberately, rather, spontaneously.'[50]). He refuses to take himself too seriously, always maintaining an ironic distance from the situations he is describing, and peppers the narrative with anecdotes that range from the amusing to the hilarious. His memories of theatre activity are invariably lighthearted in nature, and vividly convey a sense of fun and pleasure, a far cry from the intensity and self-questioning one associates with his later theatre. On the contrary, in this phase of his life, theatre seems to be all about friends spending hours together, having a good time, snacking, smoking, consuming cups of tea and dealing good-naturedly with the inevitable mishaps and obstacles that amateur productions face. And of course, theatre at this time is all about doing comedies.

Secondly, from the time when he first begins to mention plays, one notices that it is the same few plays and writers that circulate through his

[46] Sircar, *Purano Kasundi*, Vol. 1, p. 185. In 1931, a film was released with the same title, *Dena Paona*, adapted from Saratchandra's novel *Saroshi*, directed by Premankur Atorthy, produced by New Theatres and credited with being one of the first talkies.

[47] *Monkey Business*, 1952, dir. Howard Hawks.

[48] Sircar, *Purano Kasundi*, Vol. 1, p. 185.

[49] Sircar, *Purano Kasundi*, Vol. 1, trans. Anjum Katyal, pp. 185–86.

[50] Ibid., 'Preface', trans. Anjum Katyal, p. v.

theatre activity over the years. There seems to be little effort to experiment or to explore new material. This despite his mentioning that he is a keen reader in both Bengali and English, who devours books from libraries he has access to. Nor does he really mention contemporary writers, books, films or theatre happening around him, although this is a very fertile artistic and literary period in Kolkata. The years between 1940, when he was a questioning 15 year old, and 1955, when he turned 30, saw an unprecedented series of important cultural events unfold in the city and its environs, particularly for a politically aware and active person like him. The IPTA conferences of 1943 and 1946, the legendary production of *Nabanna* in 1944, Sombhu Mitra's work with both IPTA and Bohurupee, Mrinal Sen's experiments with shadow plays, Hemango Biswas's work with folk songs, Panu Pal's *pathnatika* or street corner plays, *Chargesheet* performed in Hazra Park to protest against the arrest of Communist leaders, Utpal Dutt's *Achalayatan, Macbeth, Sirajuddaulah*, are just some of these. The kind of politically conscious theatre he later took up, performing amidst the people, was already happening in the city. Utpal Dutt writes:

> *Chargesheet* ... was taken to working-class slums and remote villages, and its direct analysis of political issues was a revelation to me... [describing how Panu Pal and he] prepared the second street-corner play, and descended on the suburb of Maheshtala, where the people are mostly tailors with a sprinkling of workers from the Bata Shoe factory nearby ... playing five to six times a day at every corner of the constituency, from the gates of the Bata factory to the courtyard of a dark house where wives of Muslim tailors, who were in purdah, could watch the play from behind curtains.[51]

There is no talk in Badal-da's memoirs of any of these or indeed any other cultural activity by the city's artists or by writers challenging the status quo—not even to critique it. Did he take no interest in them or did they not affect him enough to warrant a mention? Moreover, although he repeats throughout the memoir how theatre is an attraction and a pleasure he cannot deny himself, there does not seem to be a sense of higher purpose or social change associated with it at this stage of his life. It appears to be a source of pleasure, period. This is something that is to change drastically in the 1960s and 1970s.

[51] Utpal Dutt, quoted in Samik Bandyopadhyay, 'Theatrescapes', *Seagull Theatre Quarterly*, No. 16, p. 27, December 1997.

What also comes through is a degree of comfort and belonging with his own class and milieu which one does not expect, given his stern critique of the middle class in his later work. The autobiography displays no such alienation or isolation, no such rejection. He talks of addas at home, of close friends with whom he enjoys passing time, of neighbours, colleagues, college classmates who are very much part of his everyday routine. He seems to seek the company of his fellow bhadralok rather than keep to himself, and if there is any sense of growing dissatisfaction with the parameters of his middle class social and cultural milieu, he does not discuss it in his autobiography. There are perhaps a few hints that one could interpret as indicative of an inner restlessness. For example, the frequent changes of employment, from teaching to working in a private corporation to taking a government job or his decision to go to London by himself. This move is to yield some important results in terms of his growth in theatre.

CHAPTER TWO

THE EARLY YEARS

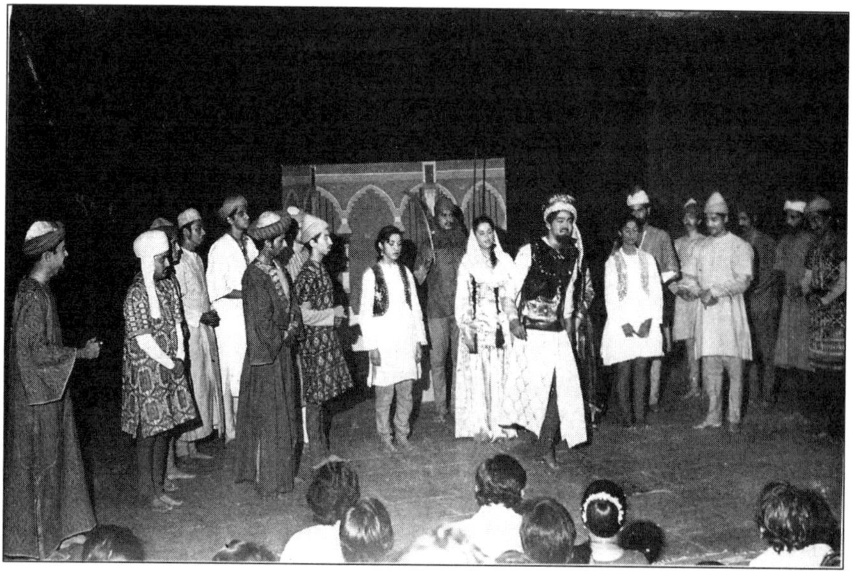

A scene from *Abu Hossain*
Courtesy: Satabdi

The sudden decision to go to London, by himself, leaving behind his wife and two small children, as well as a fairly settled professional and social life, is to my mind an extremely telling moment in terms of Badal-da's creative development. It happens when, out of the blue, he receives a lump sum of money from the Damodar Valley Corporation by way of dues he was not expecting. In his straitened circumstances, where indulgences are unaffordable, it suddenly offers a tantalising opportunity, to do something perhaps dreamed of but unattainable, or something perhaps risky and adventurous—something in any case which is out of the ordinary. He jumps at this chance. This in itself says something important about him. He doesn't use it for a better flat or a car, for example. Immediately, he thinks to himself—'I can go abroad! I'll look for a job there, courtesy my engineering and town planning training.'[1]

He starts working towards the dream—saving to supplement the windfall and make up the necessary amount, organising admission into an evening course, gathering the necessary documents. About London, he says, 'I had not the slightest wish to study there; all I wanted to do was find a job and travel around.'[2] And he repeats the clichéd dream of the educated urban middle class about Paris, the capital of the cultural world: 'Of course I must visit Paris; after reading the biographies of Van Gogh and Toulouse Lautrec, and seeing the maps, I feel I know the city already.'[3] This was a romantic getaway, then, almost an adolescent escape. 'It was like the time I set off with Kanu for Pareshnath on a whim, with no prior planning,' he says, referring to his younger days.[4] He burns his boats behind him, resigning from his post and making no concrete plans about where he'll stay or how he'll sustain himself. He blocks all attempts by his concerned father to ask about such practical considerations, insisting that he'll manage. He arranges for his wife and children to live in his father's house. And he sets off on the great adventure that is to be London. It is 30 September 1957. He is 32 years old.

The years in London were full of new experiences:

> England was not the rough seas he had feared. A year with a civil engineering firm was followed by a town planning assignment 'which I always longed for'. Soon, Sircar was sucked into London's bubbling cultural cauldron. Parallel to viewing a spate of movies at a film club[5] ... Badal Sircar's mind feverishly sponged the richness of the British stage. 'Fortunately, people on shoe-string budgets could still buy the cheapest seats', he says with a smile. 'It was quite a feeling coming face to face with theatre greats—Vivian Leigh and Charles Laughton, amongst others, live on stage. London's where I came across a Theatre in the Round. An arena version of Racine's *Phaedre*, with the unforgettable Margaret Rawlins in the lead,' he adds.[6]

[1] Sircar, *Purano Kasundi*, Vol. 1, trans. Anjum Katyal, pp. 186–87.
[2] Ibid., trans. Anjum Katyal, p. 187.
[3] Ibid., trans. Anjum Katyal.
[4] Ibid., trans. Anjum Katyal, p. 188.
[5] The National Film Society; see Sircar, *Purano Kasundi*, Vol. 2 (Kolkata: Lekhani, 2007), p. 36.
[6] See 'Badal Sircar—Off Stage'.

He also talks of watching movie after movie in the cinema halls—a cheap way of passing time while keeping out of the cold.[7] He watched the Royal Shakespeare Company perform *Romeo and Juliet* at Stratford on Avon, but the picturesque town seems to have enchanted him more than the play. Juliet did a good enough job, he felt. But nothing compared to the Theatre in the Round performance he saw, where Margaret Rawlins was simply unforgettable. 'It was my first experience of Theatre in the Round, and it left such a mark on me, that it helped bring about an important change in my acting life in Kolkata.'[8] After discovering the facility of cheap seats, his theatre-going life begins in earnest, 'something that I didn't do back home,' he admits.[9] In fact, it became like a *nesha* or addiction.[10] In London's West End, he saw John Gielgud, Michael Redgrave, Vivian Leigh, Charles Laughton. In London's East End, at the Stratford Theatre, he caught Brendan Behan's *The Hostage* directed by Joan Littlewood (an experimental production that changed every night, brought in topical and local references and often had the playwright appearing on stage.) 'It was amazing; I hadn't thought theatre could be like this! Everything was new to me—the direction, the acting.'[11] He also saw Pinter's *The Birthday Party* both acted in and directed by Charles Laughton. He had the good fortune, as he puts it, of hearing singer–actor Paul Robeson live at the majestic Royal Albert Hall, albeit from the cheapest seats![12] Alongside all this 'serious' culture, he was also watching Charlie Chaplin, Laurel and Hardy and the Three Stooges on screen.[13] He was totally entranced by Buster Keaton's films, rating him higher than Chaplin in terms of creative comedy, innovative gags and an original style of comic acting.[14]

Meanwhile, the loneliness, the dreary, grey, cold weather, the sunless days, led to the outbreak of an old fever—the impulse to write poetry. He found himself jotting down poems at work, and then carefully copying them into a notebook once he came back to his room.[15] He admits: 'I would never have written those poems had I not been away from Calcutta.'[16] These poems

[7] Sircar, *Purano Kasundi*, Vol. 2, pp. 12–13.

[8] Sircar, *Purano Kasundi*, Vol. 2, trans. Anjum Katyal, pp. 12–13.

[9] Ibid., trans. Anjum Katyal, p. 31.

[10] Sircar, *Purano Kasundi*, Vol. 2, pp. 31–32.

[11] Sircar, *Purano Kasundi*, Vol. 2, trans. Anjum Katyal, p. 32.

[12] Sircar, *Purano Kasundi*, Vol. 2, pp. 32–33.

[13] Ibid., p. 33.

[14] Ibid., p. 36.

[15] Ibid., p. 18.

[16] Badal Sircar speaking at 'Plays in a National Perspective', Round Table–I, 28–30 November 1996, organised by Natya Shodh Sansthan (NSS), at the Bharatiya Bhasha Parishad Conference Room, Kolkata. From the NSS archives (Henceforth, PNP).

were the basis of his most famous play, *Ebong Indrajit*, which 'was written from poem to poem. The poems were written between 1957 and 1959.'[17]

He touches an interesting issue here: 'I would never have written those poems had I not been away from Calcutta.' Away from the comfortable milieu in which he had grown up, confronted with a totally new cultural environment, in the absence of family, friends and the reassurance of regular adda and familiar group activity, he found himself thinking and expressing thoughts which seemed to have lain dormant thus far. He also wrote a play during his sojourn abroad—*Boro Pishima.* However, that is more along expected lines—he has been doing comedies in Kolkata, he has already written *Solution X* (1956)—whereas the poems that eventually form the spine of *Ebong Indrajit* are expressive of a new creative mindset.

In the final year of his course, amidst his incessant theatre going and cinema watching, he also wrote his first fully original, and second full-length comedy, *Boro Pishima.* This situational comedy draws on his considerable first-hand experience of doing amateur community theatre with his neighbours, colleagues and friends, both in Kolkata and Maithon. *Boro Pishima* is set in a housing colony based on where he once lived;[18] and it draws on attitudes, characters and situations all too familiar to him, in particular the experience of introducing women artistes on stage.[19] The play took him about five months to write, from April to September. As was his wont, after completing it he was eager to read it aloud to an interested listener—this was not so easy in London, but he found someone appropriate who not only listened, but also praised it highly.[20] This eagerness to find a listener seems intrinsically connected with his play writing, as we shall see later as well.

There are more cultural experiences in store for him which he writes about—a road trip through Scotland, a camping holiday in Europe, Paris and again Paris—but as his second year draws to a close he confesses that the yearning to return home was so strong as to be almost a sickness.[21] So he travels back by sea, the least expensive option he can find.

The reason why we have spent some time on his first experience of a foreign land is to try and trace the trajectory from Badal Sircar who seemed to be quite happy doing amateur theatricals with his friends to Badal Sircar, the committed theatre worker whose serious, socially-committed theatre

[17] Sircar, PNP.
[18] Sircar, *Purano Kasundi,* Vol. 1, p. 151.
[19] Ibid., p. 38.
[20] Ibid., p. 43.
[21] Ibid., p. 44.

influenced a whole subcontinent. As we have pointed out, his autobiography does not discuss milestone theatre and cinema events in his native Kolkata during his formative years, despite these being tumultuous times which definitively shaped many artists who lived through them. This is not to say that the issues, concerns, frustrations and disillusionments of these years did not find their way into his plays; but he does not talk much about the cultural ferment of the times or appear to be affected by it in terms of his creative output. In sharp contrast, the account of his London sojourn is peppered with memories of eye-opening theatre performances, and acknowledgement of how they influenced him and shaped his ideas of theatre. There is also the admission that the poetry that was to form *Ebong Indrajit* would not have been written if he had not been in foreign (and alien) climes. It seems that by the end of the London experience, Badal-da is beginning to think of himself as a playwright; this is indicated by the fact that although he may write poetry as a private activity, for his playwriting he seeks an audience. On the very first night of his return home, surrounded by family and friends, he cannot wait to read out to them his new play, *Boro Pishima*.

Badal Sircar, playwright, thus begins a career that is to establish him as one of modern Indian theatre's most important dramatists.

This time around, back home in Calcutta, there is no ambivalence in Badal-da's mind about the fact that where there is Badal, there has to be theatre ('With Badal Sircar as one of the founder members, how could we do without theatre?'[22]). After a five-month wait, he rejoins Calcutta Corporation in his previous post. His working life resumes its earlier rhythm, nothing new there. But his creative life takes on a fresh aspect. A group called Chakra is formed; they meet every Saturday. His daughter Bharati recalls,

> Initially, *Baba* asked his friends to come over for informal *adda* over tea every Saturday evening at our place. This milieu, he named Chakra...he and his friends would play indoor games, conceptualised by *Baba*. They would chit-chat and discuss anything and everything under the sun. But soon they ran out of ideas. And to keep the spirit of *adda* alive, they thought of making plays.[23]

With his typical wry humour, Badal-da claims to have begged and bullied those around him to take part in theatre;[24] at this stage, his theatre is still very

[22] Sircar, *Purano Kasundi*, Vol. 2, trans. Anjum Katyal, p. 54.

[23] Bharati Chatterjee, http://www.rediff.com/news/slide-show/slide-show-1-badal-sircars-daughter-speaks-up/20110530.htm#5 (accessed 30 January 2015).

[24] Sircar, *Purano Kasundi*, Vol. 2, pp. 54–55.

much about family, friends and friends of friends. Theatre scholar Samik Bandyopadhyay is said to have described Chakra as 'a serious group of people who did not take the theater too seriously'.[25] However, with Chakra, Badal-da's theatre activity begins to enter the larger world of the city's cultural arena. The plays are still comedies, but this time they are written by Badal-da himself.

Cultural historian Sumanta Banerjee writes:

> Badal Sircar's foray into the theatre world began with comedies. I remember having seen the first public production of his play ... way back in September 1960 when his *Boro Pishima* ... was staged in a hall in Calcutta. A humorous comedy of situations, the play was produced by Chakra, a group which was brought together by Sircar with the help of his friends and relations. The following year, the same group staged *Solution X*, another hilarious comedy written by Sircar in 1956. At around the same time, he came out with two more comedies—*Shonibar* (1959) and *Ram-Shyam-Jadu* (1961).[26]

Shanibar (Saturday, 1959), an original work, was his third play, written by him on his return to Kolkata.[27] From early 1961, Chakra began performing all three, both in Kolkata and additionally as invited or 'call' shows outside the city. Chakra also participated in a theatre competition at Theatre Centre, with *Solution X*—well-known actor and director Ahindra Choudhury[28] was a judge and won first prize. Badal-da's theatre activity had now moved firmly into—the public sphere. His fourth comedy, *Ram Shyam Jadu* (1961), was premiered in Maithon, where it was invited along with *Solution X*, in March 1962. In May that year, they performed it at both Rangmahal, Kolkata, and Minerva Theatre.

Let us take a look at this first phase of Badal Sircar, the playwright, in which he wrote four comedies, all of which were produced on stage—the true test of a dramatic text—and which are still quite popular. Badal Sircar has said, on more than one occasion, that he does not consider himself a playwright as much as a theatre worker who began writing plays almost by the way: 'Actually, I am not primarily a playwright. Primarily I am a theatre man. I started with acting, then did directing, then I wanted to produce plays. That is why I dabbled in writing.'[29] This is typical self-deprecation.

[25] Rustom Bharucha, *Rehearsals of Revolution: The Political Theater of Bengal* (Calcutta: Seagull Books, 1983), p. 133.

[26] Sumanta Banerjee, 'The Theatre of Badal Sircar,' *Theatre India*, No. 2, p. 102, 1999.

[27] Sircar, *Purano Kasundi*, Vol. 2, p. 51.

[28] Ahindra Choudhury (1897–1974), actor and director.

[29] Sircar, PNP.

Play writing was something he had attempted from a very young age, as we already know from his autobiography, *Purano Kasundi.*

Most accounts of Badal Sircar's theatre tend to dismiss these comedies with barely a mention in passing, preferring to focus on *Ebong Indrajit* as his first significant offering as a playwright. This assumption may have been supported, in all fairness, by Badal-da's own tendency to play down his playwriting in favour of his later theatre which rejected the pre-written play script. However, one cannot ignore these plays or elide over their place in his oeuvre. Firstly, they comply with the logic of his development in theatre, which began and proceeded through comedy; secondly, they are popular fare; and thirdly, they are charming and well-crafted plays with a sure grasp of the genre of situational comedy.

Pabitra Sarkar, in his introduction to the first volume of Badal Sircar's *Natak Samagra* points out the salient points of such narratives: wish fulfillment, happy endings and the neat resolution of crises. They feature stock characters driven by situations. There are no psychological explorations of the internal lives of the characters, only their behaviour in response to the circumstances in which they are placed.[30]

In his Introduction, Pabitra Sarkar says of Badal-da:

> He begins as a conventional playwright, known for his comedies ... he maintains that it is important to write good comedies; just dismissing them as non-serious plays, as a secondary art, is wrong. Reading his comedies one feels that he has got a lot out of writing them, and this enjoyment is conveyed to the audience, to the readers.[31]

Asserting the importance of good entertainment Pabitra Sarkar says that laughter gives us the stamina to deal with all our obligations and commitments and makes life easier. He provides examples of how comedy has always been popular both at times of peace and at times of war, and goes on to state that we should revisit Badal-da's comedies with a fresh eye, particularly since the Bengali tradition has just a handful of true comedies.[32]

To turn to the plays: *Solution X*, written in 1956, as already mentioned, was loosely based on the film *Monkey Business* (1952) by Howard Hawks. The plot of this one-act play has the stock comic figure of the absent-minded scientist who is so wrapped up in his scientific experiments and

[30] Pabitra Sarkar, 'Introduction', *Natak Samagra*, Vol. 1, pp. ii–iii (dui-teen).
[31] Sarkar, 'Introduction', *Natak Samagra*, Vol. 1, trans. Anjum Katyal, pp. ii–iii (dui-teen).
[32] Sarkar, 'Introduction', *Natak Samagra*, Vol. 1, pp. iii–iv (teen-char).

research that he has no time for domestic or personal life. His long-suffering wife indulges his single-minded obsession with his work. After drinking the experimental Solution X in order to help the research along, turning himself into a guinea pig in the interest of science, he regresses to childhood and gets up to all sorts of monkey business. When the effect of the solution wears off, he regains his normal persona with no memory of how he has behaved in the interim. The comedy thickens when his wife and other associates all partake of Solution X, with predictably comical results. Hilarious mayhem ensues.

Boro Pishima, as we know, was written in England in 1957, and draws on the playwright's direct experience of doing neighbourhood theatre, especially the issue of women playing women on stage, in a setting based in a typical middle-class urban housing complex. The plot revolves around a group of youngsters putting up a play and all the chaos and subterfuge that results when the heroine's strict, old fashioned, overbearing aunt arrives unexpectedly and refuses to countenance her niece acting in anything as disreputable as theatre. The various stratagems that are resorted to in order to outwit her, how they inevitably fail, and how she is reconciled in the end, form the main action of the play. The roller-coaster ride of developments, the cracking pace, the authentic characterisation and dialogue, all combine to make this a thoroughly enjoyable comedy, not least because the persons are so recognisable and true to life. Sumanta Banerjee says:

> The entire comedy of *Boro Pishima* hinges on the ingenious manipulation of a series of intricate situations to hoodwink the domineering lady, and finally ends with the winning over of the aunt. It is the stock plot of old comedies—a story of funny and surprising situations, suspense about the unpredictable, the overcoming of difficulties, and the denouncement (sic) with the reward of worthiness in the form of the engagement of the heroine with her secret admirer. But Sircar works off this plot by giving it a new twist. On the stage itself, he brings the theatre in confrontation with a real-life situation, where the characters also have to play act at another level. The intrigues that go on behind the scenes of a play within a play form the staple of *Boro Pishima*.[33]

Shanibar, a one-act play, was written in 1959, upon Badal-da's return from England. In his preface to the play in *Natak Samagra* Badal-da notes that some people feel that it is based on or adapted from James Thurber's *The Secret Life of Walter Mitty*. However, he says, at the time of writing

[33] Banerjee, 'The Theatre of Badal Sircar', p. 103.

this play, he had not encountered that work. Since daydreaming is a common phenomenon, he doesn't find it strange that there should be more than one story about it.[34] In this play, a typical middle-class clerk succumbs to vivid daydreams about office, alternating between the heady success of promotion and the nightmare of retrenchment. Appearing and re-appearing through the play is the glass of milk the concerned mother is trying to get her children to drink—a comic motif that perfectly conveys the realities of middle-class domesticity.

Ram Shyam Jadu was begun in 1957 and lay unfinished until 1961, when Chakra was looking for more material to enact. In 1962, it was performed by Chakra at Rangmahal, Minerva and a few other halls. Inspired by *We're no Angels* (1955, directed by Michael Curtiz), a Hollywood film with Humphrey Bogart, Peter Ustinov and Aldo Ray, it amusingly relates the tale of three conmen who, on the run from the long arm of the law, fall in with a kindly merchant who is facing hard times. Starting out determined to cheat him, they instead find themselves using their ingenuity and skill to help him out of his difficulties.

All these plays are set in the familiar milieu of the Bengali urban middle class, indeed Badal-da's own world. The characters, the dialogues, the sharp humour, all ring true. As comedies, they are confident, competent creations, using stock characters and devices with a sure hand and a masterful understanding of the genre. They may not be examples of earth-shatteringly original theatre, but they are thoroughly enjoyable works.

Badal-da's next creation as a playwright was *Samabritta* (lit. Concentric Circles, 1961), a crime drama—his one and only foray into this genre, he says, taken from a film he had seen but, in his typical manner, totally re-wrought into a play. It was staged in February 1963 at ABTA Hall on Ganesh Avenue.[35] *Samabritta* lay unpublished till he was over 80 years old,[36] and remains one of his little-known works, performed only once by Chakra.[37] With this, we stand poised at the watershed that was to be *Ebong Indrajit*.

A few years later, in his diary entry of 1 December 1963, while in France, Badal-da returns to his earliest plays with fresh insights:

> I'm thinking of my earlier writings. Why is *Boro Pishima* so popular? Perhaps the domestic background, recognizable characters, familiar story give it

[34] Sircar, *Natak Samagra*, Vol. 1, p. 112.
[35] Sircar, *Purano Kasundi*, Vol. 2, p. 60.
[36] Ibid.
[37] Ibid., p. 200.

> a certain authenticity which glosses over the glaring weaknesses so that spectators aren't disappointed in it. In *Ram Shyam Jadu,* the plot is strong, but I feel that my attempt to advance the storyline made the characters not that believable. If that is true (although I'm not sure about this), then *Samabritta, Solution X* and *Ballabhpurer Rupkatha* would suffer for this flaw. All of them are taken from existing stories, and in my attempt to comply with the limitations of the stage both character and atmosphere have suffered. Apart from *Boro Pishima,* my original works—*Shonibar, Ebong Indrajit,* etc.—are of a different mould.[38]

His self-criticism is not entirely supported by Sumanta Banerjee's assessment of his comedies:

> Sircar most often deals with stock situations and stereotypes as characters in these plays. At exactly the right moment, coincidences and accidents happen; the characters display their appropriate faculties, and all ends as it should happen. He uses the all too familiar device of intrigues to keep the audience in suspense and lead them on to the happy ending. But it is his acute observation of contemporary types in Bengali middle class society combined with superb theatrical dexterity and brilliant wit, that have made this group of lightweight comedies a durable part of the Bengali stage.[39]

[38] Badal Sircar, *Prabasher Hijibiji*, trans. Anjum Katyal (Kolkata: Lekhani, 2006), p. 216.
[39] Banerjee, 'The Theatre of Badal Sircar', p. 104.

CHAPTER THREE

EBONG INDRAJIT: THE GAME CHANGER

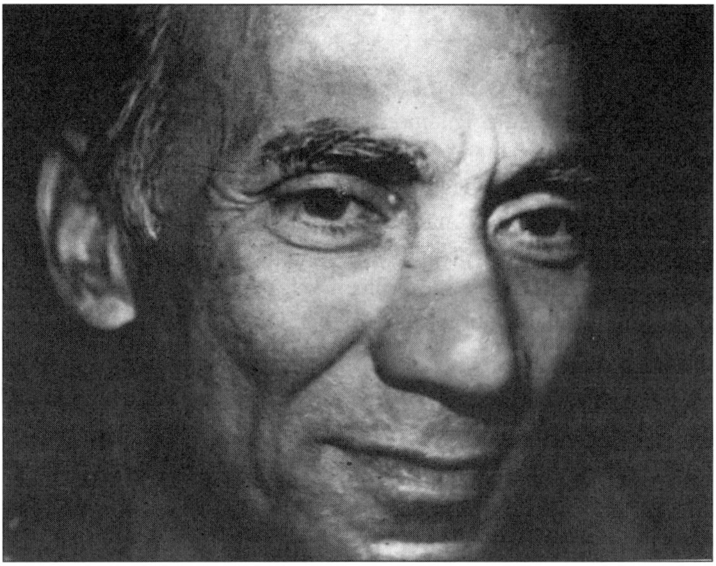

A portrait
Courtesy: Satabdi

It was with *Ebong Indrajit* that the playwright, Badal Sircar, was brought to the notice of the larger Indian theatre world. In her sensitive essay on Badal-da, Shayoni Mitra writes: '*Ebong Indrajit* is by any reckoning a hallmark in Indian dramatic history.'[1] This was the early 1960s—1963–65 to be precise. Group theatre in Bengal was already well established[2]: this was

[1] Shayoni Mitra, 'Badal Sircar: Scripting a Movement', *The Drama Review*, Vol. 48, No. 3 (Autumn, 2004), pp. 59–78.

[2] Group theatre: a post-IPTA phenomenon of theatre groups which, unlike repertories, were unable to do theatre professionally for financial reasons, whose members held day jobs

a time when Sombhu Mitra was at the helm of Bohurupee, Utpal Dutt was heading Little Theatre Group and Nandikar and Ajitesh Bandyopadhyay were already making waves. Calcutta was teeming with theatre activity of a high standard. In this setting, theatre scholar Samik Bandyopadhyay recalls his first encounter with the text of *Ebong Indrajit*. At a private gathering of a few friends, he heard Badal-da read it through. He was fascinated: 'I hadn't imagined a play like that', he said.[3] He requested the author for a copy to carry to theatre doyen Sombhu Mitra of Bohurupee, who was looking for new theatre material. But Badal-da resisted—it wasn't a play, it was not performance-worthy, it was too personal, of no interest to a broader audience. Despite his reservations, this text was to strike an immediate chord with the theatre fraternity of the time, word of mouth rapidly alerting theatre lovers to something very interesting and very different on the Bengali stage. Theatre scholar Rustom Bharucha calls it 'the *Waiting for Godot* of Bengali theatre'.[4]

Talking about the origins of *Ebong Indrajit*, Badal Sircar said:

> During my two years in London various thoughts and feelings, bits of poetry and diary entries would come to me. I thought I'd work them into the form of a play. I was convinced that I could never write anything other than plays. But the task seemed so impossible that I just couldn't begin. At last I made a beginning without thinking about it too much. I introduced a writer, like myself, who is trying to write a play, but is unable to do so. The Writer calls up four people from the audience. I had got thus far, about four or five sheets of paper, which thereafter took up permanent residence in my office bag.[5]

He narrates how one day a friend came to see him in his office while he was away in a meeting. While waiting he looked around for some reading material, found these papers in his office bag, and being a close friend, took the liberty of pulling them out and reading them. 'When I came back I snatched them from him and started scolding him, but he was not his usual jocular self, he was unusually serious. He just said—Please finish it.'[6] That very night Badal-da took out those pages along with his London notebook and

---

but worked committedly and seriously at theatre the rest of the time. Often these groups cohered around a leading actor-director, like the ones mentioned.

[3] Samik Bandyopadhyay, at his opening talk on the occasion of the Badal Utsav organised by NSS in 2009. From the NSS archives.

[4] Rustom Bharucha, *Rehearsals of Revolution*, p. 133.

[5] Sircar, *Purano Kasundi*, Vol. 2, p. 61.

[6] Ibid., trans. Anjum Katyal, p. 61.

diary, and read them over. With no clear plan in mind, he started writing. He finished it over six or seven nights.[7]

He explains:

> I never planned *Ebong Indrajit*. It was written when I was in London for two years—very poor, very lonely, very bored. So, I used to write poems. I am no poet, but I just wrote some poems. They are not love poems, nor poems on nature... but express one's thinking, when one is away, in space and time, both, for two years. I would never have written those poems had I not been away from Calcutta. *Ebong Indrajit* was written from poem to poem. The poems were written between 1957 and 1959. In 1959 I came back to Calcutta, and *Ebong Indrajit* was written in 1963. I actually sat with copies of those poems and I would write a little bit and then add a poem ... the dialogue serving as a transition from one poem to the next. That is how it was written ... I didn't know where it was going to end. Obviously, Camus. Now, I never can understand books on philosophy ... Camus' *Myth of Sisyphus*. I could never finish it ... but something affected me, moved me very much. Something somehow matched my experience. But I could not continue because it was too difficult for me. Then I read his novel *The Plague* and I thought, now I don't have to read *The Myth of Sisyphus*, the rest of it. I've got my answer ...[8]

Steeped in the conventions of the 'well-made play', he did not even consider this a complete work:

> Although I was doing plays at the time, I never thought of doing *Ebong Indrajit* as a production, because I thought it was a personal piece of writing, not a play to be produced ... and if Samik had not insisted, probably for years it would have lain in my drawer. But then it became public property.[9]

Given the importance of *Ebong Indrajit* in the canon of modern Indian plays, it is worth spending some time on its initial impact and reception.

Badal-da received a request from Bohurupee for permission to print the playscript in their journal. It was granted.[10] After the play was published,[11] Gobindo Ganguly approached Badal Sircar for permission to do a

[7] Sircar, *Purano Kasundi,* Vol. 2, p. 61.

[8] Sircar, PNP.

[9] Ibid.

[10] Sircar, *Purano Kasundi,* Vol. 2, p. 90.

[11] *Bohurupee* journal, issue of July 1965.

production. Sircar, who was in Nigeria, wrote that although he had given the permission to Bohurupee, if they didn't have an objection, neither did he.[12] For whatever reason, Bohurupee decided to allow Gobindo Ganguly to go ahead.

Thus, the first production of *Ebong Indrajit* was done by the Bengali theatre group Souvanik in 1965. It was directed by Gobindo Ganguly and staged at Muktangan, a cult intimate theatre space for alternative or group theatre in Calcutta. Despite receiving plenty of criticism from people who had read the text and expected better things from its staging, there is no gainsaying that the play had a considerable impact. With this production, Badal Sircar's entire standing and significance in the greater world of Indian theatre changed. Suddenly he is the 'enfant terrible' of the playwriting scene; great things are expected of him. A review from the period allows us to glimpse just how much of an impact he made:

> 'Badal Sarkar's entry into the circle of contemporary Bengali playwrights has been with a bang. When *Ebong lndrajit* was first published in the July '65 issue of Bohurupee magazine it evoked immediate interest, admiration and surprise. The surprise was because those who had read his earlier published plays like *Ram Shyam Jadu* or *Baro Pishima*, or had seen them on the stage had not imagined that a dramatist with only a few slender comedies to his credit could suddenly write as serious and disturbing a play as *Ebong lndrajit* and succeed at the same time with a formal experiment that was almost revolutionary. In any case acquaintance with his earlier plays could not have been wide and to most who read or saw it performed *Ebong lndrajit* was Badal Sarkar's first play.[13]

In the lacuna between writing the play and its production, while he busied himself with writing other plays, Badal-da often designed *Ebong Indrajit* for the stage, in his head and on paper, as we come to know from his diaries and letters; he had even visualised a 'theatre in the round' production of it in his imagination.[14] Yet he never embarked on a production, not even with Chakra. Inevitably, when he first heard about Souvanik's production, while he was in Nigeria, he was disappointed that the interpretation was

[12] Sircar, *Purano Kasundi*, Vol. 2, pp. 98–99.

[13] From a review of Kabi Kahini by 'A Drama Critic,' *Frontier*, Vol. 1, No. 1 (14 April 1968), p. 16. http://frontierweekly.com/archive/vol-number/vol/vol-1/vol-1-issues/1_1_14april1968.pdf (accessed 27 January 2015).

[14] See Sircar, *Prabasher Hijibiji*.

different from the way he had intended it to be: a typical dilemma for any writer seeing his or her work produced by someone else. He writes:

> Tons of news about Souvanik's *Ebong Indrajit*. A newborn child, A-B-C-D, a spirited child and so on—I haven't quite got to the bottom of it. Was I presenting a lifecycle? Couldn't understand the signal either. Yes, I did write about a railway line, but I made it clear that no train runs on it. That Indrajit, Writer, Manasi could, accepting the path ahead, leave on a train is beyond my imagination. If the 'I am Weary' poem is spoken by anyone other than Writer, particularly Amal Bimal Kamal, then the play is ruined, to my mind. I feel as if, based on *Ebong Indrajit*, they have produced a whole other play of their liking. The message of *Ebong Indrajit* is not so complex or difficult, after all. Is that why they're attempting to make it more complicated?[15]

Badal-da saw the production for himself later.[16] He is cryptic about it in his autobiography.

> It was a terrifying experience. I hadn't expected it to be so terrible ... I was intensely critical, tore it to shreds. They were quiet in response, but that wasn't good enough for me, I was uncomfortable—after all, people were coming to see it in droves, the newspapers were praising it![17]

Literary and film scholar Mihir Bhattacharya, then a 'young lecturer at Jadavpur University', who saw the Souvanik production after this episode comments: 'The group had obviously spruced up the production after the playwright's outburst, but the quality of the performance was still rather poor, and part of the audience came away unsatisfied and puzzled.'[18]

Although this production did not appear to meet with much critical approval, it certainly helped spread word about the play. Speaking in 1996, Badal-da asserted: '... that Bengali production is not my play [...]'. He further stated, 'There hasn't been a single important Bengali production of this play, although through the staging of this play in Bengali I became

[15] Sircar, *Prabasher Hijibiji*, trans. Anjum Katyal, pp. 268–69.
[16] Sircar, *Purano Kasundi*, Vol. 2, pp. 98–99.
[17] Ibid., trans. Anjum Katyal, p. 99.
[18] Mihir Bhattacharya, 'Obituary: Radical Modernist', *Frontline*, Vol. 28, No. 12, 4–17 June 2011. http://www.frontlineonnet.com/fl2812/stories/20110617281209000.htm (accessed 27 January 2015).

a playwright, as Karanth[19] said he became a national director with his production of this play.'[20]

Samik Bandopadhyay felt that the Souvanik production conveyed Sircar's alienation and feeling of being an outsider; what came through was the real anguish of a thinking, questioning, Bengali, middle class person:

> This reflected the frustration of the early sixties, of this man who would not give up his ideals despite the idealistic visions of independence crumbling, of radicalism selling out, the crisis mounting. However, that pain, that anguish, that bitterness, was lost in the obvious symbolism of a railway track, a green signal, and loud overacting.[21]

Playwright Girish Karnad, however, who had seen the production at Muktangan along with Hindi playwright Mohan Rakesh, Marathi writer Vijay Tendulkar and Marathi actor–director Arvind Deshpande when they were invited to Calcutta by cultural organisation Anamika Kala Sangam, admitted, 'I quite liked the production though I thought they overdid it a bit—they overacted.'[22] He particularly 'loved' the production 'for its use of farce, mime and improvisation'.[23]

Theatre director Rajinder Nath emphasised that it was this first production in Bengali that got the play known and talked about in Delhi.[24] After seeing that production, he managed to track down the Hindi translation by Pratibha Agarwal. 'So whether people liked the production or not, the original production of *Ebong Indrajit* created history and got the play known, after which subsequent productions took place.'[25] For Samik Bandyopadhyay, too, this first production was responsible for bringing Badal Sircar to light in a way.[26]

Sumanta Banerjee describes the reception context in which *Ebong Indrajit* was first seen by the Calcutta audience:

> Those who were acquainted with the Western philosophical trends and the new theatre movement that was developing under their influence in Europe

[19] B.V. Karanth (1929–2002), theatre director.

[20] Sircar, PNP.

[21] Samik Bandyopadhyay, PNP.

[22] Girish Karnad, PNP.

[23] E-Rang newsletter, 'Remembering Badal Sircar', No. 24, 1 July 2011. http://theatreforum.in/m/e-rang/?tab=issues&object_id=17 (accessed 27 January 2015).

[24] Rajinder Nath, Hindi theatre director (b. 1935), PNP.

[25] Nath, PNP.

[26] Bandyopadhyay, PNP.

> in the 1950–60 period, might have found the presentation of these ideas and the dramatic devices chosen by Badal Sircar in his plays to express them rather blasé, or unoriginal. The theories of Existentialism of Sartre and Camus were already familiar to the Calcutta Coffee House regulars. The Theatre of the Absurd had arrived, and the plays of Beckett, Ionesco, Adamov and Genet had reached the bookstalls. In fact, in 1965 ... Mohit Chattopadhyay[27] came out with his first absurd play, *Kanthanalite Surya*, where the hero imagines that a sun has got stuck in his windpipe and he cannot bring it out—symbolizing a mediocre person who imagines that he has all the qualities of a genius within himself, but cannot express them. The Calcutta theatre-lovers therefore were familiar with the arguments that Sircar posed in *Ebong Indrajit*. When towards the end of the play, Indrajit compared his efforts to the futile attempts of Sisyphus to lift the huge stone to the mountain top from where it always rolls down, the discerning spectators could immediately get the message and trace its source in Camus' *Le Mythe de Sisyphe*. Even the theatrical devices were old hat. The play-within-the play, the symbols and the fantasies, the poetic monologues, were worn out in the West—what with the experiments made years ago by Maeterlinck and Pirandello in devising techniques to express their metaphysical ideas, or by Eliot, Auden and Isherwood in their poetic drama.[28]

And yet Sumanta Banerjee rejects any hint that this made *Ebong Indrajit* at all derivative or inauthentic:

> Sircar brought in a new abiding flavor, where the hands of a superb playwright and theatrical technician were evident. The theatrical speech was at once colloquial and poetic. The handling of the situations was ingenious and innovative. The characters ... were located in the urban Bengali middle class environment of 1960s—a period which was an important watershed in the history of post-independence Bengal. Although Sircar's ideas might have been influenced by the West, the concerns and anxieties that they expressed were authentic, since they were being experienced by a generation of perceptive youth in Bengal, as also in other parts of India at that time. All these shook the Indian theatre-goers into a new realization of the possibilities of the drama as a means of expressing the complex spiritual anguish of the times.[29]

Girish Karnad's response to the staging was positive. In terms of playwriting, it was a major eye opener for him. During the 1960s, there was an attempt amongst writers to move away from the conventions—the scene divisions

[27] Mohit Chattopadhyay (1934–2012), Bengali playwright.
[28] Banerjee, 'The Theatre of Badal Sircar', pp. 105–06.
[29] Ibid., p. 106.

and the given 'Ibsenite' structure—of the 'well-made play'. In the circumstances, *Ebong Indrajit* was a tremendous stimulant. Karnad explained that he had focused on the fluid, unstructured movement of the text, flowing from sequence to sequence, broken by stylised interludes, interspersed with poetry, with multiple zones of action. Karnad realised that this was the fluidity of movement that one talked about in theatre. After seeing the Bengali production in Calcutta, Karnad had gone back to Madras, where he translated the play into English from Pratibha Agrawal's Hindi version. The Madras Players produced it. 'It was, I believe, one of the first modern Indian plays to be specially translated from the original language and staged by an English language group. My version shamelessly borrowed from the Souvanik production, and it was a huge success.'[30]

This experience fed directly into his development as a playwright. He says:

> For years I had been struggling with the idea of writing a play in which there were no scenic divisions and the action would flow from situation to situation, but although I discussed the possibilities endlessly with B. V. Karanth, I didn't know how to manage it. Directing *Evam Indrajit* gave me the clue, and I wrote *Hayavadana.* About *Hayavadana* I have always confessed that, 'I drew upon many different sources for my use of traditional conventions, but the form was given to me by *Evam Indrajit.*'[31]

The buzz of excitement around the text quickly spread beyond Calcutta. Director Satyadev Dubey[32] recalled that he had, in an article on Sombhu Mitra in *Dharmayug*, stated that, despite all his achievements, Mitra had never actually discovered a playwright; on his next visit to Bombay, Mitra met him and told him that he *had* discovered a new playwright, Badal Sircar, and that *Ebong Indrajit* had been published in the periodical *Bohurupee.* In 1966–67, B. V. Karanth, interviewing Dubey, also referred to *Ebong Indrajit* as a very exciting play. Dubey first accessed the text through Pratibha Agarwal's Hindi translation. 'You cannot forget certain things that become so important in your life and one of these was the translation of *Evam Indrajit* that she sent me; I loved it.'[33]

Soon, major theatre directors in different parts of the country were producing the play. We have already read about Karnad's production with the

[30] E-Rang newsletter, 'Remembering Badal Sircar', No. 24, 1 July 2011. http://theatreforum.in/m/e-rang/?tab=issues&object_id=17 (accessed 27 January 2015).

[31] Ibid.

[32] Satyadev Dubey (1936–2011), theatre director.

[33] Satyadev Dubey, PNP.

Madras Players. In Calcutta, Shyamanand Jalan[34] did a critically acclaimed Hindi production, *Evam Indrajit,* in1968 which became unexpectedly popular even with Bengali audiences:

> The whole production of *Evam Indrajit* was geared towards the discovery of images, discovery of inflexions, discovery of ways of speaking, of standing, lighting, to convey the mood and the thoughts. And for this we used circular movements. This was the first attempt on my part to convey the whole thing not through words but through movements and images.[35]

Jalan insisted that it was the visualisation in moving images that made his *Evam Indrajit* production meaningful and effective in terms of communication:

> We were not doing a play. We were conveying something to the audience—some meanings, some observations, some thoughts, in a language which they did not fully understand. And the thoughts were not very easy, they required a certain receptivity on the part of the audience, a certain intellectual standard to grasp them, and therefore we had to convey them very simply.[36]

Recalling the audience response to his production Jalan said:

> Our best audience and best response was at the show at Kalamandir, Calcutta, before a Bengali audience. That gave us so much strength because we were talking in Hindi and we had a hundred percent Bengali audience and they responded to it ... The two other performances which come to mind were in Allahabad where we had professors and students and writers in the audience, and in Kanpur where the audience was diametrically different—an audience of shopkeepers.[37]

Satyadev Dubey's production of *Evam Indrajit* (1970) had Sulabha Deshpande as Manasi, Dubey himself as Indrajit and Amrish Puri as the Writer. Dr Jabbar Patel[38] recalled the great impact of this production, not least due to the excellent performances by Sulabha and Dubey. He said:

> Dubey's use of space (I still remember Sulabha and Dubey walking with a platform behind them, and the use of different light groups as they walked);

[34] Shyamanand Jalan (1934–2010), influential theatre director and personality.
[35] Shyamanand Jalan, PNP.
[36] Ibid.
[37] Ibid.
[38] Jabbar Patel (b. 1942), theatre and film director.

> and the use of different speech patterns; and above everything else the way the whole thing was held together in a beautiful fusion.[39]

However, this was not the first production of the play in Bombay. Dubey talked of a production in Gujarati, directed by Praveen Joshi,[40] with sets designed by M. S. Sathyu.[41] He remembers that the set was full of mushrooms:

> [A]nd yet their style was a sort of Gujarati realism as in professional theatre ... I remember being able to sit through the play, not getting bored, but I said, it is a different play which they are doing ... The first production of *Evam Indrajit* in Bombay was the Gujarati production. I did it two years later.[42]

Theatre doyen B. V. Karanth did a production of the play with National School of Drama, Delhi. He recalled that in his initial reading of the text, he had found the Writer the most important character, rather than Manasi and Indrajit. But he called the play *Amal, Vimal, Kamal* and gave priority to the human relationships in the play—'no human relationship is static. This is the essence of all relationships ... it is just that we undertake journeys in vain, not reaching anywhere.' He also found the text of much literary value.[43]

Karanth recalled a Kannada production of *Evam Indrajit* directed by

> a young college student Narasimhan, in Mysore, performed in a college courtyard, with no stage lights at all. Lights from the classrooms served as the only lighting arrangement.... He laid a lot of stress on the Indrajit-Manasi relationship. His interpretation was striking because of its simplicity.[44]

From Bengali to Hindi, Marathi, Gujarati, Kannada and English—it is unusual for a regional language play to travel with such speed to different states across the country within a few years of being written. It is unusual for the leading directors of the time to respond to it almost unanimously and seek to stage it. Clearly there was something about this text that spoke to the need of the hour, both in terms of form and content. Satyadev Dubey, in his introduction to the English translation of the play, says: '... it is only in relation to Indian theatre history that *Evam Indrajit* really makes its

[39] Jabbar Patel, PNP.
[40] Praveen Joshi, Gujarati theatre director (1936–1980).
[41] Mysore Shrinivas Sathyu (b. 1930), leading film director, stage designer and art director.
[42] Dubey, PNP.
[43] B. V. Karanth, PNP.
[44] Ibid.

presence felt; otherwise it is just a very good, sensitively written play, like many others written in the last decade in India.'[45] What made this play so relevant to, and representative of, that time?

Sumanta Banerjee, cultural historian, succinctly analyses the historical context in which *Ebong Indrajit* was embedded:

> More than a decade after Independence, the 1960s appeared to the urban Indian middle class as an age that offered too much for a few instead of enough for the many. The idealism of the years immediately following Independence had dissipated and degenerated into corruption among the political leaders and cynicism among the common people. A generation of unemployed educated youth had grown up finding their ideals and hopes crashing in disappointments. It was not merely a question of jobs for them. It was a crisis of values. As in other parts of India, in Bengal also they were torn between the norms of moral integrity and responsibility, with which they grew up as children in their middle class homes in the 1940–50 period on the one hand, and the new norms of unscrupulousness that they were required to follow in their youth to survive in the commercial world of the 1960s on the other. Here they had to come to terms with bribery, nepotism, and various other forms of corruption. Those who could not cope with these, came to feel that they were unnecessary, unwanted and useless—whether in their homes, or in their careers, or in their personal relationships. A sense of utter loneliness and inexplicable alieniation gripped them. Yet, their hopes and desires were still glowing like dying embers [...]. It was this generation that discovered in Badal Sircar's *Ebong Indrajit* an indigenously designed experimental drama that gave voice to their inarticulate cries, and a certain shape to their confused ideas.[46]

Satyadev Dubey says:

> The year 1962 is important to India for many reasons. 1962 was a year of great political turmoil. But it was also the year when Dharamvir Bharati's Hindi play *Andha Yug* was performed by Theatre Unit (Bombay). *Andha Yug* was a small beginning but the seeds of creative pride had been sown and a determined effort at looking at one's surroundings was to become an imperative which went beyond the platitudinous slogan of seeking one's roots. This imperative found its first fully conscious expression the same year in Calcutta, where a lean and balding Bengali architect was fulfilling his

[45] Satyadev Dubey, Introduction to Badal Sircar, *Evam Indrajit*, trans. Girish Karnad (Calcutta: Oxford University Press, 1974), p. v.

[46] Banerjee, 'The Theatre of Badal Sircar', pp. 106–07.

assignment as an urban designer and also writing a play, later to be recognized as a milestone in the history of modern Indian drama.[47]

The play, of course, was *Ebong Indrajit* by Badal Sircar:

> With the performance of Sircar's *Evam Indrajit* in Bengali in Calcutta in September 1965, theatre practitioners all over India became aware of a major talent and a major play. The play provided for them the shock of recognition. It was about the Indian reality as they knew it; it was a theatrically effective and crystallized projection of all the prevalent attitudes, vague feelings and undefined frustrations gnawing in the hearts of the educated urban middle class.[48]

Like Sumanta Banerjee, Dubey also pinpoints that the play is about, of and for the urban educated middle class in India:

> The intellectually alive urban middle class regards itself as the backbone of the country. Their so-called middle class values have been glorified and yet their genuine and deeper values have always been attacked by those who swear by fashionable Marxist dogmas. The middle classes have been made to feel guilty for opting for stability, aspiring for culture and believing in a national identity ... *Evam Indrajit* is in some ways about the residue; the residue consists of those who have failed to adjust, align and ceased to aspire, and also those who are enmeshed in the day to day struggle for survival.... Structurally Sircar anticipates and captures the hybridization of the period; for the complexity of Indrajit's situation is such that stylistic punctiliousness must give precedence to what needs to be expressed.[49]

Rustom Bharucha, explaining why the play was 'spontaneously received by the theatrical community in Bengal' feels that they

> discovered in the protagonist Indrajit all their dreams and compromises and moments of futility. One could say that *Evam Indrajit* is about an enlightened middle-class youth in Bengal who passes through various stages in his life unable to fulfill his dreams, and yet unable to accept the triviality of the world around him epitomized by three representatives of the bourgeoisie, Amal, Vimal and Kamal.[50]

[47] Dubey, Introduction to Badal Sircar, *Evam Indrajit*, p. v.
[48] Ibid., p. vi.
[49] Ibid., pp. vi–ix.
[50] Bharucha, *Rehearsals of Revolution*, pp. 133–34.

For Shyamanand Jalan, the play spoke to the fears and insecurities of the time:

> In the early sixties people were quite concerned with [the threat of] the wiping out of the world because of the atom bomb and the hydrogen bomb. That sort of fear has become dormant now ... but it was new at that time, in the fifties and the sixties, and it was playing on our minds. And therefore the total philosophy of *Evam Indrajit* and the total content of *Evam Indrajit* became very personal.[51]

There have been many interpretations and approaches to this text as well as differing ideas about the message of the play. It is about the absence of hope, about living in a state of non-hope; it is about the journey, the process, of life; it is about holding on to your dreams despite daily life's attempts to crush you into submission; it is about daring to be different and refusing to succumb to the demands of everyday living. The motif of the myth of Sisyphus, of the boulder being endlessly pushed uphill only to roll all the way down again; the motif of the unending road; the motif of the railway tracks that remain parallel, only seeming to meet way in the past or way in the future—these have been interpreted variously in various readings of the text. Like all rich and complex works, the possibility for interpretation is endless, with each new reader bringing his or her own understanding to it.

The playwright has introduced experiences from his own life into *Ebong Indrajit*. The typical life cycle of an educated middle class boy who is expected to study, finish school, go to college, graduate, find a job, get married, start a family and produce children who will in turn study, finish school, go to college and so on, is very much his own. He knows this reality, which is also that of his friends. He also knows the aspiration for a different kind of life, something creative, risky and adventurous, which he too felt, manifest in a certain inner restlessness which kept him changing jobs and travelling to new places for new experiences—and above all, writing. Like him, Indrajit goes to Bhopal and then London. The social taboo that forbids Manasi and Indrajit from getting married is something Badal-da faced in his own life; he chose to defy it but experienced the stigma and disapproval that ensued: he alludes to this in *Purano Kasundi*. The friendship between the four lads, the fooling around and teasing which captures their closeness, is also familiar ground from his personal life. The poems, of course, have sprung from his own thoughts and feelings. The humiliating, soul-destroying job

[51] Jalan, PNP.

interview, the stultifying file-pusher's work routine, the enervating commutes to and from office—all this could be straight from his own life. He turns them into amusing, tongue-in-cheek interludes which express their essentially absurd quality:

> Writer: First files, then cha. Then files. Then tiffin. Then files. Then cha. Then tiffin. Then tram-bus-train. A bigger office. More important work. First files, then tea. Then files. Then lunch. Then files. Then tea. Then files. Then Hindustan-Fiat-Standard.[52]

The use of such 'abstractions of situations and attitudes'[53] helps him convey the empty, mechanical repetitiveness of middle-class life. His sure grasp of the nuances of language can be seen here in the shift from *cha*, the colloquial word, to the English word 'tea', and from the humbler 'tiffin' to the more sophisticated 'lunch', to indicate a rise up the corporate and social ladder. Public transport is replaced by individual cars, the Hindustan–Fiat-Standard Heralds which were the only models then available in the country. And yet the basic absurdity of the life remains the same.

It is this groundedness in experience, this first-hand knowledge of the subject and his unerring ear for the spoken word resulting in believable dialogue, that turns *Ebong Indrajit* into such a powerful text. Leading Marathi playwright G.P. Deshpande recognised this when he said, 'Badal Sarkar's [sic] Bangla is radically different from the pre-Sarkar theatre speech in Bangla. That it came close to actual speech is not its only achievement. The economy of words was unknown to several theatre traditions in India.'[54] The audience could recognise the characters, the milieu, and identify with them. It all rang true. It was witty and ironic, but it was also poignant and emotional.

Even the form of the play, with its non-linear narrative, its segueing into different sequences without formal breaks, the introduction of poetic interludes, the deft use of repetition, the piercing of the fourth wall, bespoke a contemporaneity that made this very much a work of its time.

A word here about the introduction of poetry into the play. Badal-da meant the poems to be integral to the work, as we know from his description of the writing process. In a sense, the dialogue is just what he added to

[52] Sircar, 'Ebong Indrajit', *Natak Samagra*, Vol. 1, trans. Anjum Katyal, p. 288.

[53] Samik Bandyopadhyay, 'Middle-class Responsibilities', *Sangeet Natak*, No. 22 (October–December 1971). Quoted from Bharucha, *Rehearsals of Revolution*, p. 135.

[54] G.P. Deshpande, 'Theatre of Modernity: A Celebration of Modernity?' *Theatre India*, Vol. 5, May 2002, pp. 8–14.

string the poems together, if one is to go by what he says. Sumanta Banerjee comments:

> By bringing back poetry to the theatre after many decades, Sircar to some extent was also satisfying the cravings of an audience that had been brought up on the vacuous formality of rigid prose in the theatre for much too long. Sircar's monologues in verse are of course totally different from the high-pitched melodramatic outpourings of the romantic characters of the nineteenth-early twentieth century Bengali plays ... He expresses individual and social concerns in a poetic idiom which has a rhythm that is close to contemporary speech. The sudden switch from prose dialogue to verse reflects the shift of mood and feeling of the character.[55]

Here is one example of how he uses poetry in this play, to elevate the tenor of the language from conversational to poetic, thereby causing a sudden shift in the atmosphere. The effect is to underline that the quotidian and the spiritual are linked. Ordinary, everyday words can mask a deeper, more meditative thought process.

The Writer and Manasi have just been talking about Indrajit. Manasi feels that he is still holding on to his dreams. But when they vanish, he will no longer be able to float through life clinging on to the fragile shreds of his dreams. 'What if he drowns?' asks the Writer. 'It'll be good if he does', she replies. 'Perhaps by drowning he'll learn his inner depths, touch solid ground, and then maybe his real life will truly begin.' 'How do you know?' asks the Writer. 'I don't', she replies, walking away. 'I don't know anything, I'm stupid. I just believe'. 'Believe?' He responds, 'Belief, in this underworld hell?'

Immediately, Indrajit enters and recites a poem which takes the imagery and ideas of this preceding conversation and recasts them in poetic form:

> Adrift on the waters of impoverished existence
> Resting life's burdens on the merest wisp of support
> The far bank is veiled in a weary white breath of mist
> Those golden realms so far beyond the clouds
> Those heavens that reside beside the stars
> In this other land they are a lie
> Let be the tepid words of comfort mild
> Strip off the blinkers of belief blind

[55] Banerjee, 'The Theatre of Badal Sircar', p. 105.

Plunge down, drown, plumb your own deep
Man is restless, never still
Man is a surprising soul
Who will a kingdom found even on a drowned and buried stone.

Next, the Writer approaches Indrajit and there is a series of questions from Writer countered by terse, matter of fact answers by Indrajit. We discover that he has yielded to the demands of the everyday—returned to the city, taken up a job, married a woman other than his beloved Manasi; in other words, he appears to have surrendered.[56]

This sequence shows us how the playwright plays with registers of atmosphere and meaning. The Writer's conversation with Manasi is philosophical, deep; next comes a poem which takes the very same vocabulary onto another plane of poetic expression; immediately thereafter the most banal of conversations which is yet strangely poignant.

We have seen from the early comedies that Badal-da the playwright locates his plays squarely in the middle–middle class which is his own milieu. *Ebong Indrajit* is no different. However, instead of the previous lighthearted (albeit affectionate) approach to characters and situations, here we see the first tentative step towards the politicisation of the subject. The playwright identifies the malaise of conformity which ails the middle class and exposes the banality and mechanical nature of daily existence by contrasting it with the figure of the Writer who cannot fit neatly into the structure of middle-class expectations, and the figure of Indrajit who finds himself questioning what his peers unquestioningly accept: the pressure to conform, the taboos, the social inequalities and prescriptions that make up the 'system'. The poetry that peppers the text reflects this inner questioning, serving as a marker of the inner creative life of an individual. There are shades of Rabindranath Tagore in this dichotomy between the individual soul that yearns for creativity and freedom and the repressive nature of the establishment that seeks to contain him.

Indrajit begins by confessing that he conforms out of fear of *ashanti*—unrest, upheaval. His soulmate, with whom he discusses his inner confusions, is Manasi (lit. creation of the mind); their relationship is too unconventional for a conventional resolution. He is the only one who expresses his disturbance at the injustice prevalent in the system the others accept—at the destitute shoe-polish boy trying to eke out a living or the

[56] Sircar, 'Ebong Indrajit', *Natak Samagra*, Vol. 1, trans. Anjum Katyal, pp. 303–04.

young widow disowned by her in-laws who has no place to go. He is the only one who expresses an incoherent anger at such injustice:

> Indrajit: At the bus stop where I catch my bus, a boy of about seven or eight years accosted me. To polish my shoes. He had a child with him, a year-old toddler, who was playing with the polish-rag. I didn't get my shoes polished. I didn't give him a single paisa. Just scared him off. If he had pestered me I may even have hit him.
>
> Manasi (taking his hand): Why?
>
> Indrajit: Don't know. I don't know whom I should hit. I know I shouldn't hit him. But still I might have. Because I can't accept him. A system in which a seven-year-old boy has to polish shoes for a living, with his year-old brother beside him—I can't accept such a system.[57]

This protest is still inchoate, still confused about who the hated entity is—himself for being part of such a system, the child victim, or the unjust society that perpetrates such inequity. And yet his refusal to accept is the seed of conscientisation, and thereafter politicisation. This is what makes Indrajit different from Amal Bimal Kamal. The Writer is the only sentient being who understands, empathises and then encourages the spark of protest and resistance he sees in Indrajit. But Indrajit cannot find it in him to defy, challenge or break free of the restrictions that seem to make up his life. Rather, at the end of the play, he finds himself succumbing to them, growing to accept that he is Nirmal after all. This is when the Writer steps in to guide him towards a different idea of his destiny:

> Writer: Indrajit?
> Indrajit: I'm sorry, you're mistaken. I'm Nirmal Kumar Ray.
> Writer: Don't you know me, Indrajit?
> Indrajit: Who are you? Writer?
> Writer: I can't seem to complete my play, Indrajit?
> Indrajit: So what's the point of completing it? It has no end. Its beginning and end are all the same.
> Writer: I still have to write, don't I?
> Indrajit: You have your writing, so write. It's nothing to do with me. I am Nirmal.
> Writer: But you have nothing. No promotion to plan, no house to build, no business scheme. How can you be Nirmal?
> Indrajit: But—I'm so ordinary!

[57] Sircar, 'Ebong Indrajit', *Natak Samagra*, Vol. 1, trans. Anjum Katyal, p. 279.

> Writer: Still, you're not Nirmal. I too am ordinary. But I'm not Nirmal either. Neither you nor I have the option of being Nirmal.
> Indrajit: So what then—what will we live by?
> Writer: The road. For us, there is only the road. We'll walk. I have nothing to write about, yet I'll write. You have nothing to talk about, yet you'll talk. Manasi has nothing to live for, yet she'll live. We have the road. We'll carry on walking.
> Indrajit: The God Jupiter cursed Sisyphus so that he had to keep rolling a heavy boulder all the way uphill. As soon he reached the peak, the rock would roll down again. Again he pushes it up, again it rolls down, again he pushes it up.
> Writer: We too are like the doomed Sisyphus. We too know the rock is bound to roll down again. Even as we roll it uphill we know that there is no point to it. The peak we are aiming for—it has no meaning.
> Indrajit: Yet we have to push it uphill.
> Writer: Yet we must push it uphill. Without hope, since we know what the future holds. Our past and our future are all mixed up. We know that what lay behind us also lies ahead of us.
> Indrajit: And still we must live?
> Writer: Still we must live. Still we must keep walking. For us there is no holy place, just the journey. The pilgrimage.[58]

The play ends on this note. The image of the 'path', the road, is a powerful one in Bengali literature and folklore. The figure of the traveller on the unending road holds an emotional and intellectual charge, fuelled by myriad associations: he who turns his back on society, from the rebel to the lone ascetic, the mystic, the wanderer, the seeker of truth. By selecting this as the final image of the play, the playwright is connecting with a tradition of nonconformism that his audience can immediately relate to. And for the first time, his middle-class subject, who in his earlier plays has exhibited mild symptoms of being a misfit, albeit in a comical framework, exiles himself from his social class in protest: not only in a state of non-hope, perhaps, but also in a rejection of its parameters.

In terms of style and form, this play already exhibits several of the features that are going to be characteristic of Badal-da's later theatre, including his Third Theatre, which is ironic, given that he put this play firmly and publicly behind him when he rejected the proscenium.[59] We see the fluid movement from one sequence, one tableau, to the next. We see the 'abstraction

[58] Sircar, 'Ebong Indrajit', *Natak Samagra,* Vol. 1, trans. Anjum Katyal, pp. 310–11.
[59] See PNP.

of situations' mentioned earlier: the tendency of his words to 'resonate ideas rather than personal feelings.'[60] The easy shifting between differing registers of language, from colloquial spoken speech to poetry, journalese, officialese and even gibberish; the interjection of mechanical, machine-like movements. There is the technique of 'verbal collage' where characters utter phrases and sentences which are seemingly disconnected but which build an overall coherent picture of a class, a society and a life:

> Amal: The country is full of corruption
> Vimal: This government is useless
> Kamal: Power is bound to corrupt one
> Amal: Politics is a dirty game
> [...]
> Amal: No promotion
> Vimal: Terrible living quarters
> Kamal: Business is poor
> Amal: Wife is sick
> Vimal: Child failed in school
> Kamal: Father died[61]

This juxtapositioning of seemingly disparate entities, ideas, words, is very typical of Badal-da's later work, and we see it first in *Ebong Indrajit*.

Rustom Bharucha identifies several additional 'rhetorical techniques' common to Badal-da's Third Theatre phase; we already find them in *Ebong Indrajit*. For example, the 'accumulation of phrases and non sequiturs that Sircar generally uses with ironic effect' and 'the repetition of words to create an effect of incantation'.[62] In fact, a confident playfulness with language is very characteristic of his style: internal rhymes creating interesting echoes, puns and wry repetitions.

Mihir Bhattacharya, who had not cared much for the Souvanik production, was nonetheless impressed with the text of the play:

> What stood out was the power of the text. Much of it is loosely strung free verse from the writer, but what comes from Amal, Bimal, Kamal and Indrajit and Manasi are so integrally related to the rhythm and tonality of what the writer offers, often directly to the audience, that the theatrical experience not only shatters the cherished illusionism of generations of

[60] Bharucha, *Rehearsals of Revolution*, p. 135.
[61] Sircar, 'Ebong Indrajit', *Natak Samagra*, Vol. 1, trans. Anjum Katyal, p. 301.
[62] Bharucha, *Rehearsals of Revolution*, p. 136.

theatregoers but also makes them participate in a dialogic exploration of urgent existential questions.

The technique is based on the constant evocation of the allusive power of ordinary language, much used in both modernism and folk poetry, moving instantly from the utterly mundane to the profoundly philosophical. A reminder about dinner, a job interview, a courting at the park, a litany of family woes—things that are repeated trillions of times on the terrain of the quotidian—evoke sharp interrogations of the conventions on which such speech-acts are based and lay bare the purposive illusions of facticity. And this is done by baring the device of artistry itself.

The Russian formalists used to call this ostranenie, or defamiliarisation, which shatters the facade of the familiar and makes it strange. Bertolt Brecht's 'estrangement effect' is something very much like this, and both Vsevolod E. Meyerhold and Erwin Piscator and, later on, Ariane Mnouchkine used the principle to marvellous effect.

Sircar's particular take was to make each character a shifting subject—with actors easing into different roles and interchanging them at will—so that representing the world of human beings became a universalising exercise. Each character is multiple over space and time and, therefore, ungraspable and at one with the indeterminacy of the world. Sircar's puzzles traversed the known contours of middle-class life in India with intent, as so many signposts of waste and frustration, bringing home to the audience that thinking out things meant a constant clash of ideas and identities, a continual questioning of certainties.[63]

This play is a central referent in Badal-da's creative life both as a playwright and as a director or theatre practitioner. It prefigures, as we shall see, many aspects and features of his later work. Literary scholar Sibaji Bandyopadhyay traces a trajectory of Badal-da's playwriting from *Ebong Indrajit* onwards—the move to a kind of 'structural' playwriting after his first phase of comedies was over, in answer to his own dilemma of what to do next:

> [It was] obvious to Badal Sircar [that], in order to continue one has to produce *original* plays. What counted as an original play in Bengali was the question which at one point in his career preoccupied Badal Sircar; as a matter of fact, the question almost consumed him. And perhaps this is one of the salient reasons why, of all his plays, *Ebong Indrajit* enjoys a kind of centrality in any 'Badal Sircar Study'.[64]

[63] Mihir Bhattacharya, 'Obituary: Radical Modernist', *Frontline*.

[64] Sibaji Bandyopadhyay, interview with the author, Kolkata, 17 May 2014.

He is not surprised that *Ebong Indrajit* took such a long time to emerge in a finished form—that from the initial poems of 1957–59, it finally emerged as a full-blown piece only after four further years, in 1963:

> *Ebong Indrajit* is a play about writing a play, about conceptualizing a performance-text worthy of theatre. The stellar achievement of the play was constituted by the fact that Badal Sircar succeeded in it to transform a 'personal' problem into a problematic. In trying to interrogate why it is damnably difficult to use the bhadralok world as dramatic material Badal Sircar managed to project his own angst vis-à-vis 'writing' onto a middle-class person who *fails* to craft an original play. Delegating his authorial rights to the character, Badal Sircar called him simply Lekhak or Writer.
>
> In *Ebong Indrajit* Lekhak assumes that every dramatic presentation requires some or the other 'situation' which is pregnant with a momentous 'crisis'. But, as he searches for situations amenable to the logic of dramatic 'action' in the middle-class world he inhabits, Lekhak discovers that no such occasion is forthcoming. It seems to Lekhak that the bhadralok *habitus* is far too homogenized to offer ruptures which could be effectively exploited to depict meaningful clashes or contradictions; the range of emotions covered by an average middle-class Bengali was inordinately restricted. From the point of view of Lekhak the 'crisis' thus was that being tied far too steadfastly to an already scripted narrative—a narrative marked by the monotonous punctuality of birth, rigorous but empty schooling, domesticated marriage, planned or unplanned reproduction and death—the bhadralok did not qualify to be dramatis persona. It was as though the bhadralok was ontologically disqualified to be so—you have persons, but no characters.
>
> Perennially in search of characters, Lekhak (and by extension Badal Sircar) is foiled by meeting psychologically similar persons with phonetically similar names: Amal, Bimal, Kamal. This stunning similarity implies that the members of the Bengali middle class—particularly its male segment—do not possess 'masks' donning which they can execute various roles, change registers of enunciation.[65]

According to him, hitting upon this paradox in *Ebong Indrajit*, Badal Sircar gives up on 'character' itself. 'Every character in his post-*Ebong Indrajit* plays literally shrivels up to become mere datum'.[66] And what he then seeks to dramatise is the structure itself; to be precise, 'structure without subject'.[67]

[65] Bandyopadhyay, interview with author, Kolkata, 17 May 2014.
[66] Ibid.
[67] Ibid.

The strongest thread of connection between this play and his later theatre is the searchlight on the middle class; the critique of its safe, convention-bound, approach to life; its blindness to, and acceptance of, inequity and injustice. With the Writer and Indrajit Badal-da, through his theatre, begins a long procession of awakening, of protest, of awareness building, of showing another reality, another way of living. This mission of conscientisation can be said to have begun with *Ebong Indrajit*.

CHAPTER FOUR

A CREATIVE YEAR

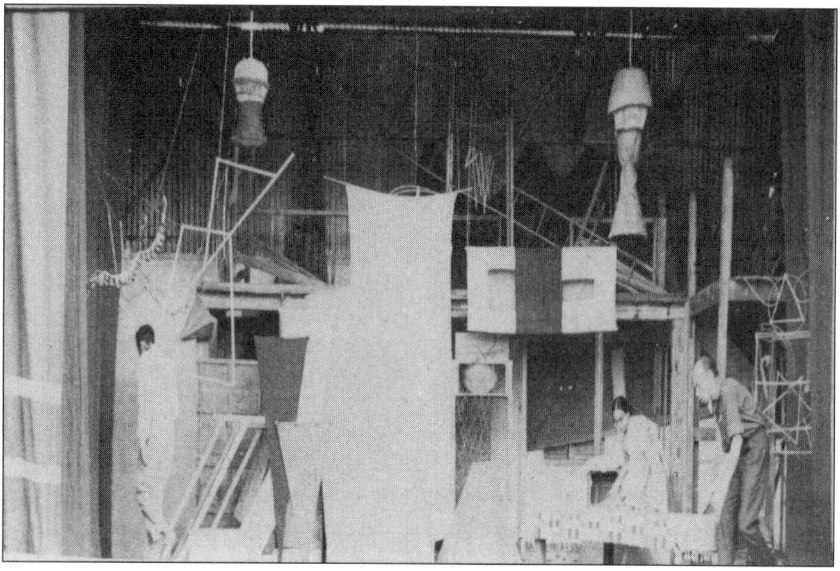

A scene from *Sara Rattir*
Courtesy: Satabdi

The year that began with *Ebong Indrajit*, 1963–64, is an important point in the trajectory of Badal-da's creative development as a playwright and theatre worker. I make this claim for several reasons. First, there was the writing of *Ebong Indrajit*. This in itself was a major shift from Badal-da's idea of himself as a writer of lighthearted comedies doing theatre with friends—theatre for fun—to a playwright other intellectuals and artistes were taking seriously. From its very first reading to a group of the city's leading cultural figures, this text began to make waves and draw critical attention. Second, there was the aftermath of the writing of *Ebong Indrajit* in terms of his own inner quest as a writer, grappling with issues of creativity and expression. Third, there is the fact that he wrote four plays in the course of this year, not including *Ebong Indrajit*. These were *Sara Rattir, Ballabhpurer Rupkatha, Kabikahini* and *Bichitra Anusthan*, in that order. From July 1963 to March 1964, he was in France; and by the time his stint there was over, he had written all these plays which, even today, are in production by various Indian theatre groups somewhere or the other in the country.

The first play Badal-da wrote after *Ebong Indrajit* was *Sara Rattir*. Like *Ebong Indrajit*, it was an intense work. Badal-da states:

> I have composed three plays in my life, during the writing of which the feelings and views were quite different from those experienced when conceiving my other plays. It was as if I was writing [these three plays] in a delirious mood of giddy rapture without planning any direction for their development. As if a ghost was shaking me by the neck and making me write. From this point of view—whatever the critics might say—these three plays have a different meaning for me. The three plays are *Ebong Indrajit*, *Sara Rattir* and ... *Pagla Ghora*.[1]

In his diary entry for 2 September 1963, the opening scene of *Sara Rattir* is described, including the rather elaborate stage directions and the main characters.[2] He completes it on 8 September, a week later.[3] And he repeatedly says that he feels driven, as if he's writing in a frenzy. 'Writing. Thinking about nothing. What to write next, how to proceed, how to end—nothing. Finished the first scene today. Twenty-six pages.'[4] Two days later, on 7 September, he writes: 'Starting is simple; ending is not.'[5] The process of writing this play is captured both in his diary entries and in a letter dated 8 September.[6] Describing the just-completed play in the letter, he says:

> I was writing about one night. About one room. I felt as if I was in that room. On just such a night. For a long time I wasn't thinking about what I was writing. I didn't stop. Didn't wonder about what I was writing, where it was heading...I don't think I can show this to anyone aside from a few of you. It is very strange. Has no value. But that's not why. It's very personal, even more than *Ebong Indrajit*. It's much less structured, less consciously

[1] Introduction to Badal Sircar, *Natya Sangraha*, Calcutta, 1995, p. 3.
[2] Sircar, *Prabasher Hijibiji*, p. 180.
[3] Ibid., p. 182.
[4] Sircar, *Prabasher Hijibiji*, trans. Anjum Katyal, p. 181.
[5] Ibid., trans. Anjum Katyal, p. 182.
[6] Sircar, *Prabasher Hijibiji*, p. 180–87.

> wrought, more narrow.... I don't feel like talking about this piece to many people. I'm not even sure if it's a piece of 'writing' or my 'diary'.[7]

Even after completing the play, he continues to brood over it and discuss it in his diary. He compares it to *Ebong Indrajit* in terms of its personal importance to him as a piece of writing. 'This too—like *Ebong Indrajit*—is mine.'[8]

For some time before this, he had felt an inability to write which seemed directly connected to *Ebong Indrajit*. In a diary entry dated 18 August 1963, he says:

> Whenever I think of writing, whenever I try to find a subject to write about, Indrajit comes and stops me. It's as if *Boro Pishima, Ram Shyam Jadu,* etc. are no longer possible. Yet Indrajit cannot be written again and again. So is it over, then? Is there anything beyond Indrajit?[9]

A week later, on 25 August, he says:

> Trying to write. Hours pass just thinking. About what to write. Thought of a play all day today. A light play.[10] Once again, a light play. But I can't seem to pin it down. Can't hold on to it. What will I do? Big question: what to do what to do what to do? Trying to forget Indrajit. I want to write as an exercise. I want to write as a journalist. But I can't. I realize that I'm not a journalist. Even when I've decided to write, I can't.[11]

Clearly the experience of *Ebong Indrajit* has caused an upheaval, leading him to question his creative practice. Is it even possible to return to the earlier lighthearted comedies that tripped off his pen? Sibaji Bandyopadhyay analyses:

> Badal Sircar claimed that he had a facility for creating scenes and situations, for coming up with spontaneous dialogues. Giving words to various characters came naturally to him. This is something he himself recognized. So in the early plays, in his 'comedies'—which I will call 'practice plays'—he tried to hone the facility he thought he had. Many of the themes were borrowed from foreign films and stories, which he then translated into the Bengali context, and they worked pretty well.[12]

[7] Sircar, *Prabasher Hijibiji*, trans. Anjum Katyal, pp. 182–83.

[8] Ibid., trans. Anjum Katyal, p. 184.

[9] Ibid., trans. Anjum Katyal, p. 174.

[10] This was *Ballabhpurer Rupkatha*, which he started and put aside. See Sircar, *Prabasher Hijibiji*, trans. Anjum Katyal, p. 192.

[11] Sircar, *Prabasher Hijibiji*, trans. Anjum Katyal, p. 177.

[12] Bandyopadhyay, interview with the author, Kolkata, 17 May 2014.

Then came the milestone of *Ebong Indrajit*, which drew on his personal experience and thoughts in a hitherto unexplored fashion, creating a work that spoke to an entire generation, capturing an angst pervasive in the milieu he was speaking of and addressing. Where was he to go from here? He tried returning to the earlier mindset but that did not work. Instead he ended up writing a play which, like *Ebong Indrajit* was deeply personal, but very different in content and form, as he himself recognised.

Sara Rattir takes place in the course of one night in one room. It is a play about self-discovery. A young couple, married seven years, takes shelter from the storm in a decrepit old house in the middle of nowhere. In a dark, shadowy and mysterious room, they encounter an unusual old man who welcomes them and offers them refuge for the night. But nothing is quite what it seems to be; and in the course of the long night, all three characters explore their innermost depths—of desire, of frustration and of bliss. It is a night they will never forget, a night that leaves them changed forever.

Like in *Ebong Indrajit*, here too the central characters are generically named. Woman (*Stree*) and Old Man (*Briddha*) crave something deeper, something beyond their mundane daily lives. *Ananda*, rather than *shanti*: bliss, rather than contentment or peace. Here too, the longing is in conflict with the expectations of the everyday which are embodied in the character of Man (*Purush*). However, the characters of the couple are more developed in this play than the symbolic characters of *Ebong Indrajit*, more three-dimensional, though the old man is a rather other-worldly presence, not meant to be seen as a flesh and blood person but rather as a sign of something else. Whereas the earlier play ranges over an entire socio-economic milieu with its tableaux and montages, this play delves deep into the psyche, its inner needs and desires.

The marital bickering between husband and wife, the pragmatic talk of dry clothes, bedding for the night and a hot meal, are in contrast to the carefully built up eerie atmosphere of the room, which, with its twisted shadows and ghostly echo, is itself a character in the play. In dramatic terms, the tension is carefully enhanced through moments of unease which seem to get resolved, but create an expectation of something momentous that is imminent. This is the late-night confrontation between the Old Man and the Woman who lays bare her deep and infinite longing for Ranjan, a longing which is expressed in mystical, almost spiritual terms, as a desire to give all of herself to Ranjan, wanting nothing in return, except an acknowledgement that she is part of his dreams. The Old Man is her path to Ranjan. It is significant that the name picked by the playwright, Ranjan (meaning 'red' or 'that which gives pleasure') is that of the famous character in Tagore's *Raktakarabi* (Red Oleanders).[13] In that play, Ranjan is a symbol of boundless love and freedom, a breath of fresh air, impossible to tie down or limit, and Nandini the pure being, who has given herself over heart and soul to Ranjan and all he stands for. In this play, too, the Woman's longing for Ranjan is a longing for a sort of infinite, all-consuming passion, a different way of living and being in this world, far from the constraints of domestic life, or even a stable marital relationship. When her husband accuses her of betrayal, she tries to explain that the two kinds of need are totally different, but he is incapable of seeing beyond the dimension he inhabits to the abstraction to which she refers.

There is a clever juxtaposition, throughout, of the minutiae of daily domesticity (the drying of wet clothes, the cooking of an impromptu meal, the water leaking from the roof) and a sense of something otherworldly and mystical (the properties of the number seven, the strange, selective echo, the ominous thunderstorm). One is kept conscious of 'something beyond' the quotidian that keeps breaking through and disrupting the 'normality' of this world. In terms of form, this is a conventional three-act play with neatly designated segments building up to a climax and some form of resolution: none of the fluid collage-like structure or innovations of its predecessor. However, there is one unusual element: in the guise of extended stage directions, the playwright introduces questions and comments, sotto voce as it were, almost like a chorus would. One wonders how he expects them to translate from the page to the stage—it is as if he is piercing through the fourth wall in the script itself, communicating directly with the reader as the authorial voice in a novel would do.

From his diary entries, it is clear that *Sara Rattir* is intensely personal, reflecting dilemmas and doubts which were haunting him at the time. He even says that the Old Man is himself.[14] However, our concern is not so much the biographical connection as the implications of this on his creative development. This moment in his career is a turning point. Both these plays, *Ebong Indrajit* and *Sara Rattir*, are expressions of his own life and experience in dramatic form. In both plays, the protagonists work through non-hope and resignation to a decision to continue, to persist, not to forget. In the latter, the Woman's final words are, 'I will not, I will not, I will not forget! This

[13] The play first appeared in 1924 in the Bengali original in *Prabasi*, a Calcutta literary monthly. The English version came out in the September 1924 issue of the 'Visvabharati Quarterly'.

[14] Sircar, *Prabasher Hijibiji*, p. 185.

night is mine! One night. All night. All night long.'[15] Sibaji Bandyopadhyay perceptively pinpoints this choice—to 'keep on carrying on' in the face of non-hope, despite the conviction of failure—as the political in Badal Sircar.[16] We will explore this aspect in greater detail in a later chapter, as we will the text of the play *Sara Rattir* in terms of gender.

On 9 September, a day after completing *Sara Rattir*, Badal-da writes in his diary:

> I will not be able to write a play like *Boro Pishima* again. I'm losing my ability to make others laugh. My writing is slowly growing darker, more intense. And gradually I'm losing my ability to write about real stories in a realistic way. They're taking the form of metaphor or poetry. My writing is becoming fantastical and abstract.[17]

On 27 September, he writes that six days previously he had started writing *Ballabpurer Rupkatha* (Ballabhpur's Fairytale, 1963–04), a rollicking comedy. He had begun it earlier, soon after reaching France, but put it aside after about five pages.[18] After re-starting, he has been writing steadily. Clearly his reservations about writing 'light' plays have been overcome, although he does say that he has to force himself to write.[19]

The following day, he writes a letter to Monu[20] detailing a list of historical information and some material he requires, and then jokes, 'You must be wondering if I've started researching ancient Bengal history sitting here in France! No, this is not for research. This is information I need for the play I'm working on. Based on a film I saw in London.'

His rejection of 'realistic' drama is explored in this farce. It begins with a direct address to the audience, setting the tone of irreverent cheekiness right from the start. This play remains popular decades after it was written, and an account of a 2005 production helps explain why:

> *Ballabhpurer Rupkatha* was ... written around the same time as his classic *Evam Indrajit*, in 1963. Sircar appears to have liked it enough to direct it himself in 1970, soon after forming his own group Satabdi, before he rejected regular auditoriums ... it is easy to understand why the play

[15] Badal Sircar, 'Sara Rattir', *Natya Samagra*, Vol. 1, trans. Anjum Katyal, p. 356.
[16] Bandyopadhyay, interview with the author, Kolkata, 17 May 2014.
[17] Sircar, *Prabasher Hijibiji*, trans. Anjum Katyal, p. 185.
[18] Sircar, *Prabasher Hijibiji*, p. 193.
[19] Ibid.
[20] Anjali Basu (Dutta), close friend and confidante.

> appealed to him. Beneath the fun and games and shades of Oscar Wilde's story *The Canterville Ghost* lies an ironic look at the changing face of society that remains relevant.
>
> Bhupati Ray of Ballabhpur has seen better days. His magnificent 400-year-old palace is on the point of collapse, and he has too many creditors. The only way out is to sell the mansion, but who will buy a crumbling edifice? That, too, with a resident ancestral ghost.
>
> Luckily, a Calcutta businessman, Mr Haldar, expresses interest because he's competing with his rival as to who can possess a more ancient building. Bhupati tries to lessen its age in order to raise the price, but Haldar's ready to pay more the older it is.
>
> He's in seventh heaven to hear that it's haunted, since his rival can't top that. Meanwhile, the ghost (a spitting image of Bhupati, but possessed of a glad eye), flirts with Haldar's daughter who doesn't know of his spectral nature. The plot thickens.... In a city where dilapidated bungalows owned by impoverished gentility are being bought and torn down by profiteering promoters every day, Sircar's play certainly resounds with echoes.[21]

This play is taking longer, with more interruptions, than *Sara Rattir* which was completed at a stretch of less than a week. We know that he began the play earlier, soon after reaching France, as his next attempt after *Ebong Indrajit*, but couldn't bring himself to persist with a comic play. Instead he plunged into the catharsis of *Sara Rattir*. Within a month of completing that, he picked up *Ballabhpurer Rupkatha* again, on 21 September 1963. In a letter to Monu on 28 September, he talks of how he is forcing himself to write. He is not in the mood, he cannot find the laughter; yet he is continuing with it as if he has to finish it somehow. He has 100 pages written, and one part to go. He feels that he can complete it without thinking too much about it. 'The experience is totally different from that of writing *Sara Rattir*. And yet, I'm giving it my time. And I'm enjoying it.'[22] On 10 and 12 October, he is still undergoing the usual process of self-doubt, self-criticism, dissatisfaction with his work, uncertainty about how to proceed, which is built into his writing process.[23] Over and over again, he records how much time the play is taking, one act at a time, till finally, on 21 October, just after midnight, he has his Hallelujah moment: 'Finished! Just now! Freedom!'[24] It has been a

[21] *The Telegraph*, 10 June 2005. http://www.telegraphindia.com/1050610/asp/calcutta/story_4851102.asp (accessed on 27 January 2015).

[22] Sircar, *Prabasher Hijibiji*, trans. Anjum Katyal, p. 193.

[23] Sircar, *Prabasher Hijibiji*, p. 198.

[24] Sircar, *Prabasher Hijibiji*, trans. Anjum Katyal, p. 201.

month of persistence, with moments of doubt along the way. Even now he feels that it needs more work:

> I had thought that I'd leave the play untouched for a month or so. But it's so weak, has such inadequate comedy, that I can't leave it as it is. With *Sara Rattir* and *Ebong Indrajit*, when I finished them, I was done. But with this fairytale, if it is to stand at all, then I have to really pummel it into shape.[25]

All along there is the comparison with the two earlier plays, as if the shadow of *Ebong Indrajit* and *Sara Rattir* is hanging over him. One feels that his creative expression is splitting into two very distinct streams. There is the intensely inward, private writing which produces texts like *Ebong Indrajit* and *Sara Rattir* (so far; others will be added to this list later), and there is the 'light' comedy that he never quite gives up writing even after he moves out of the proscenium.

His diary testifies to the doubts and inner questioning thrown up by what appears to have become a divided process of writing. On 17 October 1963, he writes:

> So many days have passed in trying to start the final part of *Ballabhpurer Rupkatha*. Hours spent thinking, time gone waste. With one urgency—I have to finish it. And start something else. My mind just refuses to accept that this kind of forced writing and thinking is not the way to do it. It's as if I'm scared of putting it aside. Suppose it's never finished? And what's the harm in that? Even this question is frightening.
>
> *Sara Rattir*, I feel, brought an end to many things, for me. Just as before it, *Ebong Indrajit* also did. With these two works, it's as if they didn't end even after I finished writing. Instead, they continued to affect me, influence me. They aged me. These two are my most authentic, personal writings. They are truly me. It doesn't matter what others think of them.
>
> I'm not really in the frame of mind for *Ballabhpurer Rupkatha*...I'm not able to put my mind to it. Its subject matter is too far removed from me. It's just because I want to do theatre that I am at all able to write this kind of play.
>
> Yet I want to finish it. Because I've begun it...It's like, having begun a course of study, one has no option but to try and pass, no matter how purposeless passing such a course may be.
>
> [...]
>
> I tried to start writing the third part of *Ballabhpurer Rupkatha*. Late at night. Chanda and Bhupathi. I got reminded of *Sara Rattir*. I realised—no

[25] Sircar, *Prabasher Hijibiji*, trans. Anjum Katyal, p. 202.

> point persisting with this fairytale now. I took out the manuscript of *Sara Rattir* and read the whole thing through.[26]

The slowly dawning realisation that these two kinds of writing, these two very different categories of output, are making contradictory demands on him, pulling him in two directions as it were, soon became a conviction. In a letter to Monu dated 28 November 1963, he says:

> I think a lot about writing. But what's the point of thinking about it? I now have another problem. The *Ebong Indrajit* brand of thought and the *Ballabhpurer Rupkatha* brand of thought are in contradiction to each other. As a result, I can't give too much thought to any one of them. At times I think, I won't write anything serious any more. I'll only try to make people laugh. A little while later I feel—I can't think of anything funny. I've even considered moving away from plays to some other genre, but I can't. I don't even want to. I'm committed to theatre as a medium. I'm obsessed with the thought of doing theatre, of undertaking a theatre project. The other day I couldn't think of anything else. Against all wisdom, against all logic, I spent the whole evening engrossed in making impossible theatre plans. Calculations. Set drawings. Giving form to a production in my mind. Thinking of the lighting. Thinking of the stage.[27]

Badal-da has already mentioned elsewhere that he finds creative satisfaction in drawing and painting, in writing poetry—but of all these mediums, it is theatre, both in terms of text and in terms of staging, that has him in its grip.

The next two plays he writes are both comedies. This is clearly the fare that comes to him most easily when he thinks of material he can turn into theatre, which is not surprising given that it is the familiar people who make up Chakra of whom he thinks when he thinks of doing a play.

Kabikahini (Poet's Tale, 1964) is written with minimum fuss and bother. On 1 December, while ruminating over his body of work to date, he thinks:

> Suppose I once again try to write a play like I did *Boro Pishima*, based on just a background and a few characters? Just as in that play there was the background of amateur theatricals and a few key characters...Since last night this idea has grown. While reading a foreign story I came upon a comic situation—not really a story, just a stray fragment. Based on that, a few characters started developing. Then a few more. I jotted down a few notes.

[26] Sircar, *Prabasher Hijibiji*, trans. Anjum Katyal, pp. 199–200.
[27] Ibid., trans. Anjum Katyal, p. 215.

> Characters. Situation. A little of the background. A beginning. A trace of a possible ending. Just a trace, nothing more, very negligible. After all I didn't have anything more than this when I began writing *Boro Pishima*?[28]

The rest of the entry traces the gradual accumulation of pages, to his relief and delight.

He begins it on 30 November and it is completed at midnight on 6 December 1963, in just six days. He congratulates himself on having accomplished it without any hiccups, any setbacks, blockages or doubts. It just flowed. That very night, he writes a letter to Monu, exulting over his 'record break': 'In six days I've completed a play! All my own idea, nothing taken from a foreign story!'[29]

With this play, he returns to the ground of his first original comedy, *Boro Pishima*. Both are set in the middle-class domestic environment.

One review says:

> *Kabi Kahini* is a satirical comedy about an aspiring political climber preparing for an election with an aspiring literary climber for a wife preparing for a literary soiree which 'the famous modern poet' Smarajit is expected to attend as the chief guest. The daughter has both suitors and secret literary ambitions. The poet does not arrive but a journalist working in the rival candidate's paper and impersonating the poet, does. With election politics, modern poetry, an imposter, one young woman and several young men, the situation is of course explosive and crackers, together with several well-timed mines planted cunningly, go off at a brisk rate.[30]

The excitement of having pulled off this comedy seems to be fuelled by his being able to imagine Chakra doing this play, as also *Ballabhpurer Rupkatha*. In the previously mentioned letter, which bubbles over with good humour and a kind of relief at having smoothly negotiated writing yet another play, he cheerfully lists the various parts which can be played by various members of Chakra, reserving a role for himself as well. Without being able to imagine it being staged, it is hard to write a play, he says. Perhaps that is what lies behind his attachment to the comedy form—a tried and tested vehicle for the theatre group he is involved with. He can

[28] Sircar, *Prabasher Hijibiji*, trans. Anjum Katyal, pp. 216–17.

[29] Ibid., trans. Anjum Katyal, p. 218.

[30] 'Kabi Kahini' by A Drama Critic. *Frontier*, Vol. 1, No 1, 14 April 1968, p. 16; http://frontierweekly.com/archive/vol-number/vol/vol-1/vol-1-issues/1_1_14april1968.pdf (accessed on 27 January 2015).

easily imagine the well-trodden sequence of events: the play-reading out loud, the group response, the allotment of roles, the rehearsals, the planning of a public performance. This is familiar ground he is confident about.

Kabikahini will be performed by Satabdi in 1968, with Badal-da playing a role. Praising it as better than the comic fare commonly seen on the Bengali stage, one critic still finds it disappointing:

> But even as ... one is genuinely amused, an undercurrent of disappointment is difficult to avoid. The characters are quite openly drawn from set types. The semi-literate candidate, the overbearing party boss, the local tough, the impossible wife, the vacuous daughter—one has met them all before. Nor are the structural levers—the election battle farce and the comedy of errors—particularly original. Even some of the scenes, as for instance, the one where the fake poet composes modern poems out of advertisements and household letters, ring a faint bell of recognition and one has an uneasy feeling that the gag has been used before. It is not suggested that there is any element of copy in the play. Its ambience is entirely indigenous and the details are both clever and fresh. Badal Sarkar's undoubted talent and competence rescue *Kabi Kahini* from being a humdrum comedy but they have not been able to transform the conventional set of comic situations into a play which one had hoped would do for the comedy what *Ebong lndrajit* did for serious drama, that is, achieve a breakthrough.[31]

As we follow the inner grappling with his creative muse and the direction in which his playwriting is progressing, it is interesting to note that for all the strong effect *Ebong Indrajit* and *Sara Rattir* have had on him, it is comedies that he deliberately turns to straight after. His next play—the final one of this formative year—is to be another comedy. In the meanwhile, however, another major event occurs, which will yield its significance years later, with his move into Third Theatre. In December 1964, about a year after the completion of *Kabikahini* he sees Theatre in the Round. In Paris.

We know that this is not his first encounter with this style of non-proscenium theatre. He has already responded to his initial experience of this form in London, and it clearly left an impact, since he says that he has read books on it and has a theoretical understanding of its features. However, this time he not only expounds at some length about the characteristics of this form but concludes that it is more effective and hard hitting than the regular theatre. He notes that there is a central performance space, with audience seated all around, gallery style; that there are six rows of seats and

[31] 'Kabi Kahini' by A Drama Critic.

room for about 300 spectators; that the entrances and exits of the actors are effected through the same doors by which the audience enters and leaves; that the closeness of the actors to the viewers greatly enhances the impact and heightens the whole experience. He comments that despite not following too much of the dialogue (the play is a French version of *The Caine Mutiny Court Martial*), he could still experience the power of the play: this despite there being no sets except for a few chairs and tables, and no costumes or make-up. 'I felt as if I was watching real people ... it was as if I was right in the judge's chamber ... I had never imagined that it was possible for actors to come so close to the spectators.'[32] And he notes that two things are essential for this type of theatre to work: the acting has to be truly, truly good and of course there can be no prompting.[33]

The experience leaves him lost in pleasant daydreams and far-fetched plans: he has designed the *Ebong Indrajit* stage and sets often enough in his head, but now he imagines the play in the round. He feels it would work much better, take up less space; he sees how Amal–Bimal–Kamal can walk in a circle instead of a straight line. In a word, it would be much more 'effective' he says, using the English word. Moreover, though no doubt it is a much more demanding form, it also offers more freedom and flexibility in terms of staging. 'However—what's the point of all these plans? Who will do *Ebong Indrajit*?'[34] Ironic, to say the least, that he is worried about a lack of interest in this, perhaps the most influential, play text of the 1960s and 1970s. Eventually, he and his group will do a non-proscenium production of this work in his Anganmancha style.

It is important to note that the desirability of non-proscenium theatre has already been felt by Badal-da, although it will take years before it becomes a fully formed rejection of the proscenium.

He takes care to mention two other significant theatre experiences. On 25 February 1964, he describes seeing a play in London which left him amazed—an anti-war piece called 'Oh What a Lovely War!' That such a deeply serious theme could be expressed through comedy, dance and music was beyond his imagination. He says that one can't quite call it a play; rather it was musical comedy. This was a piece developed by Joan Littlewood and her ensemble through a workshop process.[35] He has seen

[32] Sircar, *Prabasher Hijibiji*, trans. Anjum Katyal, p. 228.

[33] Sircar, *Prabasher Hijibiji*, p. 228.

[34] Ibid., trans. Anjum Katyal, pp. 227–28.

[35] *Oh, What a Lovely War!* was an epic musical developed by Joan Littlewood and her ensemble at the Theatre Workshop in 1963.

her work before, but this workshop production leaves a deep impact. He says, 'There is so much more to theatre than what we think of as theatre. If only one could think of, do it, be able to do it.'[36] He takes away one important realisation from this—that one can do theatre independent of the written play script; that theatre is a self-sufficient art form which is not really dependent on the playwright.[37]Another important seed has been planted which will bear fruit later.

The other experience is described in a letter to Monu dated 6 March 1964. He sees some plays by Ionesco. He finds it interesting that a new kind of play writing is taking place which completely overturns the prevalent norms and traditions of theatre. He says he was delighted to see that even non-realistic or fantastical drama has takers.[38]

Later in the same letter, he ruminates over his progress as a writer:

> I wrote *Ebong Indrajit*—good. *Sara Rattir*—also good. *Ballabhpur, Kabikahini*—nothing much in them, but good practice, I feel that I've made some progress. Bits and pieces, scattered, fragments, contradictions—but still, progress. Amal, Bimal, Kamal and Indrajit are dancing. Together. Indrajit's rhythm is a bit different, more complex. But this physics cinema literature politics, this examination interview office, this boy–girl, husband–wife, householder–housewife, this game of cards—it's all too much like a dance drama. I don't know if Badal Sircar will ever write another play. But if he does—I hope it will make the audience laugh out loud; and stop to think; and having thought, laugh again.[39]

Badal Sircar not only wrote several more plays in the years ahead—which made the audience both laugh and think—but he had also written yet another comedy, *Bichitranushthan* (Cultural Programme, 1964), before he returned to Kolkata at the end of the month.[40] He describes this as 'a lively play. A mad play. A funny play. Crazily funny.'[41]

As he returns briefly to Kolkata, before leaving for Nigeria, let us pause to look back over this rather tumultuous year in terms of his creative development. As both a playwright and a practitioner, there have been important

[36] Sircar, *Prabasher Hijibiji*, trans. Anjum Katyal, pp. 240–41.
[37] Ibid., trans. Anjum Katyal, p. 241.
[38] Sircar, *Prabasher Hijibiji*, pp. 246–47.
[39] Ibid., trans. Anjum Katyal, pp. 248–49.
[40] Sircar, *Purano Kasundi*, Vol. 2, p. 67.
[41] Sircar, *Natak Samagra*, Vol. 2, trans. Anjum Katyal (Kolkata: Mitra and Ghosh, 2010/2013), p. 2.

developments. It has been a year of self-search and obsessing over writing, of almost crippling self-doubt strenuously overcome in order to produce work, of probing self-analysis and critique. Some fresh ideas have sown seeds that will germinate and come to fruition in his later work: ideas about a theatre that allows the actor to be close to the spectator; a theatre that allows the most grim and serious subjects to be presented through farce and satire; an 'absurd' or non-realistic theatre that can yet find its own audience.

As can be expected from his eagerness to see his plays turned into actual productions, on his return to Calcutta, he reads both *Ballabhpurer Rupkatha* and *Kabikahini* to Chakra (*Sara Rattir* and *Bichitranushthan* are reserved for a more intimate group[42]) and, in the months before he has to leave for Nigeria, they begin rehearsals for *Kabikahini*. It is perhaps unsurprising that it is this play, the domestic comedy with stock recognisable characters that Chakra selects. The performance is on 1 June 1964 at the Minerva Theatre.

[42] Sircar, *Purano Kasundi*, Vol. 2, p. 77.

CHAPTER FIVE

NIGERIAN INTERLUDE

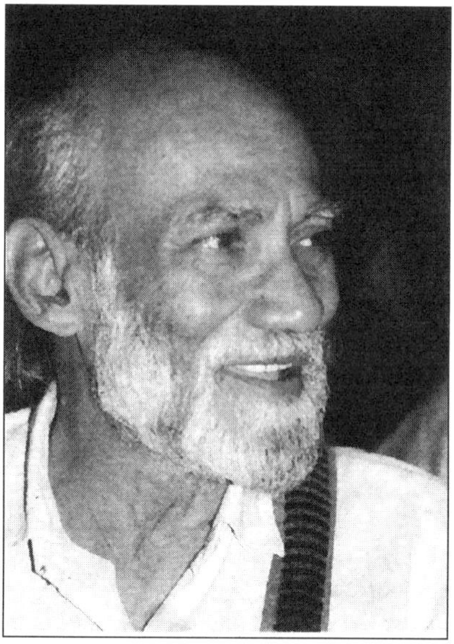

A portrait
Courtesy: Natya Shodh Sansthan

In September 1965, about a year and a half after his last play, Badal-da begins writing his next work, *Baki Itihas*. Like its predecessors *Ebong Indrajit* and *Sara Rattir*, it deals with the inadequacies and stultifying banality of a middle-class routine barricaded against the call of a larger life outside. What about the rest of history—the *baki itihas*—is the anguished cry that ends the play.

Talking about writing the play, Badal-da says:

> *Baki Itihas* needed a more conscious effort—it was one play that gave me a lot of trouble. I wrote it in Nigeria in 1964–65, the first of the six plays that I wrote in those three years. I started it and got stuck ... for months ... I had

> to invent the stories ... and I can never invent stories. Practically no play of mine has a story, for the simple reason that I can't write stories ... But the germ of the third act was already there. In a way it was a kind of ... rewriting of *Ebong Indrajit* that came out in the third act, with a difference. Not the myth of Sisyphus, but the *Baki Itihas*.[1]

In a series of letters to Monu, written between 10 September and 24 October 1965, he discusses the challenges of writing this 'totally original' play.[2] The idea of the story came to him all of a sudden, in office, and he began writing compulsively. It was a relief to write again, he says, although it felt like bitter medicine. On 2 October, he is re-writing, more than he has ever had to before. He calls it 'gruelling, boring, donkey work'.[3] In the interim, he has to cope with news of the *Ebong Indrajit* production in Kolkata, which displeases him. His mood is off. He dismisses his new play as terrible, claiming that if it doesn't improve it will be competing for last place with his least favourite work, *Samabritta*. A week later, he says that he never felt so dissatisfied upon completing a play before, although he likes the theme despite it being 'apparently morbid'.[4] And on 14 October, he writes that it is finally done, a bit improved, and its title is *Baki Itihas*.[5]

This play intensifies the central concerns of *Ebong Indrajit* by asking the question—why should a middle-class subject not commit suicide? What justifies his continued existence? His modest, measured pleasures, the reassurance of his domestic routine, his steady rise through the ranks of his profession—are these enough to block out the violence and injustice that reigns in that 'other' history?

In the final confrontation between the central characters Sitanath and Saradindu, the former accuses him:

> Sitanath: Yes, the rest of history. Which is not about examinations, not about jobs, not about marriage. Which is about oppression, violence, destruction, war, the suffering of centuries. The history of the Pandav-Kauravs, Alexander, Nero, Chengiz Khan, Napoleon, Hitler. Thousands of years of history etched into the stones of the pyramids, the sands of the Colosseum, the walls of Jalianwala Bagh, the blasted earth of Hiroshima. Thousands of years of another history.

[1] Sircar, PNP.

[2] Badal Sircar, Mukhbandh (preface) to 'Baki Itihas', *Natak Samagra*, Vol. 2, trans. Anjum Katyal, p. 40.

[3] Sircar, *Prabasher Hijibiji*, trans. Anjum Katyal, p. 269.

[4] Sircar, *Prabasher Hijibiji*, p. 269.

[5] Ibid., pp. 268–70.

> Saradindu: But what can I do about that?
> Sitanath: No, you can't do anything. I couldn't do anything. No one can do anything. Oppression, murder, violence, war will continue, all carried out by man, but still there's nothing man can do. The very man who's content with his two meals a day will stab another through the belly. The same scientist who cannot bear to see an animal in pain will invent a weapon of mass destruction to annihilate millions. These are all men. Like you. Like me. They have all tried to find a meaning in life in order to carry on surviving.
> Saradindu: But they're surviving, aren't they?
> Sitanath: It's a pretence of survival. When existence has no meaning, then one turns to habit to help one go through the motions of survival. Like I did. Like you're doing.
> Saradindu: No, it's not true. There's another side to history. There's peace as well as war, love as well as oppression. It has to be. Otherwise there would be no option but to kill oneself. Why did you kill yourself? Couldn't you have carried on living? Like other people do?

But Sitanath turns the question on him: 'Why didn't you end *your* life, Saradindu?[6]

After this encounter with what is essentially part of his own psyche, Saradindu seems to make a move towards ending his life, taking the electric lamp cord in his hands, but is interrupted by the news of an imminent promotion—and an abrupt return to the reality of domesticity. A garrulous visitor, cups of tea, conversation and chatter. Yet the traces of unease remain. He says, 'It was just a nightmare, a bad dream. A useless, false, meaningless nightmare.' Yet his last words in the play are a cry of *baki itihas*—the other history that, once having intruded, can never quite be ignored.[7]

Like in *Ebong Indrajit*, here also Badal-da confronts his own class, his own milieu, with its blinkered existence; but the politicisation of the subject has moved one step ahead. In the earlier play, the process of politicisation was begun, with a questioning and refusal to conform. Here, the demand is more intense—is the choice to be between action and suicide? Is the domestic middle-class round of daily existence a denial of reality? Whereas action—intervention—was not even a possibility for the protagonists of *Ebong Indrajit*, who were struggling merely to find a reason to carry on, the subject in *Baki Itihas* faces the harsh choice between his personal, everyday routine and the demands of that other, violent, history. Is suicide the only option, then, for the aware middle-class subject? 'Guilt reproduces

[6] Sircar, 'Baki Itihas', trans. Anjum Katyal, pp. 93–95.
[7] Ibid., pp. 95–97.

itself in each of us,' says Theodor Adorno in *Negative Dialectics*.[8] 'If we ... knew at every moment what has happened ... and how our own existence is interwoven with calamity, even if we have done nothing wrong ... if one were fully aware of all things at every moment, one would really be unable to live.'[9] It is this human interconnectedness with which Sitanath is identifying when he evokes the whole history of unfair suffering in the world, leading to the fatal realisation that staying alive is not possible in the light of such knowledge.

Badal-da is continuing to mull over this question of the literate middle-class subject and his ability for action or heroism. After reading a play by Sombhu Mitra, *Ghurni*, he finds himself pondering:

> This educated Bengali middle-class's blind groping quest to discover where strength lies, where courage lies—even if one were wiped out, destroyed in the process, one would still find in this some meaning to existence. Staying alive at Nature's urging, whether it's as an animal, or vegetable, or some misshapen idol. Just staying alive. And somehow finding some meaning in this, some value in this. This then is our heroism, ours and that of our Indrajits ... these unheroic characters' blind but still somehow heroic quest and effort—this is the heroism of heroes in plays written by playwrights like us.[10]

In *Sara Rattir,* this quest for meaning is highlighted in the split between two realities, contrasting the reassuring securities of domesticity with the yearning for something deeper, larger, beyond the self, through the figure of the other-worldly old man with all-seeing eyes. There too, as in *Baki Itihas*, the subject eventually surrenders to the pull of the everyday, although she will carry the memory of her epiphany with her. However, there is a marked difference between the spiritual yearning of that play and the harsh history of oppression and violence referred to here, in sharp contrast to the middle-class ethos of getting by and getting ahead.

In terms of form, the structure of *Baki Itihas* is experimental, with two acts spinning out two versions of the story behind Sitanath's suicide, and the third act confronting the limited mindset which is unable to imagine that the motivation for suicide may have been not a personal tragedy but a total rejection of middle-class existence. One does not expect this sudden escalation onto the plane of philosophy, and it adds gravitas to the

[8] Theodor Adorno, *Negative Dialectics* (London: Routledge and Kegan Paul, 1973), p. 156.
[9] Ibid.
[10] Sircar, *Prabasher Hijibiji*, trans. Anjum Katyal, pp. 271–72.

play. The playwright balances pace and tension deftly throughout, and, as always, his sure grasp of the milieu, the rhythms and the language of his middle-class characters comes through.

By the time *Baki Itihas* reached the Kolkata audience (it was published in the *Bohurupee* journal),[11] *Ebong Indrajit* was already making waves and Badal-da was already known as a playwright to watch out for, as we know from this review:

> With Bahurupee's production of his next published play *Baki ltihas* his reputation as a serious and gifted dramatist became secure and he came to be regarded as one of the most important of contemporary playwrights whose modernity and inventive command over form were beyond dispute.[12]

Like with *Ebong Indrajit*, this play too resonated with leading playwrights across the country. Satyadev Dubey talked of visiting Calcutta in 1967–68, and attending a rehearsal of Sombhu Mitra's production of *Baki Itihas.* The play impressed him: 'I eventually took the script and got Arvind and Sulabha to do it for which incidentally the set design was mine, though I didn't take credit for it.'[13] Rajinder Nath also did a production of *Baki Itihas.*

In a few months, while visiting Calcutta on leave, Badal-da writes his next play, *Bagh* (Tiger, 1965), within a span of two days. He had earlier read and liked a play called 'The Tiger' by Murray Schisgal[14] but held back from working on it because he felt that it exuded too strong a 'foreign smell' (*Ingrijir gondho*) for him to be able to turn it into a play that sounded and felt Bengali (He says that he only adapted a foreign play if he could manage to make it so authentic that no one could tell that it was not originally a Bengali play[15]). *Bagh* was completed by December 1965. Badal-da identifies friendship as the main theme of the play.[16] It traces the relationship between a Tiger and a young woman (designated as Bagh and Meye or 'girl', respectively) from one of oppression (Tiger has her bound

[11] *Bohurupee,* No. 27, September 1967.

[12] From a review of Kabi Kahini by 'A Drama Critic', *Frontier*, Vol. 1, No. 1 (14 April 1968), p. 16.

[13] Dubey, PNP.

[14] Murray Schisgal (b. 1926), American playwright whose 1963 play 'The Tiger' won him the Drama Desk Award.

[15] Sircar, *Prabasher Hijibiji*, p. 99.

[16] Badal Sircar, Preface to 'Bagh', *Natak Samagra*, Vol. 2, p. 100.

and tied in his den) to one of equality. In the course of the play, Girl seizes agency, moving from helpless victim to teacher, voluntarily offering him her friendship, time and expertise. By the time she leaves, promising to come again soon, the two are good friends. The characters bond over their mutual dissatisfaction with the constraints of their limited lives. For Tiger, there is far too much empty talk in the world—*bak bak bak bak*—it alienates him, and he withdraws into a solitary life with just his books for company—literature, philosophy, Tagore, history. For Girl, life is much bigger than narrow domesticity. She is already seeking something—she is part of a women's group (*mahila samiti*) and attends their meetings. She frankly admits that she cannot really talk to her husband:

> Girl: .... What can I talk to him about? Will he understand? As Latika-di says, life cannot be bound by a syllabus, it's much much bigger, more complex—he just doesn't get it, you know? Doesn't understand. Just laughs it off.
> Tiger: And you? Do you understand?
> Girl: Whether I understand or not, at least I try. Just the other day I was telling Karuna-di of the women's group—she doesn't come to our meetings, it's always some excuse, the household, children, her in-laws—that there's a whole world outside the home and family, a huge world. A life which means something—something—else ...[17]

Their conversation progresses to a sharing of ideas and the start of a friendship:

> Tiger: What does life mean?
> Girl: Whatever it may mean—it is something else. Something different. Much bigger.
> [...] You know, as you were saying—Work. The real thing. But what is this work? Which is the real thing? That's what we have to find out. All this third-rate, meaningless talk, what you call—what's it you say?
> Tiger: Bak bak bak bak bak bak
> Girl: Yes! Blah blah blah!
> Tiger: Blah blah blah! You're born, you grow up—you go blah blah. You're doing a job, having a family, you're doing blah blah. You're growing old, falling sick—you're going blah blah. You're lying in bed going blah blah. Not once do you stop to think, not once do you stop going blah blah long enough to think—is there something you can actually do.
> Girl: Right. They never stop to think—is it just to go blah blah that God put man on earth?

[17] Sircar, 'Bagh', *Natak Samagra*, Vol. 2, trans. Anjum Katyal, pp. 115–16.

> Tiger: God? God is just more blah blah. God is the excuse to go blah blah. Can't get enough to eat, can't manage to study—well, it's God's will, blah blah. Year after year things grow worse—it's God's blessing blah blah. Violence breaks out, wars rage—it's God's plan blah blah.
> Girl: Yes, yes! Violence, war—why? They could just sit at home and go blah blah. But they also want to attack and wage war—that too not with simple guns, but with the atom bomb!
> Tiger: Atom bomb! They're making the atom bomb! They want to annihilate the world! And then? Where will they live? Why—on the moon, of course! Do you know how much it costs to send just one rocket to the moon? For that much money they could feed every single person on earth one full meal.
> Girl: And still so many people go hungry. Sleep on the footpath. No one seems to think about these things. But even thinking about it doesn't help, does it?[18]

We notice the now familiar issues that haunt Badal-da's non-comedies from *Ebong Indrajit* onwards: the limitations of the blind routine-bound middle-class worldview; the presence of a larger, more meaningful life beyond the individual's self-serving existence; social injustice, oppression, violence and war; and the ultimate weapon of total destruction, the atom bomb.

We know that war, the death and destruction it causes, and the horror of the nuclear bomb have been an important part of his consciousness since his time in France over a year ago. He has already ruminated on the intensity with which the effects and evils of war are felt in Europe, in a different way than he sees at home—a different relationship with violent, untimely death which is not part of the biological lifecycle.[19] The destruction of war becomes a repeated reference in his plays thereafter. And not just regular war—the total annihilation portended by nuclear warfare. This single fact—the existence of the atom bomb—comes to dominate his outlook on the meaning and purpose of life. We will study the significance of the nuclear threat in his work in greater detail later.

Next begins a year in Nigeria—-1966—which, like the year which began with *Ebong Indrajit*, is one of intense playwriting. He describes it as 'the most fruitful period of my playwriting life'.[20] He writes five plays in this year: *Porey Konodin*, *Jodi Aar Ekbar* (If Only Once More, 1966), *Pralaap* (Delirium, 1966), *Tringsha Shatabdi* (Thirtieth Century, 1966) and *Bibar* (Hollow, 1966–07). There is one significant difference between this burst

[18] Sircar, 'Bagh', *Natak Samagra*, Vol. 2, trans. Anjum Katyal, pp. 115–16.
[19] Sircar, *Prabasher Hijibiji*, p. 248
[20] Sircar, *Purano Kasundi*, Vol. 2, trans. Anjum Katyal, p. 101.

of creativity and the previous one—by now, he has become a recognised playwright. He is being talked about in theatre circles, and permission to do his plays has been sought by Bohurupee, the leading group theatre of Kolkata under the respected Sombhu Mitra. Chakra is no longer the only vehicle for his plays.[21]

Interestingly, in terms of genre and form, each of the five plays is different. He moves from science fiction back to domestic comedy to docu-drama to the adaptation of a novel. He seems to be restlessly seeking, or maybe keeping his hand in, practising as it were. All these plays are based on outside sources which he adapts and totally changes to his own ends. He crows about tossing off the science fiction play (*Porey Konodin*) in just a few days—'I started (Later Someday, 1966) on the 6th at ten o'clock at night, and finished on the night of the 8th–9th at three in the morning'.[22] About *Jodi Aar Ekbar* he has this to say—'I was inspired to write this by an English play I read. The story, characters, verses are all mine.'[23] Two married couples and a single working woman, all dissatisfied with their lot in life, are gathered at a seaside resort managed by a kindhearted resort manager and a caretaker who dreams of a successful business empire. All of them wish that they had a chance to make life choices one more time. A helpful genie grants them their dreams, with unpredictable results. The next play, *Pralaap* is totally different—an absurdist play about playwriting which he writes between 5 and 8 May 1966,[24] a farcical roller-coaster ride in which a playwright and a cast of uncontrollable characters fail to mount a play before an audience to which they allude frequently, and whom they address whenever they wish, even asking for a match and offering them cigarettes. The playwright character is desperately trying to convey the story of an ordinary middle-class man whose 50-year life span—he is born in 1912 and dies in 1962—has been totally banal and ordinary. Shades of the playwright's struggle in *Ebong Indrajit*. Of course he fails, but this time his characters escape the framework and the play becomes a spoof on 'conventional' playmaking itself.

It is with *Tringsha Shatabdi*, Badal-da's next play, that he returns to the fulminating issue that has been a slow burning fuse from *Ebong Indrajit* through *Sara Rattir*, to *Baki Itihas* and *Bagh*, gathering intensity along the way. Once again the playwright addresses the middle-class subject, his own class—but this time, he has moved from talking of guilt

[21] Sircar, *Purano Kasundi*, Vol. 2, pp. 99–100.
[22] Sircar, *Prabasher Hijibiji*, p. 271.
[23] Badal Sircar, Preface to 'Jodi Aar Ekbar', *Natak Samagra*, Vol. 2, p. 176.
[24] Sircar, *Prabasher Hijibiji*, p. 275.

to talking of responsibility. The guilt that Sitanath of *Baki Itihas* felt he should assume for the violence in the world is here explicitly assumed by Sarat, the protagonist, standing in for Everyman. And along with the guilt comes responsibility.

Let us turn first to the writing of this play. On 24 March 1966, in a thoughtful letter to Monu Badal-da discusses the concept of heroism as it pertains to people like him, ordinary middle class folk; the letter continues on to talk of Sartre's play *The Condemned of Altona*[25] which he is reading:

> Whether I am able to write or not isn't the important question. But whether I am still alive, whether I am thinking about the whole question of existence, whether I'm trying to find the meaning of life—that's the main thing. *Altona*'s crazy hero alone assumes full responsibility for his times, and in the courtroom of the thirtieth century human being tries to defend himself, and his century. He says—I, Franz von Gerlach, here in this room, have taken the century upon my shoulders and have said, 'I will answer for it. This day and for ever'.[26]

This is all incorporated by him in *Tringsha Shatabdi* when he comes to write it, about two months later, including the address to thirtieth century man. In between, he writes the farcical *Pralaap* in the course of a few days. On 30 May 1966, he mentions a book he has been trying to translate: 'A French journalist has put together a document after much travel, meeting and talking to many people, reading many papers and books. The subject – Hiroshima, Nagasaki, Bikini'.[27] The book in question is Fernand Gigon's *Formula for Death—E = MC2.*[28] He says that this book shook him, affected him profoundly.[29] He wants to translate it into Bengali. But he just can't make himself do a straight translation. He finds himself turning it into a script for a play. 'I know that a documentary play is not a play, it will never be staged. Even if it is, no one will come to see it ... moreover, it will have American and Japanese characters but the play will be in Bengali'.[30] Despite these misgivings, he continues. On 6 June, he completes the second part

[25] Jean Paul Sartre's play *The Condemned of Altona*, known in the UK as *Loser Wins*, was first produced in 1959 at the Théâtre de la Renaissance in Paris.

[26] Sircar, *Prabasher Hijibiji*, trans. Anjum Katyal, p. 272.

[27] Ibid., trans. Anjum Katyal, p. 277.

[28] Fernand Gigon's *Formula for Death—E = MC2*: *The Atom Bombs and After* (New York: Roy Publishers, 1958).

[29] Badal Sircar, Preface to 'Tringsha Satabdi', *Natak Samagra*, Vol. 2, p. 296.

[30] Sircar, *Prabasher Hijibiji*, trans. Anjum Katyal, p. 277.

of the play and wonders whether he should end it there, although he had planned a third part. He thinks of calling it *Hiroshima Chhariye*. Or, alternatively, *Vichar*. He is still trying to convince himself that this is, after all, supposed to be a play; one can have a documentary film, but a documentary play?[31] And yet, there it is: his first documentary drama, a forerunner to his later non-proscenium productions in terms of form and content.

In fact, this play has two versions. The earlier, proscenium, version began with two characters from *Baki Itihas*—Saradindu and Basanti—indicating a clear link between the concerns of that play and this. This was an attempt to build a connection between the nuclear bombings in Japan in World War II and everyday life in middle class Bengal, by containing it 'within a domestic framework'.[32] In the prologue to the first version, a visitor arrives, a friend who has been in France for a year. Basanti asks him to recall the subject of the conversation he and her husband Saradindu had held on his last visit. Apparently, ever since then Saradindu has been profoundly disturbed. 'More inexorably than the Sharadindu of *Baki Itihas*, the Sharadindu of *Tringsha Satabdi* is unable to accept the violence of his century.'[33] The friend begins to recall the conversation, the prologue ends and the enactment of the Hiroshima attack begins. Later, Badal-da did away with this beginning. 'Our first enactment of this play was in the *anganmancha*. As a result, it was much condensed. Some characters were dropped ... By an amazing coincidence, our first show was held in 1974 on 5th August—the date the bomb was dropped on Hiroshima'.[34]

A relentlessly hard-hitting account of the nuclear bombing of Japan, and the hydrogen bomb test in Bikini atoll, the narrative is constructed from documentary evidence: child survivor testimonials, accounts by the American officer present and the ex-wife of the pilot of the plane, testimonies by Japanese scholars, doctors, victims. It is structured in the form of a trial, with witnesses being called to the stand to testify and be interrogated. The play begins with a direct address by Sarat, locating the play in time:

> So many years after that occurrence, we are presenting *Tringsha Satabdi* to you today. The main question this play asks is—America dropped an atom bomb on Japan's Hiroshima; do we, ordinary Indian citizens, have any responsibility in this matter? We weren't in the war, we didn't drop the

[31] Sircar, *Prabasher Hijibiji*, p. 278.
[32] Bharucha, *Rehearsals of Revolution*, p. 140.
[33] Ibid.
[34] Sircar, Preface to 'Tringsha Satabdi', trans. Anjum Katyal, p. 296.

> bomb. This play was written in 1966. This question has gained in intensity after 18 May 1974 when the Indian government tested its nuclear bomb in the Rajasthan desert. Again in the year 1998 on 11 and 13 May, a series of five atom bombs and one hydrogen bomb were tested in the same location. This means that the central subject of this play is even more relevant today.[35]

'This is not a pretty play. We don't know how to make this a pleasing play. We aren't interested in trying,' states the character who starts the performance.[36] 'Instead of dealing with the obvious contradictions an artist faces when he aestheticises calamities like Hiroshima, Sircar is content with the more simple task of disseminating certain facts and attitudes relating to Hiroshima and its effect on our lives today,' says theatre scholar Rustom Bharucha.[37] And yet the playwright has given adequate thought to how to keep dramatic interest alive: a chorus that acts as witness and enacts and dramatises the documentary evidence; a range of characters who take the stand to answer rapid fire interrogations; and a register that moves back and forth between the military facts and the intensely personal human experience in a continuous flux that keeps the audience engaged throughout.

There is no ambiguity about whom this play addresses, and whom it indicts. Sarat, the protagonist is a 'bhadralok—a gentleman. A Bengali bourgeois. Like all of you. Like me'.[38] This is a play of, by and for the middle class. His friend Sadhan, who has the expected middle of the road attitude to this whole question of guilt and responsibility, is the perfect foil for Sarat. He asks, Why is Sarat bothering so much about all this? In return Sarat asks him—'Tell me one thing. America drops an atom bomb on Hiroshima in Japan—don't you and I have any responsibility in this?' Sadhan argues—after all, not every person in America is guilty, only some are. 'Can one say for sure that no one in our country would ever commit the same crime?' counters Sarat. So are you saying that it's mankind that is responsible, asks Sadhan. The answer is yes.[39]

Later in the play, Sadhan tells him to forget all this, to turn his mind to other things. Here, the playwright introduces another important question,

[35] Badal Sircar, 'Tringsha Satabdi', *Natak Samagra*, Vol. 2, trans. Anjum Katyal, p. 299.
[36] Sircar, 'Tringsha Satabdi', trans. Anjum Katyal, p. 299.
[37] Bharucha, *Rehearsals of Revolution*, p. 164.
[38] Sircar, 'Tringsha Satabdi', trans. Anjum Katyal, p. 300.
[39] Ibid., trans. Anjum Katyal, p. 301.

voiced by Sarat—'Do you and I have the right to forget?' Sadhan asserts that since there is nothing they can really do, they are absolved. But Sarat is not buying that.

> You and I are passengers on a bus which is careening out of control. Can't we rebuke the driver, tell him to drive safely, slow down, watch out for children in his path? Can't we find out if he has a valid license, if he's of sane mind, if he's blind? Or should we turn our minds to other things, look out of the window and admire the scenery?[40]

He insists, 'Who says I am not responsible? I am responsible for two reasons. One—both I and the driver belong to the same human race. Two—we were both born in the same century, this, the twentieth century.'[41]

The play closes with the middle-class subject literally standing up to be counted. 'I, Sarat Choudhury, am here. I, Sarat Choudhury, will answer for my time, for my century. Today! Tomorrow! Always!' Addressing members of the audience directly, he asks, 'And you? What have you decided to do? You? What about you?'[42] The gradual process of politicisation of the subject has taken a substantial step forward in *Tringsha Shatabdi*.

After completing writing the play, Badal-da is still in the grip of its intensity:

> I'm not being able to write a funny play, you know? Somehow I'm feeling too severe, grim. I want to make people feel pain, rather than make them laugh. No, that's not quite it—I feel like making them laugh, but I can't do it ... I've completed my documentary play. Although I feel it's not quite ready. Even so, I feel that I want to show it to people free of charge, I feel it's only right, somehow.[43]

This thought, that the nature of the content, the message, makes it only right, or appropriate, to perform it free of charge, to take it to people without expecting them to pay to see it, is significant, given his later decision to make his a 'free' theatre. Once his theatre becomes all about the message, he does not feel it correct to charge a ticket price for it. We see the seeds of this principle here.

[40] Sircar, 'Tringsha Satabdi', trans. Anjum Katyal, pp. 332–33.
[41] Ibid., trans. Anjum Katyal, p. 333.
[42] Ibid., trans. Anjum Katyal, p. 334.
[43] Sircar, *Prabasher Hijibiji*, trans. Anjum Katyal, pp. 278–79.

The next play continues the exploration of different and challenging forms that characterise this period of his playwriting. In an Autumn or Puja issue of *Desh*, a Kolkata literary magazine, he comes across a novel by well-known writer Samaresh Basu, *Bibar*.[44] 'At the time the novel was notorious, considered obscene; but its underlying message really shook me.'[45] He is determined to turn it into a play, although he fully realises the difficulties of this task, since he will have to find a way of translating the characters' thoughts into dialogue and the spoken word. But—'Doing something that is considered impossible, never-done, has its own attraction ... like a high, an infatuation. The irresistibility of a challenge.'[46] On 31 December 1966, he is immersed in this challenge—'this afternoon, sketching the set. Evening, putting pen to paper, beginning.' He is restless, dissatisfied with what he has written, unable to focus on office work.

> I left a lot unsaid, much of what I wrote is not a play, the scenes are ending in the wrong place, what remains cannot be brought into the play form. However, even now I have faith in that which seems impossible. I mean, the challenge still exists.[47]

The next day, 1 January 1967, it's completed. It's taken him less than three days. 'Actually, I've realised, if the theme doesn't grip me, it's impossible for me to write. Yet, if the theme appeals, I can write very fast, it just flows out'.[48]

What is it about this theme that so appealed to him? The controversial novel, attacked as pornography for its sexual content at the time, is described as an unabashed dissection of the Bengali middle class, an expose of its mores, values and shameless pursuit of self-interest. The protagonist is bent on freeing himself from the restrictions of domesticity, job, politics and family obligations. These are concerns close to Badal-da's own heart.

> The more I read, the more I feel as if my brain that, drugged by my life in Nigeria, had fallen into a stupor, and that I had almost forgotten existed, is coming back to life. Not analyzing *Bibar*, not rating it a classic, just being moved, affected, touched.[49]

[44] Samaresh Basu (1924–88), Bengali writer.
[45] Sircar, Preface to 'Bibar', *Natak Samagra*, Vol. 2, trans. Anjum Katyal, p. 336.
[46] Sircar, *Prabasher Hijibiji*, trans. Anjum Katyal, p. 285.
[47] Ibid., trans. Anjum Katyal, p. 286.
[48] Ibid., trans. Anjum Katyal, p. 288.
[49] Sircar, *Prabasher Hijibiji*, trans. Anjum Katyal, p. 287.

And yet, this play is to have a strange destiny. Upon completing it, Badal-da says that

> writing it felt amazingly wonderful. At least I managed to pull it off! It may not be a play at all, but at least it has the form of a play! If so desired, it can even be put on stage, whether or not it gets an audience ... the main thing is, I have got great satisfaction from this work. I haven't felt this degree of satisfaction from any of my other plays written during this stint in Africa, except for *Pralaap*.[50]

Later, he read it to Samaresh Basu who apparently approved of it, saying that the essence of his novel had been retained.[51] And yet, in the preface to its publication, written in April 2010, Badal-da says that for the past 42 years, he hasn't published this work, out of the fear that its more sensational aspects will be played up. And he categorically states that he does not want this play produced.[52]

The final play written during his years in Nigeria, although not within 1966, like the preceding ones, is one of his best known. *Pagla Ghora* was written in January 1967 at the tail end of his African stay. He is both excited and nervous about returning to Calcutta after having lived away for several years; both eager and loathe to leave Africa. It is during this restless, unsettled emotional phase that he plunges into writing *Pagla Ghora*, his first totally original play of this period. He tries to convey the essence of what the play is about:

> The life of a human being, human relationships. Loving, not loving, staying together, living apart, all the complex nuances and impact of human relationships, the suffering, the joy, the sorrow. Inextricably linked with this is the aspect of analysis, to view things from the outside, above, to test, to determine its value and meaning, to introduce the perspective of the outside world. These two aspects cannot be separated, they are inseparably connected. And the play is being created out of all this. Just scenes from life would not have made a play; only analysis would not have been enough for a play; but with both these together, side by side, grappling with each other, the play is coming along. Imagine a woman. A moment from her life. Or just after her death. Her childhood, her growing years, her various relationships, the

[50] Sircar, *Prabasher Hijibiji*, trans. Anjum Katyal, pp. 287–88.
[51] Sircar, Preface to 'Bibar', *Natak Samagra*, Vol. 2, p. 336.
[52] Ibid.

> different sides to her life—like a kaleidoscope of images which are also being analysed, discussed. And the person emerges, and a life emerges, because there is nothing like death to bring a life into focus.[53]

Ten days later, he is still immersed in his writing.

> Malti, Milli, Lachmi are living people for me now, I can see them in front of me. Have I ever really seen them as separate individuals? But little bits of them were there in all those others – Malti, Milli, Lachmi, and the woman without a name, who is all three of them in one. Himadri, Shashi, Satkari, Kartik—have I seen them? No. Are they coming through as men, as individual persons? Probably not. There's no need. I am not writing this play with the purpose of creating characters. Then what is my purpose? No purpose. No facts. No theory is being proved here. I leave it to the pundits to find a theory in all this. Still, I'm writing. And being able to drown in the process of writing. I feel as if I'm writing what is known to me. I know all this.[54]

That same night, on 25 January 1967, he makes an entry in his diary: '11 o'clock. I just completed *Pagla Ghora*.'[55]

About a month later, he writes, '*Pagla Ghora* will remain one of my most favourite plays. I was totally immersed in it while writing it. Only one other play engulfed me as completely as this—*Sara Rattir*.'[56]

This emotional validation notwithstanding, *Pagla Ghora* does not quite live up to the description that the playwright himself provides while in the throes of writing it. Like *Ebong Indrajit*, the play once again indicts the middle class male's inability to break out of society's chains and dare to take an emotional risk; like *Sara Rattir*, it once again depicts the middle class woman as the one more emotionally honest and true to her inner being, able to give of herself without thinking only of self-interest. Yet none of the characters emerge as living and three-dimensional, neither the women nor the men. Rather, one sees only single aspects of them all. The play sets out to make a point—that Bengali middle-class men of Badal-da's own class are social and emotional cowards, forever ruled by the fear of 'what others will think', and given to calculation rather than passion; and that as a result they do not have the capacity to truly love, since love demands passion, that one lose oneself in something much bigger than oneself. In the course of making

[53] Sircar, *Prabasher Hijibiji*, trans. Anjum Katyal, p. 288.
[54] Ibid., trans. Anjum Katyal, p. 289.
[55] Ibid., trans. Anjum Katyal, pp. 289–90.
[56] Ibid., trans. Anjum Katyal, p. 290.

this point, however, the portrayal of the women is very one-dimensional. This thought will be explored in more detail when we study the gender aspect of Badal-da's work in a later chapter.

This is also the most melodramatic of his plays thus far. The leitmotif of the *pagla ghora* is taken from a popular Bengali rhyme or *chhara* in which the wild or mad horse signifies a force out of control, unpredictable and terrible in its untamed beauty. This force, which can literally sweep one off one's feet, is repeatedly invoked with equal longing and dread by the Woman who has never known passion. This *pagla ghora* is the exact opposite of the careful, cautious men characters who do not dare to take a risk in fear of social disapproval.

There is also a tribute to Rabindranath Tagore in the poetic yearning of this unnamed Woman, whose description of the colours of the evening sky which, seen from her window, fill her heart with joy, uncannily echoes Tagore's lines 'Clouds come floating into my life, no longer to carry rain or usher storm, but to add color to my sunset sky.'[57] In *Sara Rattir* too, as we recall, the ineffable force or source of beauty which infuses some meaning into the woman protagonist's banal existence—in that case, Ranjan—is a direct reference to Tagore's *Raktakarabi*. This cannot be mere coincidence. The persistent theme that runs through several of Tagore's dramas, of the freedom of the individual soul in conflict with the repressive forces of society, clearly holds meaning for Badal-da at this stage of his playwriting.

[57] Rabindranath Tagore, Verse 292, *Stray Birds*, 1916.

CHAPTER SIX

AN ESTABLISHED PLAYWRIGHT

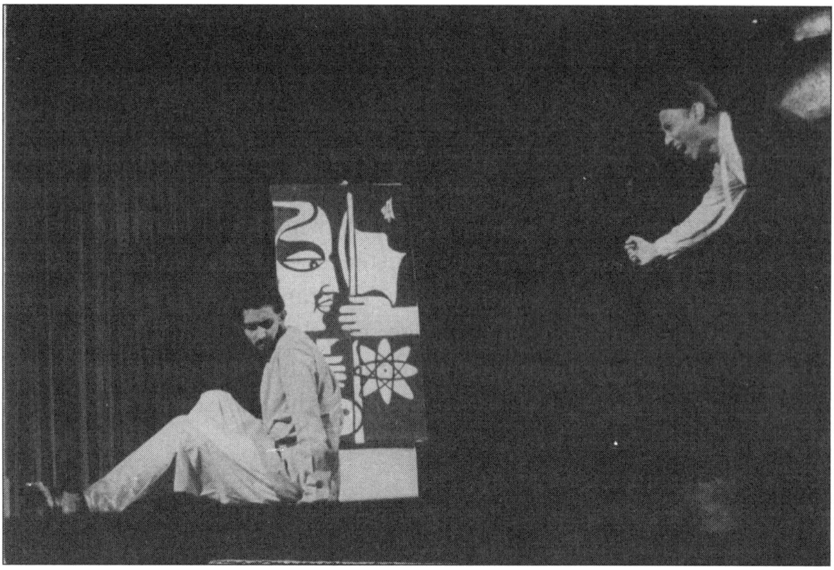

A scene from *Shesh Nei*
Courtesy: Satabdi

When Badal-da returns to Calcutta in early June, 1967, it is to a theatre world that expects great things from him. His *Ebong Indrajit* alone had catapulted him firmly into the circle of leading contemporary theatre persons; subsequently, *Sara Rattir* and *Baki Itihas*, have built up further anticipation. But he himself has returned in an ambiguous frame of mind concerning his future direction. Although theatre holds a great attraction, his profession of town planning also draws him, though he does not have a job yet. And he has plans to launch a periodical for children, or perhaps youth. He has drawings, writings and even names ready—*Chiching Phank* for the kids' magazine and *Satabdi* for the youth venture.[1] The latter, of course, is to become the name of his theatre group.

He moves into the family home on Peary Row, where he grew up and made his first foray into theatre as a child. This address, firmly identified with him, is to be his for most of the rest of his life, and much of his theatre activity happens from here in succeeding years. He tries to pick up the threads of his pre-Nigerian Calcutta life—for six Saturdays in a row he reads aloud his Nigeria plays to his old group, Chakra. He goes to see Bohurupee's production of *Baki Itihas* and comes away with admiration for the direction by Sombhu Mitra and the competent acting but reservations about the interpretation, which he feels changes the intended meaning of the play—a universal writers' grouse.

Meanwhile, Badal-da feels that rather than plunge into setting up his own theatre group—a dream from his days in France—he may be better off linking himself with Bohurupee, a group which likes his plays and wishes to produce them, and one from which he can learn a lot about direction and acting.[2] So, he decides to test the waters by directing *Pralaap* for them.

This is a period of intense theatre activity in Calcutta. The previous year had seen Bijan Bhattacharya's[3] *Debi Garjan* being staged. In 1967 itself, Bohurupee staged *Baki Itihas* at New Empire, Little Theatre staged *Tir* at Minerva and Utpal Dutt's *Kallol* was published. The group theatre was producing some of its most renowned productions around this time.

But Badal Sircar was no longer just a playwright for Bengal. He was claimed by a larger national theatre scene, as one of the four major contemporary playwrights everyone was talking about. By now, three other playwrights had emerged on the Indian scene. Mohan Rakesh, Vijay Tendulkar and Girish Karnad were producing works that challenged middle-class values in terms of content and explored new ground in terms of language and form. Hindi playwright Mohan Rakesh, born in 1925, which made him Badal-da's exact contemporary, had written *Ashadh Ka Ek Din* (*One Day in Ashadh*) in 1958, and it was first performed by Shyamanand Jalan and the Calcutta Hindi theatre group Anamika as early as 1960, followed by a production by Ebrahim Alkazi at National School of Drama in 1962. His *Adhe Adhure* (*The Incomplete Ones* or *The Halfway House*), depicting the dissolution of

[1] Sircar, *Purano Kasundi*, Vol. 3 (Kolkata: Lekhani, 2008), p. 10.
[2] Sircar, Purano Kasundi, Vol. 3, p. 11.
[3] Bijon Bhattacharya (1917–1978), Bengali playwright, best known for his *Nabanna*.

a middle class family, created a major impact in 1968 when it was staged. Manipuri theatre director Heisnam Kanhailal recalls:

> I heard the names of two playwrights being talked about in the late sixties: Badal Sircar and Mohan Rakesh. When I was in Delhi I saw *Baki Itihas*, Badal's play, in Sombhu Mitra's production, featuring Kumar Ray and Tripti Mitra. The production was fascinating and inspiring, particularly the acting by Tripti and Kumar. The simple stage design that suggested a room was also fascinating. When I was in Imphal I wrote a play *Wahang Ama* (One Question) inspired by *Baki Itihas* and made Sabitri perform in different roles following Tripti Mitra.[4]

Marathi playwright Tendulkar, born in 1928, had written *Shrimant* (1956) in which a single mother decides to keep her child while her rich father schemes to buy a husband to cover her shame and his social disgrace; *Gidhade* (Vultures, 1961), which explored the theme of violence; and, inspired by a Friedrich Dürrenmatt story and other sources, his famous *Shantata! Court Chalu Ahe* (Silence! The Court is in Session) which was produced in 1967 and caused an immediate sensation, dealing as it did with society's hypocrisy in relation to women's lives. Kannada playwright Girish Karnad (born in 1938) had written *Yayati* (1961) and *Tughlak* (1964), and we have already read about how he wrote *Hayavadana* after being inspired by the fluid structure of *Ebong Indrajit*. Together, these four were being vaunted as the Young Turks of Indian playwriting. 'If there was a renaissance in modern Indian theatre, it was these four who made it happen.'[5] Along with the playwrights was a group of directors and actors who were excited by their new material, and helped bring it to the stage and thereby to a large audience.

After his brief experience with Bohurupee, Badal-da decides that he wishes to form his own theatre group after all. He will call it Satabdi, and begin with a handful of close people with whom he is already doing theatre. Himangshu Chatterjee is one of them, Ashok Chatterjee another. His wife Putul, and some acquaintances of hers, add to the numbers. An advertisement in the newspaper draws an overwhelming 900 applicants! Some are selected from these, but most of them do not last long. Deben Ganguly is one who does. As Badal-da writes in his *The Third Theatre*:

> [O]ur theatre group Satabdi was established in 1967. We also took proscenium theatre, sets and lighting for granted. Satabdi at that time was no different from any other group theatre in Calcutta. The advantages we had

[4] Heisnam Kanhailal, email communication with the author, 9 August 2014.

[5] Shantanu Datta, http://www.indianexpress.com/oldStory/54083/. Posted: 30 August 2004 (accessed 29 January 2015).

over most of the other groups was that I had saved some money from my job in Nigeria which I could use as the initial capital and that I had written a number of plays which could last us for several years.[6]

The first play they present is his comedy *Kabikahini*. After two invited shows outside Calcutta, they hold their first city show on 3 March at the Rabindra Sarobar hall in south Calcutta. A review gives us a good idea of how the theatre aficionado received this offering:

It came ... as a surprise to many when, a few months ago, Badal Sarkar announced that a new theatre group formed by him, Satabdi, would produce a new play by him, *Kabi Kahini*, with two shows every Sunday on the Rabindra Sarobar stage. The news naturally raised considerable hope and expectation. But at the same time it was not without some apprehension that one went to see the play which one had already heard described as a 'light comedy'. It need not be a paradox that, as it turned out, while the expectation was at least partially fulfilled, the apprehension was found to be iustified as well. *Kabi Kahini* is in the vein of the author's earlier comedies. The author has found it necessary to print a statement in the programme notes to say that *Kabi Kahini* was written after and not before *Ebong lndrajit*. One sees his point but chronology does not disprove a reversion and if in *Kabi Kahini* there is ample evidence of the author's remarkable grasp over the craft of playwriting—his unfailing sense of the theatre, his easy build-up [of] situations, his sureness of touch in writing theatrical dialogues and his nimble wit—it reveals at the same time a certain care for safety and a regard for caution, if not actually for the conventional. *Kabi Kahini* is a very well-made play but well-madeness is not exactly what one hopefully goes to look for in a new play by Badal Sarkar.[7]

For 18 Sundays at a stretch, the new Satabdi presented its repertoire of three plays, all comedies by Badal-da: in addition to *Kabikahini*, the two-hander *Bagh* (Tiger) and *Bichitranusthan*. It was hard work, but Badal-da confessed that he got 'a strange kind of pleasure from those Sundays, it was like a picnic atmosphere.'[8] No doubt it was like a throwback to the earlier days of doing theatre at Maithon and with Chakra, with everyone pitching in and working together, roughing it out but having fun. A far cry from the strict discipline of rehearsals and the fairly rigid hierarchy he had seen at Bohurupee.[9] For all the buzz around his serious plays, when it comes to doing productions,

[6] Badal Sircar, 'The Third Theatre', *On Theatre: Selected Essays*, p. 8.

[7] A Drama Critic, review of Kabi Kahini, *Frontier*, Vol. 1, No. 1, 14 April 1968, p. 16.

[8] Sircar, *Purano Kasundi*, Vol. 3, trans. Anjum Katyal, p. 15.

[9] Sircar, *Purano Kasundi*, Vol. 3, pp. 11–12.

his own choice continues to veer towards comedy, despite starting from scratch with a new group, despite the intellectually charged atmosphere of the time and his own plays, such as *Tringsha Satabdi* and *Pagla Ghora*, which are lying unproduced.

In 1968, he was awarded the Sangeet Natak Akademi award for playwriting, a big honour for an artist. In 1969, at the award function in Delhi, Bohurupee's production of *Baki Itihas* was invited to perform. At the same time, Satabdi managed an invitation from a Bengali organisation to perform *Kabikahini* as well. But something was wrong. Perhaps he was no longer enjoying the routine of doing theatre with Satabdi. Or perhaps the reason was financial. 'Within a year I ran out of the money I could spare to lose on theatre and the group practically disintegrated due to various reasons,' he writes in *The Third Theatre*.[10] In his autobiography, he says, 'For a variety of reasons, the group began to displease me. I felt more and more irritated. Finally, saying, "I don't want to do any more theatre" I dissolved Satabdi.'[11] Some of the members joined Nandikar and Bohurupee; but some—he mentions Deben, Pankaj and a few others—continue to hang around, hoping to persuade him to change his mind. 'They knew perfectly well my weakness for theatre.'[12] '1968, mid-year,' he writes in *Voyages in the Theatre*:

> A number of young members of Satabdi refuse to accept the termination of the group, refuse to accept my retirement from theatre. A series of study circles on theatre begins followed by some rehearsals for a play with the specific understanding that the play will never be staged.[13]

Shades of the rehearsal club at Maithon. And we know how that ended up.

His restlessness manifests itself in his trying his hand at different mediums. He gets involved in a low-budget film being made by a friend and filmmaker, of his script *Shanibar*. When writing about the experience of visiting the studio and playing a small role in the movie, he comments favourably on the teamwork and camaraderie on the set, how it's a collective enterprise, very democratic in nature.[14] This is a quality that has always attracted him in the theatre, as we have seen. He gets a job as a training advisor with CMPU. And then he gets the opportunity to visit Russia, Poland and Czechoslovakia

[10] Sircar, 'The Third Theatre', *On Theatre*, p. 8.
[11] Sircar, *Purano Kasundi*, Vol. 3, trans. Anjum Katyal, p. 18.
[12] Ibid., trans. Anjum Katyal, p. 19.
[13] Sircar, 'Voyages in the Theatre', *On Theatre*, p. 95
[14] Sircar, *Purano Kasundi*, Vol. 3, p. 22.

for a two-month trip, under the cultural exchange programme of the government. He jumps at the chance.

He goes on this trip with a single-minded agenda: to see as much theatre as possible. Before leaving, he is given some suggestions by, amongst others, Samik Bandyopadhyay, as to interesting work he should try and observe; in other words, he goes prepared. For someone who has just publicly stated that he does not want to do theatre anymore, he is certainly determined to learn as much as he can about theatre in Eastern Europe, which is experimentally and culturally very alive at this time. 'I don't know what sort of programme you've drawn up for me, but I want to see a play every day. If not, then the circus,' he informs his interpreter and guide in Moscow upon reaching. He is asked if he also wants to visit the ballet, or the opera; but he has seen plenty of ballet in London, and he doesn't enjoy opera. 'I'm a theatre person, I'm here to learn about theatre.'[15]

His first theatrical experience of the trip is watching a rehearsal of Gorky's *Mother* at Lyubimov's Taganka Theatre.[16] Although he is scheduled to stay only till the lunch break, he is so engrossed that he chooses to spend the whole day there. He observes an intimate performance area, with seating for about 300 persons, with no curtains masking the stage, the back wall with its metal ladders and light switches fully visible, 'and even the gantry which the theatre hands use to climb up and down being used for the performance.'[17] He is impressed with Lyubimov's use of light, the spotlight in particular; with the innovative and dramatic utilisation of space (he sees the Mayday procession scene in which the gantry is pressed into use as a 'balcony' overlooking the street); the employment of real soldiers to play soldiers in the play; the way actors' bodies become prison walls. All these elements remain in his memory.[18] There is no attempt at naturalism; time and space are elastic and fluid; and above all, one does not need spoken language to grasp this theatrical language.[19] Next he sees a production of *Ten Days that Shook the World* by the same director. Again he vividly recalls the dramatically poetic and innovative use of his theatre language.[20] 'I learnt so much from watching his rehearsals and his theatre, it stayed deep in my

[15] Sircar, *Purano Kasundi,* Vol. 3, trans. Anjum Katyal, p. 28.

[16] Yuri Petrovich Lyubimov (b. 1917), leading stage actor and director, founded the internationally-renowned Taganka Theatre in 1964.

[17] Sircar, *Purano Kasundi,* Vol. 3, trans. Anjum Katyal, p. 32.

[18] Sircar, *Purano Kasundi,* Vol. 3, pp. 32–33.

[19] Ibid., p. 34.

[20] Ibid.

mind. I didn't directly copy him, but in my later life in theatre, a lot of what I learnt here came out in my work.'[21]

He also encounters Grotowski,[22] whose idea of a 'poor theatre' has so often been asserted as being a major influence on Badal-da's own formulation of a *Third Theatre*—an assertion we shall analyse when we come to that phase of Badal-da's theatre. In preparation he reads Grotowski's text 'Towards a Poor Theatre', and goes to see a Theatre Laboratory production.

> What went through my mind, I'll never forget as long as I live. I felt a fear, a numbing terror that engulfed me. Not for myself—but I felt that something horrifying was going to happen in that room to which I would be forced to bear witness for the rest of my life. Yet I couldn't leave. I was unable to move, let alone leave![23]

He also remembers the actors using the voice and vocal chords in an awe-inspiring way. That theatre could have such a powerful emotional impact is an important learning; and this effect is something he aims for in some of his later works, including the use of the human voice and sound. He also realises that the impact is to a great extent a function of space. This performance is unfolding in a small room with proximity between him and the performers. These are all things he takes away from this experience.

Later that evening, he meets Grotowski as planned, at the Writers' Union café. In answer to a question about the kind of playwrights whose plays he chooses, Grotowski answers at length: 'Two types—first, literary works by the best writers, even if they are not plays, like Leo Tolstoy or Jean Genet … Second, the theatre workers' own material.'[24] This answer rings a bell. Badal-da decides he should continue doing plays by theatre workers or himself. Grotowski remains a figure of interest—as Badal-da says, he read whatever he could on and by him—essays, interviews—and learned a lot from him.[25]

When he returned to Calcutta two months later, he has, in the words of Rustom Bharucha, seen 'some of the most innovative theatre in the world … It is not surprising that Sircar realized that he had to do something radically different in the theater.'[26]

[21] Sircar, *Purano Kasundi*, Vol. 3, trans. Anjum Katyal, p. 35.

[22] Jerzy Grotowski (1933–99), Polish theatre director and innovator of experimental theatre, the 'theatre laboratory' and 'poor theatre' concepts.

[23] Sircar, *Purano Kasundi*, Vol. 3, trans. Anjum Katyal, p. 51.

[24] Ibid., trans. Anjum Katyal, p. 54.

[25] Sircar, *Purano Kasundi*, Vol. 3, p. 54.

[26] Bharucha, *Rehearsals of Revolution*, p. 143.

Satabdi was waiting. In Badal-da's own words, 'We began again. Most of the members were new—younger than the previous members and had more enthusiasm and determination. That was 1969.'[27] He starts work:

> The first production of the reorganized Satabdi was *Pralaap* (Delirium) ... produced just after my return from a tour of the USSR, Poland and Czechoslovakia on a Cultural Exchange Programme. Yuri Lyubimov's productions of *The Good Person of Schezwan*, *Galileo* and *Ten Days that Shook the World*, and a rehearsal of Gorky's *Mother* at his Taganka Theatre in Moscow, Jari's pantomime and Cinoherni Klub's productions in Prague, and Grotowski's work and his comments on theatre were fresh in my mind. Not much of those was reflected directly in our production of *Pralaap* and the subsequent productions of *Sararattir* (Through the Night), *Sesh Nei* (There's No End) and *Ballavpurer Rupkatha* (The Fairytale of Ballavpur), except one vital principle—the concept of the Poor Theatre.[28]

In *Voyages in Theatre*, he explains his approach to theatre at the time:

> When Satabdi in its new incarnation began its voyage, the concept of free theatre did not feature even in our remotest thoughts. Like several others of our class and kind, we did not believe that a free theatre was possible. We had accepted the city theatre—the proscenium stage and the auditorium, the sets and the spotlights, in short, the theatre imported from Britain more than a century ago—and thereby we had accepted the fact that theatre actually cost money. But we were frantically trying to reduce the cost of production. On principle we decided not to spend more than ₹100 on sets, props and costumes for a new production. We recycled the set elements from one production to the next by making platform modules. We met the challenge by spending only ₹65 in creating the sets for *Ballavpurer Rupkatha*—three fluted columns and a throne in the court of a dilapidated palace. *Abu Hossain* demanded sets for court and garden, parlour and street, and we needed less than ₹100 for all that. We learnt to use our imagination and the imagination of the audience. We did all this not with the thought of a free theatre but in order to survive as a theatre group. Believe me, it is difficult to survive.[29]

He explains how he applied the concept of a 'poor theatre' to the productions he was now doing:

> The term is borrowed from Grotowski; but his concept of the Poor Theatre is that of going against the enrichment of theatre by borrowing from other

[27] Sircar, 'The Third Theatre', *On Theatre*, pp. 8–9.
[28] Ibid., p. 18.
[29] Sircar, 'Voyages in the Theatre', *On Theatre*, pp. 96–98.

> art forms and techniques, like background music, lighting, sets and costume; of impoverishing theatre to the extent of reducing it to the unadorned body of the performer, of going to the root of theatre—the rituals. We gradually reduced the use of sets, lights, costume and background music, decided never to use mechanical devices like tape recorders and projectors; but we also adopted the concept of Poor Theatre in the literal sense—that is, inexpensive theatre. Our group was poor, so are our countrymen, but we wanted to *utilize* poverty and turn it into an advantage instead of allowing it to be a restriction. This concept was discussed at length in our group, adopted as a principle, and applied in practice ... And it paid off, for this was the first time our sets (or the absence of them) were being praised by the audience and critics alike for being imaginative.[30]

He concludes:

> So, from the inception of our theatre group Satabdi, we worked through seven full-length plays and two short plays, progressively reducing the cost of the production, working hard on preparation, badgering our friends to buy tickets, until we arrived at that point of success when the city show itself became self-supporting.[31]

Shesh Nei (Without End) was written in 1970, and it extends the theme of guilt and responsibility that we have seen developing through *Baki Itihas* and *Tringsha Satabdi*. 'Instead of abstracting them, it concentrates them in the analysis of one character, Sumanta.'[32] A successful writer finds himself on trial as people who have been part of his life accuse him of different kinds of crimes. Scholar Sumanta Banerjee reads it as an 'unequal contest between a rebel and a hostile social environment.'[33] Sumanta the writer is accused of neglecting his mother, abandoning his political party and comrades, disappointing his teacher by rejecting a career in academia, throwing away the chance of a job promotion and betraying the women who loved him. He faces these charges with an assertion that conforming to their expectations would have imprisoned him in a role from which he has successfully escaped by choosing poetry as his medium of self-expression. He then begins to re-define the concept of guilt and innocence in the middle-class context.

> Five anonymous figures emerge from Sumanta's troubled psyche and accuse him of his essential cowardice as a writer. They remind him of all

[30] Sircar, 'The Third Theatre', *On Theatre*, pp. 18–19.
[31] Sircar, 'Voyages in the Theatre', *On Theatre*, p. 98.
[32] Bharucha, *Rehearsals of Revolution*, p. 141.
[33] Banerjee, 'The Theatre of Badal Sircar', p. 109.

> the unpleasant realities he has so scrupulously avoided—the beggar in the street, the unemployed worker, the victim of a communal riot, the survivor of an atomic explosion.[34]

He in turn asks—what justice is there for them? Who is responsible for their suffering? By what set of laws should he, as a writer, write? 'We are all the accused,' he says. 'Each individual is the accused and the judge at the same time ... It is a continuous process of self-evaluation and social criticism. Thus, there is no end to the trial—*shesh nei.*'[35]

According to Rustom Bharucha:

> Though he has diverted considerably from the dramatic structure and the characterization of *Shesh Nei* [in his non-proscenium work], Sircar continues to return to the same questions raised in that play: What is the responsibility of the middle class to the pervasive terror and injustice of this world? What is the role of the individual in collective action? How does one make another person confront his or her guilt without in some way concealing one's own? These are difficult questions, which Sircar continues to grapple with in his exploration of the Third Theatre.[36]

Shesh Nei ran for eight shows; it did not attract any call shows.[37] This paucity of shows spells a crisis for Satabdi; the economics of group theatre demand more shows to break even and keep going. They decide to do *Ballabhpurer Rupkatha* next, and go all out personally trying to 'push' ticket sales to ensure that they get enough of an audience. It works, and, as Badal-da says, from this moment, the wind changes for Satabdi.[38] This popular comedy saves the day; it chalks up 31 shows at theatres across the city and also travels to many cities and small towns scattered throughout the country. Thus encouraged, the group next essays *Sagina Mahato* (1970), on 8 August 1971 at the Pratap Memorial Hall.[39]

Also written by Badal Sircar in 1970 after *Shesh Nei*, this is an adaptation into play form of a story by Gourkishore Ghosh[40] about the life of a worker who becomes a trade union leader, the subsequent changes he goes through both in his attitude and way of life due to the policy of expediency

[34] Bharucha, *Rehearsals of Revolution*, p. 141.
[35] Banerjee, 'The Theatre of Badal Sircar', p. 109.
[36] Bharucha, *Rehearsals of Revolution*, pp. 141–42.
[37] Call show is a term for an invited or sponsored show.
[38] Sircar, *Purano Kasundi*, Vol. 3, p. 65.
[39] Ibid., p. 67.
[40] Gourkishore Ghosh (1923–2000), well-known Bengali writer and journalist.

the leaders of his party practise, and his attempts to survive. This is the first overtly political story Badal-da tackles as a playwright. He says:

> When I wrote *Sagina Mahato* ... my thinking had sufficiently progressed to make it fundamentally different from my previous plays. I dispensed with the mechanical division of the play into scenes and acts, the sequence of time and the barriers and limitations of space. I used the stage to show different locales and different times *simultaneously*. Also, I emphasized group acting, pantomime, rhythmic movements, songs and dances and thereby considerably reduced the importance of language. Sets were of the simplest kind that could easily be carried about and erected.[41]

In fact, many of these formal innovations are not new to his plays—some like the fluid structure, the flexible treatment of time and space, multiple zones to show simultaneity, group acting and rhythmic movements have been introduced much earlier, in *Ebong Indrajit*, for example, or *Pagla Ghora*, or *Tringsha Satabdi*.

Sagina Mahato is important for another reason. Although it begins its life as a proscenium production and runs for 23 shows on stage,[42] it is also to be Satabdi's first non-proscenium production, which we will discuss in detail in the next chapter. With this play, Badal-da decides that the future of his theatre lies outside the proscenium; however, in the months spent in the search for a suitable space for such theatre, he mounts another play, destined to be his last proscenium production: *Abu Hossain* (1971).

In the group theatre scenario, Satabdi is now on a roll; with this next stage production, *Abu Hossain*, their reputation grows. According to Shyamanand Jalan, they are at the top of their form.[43] Badal-da describes the thinking behind this play:

> During this period, three months after the production of *Sagina Mahato* at the ABTA hall, we were busy preparing our new production—*Abu Hossain*, of which some description is necessary. Although it was first produced on the conventional proscenium stage, it contained many elements that reflected my ideas about the Third Theatre.
>
> *Abu Hossain* is a music farce written nearly 80 years ago by Girish Chandra Ghosh—the great playwright-director-actor who dominated the Bengali professional theatre for over 30 years before his death in 1912. But his plays

[41] Sircar, 'The Third Theatre', p. 19.
[42] Sircar, *Purano Kasundi*, Vol. 3, p. 66.
[43] Ibid., p. 67.

> have very rarely been produced in the last three decades, as his language and themes were considered outdated. I found the humour of *Abu Hossain* surprisingly fresh, and the difficulties the play presented—numerous changes in scenes, a large cast, costume, songs, dances, etc.—appeared to me as a worthy challenge which had to be addressed with the new ideas of theatre. We met the challenge, firstly, by using modern daily wear instead of costume, although the play is based on an *Arabian Nights* story. Secondly, instead of using a number of platforms, we used a frame (3 ft. wide and 4 ft. 6 in. high) on which were hung painted canvas sheets to suggest different locales. These 'scenes' were changed in full view of the audience...Abu Hossain was first produced on 9 February 1972, and the response was tremendous. It subsequently proved to be the most popular of our productions and helped to solve some of our financial problems. But it was fated to remain bound by the conventional form of theatre for a long time, for our efforts to find a suitable space for the Third Theatre were still to no avail.[44]

In his Preface to the play's publication as part of his *Natak Samagra* (Volume 3), Badal-da says that this play was 'a great favourite'.[45] 'I heard this play often as a child, over the radio ... the message and the humour are quite contemporary.'[46] Nineteen shows into the production, Badal-da decides to quit proscenium theatre for theatre in the round. From now on, he will work only in the non-proscenium space.

This is a good juncture at which to look back over his career as a playwright thus far. In his astute essay on Badal-da's theatre, Sumanta Banerjee says:

> The appeal of Badal Sircar's plays of this period among the perceptive sections of the Indian urban middle-class audience lay in his ability to rescue some pattern and significance for human life out of the utterly dismal scene of disillusionment and failure that surrounded that audience. The adventure of self-discovery through confrontation with the grim reality, and defiance of it at every stage, was projected by Sircar as the individual rebel's only way of triumphing over the hurdles created by society ...
>
> In almost all his plays of this phase (1963–70), at the end, the protagonists, despite their bitter disappointments in life, the collapse of their ideals and their reconciliation to defeat continue to live with a purpose—although without any illusion. They try to rescue from the wreck some human value that one can yet cling to. And at the end, they hold up for us that value like a drowning man clutching at a life buoy.[47]

[44] Sircar, 'The Third Theatre', *On Theatre*, pp. 21–22.
[45] Badal Sircar, Preface to 'Abu Hossain', *Natak Samagra*, Vol. 3, trans. Anjum Katyal, p. 62.
[46] Ibid., trans. Anjum Katyal.
[47] Banerjee, 'The Theatre of Badal Sircar', pp. 107–09.

We have already noticed a growing politicisation in the content and message of his plays from *Ebong Indrajit* onwards; a preoccupation with social issues including injustice and inequality regarding women and the poor, violence and war, nuclear armament. His plays are intended for his own class to examine their own lives and norms, and raise questions about the status quo. Slowly the middle class subject of his plays has begun to act rather than just react. As he begins the non-proscenium phase of his play-making, this political aspect increasingly gains in importance.

Interwoven throughout his oeuvre is the aspect of humour and the comic, an important element of his play making. Not only is it ubiquitous in his work, from the very beginning to the end, but he also has strong views on the use of humour in theatre. Moreover, there is an element of ambiguity to his views on the place of humour in his own plays, which makes the exploration of the comic vein all the more interesting. We see an evolution of this aspect of expression—which he holds as very important—across the years.

From his childhood, Badal-da professed a love for the comic, as testified by his autobiographical *Purano Kasundi*, amongst a host of other sources already referred to. Comic characters were always his favourite, he enjoyed reading comedies, and even his Preface to *Purano Kasundi* disclaims any attempt at an overly serious account of his life. Since this was written when he was over 80 years old, clearly this penchant for humour lasted his lifetime. Those who knew him can vouch for his sardonic, wry sense of humour, while his wit and irony are in evidence in his plays.

We know, of course, that he began his life as a playwright writing comedies. He displayed quite a facility for this, with a keen sense of comic timing, ability to pace developments with deftness and skill, and a sharp ear for dialogue that rang true. His characters, drawn from his own middle-class milieu, were stock figures, but they served the purpose of advancing the storyline admirably. These initial comedies were popular fare and indeed continue to be done by groups looking for authentic comic plays to produce, even today.

Pabitra Sircar, in his Introduction to the first volume of Badal-da's *Natak Samagra* (Collected Plays) pays tribute to these early comedies. He is glad that Badal-da supports the art of comic writing:

> He maintains that it is important to write good comedies; just dismissing them as non-serious plays, as a secondary art, is wrong ... Reading his comedies one feels that he has got a lot out of writing them, and this enjoyment is conveyed to his viewers and readers. When we read these plays, we are compelled to think that they should have played a far bigger role in the

greater field of theatre development. Perhaps they have. Theatre is definitely a weapon. Badal babu will move increasingly towards this aspect of theatre; for a while perhaps he'll also be writing both entertainers and social plays. However social philosophers may say that pure entertainment has no value for society, we believe that entertainment has an important contribution in helping people bear up with their problems, even deal with their obligations and commitments more easily.[48]

He offers proof of this with the example of how, at times of war, light films and plays are much more popular than serious fare.

It was after his *Ebong Indrajit* took the theatre world by storm, and he began to consider himself a serious playwright, that his penchant for comedy became problematic. We know from his diaries and letters, published as *Prabasher Hijibiji*, that he was torn between two very different kinds of writing: the light, comic vein and the serious, intense, play with a message, or at the very least, a question. He mentions this inner struggle over and over. He takes up a comic play, *Ballabhpurer Rupkatha*, puts it aside as *Sara Rattir* comes pouring out of him, then returns to it and completes it. It remains till date one of his most widely-produced entertainers. Soon after, he writes *Kabikahini*, another piece of entertainment which, however, introduces a new note into his comic writing:

In Kabi Kahini (1964), the spectators see the lineaments of contemporary society, where a poor school teacher gets bewildered by the chicanery of self-seeking rival politicians during the election, and is soon embroiled in their petty exaggeration, and it approaches the level of the serious where no careful spectator can fail to read the bitter cynicism under the mask of the comic—a mood that was to return with a sharper political perspective in the later phase of Sircar's 'Third Theatre'.[49]

It is when *Kabikahini* is being produced by Satabdi that Badal-da decides to comment, rather sharply, in defence of his own comic writing:

According to many people, I first wrote comedies, honed my craft, and then started to write 'Ebong Indrajit', 'Baki Itihas' etc, so-called *bhalo* or 'good' plays.

I object to this on two grounds. First, it isn't really correct. I wrote *Kabi Kahini* and a few other comedies after I wrote *Ebong Indrajit*. If I can, I'll

[48] Sircar, Introduction to Badal Sircar, *Natak Samagra*, Vol. I, p. iii (teen).

[49] Banerjee, 'The Theatre of Badal Sircar', p. 104.

> write more. Second, it seems to indicate that comedy is somehow a lesser form. I don't think so. Even if I was to accept that comedies have no message, no engagement with contemporary issues, no voice, the value to me of the comic or indeed laughter is not thereby any the less. That we Bengalis love to weep and are embarrassed to laugh—even this is something I am reluctant to accept. In fact I'd rather say—we can smile even from the depths of grief, we can laugh when faced with terrible tragedy, we can overcome the most complicated problems through the medium of laughter. So I hold laughter dear. If laughter is healthy, if I can make others laugh without resorting to buffoonery, grotesque mannerisms or grimaces, I believe it can never be pointless.[50]

This note sounds defensive, even more so when read alongside his outpourings in *Prabasher Hijibi* where his own confusion over his 'serious' and 'comic' is explored quite intensely. On 21 November 1963, he embarks on a bout of soul searching:

> Life offers us lots to laugh about. Lots of material for laughter in life. Any human being can be comical. Ludicrous. Many human beings together—even more ludicrous. Whatever morals, laws, rules mankind has created, all have a ridiculous side to them. And many men follow them with such amusing solemnity, even worship them.[51]

He continues to question himself.

> Am I then alienated from life? Most definitely not. As a human being who has been granted life, I don't have the option to opt out. Will I be able to laugh? It's not as if I can't. I have in the past. And today, if I wish it, surely I'll be able to? So then, what are these poems? This deep dark dramatic poetry? Are they, too, alienated from life? Only imaginings? And dreams? But both the imagination and dreams are part of life, aren't they? Both laughter and poetry are part of the same life.[52]

He turns to the characters of his plays:

> Dibyendu of *Shonibar* is a comical figure. I said, let people laugh at him. Someone or the other commented—in that case, the play is sunk. Is that so?

[50] Badal Sircar, Playwright's note, brochure for 'Kabi Kahini', reproduced as the preface, 'Kabi Kahini', *Natak Samagra*, Vol. 1, trans. Anjum Katyal, p. 450.

[51] Sircar, *Prabasher Hijibiji*, trans. Anjum Katyal, p. 211.

[52] Ibid., trans. Anjum Katyal, p. 212.

> Can't Dibyendu be amusing? Isn't man funny? Can man not laugh at himself? Will people laugh at Indrajit? Probably not. But they should. Indrajit is also comical. Why didn't I make them laugh at him, allow them to laugh at him? We want to laugh at others, but never at ourselves. We can't bear to think of ourselves as ludicrous.[53]

It is not as if *Ebong Indrajit* is a humourless play. It offers moments of satire and irony, it is witty in its stylisations, some of the sequences are funny in their sharp enunciation of an absurd reality; but Indrajit himself is not a comic figure. And yet, argues Badal-da more and more frequently, he could have been, perhaps even should have been. Watching absurd theatre, farces, musicals, during his time in England and France, he sees how serious subjects can be treated with lightness and humour. War, death, violence, suffering and tyranny—can all be conveyed with generous doses of laughter. He comments on this. He feels that there is more truth and a 'greater reality' in the Absurd.[54] So much so that he confesses on 6 March 1964 that he feels it was a mistake to make *Ebong Indrajit* so serious. 'If I could rewrite it as a comedy that would be a job well done. And it's not impossible at all, in fact it is probably more appropriate. I had thought this even before I saw Ionesco's plays—in fact I had written as much in my diary last November.'[55] Having said this, he launches into an analysis of the Absurd theatre movement in Europe. After living in the midst of a soul-destroying war, after seeing young men and women dying by the thousands, Europe resorts helplessly to laughter as the only resort. When life itself is absurd, is there any more appropriate response? And so you get the comedy of a play like 'Oh, What a Lovely War'.[56] It is this black humour that attracts him. On 12 May 1966, he returns to the idea of rewriting Ebong Indrajit as a 'roaring farce'. Should he do it? Dead serious subject matter, slapstick treatment.[57]

Two years later in the *Illustrated Weekly of India,* he is talking about the 'modern' playwright's search for sanity, in the course of which:

> [H]e often has to delve deep into insanity. It is often difficult for him to keep his play 'straight'. His play may go awry, go mad, but he is fully justified if his search for sanity is genuine. Often, in his search for sanity, the 'modern' playwright has to laugh. The world has become so full of anomalies and

[53] Sircar, *Prabasher Hijibiji,* trans. Anjum Katyal, p. 212.
[54] Ibid., p. 247.
[55] Ibid., trans. Anjum Katyal, pp. 247–48.
[56] Sircar, *Prabasher Hijibiji,* p. 248.
[57] Ibid., p. 276.

> absurdities that we have to laugh sometimes to see it in the correct perspective. The problems and tragedies of modern life may be very real, but the root causes of these ... appear to be so ludicrous that the playwright finds it difficult to express them without laughing. We should not be surprised if humour gradually becomes the main vehicle of the *new play* ... Even a play that does not do anything but make us laugh appears to be useful to a man of the 'modern' world.[58]

His desire to write a black comedy finally finds expression in *Khat Mat Kring* (1983). Speaking of this play, he says:

> To be able to write a play on violence, ranging from bride-burning to gas chambers and nuclear holocaust, in the medium of slapstick humour—that was a great voyage, at least for me. That was something I wanted to write for years, for I believed that such grim themes can be made more intense and poignant if humour is used. I wanted, but I never had any success before I wrote this play.[59]

By linking the serious, the deeply emotional, the intense, with the absurd, ludicrous, comical, one feels that Badal-da is working out a solution to his own impasse, the repeated inner questioning he goes through in the 1960s, torn between his inability to write light and humorous plays and his desire to focus on socially meaningful material. From his Anganmancha period onwards, we see plenty of humour in his productions, but we do not see the lightweight domestic entertainers he churned out earlier. *Ebong Indrajit*, his first 'serious' play, which is largely seen as an angst-ridden text, is shot through with a sardonic irony and wit. *Michhil* has moments of savage comedy in the vignettes on *netas* and gurus. Brecht comes to mind, with his sharp use of humour as part of the 'alienation effect'. There are echoes of this strategy in the documentary plays of Badal-da's Third Theatre phase, as Sumanta Banerjee recognises:

> Satire adopts a fantastic garb. Underneath the seeming gaiety, horrors of the pit are suddenly exposed. The comic in Badal Sircar has turned a full circle—but this time with a mission. It often appears first in the guise of fantasy, and then gradually shows its fangs which tear apart the ridiculous pretensions of politicians, the greed of the multinationals, the crimes of the war-mongers.[60]

[58] Badal Sircar in *Illustrated Weekly of India*, 2 June 1968.
[59] Sircar, 'Voyages in the Theatre', *On Theatre*, p. 144.
[60] Banerjee, 'The Theatre of Badal Sircar', p. 116.

Sumanta Banerjee reminds us also of Badal-da's use of

> satirical skits based on historical and current social and political problems. *Sukhopathhya Bharater Itihas* (1976), which deals with past episodes from Indian history, is an interesting example of this…it is a satirical exposition (in the form of school lessons) of the history of British colonial exploitation of India. Similarly, *Khat Mat Kring* (1983) moves through a series of short satirical skits which juxtapose fleeting glimpses of political murders and street rowdyism in modern Calcutta with scenes of anti-Jewish Nazi propaganda in Germany in the 1930s and anti-Shudra acts of Rama in Ramayana. In a sort of stream-of-consciousness burlesque, one dialogue or an incident sparks off memories of similar historical events of the past, the association of one leads to that of another. As a result, the scenes keep on shifting rapidly from the immolation of Joan of Arc to the burning of a bride for dowry, from the competitive environs of a modern commercial office to the nuclear race in the international arena which leads to a future world where men have killed themselves and only cockroaches survive.[61]

This is political humour in the tradition of the cartoon, the satire, with deliberate exaggeration to enhance the point being made. Sumanta Banerjee finds it 'a brilliant caricature of the impotence of the old liberal standpoint in dealing with today's problems of criminalisation of politics, corruption of society, the rise of neo-fascist forces and the threat of the looming nuclear war.'[62]

Another tradition Badal-da mined was that of the lighthearted 'folk' play or fairytale with a moral or a message. For example, his *Hattamalar Oparey* which, he says,

> [H]as a fairytale base with humour as its medium and the colloquial dialogue [that] goes well with every situation. It works equally well in the anganmancha and the open air, in towns and in villages, with adults and with children. The subject is the ultimate desired and envisioned form of society where each will work according to his ability and will receive according to his needs, thereby rendering the use of money unnecessary.[63]

The two lovable thieves Kena and Becha (Buy and Sell) who land up accidentally in a Utopian land where no one needs money, and therefore no one needs to steal, find their noses sadly out of joint until they too see the benefits of this humane social system. Full of funny situations and comic

[61] Banerjee, 'The Theatre of Badal Sircar', pp. 113–14.
[62] Ibid., p. 114.
[63] Sircar, 'Voyages in the Theatre', *On Theatre*, p. 122.

moments, it is a delightful play on a thought-provoking subject. Badal-da says, 'I would still like to be able to write a play of that kind, but it probably happens once in a lifetime.'[64]

Sumanta Banerjee speaks appreciatively of this ability to employ traditional folk forms, replete with 'absurd and extravagantly comic characters' which in his hands turn into 'a grand mixture of serious poetry, parody, caricature, burlesque and various folk media styles, with a sharp political message'.[65] A perfect example of this, he proposes, is *Lakshmichharar Panchali* (Ballad of the Unfortunates, 1974), which is in the form of a *kobi gan*, a traditional Bengali folk form of a poetic debate between two parties, who improvise verses on either contemporary political happenings or mythological subjects in the form of a verbal duel. 'In this play an elderly *kobi* or versifier contends with a younger one. The debate between the two moves on to questions like why do the poor farmers lose their land and suffer illiteracy, why they cannot compete in a free market economy etc.'[66]

Two scholars with a close knowledge and understanding of Badal-da's oeuvre have expressed a view that he does not have humour in his work. Sibaji Bandyopadhyay, in an interview with me said, 'His sense of humour and irony is not fully developed. He becomes over serious.'[67] And Rustom Bharucha too, while discussing his work with me, said that he felt Badal-da did not have the playful touch or lightness of approach that one finds, say, in Utpal Dutt.[68] One can tell where these opinions are coming from, and it is possible to see, in Badal-da's overall oeuvre, a miasma of dark seriousness and intensity which blots out his comic pieces. However, if we examine the plays one by one, we notice bits and segments of the funny, the lighthearted, the ludicrous, the farcical and the outright ironic, interwoven alongside the earnest tone of even the darker plays like *Bhoma* (1975).

Badal-da's sense of the ridiculous and absurd, his ability to find human beings ludicrous and comic, was an integral part of his temperament, I feel. It could have led to a cynical detachment but instead, combined with his well-developed humanitarian conscience, it fused into a keen sense of irony and satire. This combined well with the political and social concerns of the bulk of his theatre work, and as a result, we see a strong streak of humour running through most of his oeuvre, from the cartoon to the spoof to the sardonic wit of sharp critique.

[64] Sircar, 'Voyages in the Theatre', *On Theatre*, p. 122.
[65] Banerjee, 'The Theatre of Badal Sircar', p. 112.
[66] Ibid.
[67] Bandyopadhyay, interview with the author, 17 May 2014.
[68] Rustom Bharucha, interview with the author, 5 May 2014.

CHAPTER SEVEN

PROSCENIUM FAREWELL

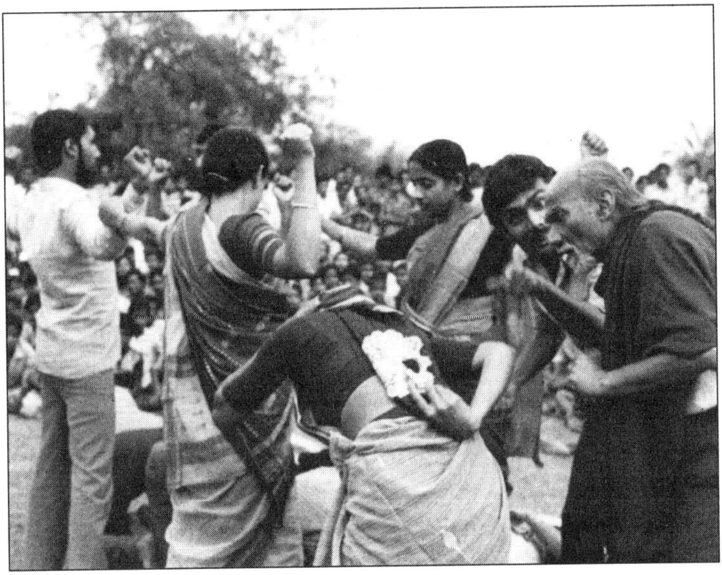

A new form
Courtesy: Satabdi

In 1971 and 1972, when Badal-da was exploring new spaces to present his alternative theatre-in-the-round, the city of Calcutta was in the grip of upheaval. The Naxalite Movement had led to a sharp crackdown by the establishment and the widespread use of State terror to counter the insurgents. Youth from the same urban educated middle class that Badal-da had addressed in his plays about guilt and responsibility were drawn to this militant, radical left movement out of a combination of that very guilt and responsibility, almost as if in answer to the questions he raised in *Baki Itihas*, *Tringsha Satabdi* and *Shesh Nei*. Of course his vocabulary was more

Christian and humanistic, a far cry from the extreme left political language and formulations of this movement, but the underlying motivation was the same—an alliance with the suffering and the oppressed across the world, an insistence that each one had to take responsibility and make a change. Finally, his middle-class subject, whom he had deemed boringly incapable of action, was acting. It was almost as if the culmination of the growing politicisation of the protagonist/subject of his plays was being enacted in the streets, as thousands of young men and women left their classrooms and their homes to join the fight for their dream of a more just and honest society.

This was also the year of the Bangladesh Liberation War, with its immediate impact on Calcutta as hordes of destitute refugees streamed into the city, fleeing from the persecution across the border. Impossible to remain untouched or unmoved as Calcutta erupted in tumult and turmoil, especially if you were, like Badal-da, already in a questioning frame of mind. From now on all his work is going to reflect a political awareness in terms of content as well as form.

Sumanta Banerjee describes the contemporary socio-political scenario:

> While his plays of introspection were shaped by the concerns and conditions of the Calcutta middle class youth of the 1960s, the Third Theatre took birth in the tumultuous decades of the late 1960s-early 1970s period, when the Naxalite movement was shaking up the status quo by raising a number of fundamentally important political and social questions. It challenged the traditional interpretation of Indian history by questioning the role of the national leadership in relation to the rural poor during the anti-colonial movement. It exposed the opportunism and expediency of the existing political parties in the history of post-Independence India. It defied the conventional middle class-dominated conservative social norms and values. The exodus of a large number of these defiant youth from the middle class homes to the villages, inspired by the Naxalite ideology of agrarian revolution, drew public attention to the hitherto neglected needs and aspirations of the rural poor. In the context of West Bengal, along with the politics of agrarian revolution, the rich cultural tradition of the numerous Bengali rural folk forms also attracted the attention of politically committed dramatists during this period. It may be recalled that Utpal Dutt took up the popular rural theatre form of *jatra* at this time to stage his political plays like *Rifle* (1968), *Jalianwala Bag* (1969), *Dilli Chalo* (1970), *Sannyasir Tarbari* (1972) and *Mao Tse Tung* (1974).[1]

[1] Banerjee, 'The Theatre of Badal Sircar', pp. 110–11.

Utpal Dutt's group also presented *Tiner Talwar* (Tin Sword) on the vast stage at Rabindra Sadan in September 1971, while a cluster of women-oriented plays appeared in quick succession, three by Bohurupee—their production of Badal-da's own *Pagla Ghora* in February 1971 at Academy of Fine Arts, Tripti Mitra's two-hour long monologue, *Aparajita*, which reportedly held the audience spellbound, in August of the same year, and Tendulkar's landmark play *Chop, Adalat Cholche* (*Silence! The Court is in Session*) in December 1971, at Kala Mandir—followed, a year later, by Nandikar's *Nati Binodini*.

Add to this the cinema being produced by alternative filmmakers, such as Mrinal Sen, Ritwik Ghatak and Satyajit Ray, all making films that grappled with the reality of the city, its politics and the socio-economic landscape, and we have a charged cultural atmosphere prevailing at the time.

In fact, according to an article on street theatre in Bengal:

> The 70s may be termed a decade of theatre movement in Bengal, among other things. Alternative theatre crystallized into a definite movement during this decade. Because theatre is such a directly life-oriented art form, turmoils of everyday living get reflected intimately in this form, mirroring the frustrations and dreams of ordinary people. During the 70s, the frustrations were over the existing social situation and the dreams were of revolutionary social change. Whether or not the street theatre activists of this decade were members of a wing of the Communist Party, their plays were uniformly influenced by leftist ideology, depicting the distress and aspirations of the times. Most of them were powerful critiques of the contemporary administrative system and State structure. Naturally the State didn't look kindly upon these theatre activists; repression and police torture was the fate of many. In 1972, Ashis Chatterjee of Theatre Unit died of police bullets while acting in *Lash Bipani*. Police atrocities killed Prabir Datta, another street theatre activist, at Curzon Park in Calcutta in 1974 ... It was this kind of State and inter-party terrorism, and its reflection in plays, that turned the 70s into the decade of street theatre in West Bengal. For the theatre workers of this period, political commitment and commitment to theatre didn't mean different things. Dreams of revolutionary social change were fused equally into both these commitments and the veering from the proscenium towards street theatre was but one aspect of rejecting the prevalent norms and values. The need was to reach the rank and file at close quarters with Marxist messages of class struggle and change, and street theatre as a distinctive art form was born in Bengal out of this need. That is why many of the street plays of this decade could so powerfully touch people's hearts.[2]

[2] Bulbuli Biswas and Paramita Banerjee, 'Street Theatre in Bengal: A Glimpse', *Seagull Theatre Quarterly*, No. 16, December 1997, pp. 35–36.

This was the city landscape in which Badal-da was to start his non-proscenium productions; his mental landscape had been harbouring this idea for a long time:

> Once [at the American Centre library] I found a book called Theatre-in-the-Round.[3] Reading it wasn't just enjoyable, it was very exciting. I even discussed it in Satabdi's study circle. Later, I saw this kind of theatre in London and Paris . . . I kept doing theatre for the proscenium, but thoughts of this theatre have been lurking at the back of my mind for a long time. Then I read about Café Theatre's La-Mama productions in America, and was very interested in that too.[4]

One could add to this his more recent experiences in the USSR, Poland and Czechoslovakia.

With *Sagina Mahato*, Badal-da felt he had reached a turning point. It is best described in his own words:

> When *Sagina Mahato* was produced, I realized that the time had come to leave the proscenium theatre, and that this was a play eminently suited for that decision.
>
> The first experimental production of the play outside of the proscenium theatre took place on 24 October 1971,[5] at the All Bengal Teachers' Association (ABTA) hall in Calcutta. It is a small hall with a tiny stage on one side, seating about 200 people when used as a conventional auditorium. We arranged the chairs in the hall and on the stage in such a manner that a central arena was obtained for acting. But we did not restrict the production to arena-acting or theatre-in-the-round but created acting areas amidst the spectators. Thus, the separation of the spectators from the performers was further broken, and a sense of being 'within' the performance was imparted, helping induce a considerable degree of involvement.[6]

[3] There is a book called *Theatre-in-the-Round* by Margo Jones which was published in 1965 by McGraw-Hill. Perhaps this is the title referred to here. Jones suggests that due to the intimacy of theatre-in-the-round, furniture should be minimal, properties and costumes naturalistic, makeup and movement subtle. Plays for this format should resemble sculptures instead of pictures, imagined from above instead of from the sides, that is, three-dimensional. She suggests that with creative problem-solving and simplification, any play can be done in this configuration.

[4] Sircar, *Purano Kasundi*, Vol. 3, trans. Anjum Katyal, p. 67. The reference is to Café La MaMa, the iconic alternative, experimental theatre space in New York of the 1960s.

[5] There is some confusion about the date of this first non-proscenium production. In his autobiographical *Purano Kasundi*, Vol. 3, Badal-da writes: 'On 18 June 1972 in ABTA Hall a test show of *Sagina Mahato* done in this new style was held' (p. 67); and 'Another show like this was held in ABTA hall on 10 October' (p. 68), trans. Anjum Katyal.

[6] Sircar, 'The Third Theatre', *On Theatre*, pp. 19–20.

According to him, audience members who had seen the proscenium production professed to like it better in its new form. 'There were about 120 spectators and we had a discussion with almost everybody after the show, asking them to write their comments for us as well; hence we have quite a comprehensive idea of their reactions.'[7]

He makes a point of mentioning a particular occurrence that was a real eye-opener for him:

> ... we learnt much more from a little accident during the show (for which I was thankful later although I cursed it at the time)—the electric fuse blew at a particularly interesting moment in the play but the performers continued without a break; for half a minute, the performance went on in complete darkness. Then the house lights came up—a few neon tubes on the ceiling which were very different and ordinary compared to the spotlight arrangement we had devised for the production. We continued acting in this light for at least five minutes, after which the theatre lights came up. During this period, there was not a comment, not a murmur, not even a sigh or rustle of movement from the audience. And in our discussion after the show, none of the spectators referred to the incident—even in sympathy. This incident confirmed my idea more than anything else that the involvement achieved by this form is much more than that of the conventional stage production. It also gave me the courage to simplify lighting to a great extent in subsequent productions.
>
> After this production, I was convinced that I was on the right path towards the creation of the Third Theatre and that our group should be geared fully to this form. It opened out entirely new possibilities in the field of theatre and it seemed that no other group but ours was thinking of exploring them.[8]

Although Satabdi returned to the proscenium with *Abu Hossain* in early 1972 and did a series of well-attended shows, Badal-da had already committed himself to moving out of the conventional stage. According to American theatre director Richard Schechner, who was soon to become a friend and source of inspiration, 'Badal knew that the "modern theatre" of psychology, drama, the spoken word, the proscenium stage, the box set, and the separate audience was dead. Worse, it was rotting.'[9] Now it was just a question of finding a suitable performance space and developing a like-minded group

[7] Sircar, 'The Third Theatre', *On Theatre*, p. 20.

[8] Ibid.

[9] Richard Schechner, *Performative Circumstances: from the Avant Garde to Ramlila* (Calcutta: Seagull Books, 1983), p. 25.

of fellow enthusiasts who would be equally committed to this alternative form of theatre. Inevitably, many members of the group were reluctant to forego the pleasures and rewards of mainstream proscenium theatre, and this was to cause a major split in Satabdi.

The previous year, Badal Sircar had decided to resign from a dissatisfying job in town planning. Soon after submitting his resignation, he was awarded the prestigious Nehru Fellowship offered by the Jawaharlal Nehru Memorial Fund on the basis of a project entitled 'Workshop for a Theatre of Synthesis as a Rural–Urban Link.'[10] This Fellowship was for a two-year period, starting June 1971, and it enabled him to devote himself single-mindedly to the exploration of his theatre ideas. As he stated in his essay *Third Theatre*:

> This is not a project taken up specifically for the purpose and the period of the Fellowship. The project began before I got the Fellowship, and will continue as long as I retain an interest in theatre. Even if I had not received the Fellowship, I would have gone on with the same ideas, but at a slower rate. The Fellowship gave me the opportunity of devoting my whole time to the project and to give it a more concrete and organized shape. It also allowed me to take the financial risks inherent in any experiment in the field of theatre and under the conditions prevailing in our country.[11]

The search for a viable and financially sustainable space for his non-proscenium theatre was finally rewarded when a chance meeting led to Lady Ranu Mukherjee[12] offering him a hall at the Academy of Fine Arts at a subsidised rate. This was in June 1972:

> We made an arrangement to hire a room of 850 square-feet area on the second floor of the Academy of Fine Arts for three consecutive days of the week—Sunday, Monday and Tuesday. The Academy of Fine Arts has a good theatre hall which has become quite popular with theatre-lovers in Calcutta. This was advantageous to us, as our theatre would be in the same building. The room would accommodate 60 to 75 spectators, depending on the play presented.[13]

[10] According to the Nehru Fellowship website (http://www.jnmf.in/flist.html), the initiation date of his fellowship was June 1971. Others awarded the same year included fellow playwright Mohan Rakesh (who unfortunately passed away the following year) and visual artist Haku Shah.

[11] Sircar, 'The Third Theatre', *On Theatre*, pp. 3–4.

[12] Lady Ranu Mukherjee (1907–2000), a Calcutta-based connoisseur and patron of the arts, who helped establish the Academy of Fine Arts in 1933.

[13] Sircar, 'The Third Theatre', *On Theatre*, p. 30.

Finally, he was about to begin his experiment with non-proscenium theatre in earnest.

However, there were still some months to go before the space was ready to be occupied by them and before they could begin working there. Two extremely significant things happened in these intervening months of 1972. First, he wrote and developed *Spartacus* (1972), his first play wholly conceived for the non-proscenium space, utilising his ideas about the nascent Third Theatre, and working with his group to effect the shift from the demands of a proscenium-style production to a theatre-in-the-round style production. Second, he embarked on a two-month study tour of the USA, responding to an invitation from Richard Schechner. Both these developments were of immense importance in the formulation of his Third Theatre philosophy and practice.

Let us turn to *Spartacus* first. 'Spartacus from its inception had to do more with the political objectives I sought outside the theatre than with creating merely good theatre—it was a departure,' Badal is quoted as saying.[14]

He describes the whole process of writing this play in some detail in *The Third Theatre*:

> For a long time in the history of theatre, particularly in our country, a play depended mainly on two factors: (a) story and (b) characters. The usual approach was to present certain *characters* with definite identities and a *story* developed through the interaction between these characters. It was done with the idea that the spectators would recognize or identify themselves with the characters on the stage and get involved with their problems and emotions. Social problems were posed as extensions of the problems of the individual characters in the play. This is all very well but this certainly is not the limit of theatre. For a long time, I have been trying to break away from this system of story and characters.'[15]

This claim is certainly substantiated if one looks back at the list of plays written to date: few of them have bothered with fully fleshed out three-dimensional characters; rather, they have preferred to present ideas and issues in a theatrical manner, using characters to embody and symbolise them, and poetry, montage and repetitive movements to express them. His comedies are more typical—they belong to the genre of the situational

[14] Badal Utsav pamphlet brought out by Natya Shodh Sansthan on the occasion of Badal Utsav, Kolkata, 15–19 July 2009, p. 9.

[15] Sircar, 'The Third Theatre', *On Theatre*, pp. 22–23.

comedy, peopled by stock characters who, however, once again remain two-dimensional in service to the plot. He continues:

> Working on the Third Theatre, I began discovering new possibilities of using groups more than either characters or types; using words addressed directly to spectators more than dialogue between stage characters; using physical acting more than language. Writing *Sagina Mahato* and producing it first on the proscenium stage and then in the new form opened out a new vista in theatre that gave me a conviction that any theme can be presented in theatre—even highly complex epic themes.[16]

Once again, we can turn to his body of plays to see that none of this is totally new to him as a playwright: in *Ebong Indrajit* and *Tringsha Satabdi,* he has introduced both groups and direct address to the audience; he has already grappled with complex and epic themes in plays such as *Baki Itihas* and *Tringsha Satabdi*. The journey to this point started many years ago, whether he recognises it or not.

Sagina Mahato, he says, gave him the courage to make a play out of Howard Fast's *Spartacus* which he did in January 1972:

> The novel always fascinated me but it seemed impossible to present in theatre, the canvas being so vast and the theme so complex. I realize fully that I could not have written it at all if I had not realized the possibilities of the Third Theatre. That is why writing, preparing and producing *Spartacus* has become perhaps the most significant event in my development.[17]

The whole process of preparing this production took a year and involved the entire group:

> When I wrote the play, I was far from satisfied. It appeared inadequate in relation to the theme and I was very doubtful about its production. Apart from the fact that this was the first play I had conceived entirely for the Third Theatre (and the fullest use of *groups* had been made as opposed to individual *characters*), it was also significantly different from the conventional plays in its use of physical action to express themes that cannot be expressed effectively by the spoken word and the strengthening of the spoken word at places where, by itself, it would have been inadequate. To deal with these, the group needed special training.

[16] Sircar, 'The Third Theatre', *On Theatre*, p. 23.
[17] Ibid.

> In February 1972, we began working on *Spartacus* and thus began a fascinating process. Instead of revising and editing the script myself, I put it to the group who confronted the script, tried it, tested it, accepted, enriched and rejected it and gradually began to build a structure that was much more than the written script. Through the process, the group was transformed into a workshop in the true sense of the term. The performers explored and discovered the hidden potential of their bodies, of their voices. Basic exercises were learnt and new exercises evolved from them to suit our needs.[18]

This was when he met Anthony Serchio—'a director of the La MaMa theatre of USA which has contributed so much to the experimental theatre.'[19] In March, the group took part in several workshops under Serchio where they learnt, among other things, 'the set of basic exercises known as the "cat series" evolved by Grotowski.'[20]

Badal-da describes the important changes the workshop approach brought into the group:

> Formerly, only those members who had a part in the play under preparation worked in the rehearsals. The others watched either with passive interest or with no interest at all ... In the workshops, everybody felt equally important and this created a universal interest.
>
> Those who were considered (by others and by themselves) as bad actors quite often proved to be very good at physical acting, a factor which had become more important in the workshops.
>
> One of the principal enemies of an actor—inhibition—was removed to a large extent. Psychological blocks were also being removed, and the individual was being benefited not only theatrewise but in his or her personal life as well.
>
> Instead of imitating certain stage voices and stage movements, the performer began giving more from within. This meant replacing the fake in theatre by a true expression of the self.
>
> There was much more participation on the part of the performer in the process of preparing the play instead of following the director unquestioningly as had been the practice so far.
>
> The whole process was necessarily slow; we were not just *rehearsing* a play set down in definite terms by the playwright but *confronting* a script to create live theatre out of it. What we were learning was useful not just for this play, but for other plays to be taken up in future. We were preparing a

[18] Sircar, 'The Third Theatre', *On Theatre*, pp. 23–25.

[19] Anthony Serchio was manager of The Poor Theatre Company, created in 1968 in New York.

[20] Sircar, 'The Third Theatre', *On Theatre*, pp. 23–25.

> base whereby the next play may not be *written* by Badal Sircar or any other playwright but *created* by Satabdi—the entire group.[21]

He not only found the work challenging and very exciting, but also felt that he was inadequately trained in the kind of physical acting and workshop exercises this theatre demanded. In order to really guide his group, he himself needed to learn more. Soon the opportunity came in the form of an invitation to visit the USA, from Dr Richard Schechner and his wife Joan Macintosh of The Performance Group, whom he had met when they visited Calcutta in 1971. They suggested that he observe their work and participate in their workshops. Since his Fellowship grant could cover part of the expenses, he decide to seize this opportunity and left for New York on 1 July 1972.[22]

This brings us to the second important development. The USA he visited was quite a radicalised place, not least in the area of arts. The previous decade had seen an explosion of anti-establishment activity, centring on the civil rights movement, the anti-Vietnam war protests, the sexual revolution, the feminist movement—and all this was reflected in the world of arts which was daring, experimental and alternative, and demonstrated a strong social commitment and consciousness. Thanks to the Schechners, Badal-da was able to meet some of the country's most dynamic and avant-garde theatre artists and performances, and the learning from this fed directly into his formulation of the Third Theatre on his return. On this visit to the USA and Canada, he saw theatre productions, attended rehearsals, observed and participated in workshops, held long in-depth discussions with other theatre directors, and learned exercises and processes that he later adapted to his own use. 'On the whole, my experience in New York was very useful in formulating and defining my ideas of the theatre, sometimes in agreement but mostly in terms of reaction,' he says in retrospect.[23]

His weeks in New York were spent immersed in theatre, living in Richard Schechner's flat, sleeping on the living room sofa and seeing plays both off-Broadway and off–off-Broadway, including Richard Schechner's *Commune* by The Performance Group. He saw how their Environmental Theatre crafted each show to suit the space, changing the whole experience in different environments. He says, David Rabe's[24] *Sticks and Bones* was a play that

[21] Sircar, 'The Third Theatre', *On Theatre*, pp. 23–25.

[22] Sircar, 'The Third Theatre', *On Theatre*, p. 25.

[23] Ibid., p. 27.

[24] David William Rabe (b. 1940), American playwright and screenwriter. His *Sticks and Bones* won the Tony Award for Best Play in 1972.

he really liked.[25] He makes special mention of *And They Put Handcuffs on the Flowers*, written and directed by Fernando Arrabal,[26] and of a dramatic presentation of Leo Tolstoy's *Anna Karenina*:

> The first was about imprisonment, and it aimed at a violent and raw emotional impact. The latter was a fine example of bringing out the essence of a great (and long) novel, and the precision and theatricality with which it was done was superb. Although the two productions were very different from each other, both aimed at theatrical experience and storytelling played little role in either.[27]

He recalls that *Anna Karenina* was presented by a middle-aged woman of Russian origin (whose name he cannot remember), who played both the scriptwriter/adaptor and the director, and who interspersed performance with talking to the actors about the essence of the work and the adaptation process. Badal-da is very taken with this juxtaposition of discourse and enactment, and the expertise with which such a vast novel is turned into a two-hour show which includes talking about its own making process:

> Discussion and performance were wonderfully intermeshed and flowed smoothly from one to the other. Anna Karenina's suicide scene left a huge impact on me. A train was formed by the actors standing in a line, the one in front had a lit torch on his forehead. Anna leapt in front, fell. The 'train' skirted her fallen body which we continued to see lying there. I can't describe it in words. But I realised that [the director] had real craft, like I had seen in Joan Littlewood, in Lyubimov.[28]

Another production which left an impact was that of *Commune* in Berkeley, near San Francisco. The performance at Berkeley took place on a conventional stage but with a twist:

> The spectators were accommodated entirely on the stage itself, ignoring the vast auditorium. They sat on platforms and gangways at different levels on the floor. Although there was a central performing area, the performers quite often used areas within, behind and above the spectators. The environment encompassed the whole space and was by no means confined to the central

[25] Sircar, *Purano Kasundi*, Vol. 3, pp. 83–86.

[26] Fernando Arrabal Terán (b. 1932), Spanish playwright, screenwriter, film director, novelist and poet.

[27] Sircar, 'The Third Theatre', *On Theatre*, p. 26.

[28] Sircar, *Purano Kasundi*, Vol. 3, trans. Anjum Katyal, pp. 86–87.

> performing area and the spectators constituted a part of it. In other words, the experience of any spectator did not come only from the performance and the decor of the stage (as happens in the proscenium theatre), but from other spectators as well. The spectators were never *manipulated*, but their *participation* was apparent by their very presence in the *space* encompassed by the *environment* of that particular theatre. Altogether, it was a new *language* of communication.[29]

This was another consideration he carried into his Third Theatre.

He was privileged to observe rehearsals of The Performance Group, and Julian Beck and Judith Malina's *The Living Theatre*:

> The Living Theatre is considered to be the first principal initiator of the new theatre in America. The Living Theatre very rarely uses theatre halls; even when it does, the distinction between the stage and the auditorium is completely ignored. As a matter of fact, the distinction between the performers and spectators is more or less done away with; the performers go to the auditorium and the spectators find a way of going on stage to participate. At that time, the whole group was residing together as a community in a dilapidated house in the working-class area of Brooklyn in New York, preparing a new project called the Legacy of Cain—a series of plays dealing with money, love, war, etc., their inter-relationships and their relationship with man. I attended one of their discussions and was impressed by their involvement and seriousness of approach. The Living Theatre is openly and frankly political. The politics, however, is not what is commonly found in propaganda and poster plays but have more to do with basic political philosophy, with man's consciousness and responsibility. I did not realize at that time but, later, the sole purpose of my theatre was to become almost exactly that, although my philosophy as well as my theatre differed considerably from that of the Living Theatre.[30]

He also spent some time with San Francisco-based Firehouse Theatre, attending one of their workshops and engaging in discussion with the director and the performers. Like the Living Theatre, they too lived together as a community. Theatre for them was a way of life rather than a profession or a pastime.

He participated in workshops and rehearsals which were intense, rigorous and demanding. In Vancouver, the Performance Group lived in a rented house over the summer holidays, and Badal-da stayed with them.

[29] Sircar, 'The Third Theatre', *On Theatre*, p. 27. Emphases in original.
[30] Sircar, 'The Third Theatre', *On Theatre*, p. 26.

They worked all day, eight hours at a stretch with short breaks of not more than an hour in total. Alongside the workshop with students, there was also preparatory work on the play *Commune* of which they had six shows during that period:

> Richard is an excellent teacher and I learnt a lot from those workshops. But watching a play being prepared was a still greater experience. I have used the term rehearsals before but the work of the group had little resemblance with what we understand by the term. At that time, they were preparing two plays simultaneously. I mostly attended the rehearsals of Sam Shepard's *The Tooth of Crime* directed by Richard Schechner. The script was being followed (that is to say, it was not to be an improvised performance), but follow is hardly the term that can be applied. Actually, the script was being confronted. Not limited to finding out the best way to project the lines of the script, it was a process of confronting, exploring and assimilating the meaning of the whole play through every situation, every line—till the script was no longer something written by a playwright; rather, it became a play *felt* and *made* by the performers themselves. To achieve this end, very frequently the group went into a workshop situation where the *inside* of the performer in relation to the play was explored rather than the play itself. It was not limited to an intellectual process. As a matter of fact, the process involved *feelings* much more than intellect.[31]

This process of *confronting* the script, and of the actors bringing their inner selves to the performance, is directly related to the way Badal-da has been working on *Spartacus*, and will continue to work on further productions.

By end of August 1972, he is back in Calcutta. He comes home with a head full of ideas, experiences and observations that were to find their way into his future work. In conclusion, he says:

> Though short, my stay in America and my contact with the people of the new theatre there drove at least one important point home—that theatre cannot be done without intense training. It is true for all art media, but so many theatre people in our country believe that they are born artistes and need little training that realization in this respect comes slowly. An average theatre worker in India (not excluding myself) would shudder at the thought of devoting as much time and energy for training as one has to devote in order to master Bharatnatyam or the sitar or sculpture.[32]

[31] Sircar, 'The Third Theatre', *On Theatre*, pp. 28–29.

[32] Ibid., p. 29.

Badal-da plunges straight into the logistics of his new theatre space, group and practice. The Academy room was being prepared. They would not get possession of it before October since a green room and a toilet had to be constructed. So, productions there would have to begin in November, not before:

> An intense membership drive began. Planning of furniture and lighting took up much of our time, particularly as we had to work on a very limited budget. In October, we began furnishing the room, fixing lights and making arrangements to improve the acoustics which were very bad. Also, we conducted intense rehearsals in the room on the days available to us.[33]

Over and above this, there were additional commitments. In October, they had an invitation from the Manipur State Kala Akademi to visit Imphal in Manipur to participate in a theatre festival where Satabdi would present *Ballabhpurer Rupkatha*, *Sesh Nei* and *Ebong Indrajit*. The festival was from 25 to 31 October. A month later, in the last week of November, Dishantar of Delhi had invited them to stage two shows each of *Sagina Mahato* and *Abu Hossain* at the Triveni Garden Theatre.

In these past few years, on his travels, Badal-da had encountered a very different kind of theatre than he was used to seeing around him. Different from the Group Theatre process which he knew intimately, which was premised on the passion and dedication one brings to a deeply serious hobby or special interest, in the company of fellow enthusiasts, but which remains at its core an 'addition' to one's daily life of job, career, family and home. Different from the political plays of, for example, Utpal Dutt, which were spectacular and theatrical but spoke from the elevated distance of the proscenium. Different from the rural-based folk performance forms in which the (usually) hereditary practitioners may live their whole lives not only within their profession but also within the confines of prescribed social and cultural custom; these forms had many of the characteristics of the theatre to which Badal-da aspired, like flexible performance spaces in the midst of the audience, spontaneity and improvisation, humour and satire; but they did not speak adequately to the urban educated middle class which was both Badal-da's subject and his chief audience, nor was their standard fare really relevant to contemporary urban middle class issues and concerns. And different also from the Jatra, that hugely popular hybrid professional travelling theatre which dished out commercial fare with generous doses

[33] Sircar, 'The Third Theatre', *On Theatre*, pp. 31–32.

of melodrama, pathos, music, song and spectacle. What he encountered was an approach which assumed that theatre was a serious art form and as such demanded rigorous training, that it was a form of socially committed communication, that it could be used to intervene and help bring about change, and that its practice and process could make a difference both to one's own self and to the audience.

This approach speaks to something deep within him. We have already seen that he was happiest doing theatre as part of a team, a collective, and that the splendid isolation of the Director who is the all-in-all authority in the group did not suit his temperament (he had a taste of this when he was directing *Pralaap* for Bohurupee, and it clearly was not his cup of tea; in fact, tea plays a big part in this experience, which he recounts with tongue firmly in cheek in his autobiography).[34] We have also seen that his plays have been growing increasingly political in grappling with questions of socio-economic injustice and inequality. Banerjee recognises this trajectory:

> A theatrical problem which had exercised Badal Sircar's mind for quite some time during his experiments with a variety of technical devices in the 1960s in plays like *Ebong Indrajit*, *Baki Itihas*, or *Tringsha Shatabdi*, was how to bridge over the distance between the play and its audience, the performers and their spectators. This urge was further accentuated by the increasing infusion of political ideas in his plays. It grew out of the realization that the theatre should not only reflect human condition, but should also endeavour to make the audience aspire to change the present condition.[35]

Badal-da is now ready to commit himself wholly to a theatre of social engagement, a theatre which questions and challenges the comfortable parameters of middle-class life; and he hopes to be part of a group that does this together. This is what he wants Satabdi to be. This decision is going to become the defining moment of his theatre life.

[34] Sircar, *Purano Kasundi*, Vol. 3, pp. 11–12.
[35] Banerjee, 'The Theatre of Badal Sircar', p. 110.

CHAPTER EIGHT

INDOORS AND OUTDOORS

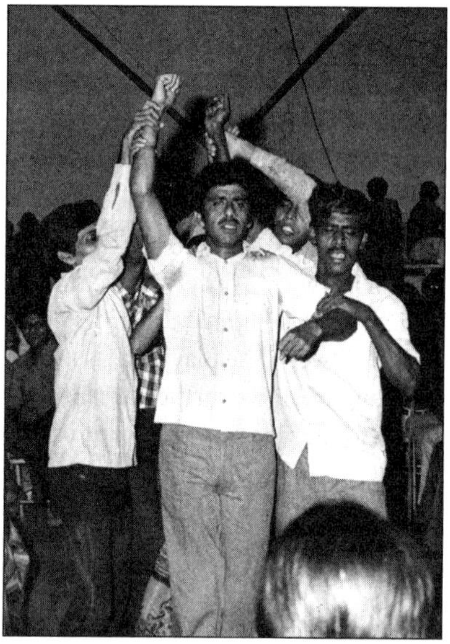

A scene from *Michhil*
Courtesy: Satabdi

Finally, we come to what is widely viewed as the real beginning of Badal Sircar's theatre practice: his initiation of a non-proscenium, intimate theatre space named Anganmancha 'which roughly means "space theatre"'.[1] It was a big moment. They had an inauguration. They printed a manifesto.

He says:

> We opened Anganmancha on 5 November 1972 on the first Sunday of the month. Instead of having a formal opening ceremony, we declared an open

[1] Sircar, 'The Third Theatre', *On Theatre*, p. 30.

house on 5, 6 and 7 November from 3 P.M. to 8 P.M. We had intermittent musical programmes given by the members of Satabdi; the rest of the time, we held discussions with our new members and prospective members, explaining the ideas of the theatre we were trying to establish and answering their questions. One of our main ideas regarding Anganmancha—to build up a community of theatre workers and theatre-goers—was put into practice during this informal opening.[2]

The manifesto drafted by Badal-da outlined the principles of their theatre:

- Anganmancha, run by Satabdi, is an intimate theatre in flexible form where performers and spectators are much closer, sometimes intermingled, so that the barriers and the distance between them are minimized.
- Anganmancha is run not as a commercial theatre house, but as a theatre established and developed by the efforts of a community of theatre-lovers comprising performers, organizers and spectators. Hence the usual ticket system is replaced as far as possible by a system of membership.
- Although the terms of membership have been kept at a minimum to enable all genuine theatre-lovers to participate, it is expected that a member joins the organization as a positive participant in this community effort of building a new theatre, and not in the spirit of calculating value for money.
- In a year, a minimum of three plays will be presented in the new form, and regular shows will be run each week. The number of shows per week will depend on the response of members.
- Every attempt will be made to arrange more than the minimum of three productions, either by Satabdi or by other theatre groups interested in experimenting in this new form.
- The membership subscription is ₹6 annually. The admission fee is ₹4 for the first 300 members, and ₹6 for the next 200 members. If the organization can later cope with more than 500 members, the admission fee for the new members will then be fixed accordingly.
- Each member is entitled to free entry to three shows of Anganmancha within the membership period. Thereafter a nominal entry fee of ₹1 for each show is charged. Booking is made on a first-come first-served basis, but it is endeavoured to give all members a chance to see a new production before any member sees it more than once.
- Guests accompanied by members can see any show on payment of ₹3 each. The number of guests may have to be regulated in the case of a new production till all members get a chance to see it.

[2] Sircar, 'The Third Theatre', *On Theatre*, p. 32.

- A non-member is to pay ₹5 for entry to a show provided seats are available after serving members and their guests.
- A life-member is to pay a total of ₹200. A life member can see any show with one companion without having to pay any entry fee.[3]

It should be noted that there is no mention of a free theatre yet. In fact, the major portion of the manifesto deals with membership fees and deliverables which are part of a 'contract' between Satabdi and its audience, so much so that it includes a plea that 'it is expected that a member joins the organisation as a positive participant in this community effort of building a new theatre, and not in the spirit of calculating value for money.' This is in contradiction to one of the fundamental principles of the later Third Theatre which explicitly eschews buying and selling in theatre. Having said that, however, it is important to acknowledge that the fees mentioned are reasonable and quite affordable even for those on low budgets. Nonetheless, it tells us that this is still clearly a middle-class oriented theatre; its prospective members and supporters can afford to spend, however, minimally, on extras like going to the theatre.

One can appreciate that the move to the membership model from the ticket-sale model was an attempt at building a community of people who were committed to this form of theatre, and who were, therefore, willing to sign up and pay in advance to be counted as members. But perhaps there are other ways of building such a community. For example, one Bangalore-based theatre group asks its members to contribute not money but their time, a certain number of hours a month, by volunteering or helping in other ways.

Sumanta Banerjee points out:

> [F]rom his writings … in 1971 (when he had just started experimenting with [Anganmancha]), it appears that he was more driven by the need to reach an audience directly, and thus more concerned with the technical device of the 'theatre-in-the-round' in order to gain that objective. It was only later that Sircar, in his writings on drama, came out more explicitly on the political messages that he wanted to convey through Third Theatre.[4]

This is borne out by the manifesto which speaks about performers and spectators being 'much closer, sometimes intermingled, so that the barriers and the distance between them are minimized.' There is no mention of political messages or social change in the manifesto.

[3] Sircar, 'The Third Theatre', pp. 30–31.
[4] Banerjee, 'The Theatre of Badal Sircar', p. 111.

In his 'The Third Theatre', Badal-da sets out in some detail the physical attributes of the Anganmancha performance space. No chairs are to be used, 'as chairs emphasize special sitting areas for the spectators, thus separating them from the performers.' Instead, benches in three different heights are used for seating, laid out in two or three rows, placed side by side to create a 'continuous platform', 'thus eliminating the auditorium-like appearance and bringing the spectators within the theatre.' The seats would be re-arranged for each play, thereby changing the performer–spectator relationship. For lighting, they opt for 'ordinary lights from many sources' instead of spotlights.

> We fixed a grid of wire-ropes near the ceiling and hung 16 specially constructed lampshades with clamps. The shades could be shifted along the wire grid to different positions and the clamps allowed them to be turned at any desired angle. We used 100w, 60w and 40w bulbs. We had five switch controls which gave us considerable flexibility. To simplify lighting and to save cost, we did not use dimmers. The total cost for installation did not exceed ₹300.

Light controls were handled by group members who were clearly visible. Economical solutions were found for other technical challenges as well, such as the echo which hampered clarity of sound. 'Instead of going for costly acoustic treatment, we hung pleated hessian curtains on the blank portions of the walls.'[5]

The response to Anganmancha was quite favourable, with 325 ordinary members and 14 life members joining them; and from 12 November 1972, they begin regular weekly shows every Sunday for the next two years.

Badal-da would have liked to have launched Anganmancha with his *Spartacus*, written, as we know, especially for theatre-in-the-round. However, the play was not ready, so they began with something that was already prepared, a play that had been done outside the proscenium earlier: *Sagina Mahato*.

A review of this play, albeit done several years later, says:

> Sircar shows imagination in breaking up the small rectangle with the audience sitting around it into a number of areas with a few neutral wooden blocks scattered here and there and actors standing upon one or the other [...] all excellently controlled by the director Sircar in a masterly handling of gestures, movements, rhythm and time [...] Sircar's mastery over form never takes away from the complexity of the situation.[6]

[5] Sircar, 'The Third Theatre', *On Theatre*, pp. 33–34.

[6] Review of 'Sagina Mahato', *Hindusthan Standard*, 24 July 1981. From the NSS archives.

The next play they presented was *Ebong Indrajit*, on 17 December. Before this, Satabdi had done the play in Imphal, so this too was familiar fare. Badal-da says:

> In the Anganmancha production, we kept a small inner arena with some low seats placed around it. Behind these seats, we kept an acting space in the form of a ring, and the rest of the spectators were seated around this ring. Three spaces within or behind the seating areas were also used for acting. In one of these spaces at a corner, two levels were formed by some platforms we already possessed. Only one percussion instrument—a dhol—was used for music, and that too in full view of the spectators. The arena and the ring were very suitable for the circular movements needed so much in this play. The production was simple and intimate, but mobile, with almost continuous movement; and the spectators were given a feeling of being encompassed by the performance.[7]

We know that he had long dreamt of doing *Ebong Indrajit* as theatre-in-the-round; finally, he was able to see the result of his imagined design.

And now, finally, they were ready with *Spartacus* which opened at Anganmancha on 28 January 1973.[8] This production had a huge impact when performed, and as Badal-da's first script written for the Anganmancha, it is fitting that we spend some time on the details of it.

Badal-da claims this novel by Howard Fast as one of his most favourite books ever. According to him, he had often dreamt of dramatising it, but didn't have the courage until he left the proscenium for the Anganmancha.[9] What drew him to this work? First, let us begin with the writer and the novel. Howard Fast was the son of poor Jewish immigrants who grew up in poverty, forced to earn his own living from the age of nine. His career is marked by left-oriented activism through his novels and other writings. In 1943, he joined the Communist Party USA. In 1950, summoned before the House Committee on Un-American Activities, he refused to disclose any names and was given a three-month prison sentence for contempt of Congress. In jail, he began writing his most famous novel, *Spartacus* (1951). He was forced to publish it himself but it managed to sell well. Filmmaker Stanley Kubrick turned it into a film by the same name, released in 1960. It is not surprising that this writer and this novel should attract Badal-da

[7] Sircar, 'The Third Theatre', *On Theatre*, p. 44.
[8] Ibid., p. 37.
[9] Badal Sircar, Preface to 'Spartacus', *Natak Samagra*, Vol. 3, p. 122.

enough to consider adapting it into a play in Bengali. It is interesting to see what the subject of this book means to him. In his own words:

> *Spartacus* is the story of the great slave revolt that began in BC 71 and shook the mighty Roman Empire for four long years. Although it began from a spontaneous upsurge in the gladiatorial school of Capua, it did not remain so for long. Under the able leadership of Spartacus, the gladiator, the handful of rebels soon transformed into an organized slave army of thousands which fought for something unheard of by any other army the world had seen so far. In the words of Howard Fast ... it was an army which fought for freedom in the most simple and unvarnished terms. In the past, there have been armies without end, armies which have fought for nations or cities or wealth or spoils or power or control of this or that area; but here was an army which fought for human freedom and dignity, an army which called no land or city its own because the people within it came from all lands and cities and tribes, an army where every soldier shared a common heritage of servitude and a common hatred of men who made other men slaves. This was an army which was committed to victory, for there were no bridges over which it could retreat, no land which would give it shelter or rest. It was an army which suddenly had the knowledge that the victory to which it was committed must change the world and, therefore, the army must change the world or have no victory. The army was crushed ultimately because the majority of the slaves would not or could not join it; apart from thousands killed in the fields of battle, over 6,000 captured slaves were crucified along Via Appia as punishment.[10]

The message of this history, and what makes it relevant to him, is this:

> But the war of the oppressed against those who oppressed them went on. It was a flame which burned high or low but never went out—and the name of Spartacus did not perish. It was not a question of descent through blood but of descent through common struggle. And this descent of Spartacus makes the story relevant in any part of the world at any time.[11]

This is the essence of what Badal-da culls from the novel, and that he wishes to convey through his play. There is another point in the novel that he wants to emphasise in his production: 'Spartacus was no hero in the conventional meaning of the term; he could be any slave at any moment in history. That

[10] Sircar, 'The Third Theatre', *On Theatre*, pp. 34–35.
[11] Ibid., p. 35.

is why the most important role in my play is played by a group of slaves, and not by one slave.'[12]

As the first script written specifically for the Anganmancha, the whole process of preparing the play is interesting to learn about. Badal-da says that his first draft was impractically long, almost four hours, and that too after reluctantly leaving out some sequences and characters which seemed important to him. He did not attempt to prune and edit the script himself, but plunged straight into working with the group to see what would happen to the text. A whole new working methodology was being evolved between him as the director and the group. He began to apply the workshop process he had picked up from experimental theatre and dance workers in the west. Let us hear from him how he changed in his approach as a director:

> When I began dabbling with theatre in the early 1950s, I was enamoured by the Western method of 'production notes'. I would chart the complete choreography with the help of notes, diagrams and models even before rehearsals began: walk three steps downstage left, turn, say the line, move upstage to sit on Chair 3—that kind of stuff. The participants in the production were, on the whole, happy for they did not have to think as far as their movements were concerned; they just had to follow the directions already chalked out for them. Changes in the prefixed scheme were made only when an unforeseen problem came up and, then too, it was left to me to come up with the required solution.
>
> By the time we took up *Spartacus*, I had assumed an almost diametrically opposed position as a director. I did not put down anything in my notes in the form of signs or diagrams. Even when I suggested the choreography for a particular scene during rehearsals, it would be incorporated through a trial-and-error method with comments and suggestions from group members leading to modifications. Sometimes alternative choreographies suggested by group members would undergo the same process before getting absorbed into the structure of the play. The final choreography would depend on the decision of the group rather than that of the director, except in rare cases of unresolved controversy.[13]

In addition to their growth as 'physical' actors, an additional benefit of this approach was felt in the shrinking verbosity of the script, as page after page began to be replaced by 'expression through sound, movement and

[12] Sircar, 'The Third Theatre', *On Theatre*, p. 35.
[13] Sircar, 'Voyages in the Theatre', *On Theatre*, p. 103.

energy.'[14] As the workshop progressed, Badal-da found himself deleting sections and lines without compromising the content. 'Thus, the script gradually got pruned.'[15]

Interestingly, this workshop way of developing the script also resulted in a structure that looked very experimental and avant-garde, although that may not have been the motivating reason. As Badal-da says,

> There is no sequential narrative; the events jump from one space to another, forward and backward in time; sometimes, two different spaces and times are put together in the same scene. Spartacus is not projected as an individual hero—the lines of his most crucial speech are divided between all the slaves.[16]

Badal-da has already stated that he wrote this play for the Anganmancha, which meant keeping the features of theatre-in-the-round in mind. For him, in terms of form, this includes the following, much of which emerged collectively through the preparation process:

> The play is not based on characters, which means that group acting and not individual acting is important. There are two prominent groups—the slaves and the Roman soldiers, and a few Roman characters who are more prototypes than characters.
>
> The play does not follow the conventions of acts or scenes and is composed of short scenes (sometimes very short, taking not more than a minute or two) linked together. The same space represents different locales without using any sets or props. In fact, not a single element of set or property was used in our production. Modern Indian costume was used by the Romans. The slaves were bare bodied, with knee-long shorts of cheap coarse cloth. There is one woman slave in the play who wore short pants extending a few inches below her knees and a shapeless shirt of the same coarse material. Flat lighting was used throughout, except for a single blue light used twice.
>
> In the production, action was emphasized more than words. The play began with five action scenes (taking about 10 minutes altogether) depicting respectively—(1) people being captured to be sold as slaves (2) slaves being sold in the market (3) slaves toiling (4) gladiator–slaves fighting in the arena and (5) a slave being crucified for an act of defiance. In these scenes, cries, shouts and noise were used but not a single sentence; they were expressed entirely by physical acting. There were many action scenes like these within the play as well.

[14] Sircar, 'Voyages in the Theatre', *On Theatre*, p. 104.
[15] Ibid.
[16] Ibid., p. 105.

> The only music used was a refrain without words sung by the group of slaves without any instrumental accompaniment. This refrain played a very important role in the play and had been used three times in such a manner that it expressed much more than several pages of dialogue.

The other major shift was in terms of the relationship between the actor and the audience:

> The spectator–performer relationship deviated from what we had done before in this theatre. For this production, groups of spectators were seated at different places, like islands, one group being right at the centre of the room. The spaces in-between were used for acting. As the room was very small, the creation of these islands could not be done the way we had hoped to, but we came to know what could be done in a bigger space.
>
> The island arrangement of seats brought the spectators within the performance, instead of keeping them in detached sanctuaries from which they could just watch. Here, I thought, we could give them a theatrical experience, not just a spectacle, and that was a long step forward to the Third Theatre.[17]

Finally, he comments on the experience of physical acting:

> *Spartacus* was based mainly on physical acting, and the performers had to go through certain physical exercises and acquire some basic parade training. It was hard work, but the group responded wonderfully to it. Toil, struggle and hope were the keynotes of the play, and physical acting was used mostly to express these. The nearness of the performers could allow a degree of direct communication with the spectators that was impossible to be had in a conventional proscenium stage production.[18]

Another important factor was the sincerity and honesty with which the actors conveyed the experience of the play:

> The essence of the play consisted of the sweat and blood of the slaves and their revolt. We took as much care as possible to avoid faking. In our workouts, a slave who would mime carrying a load practised carrying another person on his back (mostly me), and he would exert himself just as much during a performance when he would actually be carrying nothing at all. The slaves combined themselves in such a way that each step taken by the group was

[17] The detailed description above is from Sircar, 'The Third Theatre', *On Theatre*, pp. 35–37.

[18] Ibid.

> really painful for the actors and that was how we tried to convey the impression of chained slaves being led over the hot desert sands.[19]

It took Satabdi about a year to prepare the play. It was clearly worth it. Badal-da writes that the 'audience reaction to Spartacus was overwhelming' and that people said that 'they felt the direct impact of the play in a way that they had never experienced in theatre before.'[20] From all accounts, this is true. Every single viewer whom I have spoken to about this production has said how powerful it was. Innovative, moving, intense, disturbing are the adjectives that have repeatedly been used; and this includes persons who were regular theatregoers and who, indeed, had watched avant-garde productions in different parts of the world as well. Rustom Bharucha says, 'As a production, *Spartacus* had no precedent in the contemporary Bengali theatre.'[21]

Given its importance in the history of alternative theatre in India, this production deserves to be revisited as completely as possible, to fully grasp the experience of the play. There is no doubt that it was a landmark in its time. Unfortunately, I was unable to access any available audiovisual documentation of an early production done in Anganmancha. In the absence of this, one can turn to written descriptions or oral first person accounts. Even photographs are too static to convey the full experience of a production. One viewer response we have, by Ranjan K. Banerjee, is included here:

> You climb a narrow staircase on any Sunday evening to see Sircar himself at the box office. Someone shows you in; you're struck by the bareness of the room. A few stern-looking benches, a couple of tables and a number of wooden planks are just about all the gadgets of Sircar's intimate theatre [...] With the soldiers marching past, the gladiators falling dead at their feet, and the senators sharing with them their wicked thoughts, the spectators are increasingly caught in the cobweb of a blood-spattered human situation until a perceptible slowing down of movement and dimming of lights mark the denouement. And in the dying light, one of the revolting slaves slowly crawls to you to whisper that he will come back one day a thousand times stronger.[22]

[19] Sircar, 'The Third Theatre', *On Theatre*, p. 105.

[20] Ibid., p. 37.

[21] Bharucha, *Rehearsals of Revolution*, p. 149.

[22] Ranjan K. Banerjee, 'Angan Mancha: A New Theatre of Involvement.' Source NA. From the NSS archives.

Theatre critic and scholar Ananda Lal was an impressionable teenager with a keen interest in theatre when he went to see *Spartacus* at the Academy of Fine Arts Anganmancha. He vividly recalls the impact. 'Suddenly we heard a growl of voices outside, intensifying rapidly, then the slaves rushing into the room and collapsing all over us. My toes curled inwards instinctively as one slave fell on my feet. I realised later how effective such shock tactics could be.'[23]

Theatre director Probir Guha, whose own Alternative Living Theatre continues to do alternate theatre on the outskirts of Kolkata, recalls the impact on him of *Spartacus*.[24] Growing up as he did in remote villages, politically on the left, brimming with the youthful ambition to do meaningful theatre that could express his views and speak to the common man, he had never experienced theatre like it. 'My hair stood on end. Even today I can remember every scene.' He visibly shivers recalling the physical and emotional impact of a young actor playing a slave grabbing his leg as she fell against him. 'This, this is the theatre I'm searching for, the theatre I want to do! So inexpensive, so strong, such a politically direct theatre—this is my theatre.'

Rustom Bharucha also describes the production vividly:

> To describe it as an intimate experience is, perhaps, to understate the torrential immediacy of its impact. It is difficult to imagine a production so violent and yet so rigorous in its orchestration of movement. In the very first moment of the play, one is simply thrust into a world of terror and brutality as the slaves rush out in a mass from a single entrance and swarm around the audience ... The proximity of the spectators and the audience increases the physical intensity of the first ten minutes of Spartacus. There are no words but a steady crescendo of rhythmic pants that becomes deafening in the small room. The relentless movement of the actors as they raise their hands and thrash them down in unison conveys the sheer agony of the slaves' labor. Apart from watching them toil, we see the slaves being captured by a group of anonymous Roman soldiers who look like the military police in Calcutta—impassive, steely eyed, and ruthless. Once caught, the slaves are sold in the market where patrician like figures clad in the spotless kurtas and pajamas of the Bengali aristocracy examine the teeth and limbs of the slaves with brutal gestures. The most savagely choreographed scenes depict the fight of the slaves in the arena. There are no gladiatorial movements, no virtuosic

[23] Ananda Lal, 'He who took portable drama to where no group had gone', *The Telegraph* Metro, 15 May 2011.

[24] The following account is from an interview with the author, trans. Anjum Katyal, Kolkata, 28 February 2015.

somersaults and throws, no sadistic tortures of limbs. Sircar's actors fight with their bare hands. They use few gestures, which are violent in their starkness and momentum. After the fight, a slave is crucified for an act of defiance. The raising of his body in the air, the outstretched hands of the slaves in a semicircle, their faces turned upwards—all are images that remain with the audience long after the production of *Spartacus* ends.[25]

In terms of the political message of this play, Sumanta Banerjee comments:

> It ends with all the slaves rising together in a rhythmic gesture that symbolizes Spartacus, their hero who had become a martyr. They speak in the voice of Spartacus, asserting that he will always be wherever people struggle till they achieve liberty, and that he will come back, reborn among millions of people.[26]

Till now in Badal-da's plays, we have seen his middle-class subjects raise the question of guilt and responsibility, but this play, through the composite figure of Spartacus, who stands for all rebels, asserts a direct alliance with the oppressed throughout history, right till the present. To Rustom Bharucha:

> There is an ideological thrust, however naïve, that underlies the frenetic action of the play. The central idea of the Spartacus legend that concerns Sircar is what Howard Fast describes as its 'descent through common struggle.' The war of the oppressed continues in our century in Cambodia, Afghanistan, and elsewhere in the world, while repressive regimes have survived the rising of the proletariat. Sircar finds an immediate political significance in the great slave revolt led by Spartacus in 71 B.C. and its eventual destruction by representatives of the empire. He does not, however, elaborate on this significance by inserting contemporary political parallels into the dramatic framework of the play ... He does something more subtle: he abstracts the essence of slavery and oppression in history by finding appropriate visual images and words for it ... by universalizing it.[27]

Bharucha finds it significant that:

> [T]he Spartacus in Sircar's production is neither a Roman gladiator, nor is he an allusion to any particular political leader in Bengal. He is represented

[25] Bharucha, *Rehearsals of Revolution*, pp. 149–50.
[26] Banerjee, 'The Theatre of Badal Sircar', p. 111.
[27] Bharucha, *Rehearsals of Revolution*, pp. 150–51.

> as a *group* of slaves.... The most arresting moments in the production occur when they lie in a circle with their faces buried in the ground and intone their freedom chant.[28]

By causing two groups of society—the Romans and the slaves—to confront each other, rather than individual 'heroes' and 'villains', Sircar highlights the systemic aspect of power and oppression, and the class aspect of resistance and revolt. By making the slaves symbolic of the underclass that has risen in rebellion throughout the centuries, he emphasises the historic continuity of inequality and exploitation. By putting the actors into contemporary costume, he indicates the direct relevance of this historic tale to his immediate audience.

However, as we can see from the following dialogue uttered by the slaves, despite these aspects of political thought, there is both an overly simplistic analysis of historic process and a naïve Utopianism about the dream of a better tomorrow:

> At the beginning of creation all men were equal. Today because of Rome
> Man has two classes—Master and Slave.
> But we are many more than you. We are much better than you.
> Whatever is good in mankind is now with us ...
> You set man onto man like fighting dogs for your own pleasure
> You have turned our world into a filthy garbage dump
> You have turned men into beasts
> You have turned weapons into toys
> But no longer, that's all over ...
> We will destroy your Rome
> We will wreck your Senate
> We will clean up your garbage dump
> Then we'll build a beautiful town
> A beautiful village
> Without walls or barriers
> Without conflict
> Without masters or rulers
> Without subjects or slaves
> Only peace and happiness.[29]

Still, despite the rather unrealistic nature of the ideal world being envisaged, there is no doubt that the play, with its unsettling atmosphere of violence

[28] Bharucha, *Rehearsals of Revolution*, p. 151.
[29] Sircar, 'Spartacus', *Natak Samagra*, Vol. 3, trans. Anjum Katyal, pp. 162–63.

and pain, suffering and oppression, all expressed in a powerfully physical theatrical language, had a strong emotional impact on its audience. Rustom Bharucha recalls:

> [W]e see a line of slaves torturously moving around the space in the room. Their hands, arms, and legs are interlocked as they drag their bodies along. The heightened physicality of this image reveals as much about their state of oppression as the single refrain that is sung by the slaves at significant moments in the play. Sircar does not exaggerate when he says that this refrain—a haunting melody that uses barely six or seven notes—expresses the suffering and determination of the slaves more effectively than pages of dialogue.[30]

The play ends on a note that is both a promise and a threat. Samik Bandyopadhyay recalls:

> [How] after the revolt had been crushed, the actors crawled through the lanes, their faces almost touching our knees as they whispered into our faces, *abar phire ashbo* (*we will return*) ... the closeness of it, the way it hit you sensually, the actors becoming a physical transmission of the concept, was very powerful. I remember it as one of the greatest moments of theatre. We were drawn into the theatre space.'[31]

'We will return. Lakhs and crores of us. We will return.' Given the current political situation in Kolkata of the early 1970s, this muttered—vow? warning?—must have resonated with the audience and, depending on their political inclinations, lit a spark of hope or a fuse of fear.

Theatre workers who were also involved in alternative and political theatre heard about this play and came to see it; they identified with it and soon it became popular on the Third Theatre circuit. Writing in the twenty-first century, Badal-da says, in his Preface, that Satabdi alone has done 90 shows of the play, both indoors and outdoors, while Pathasena, one of Satabdi's sister groups, has done over 100 shows.[32]

Within a few weeks of opening *Spartacus* at Anganmancha, Badal-da decides to try it out in a very different setting. This was in the free outdoor performance space in Surendranath Park, also known as Curzon Park, in the heart of the commercial area of Kolkata, Esplanade. Thronging with

[30] Bharucha, *Rehearsals of Revolution*, p. 152.
[31] Samik Bandyopadhyay, interview with the author, 9 February 2009.
[32] Sircar, Preface to 'Spartacus', *Natak Samagra*, Vol. 3, p. 122.

office-goers, vendors, traders, workers and casual passers-by, noisy with traffic, horns, voices and street sounds, it was a chaotic, vibrant space totally different in character from the small, intimate, quiet and controlled ambience of Anganmancha. In the latter, the audience chose to come. In the former, the theatre went to the audience, who stopped their busy lives momentarily to see a play, and if they got interested, watched till the end. The audience demography was also completely different. The former catered to the middle-class, urban educated theatre-going crowd, including students. The latter included the very poor; uneducated, illiterate people who were never going to enter the Academy of Fine Arts. What was the spur that prodded Badal-da to move into the open-air space?

> A theatre group named Silhouette initiated this movement by performing there every Saturday afternoon. It was an absolutely open theatre, without any stage, curtains, dressing room or sets, and the performance was in daylight... We invited them to perform at Anganmancha, and we were invited by them to perform at the park. On 17 March 1973, Satabdi performed *Spartacus* at Surendranath Park. We used a shorter version of the play which ran for eight minutes. Our original production was 110 minutes long but this shorter version was a self-contained play as well.[33]

In fact, the whole process of creating this shortened version was a major learning process for Badal-da and the group:

> Through workshops and rehearsals, the play was condensed with the dialogues giving way to non-verbal modes of presentation. *Spartacus* was thus a landmark for me as a playwright and for my group as a team. I could feel that with *Spartacus* we made a giant leap towards a closer relationship with the audience.[34]

Bharucha lauds the condensed version, finding the longer play a little too verbose, and the rhetorical passages featuring the Roman patricians too clichéd and reminiscent of any 'conventional historical play about Spartacus.'[35]

The decision to present *Spartacus* at the park was made with much trepidation. Would this play work in such a setting, and for such a mixed audience?

[33] Sircar, 'The Third Theatre', *On Theatre*, p. 37.

[34] Badal Utsav pamphlet brought out by Natya Shodh Sansthan on the occasion of Badal Utsav, Kolkata, 15–19 July 2009, p. 9.

[35] Bharucha, *Rehearsals of Revolution*, p. 152.

> In many ways, *Spartacus* differed from the plays which were then being performed at the park. It was more complex and sophisticated in structure and seemed to need an intimate atmosphere as was obtained at Anganmancha. This made me somewhat doubtful about its acceptance by the audience of the open-air theatre, at that time composed mostly of casual visitors to the park, gathering around the theatre out of curiosity. It seemed to me that a more direct and straightforward approach would be needed than was afforded by *Spartacus*.[36]

But he was proved wrong. At the very first show, there was an audience of over 500 people, who watched the whole performance in total silence and focused concentration, despite the manifold distractions all around. Badal-da and his group realised that this was not entirely a casual passers-by crowd. It included people who were regular attendees of this weekly event. 'Slowly but surely, a serious and regular theatre audience was developing at Surendranath Park.'[37]

For the performers too, this environment offered fresh challenges and rewards. Badal-da describes it as

> a new kind of involvement. The grass-covered earth, the sun in the sky, the people sitting on the ground—all these gave a new meaning to the play, particularly for those who played the role of slaves. The bits of dry grass and patches of dirt on the bare bodies of the slaves covered with sweat, accentuated by spots of blood from the scratches caused by pebbles on the ground, made it a play of blood and sweat as it was supposed to be.[38]

So within a few months of initiating his non-proscenium theatre practice, Badal-da has settled into two very different kinds of performance: closed indoor and open outdoor. He analyses the difference between the two. Anganmancha has the look of an intimate theatre, with a small audience in close proximity to the actors, on the same level in a lighted area. The actors can be behind or beside the spectators, look into their eyes and communicate with them individually. The audience can be touched and felt. Muktamancha or *Maather-natak*, consisting of outdoor performances in the round, does not aim for such intimacy with the audience. It can be performed in a village field, a marketplace, slum yard, school compound or any open space used by the common people. Often the audience is in

[36] Sircar, 'The Third Theatre', *On Theatre*, pp. 37–38.
[37] Ibid., p. 38.
[38] Ibid., p. 38.

the thousands. Naturally, the actor cannot establish a direct communication with individual members of such an audience, most of whom are inaccessible to the actors. The intensity and depth that is achieved in the Anganmancha is compensated in the Muktamancha by a greater reach; its message is more extensive. Samik Bandyopadhyay makes an important distinction between the two. He feels that in Anganmancha, there was more of a confrontation with the audience, an impulse to challenge set beliefs, while with Muktamancha, the aim was a more general sort of conscientisation and sharing.[39]

Meanwhile, Satabdi's regular shows continue as promised to their members. According to a leading newspaper, 'The Anganmancha has become now a permanent centre for the experimental theatre in the true sense of the term—a theatre that questions the basic established conventions of the theatre, in terms of an original approach to the theatre.'[40]

The fourth production at Anganmanch is an invited show. Silhouette, the group that performs regularly at Curzon Park and that invited Satabdi to perform there, is asked to present their play *Abritta Dashamik* (lit., recurring decimal). Badal-da finds this event significant, because to him it signals the start of a theatre movement, with 'at least one other theatre group experimenting in the field of the Third Theatre.'[41] In June 1973, *Abu Hossain* is produced here, yet another play which has been adapted from the proscenium to Anganmancha, like *Sagina Mahato* and *Ebong Indrajit*. It is worthwhile to reproduce some reviews of the play to convey an idea of how this theatre was being received by discerning theatre-goers:

> Had there been no *Sagina Mahato* one would have grown ecstatic over Badal Sircar's latest offering at the Academy of Fine Arts Auditorium. The Satabdi production of *Abu Hossain* is burlesque of a kind seldom seen on the Bengali stage. The artistry which lies behind this bit of nose-thumbing at a favourite of a bygone age convincingly proves Mr Sircar's superiority over the so-called social dramatists. The production also demonstrates that reworking of old Bengali plays can provide better entertainment than incompetent adaptations of foreign classics. Yet it must be denied the ultimate accolade which the earlier play alone deserves for its breathtaking audacity and organic unity.[42]

[39] Samik Bandyopadhyay, interview with author, 9 February 2009.

[40] Quoted in Sircar, 'The Third Theatre', *On Theatre*, p. 54. From *Hindustan Standard*, 23 February 1973.

[41] Sircar, 'The Third Theatre', *On Theatre*, p. 44.

[42] Quoted in Sircar, 'The Third Theatre', *On Theatre*, p. 53. Source unknown.

Another reviewer says:

> The Satabdi production of *Abu Hossain* breaks new ground and establishes Sircar as a creative director in a comic mode full of surprises. *Abu Hossain*, with first rate entertainment values, will interest serious theatre-goers and the larger audience at the same time, opening out new possibilities in the style . . . Sircar avoids spectacle, and makes it almost a dialogue with the audience . . . With the nearness of the audience, the production achieves a bareness and a dimension of direct and immediate thinking; with the two rows of spectators arranged around the acting area, the actors move or stand between the rows at times, and the closeness itself becomes an experience that makes the issues more real; and the doubts and uncertainties are communicated more sharply . . . Economy becomes the keynote in the Anganmancha, and the stylization is unelaborate and precise . . . the mimetic gestures become mobile sculptures in the generally bare pattern of production. It is a pleasure now to see the Satabdi ensemble creating moments of visual structure almost out of nothing; in terms of physical acting on an unspectacular plane they have now achieved a rare discipline, which is not marred by the individual imperfections that are still there.[43]

However, things are not going smoothly with Satabdi. There is growing dissension within the group. Several of the members are unhappy with the total break with proscenium and with the direction in which Badal-da's theatre work is proceeding. Badal-da gives us his perspective on the reasons why:

> When I first discussed my ideas on the Third Theatre within our group, the ideas were received enthusiastically. Satabdi as a group was still struggling for its existence, and struggle always ensures health and dynamism in a community of workers. The actual initiation of Anganmancha, however, coincided with the success of Satabdi with three consecutive productions on the proscenium stage—*Ballavpurer Rupkatha*, *Sagina Mahato* and *Abu Hossain*. The last was so well received that the possibility of the recognition of Satabdi as a successful group in the conventional theatre scene was becoming evident. Some members of Satabdi, particularly those who were developing as good actors, began to find the switchover to Anganmancha a deterrent to their acting careers. To them, it was like throwing away the success achieved through a long and hard struggle. In a way they were correct. If a person in theatre is in search of success, establishment, fame and a career (and the

[43] Quoted in Sircar, 'The Third Theatre', *On Theatre*, pp. 53–54. From *Hindustan Standard*, 23 February 1973.

> matter of money lurking behind all these)—then the switchover to the Third Theatre at that point was certainly disastrous for him or her.[44]

There could be other reasons as well. Badal-da himself has noted earlier that not all the actors found it easy to switch to the kind of physical acting demanded of them. The close proximity to the audience, the deliberate dismantling of the comfortable distance between actor and audience which the proscenium offers, the consequent feelings of being exposed and vulnerable may not have been as acceptable to every member of the group. It may not have been just a question of seeking fame or money; it may have been a discomfort with this hugely demanding—both psychologically and physically—form of performance, which led to their wishing to opt out.

Whatever the reason, or combination of reasons, the polarisation within Satabdi became increasingly obvious as the months passed. According to Badal-da, an attempt at compromise was made by including a few proscenium stage productions along the way, no doubt as a sop to those who hankered for them. But, as he states:

> [A]t last, I for one realized that it was not possible to go on doing both at the same time. However, we did not fight but sat down and faced the problem squarely. And we came to the decision of going our separate ways by unanimous agreement. A date was also fixed until when the existing group would carry on its shows.[45]

This civilised way of dealing with dissension through dialogue and discussion was to become a feature of the group.

Those who had signed up for membership of Anganmancha had been promised at least one show a week and three productions a year. This put a lot of pressure on the truncated Satabdi, now consisting only of those who had wholly committed themselves to 'Third Theatre, to come up with a new play within two months' time.

By now, Anganmancha is well established, but there is still the practice of a fixed entry fee. Until this is dispensed with, one of the fundamental tenets of Badal-da's Third Theatre (later known also as 'Free' Theatre) is not yet in place. Let us move on to the ideology and principles of the Third Theatre as articulated by Badal-da, with its defining features.

[44] Sircar, 'The Third Theatre', *On Theatre*, p. 45.
[45] Ibid.

CHAPTER NINE

THE THIRD THEATRE

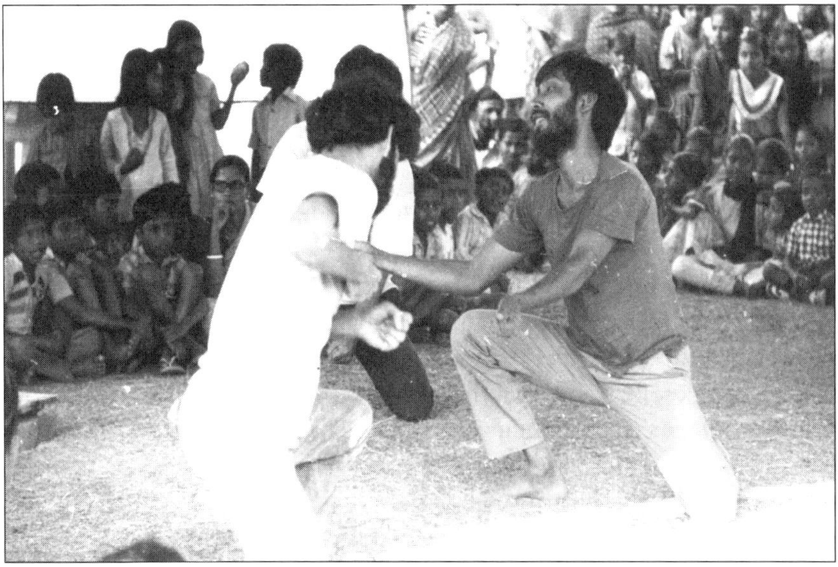

A scene from *Sada Kalo*
Courtesy: Satabdi

Tringsha Shatabdi, written in 1966, ends with the protagonist addressing members of the audience: 'And you? What are you going to do? Have you decided? You? You? You?'[1]

Two aspects of this—the direct personalised address to the audience and the inciting of the spectator to a moral decision leading to action—are to become important features of the Third Theatre. Clearly the urge to engage the audience directly was present even then. As we have discussed in Chapter 8, when Badal-da moved out of the proscenium into Anganmancha, the primary

[1] Badal Sircar, 'Tringsha Satabdi', *Natak Samagra*, Vol. 2, trans. Anjum Katyal, p. 334.

consideration seemed to be around the issue of direct communication, the removal of barriers between the actor and the spectator. It was more to do with form than content. But soon the politics of Third Theatre crystallised, and the ideology of this form became fully articulated. Let us now take a close look at this important contribution to Indian theatre—Third Theatre or Free Theatre—a major constituent of Badal-da's legacy, which has been extensively written and spoken about, both by Badal-da himself, in writings in Bengali, English, interviews and talks, and by anyone who has ever written even an essay on Badal-da.

Rustom Bharucha, in his study of Badal-da's theatre undertaken in the 1970s and early 1980s, describes it as follows:

> The emergence of the Third Theater is a significant development in the contemporary Bengali theater ... it is a movement barely ten years old that challenges the premises of the commercial theater and indirectly questions the validity of the revolutionary theatre practised by Utpal Dutt. It is the most rigorously non-commercial political theater in India today.[2]

Badal-da describes the thinking process that led him to formulate this alternative to the mainstream, conventional proscenium stage in his treatise, The Third Theatre.[3] In a nutshell, there is a dichotomy between the existing rural, folk, traditional theatre (which is the First Theatre) and the Western-influenced, proscenium stage of the city theatre (which is the Second Theatre); his attempt is to explore the possibility of a synthesis between these two—a Third Theatre.

> The dichotomy in the cultural field cannot be removed without a fundamental change in the socio-economic situation, and I have no illusion that it can be done simply through theatre. But I do believe that theatre can be one of the many facets of a movement that is vitally needed to bring about the desirable change, and that makes the idea of the Third Theatre meaningful to me.[4]

There is an indication of the political aspect of this theatre here: he sees it as part of a movement to bring about a change in the socio-economic status quo through cultural action.

[2] Bharucha, *Rehearsals of Revolution*, p. 127.

[3] Sircar, 'The Third Theatre', *On Theatre*. Based on a project entitled 'Workshop for a Theatre of Synthesis as a Rural–Urban Link' carried out with the assistance of a Jawaharlal Nehru Fellowship (June 1971–May 1973). First published in August 1978, Calcutta.

[4] Sircar, 'The Third Theatre', *On Theatre*, p. 3.

However, he says, theatre itself is losing out to cinema in terms of audience, and in trying to imitate the spectacle, the illusion and glamour of cinema is weakening its own inherent strength, which lies in its live immediacy: 'In theatre a live person communicates directly to another live person.'[5] 'People do theatre; people watch it. Theatre talks about people; there is an active communication between one man and another through theatre.'[6] It is this here-and-now link between actor and audience that is fundamental to theatre:

> In the matter of direct communication, the personality and the body (which includes the voice) of the performer becomes supremely important. The language of theatre should therefore be such that the performer gets ample opportunity for projecting himself; in other words, it should be theatrical.[7]

Further, theatre should be inexpensive, in order to free itself from the pressures of sponsorship and the marketplace, 'the clutches of big business and commercial interests.'[8]

Typically, Badal-da hastens to add that none of these ideas are new or original—many theatre practitioners have already started acting on them in different ways, including breaking through the 'fourth wall' of the proscenium stage as he himself has done in his earlier plays.

From here, he moves on to analyse the 'obstructions' that the proscenium stage erects between the performer and the viewer:

> Let us now think of the popular urban theatre; let us consider its form. The people in whose presence this whole spectacle called theatre occurs are divided into two groups. The two groups occupy completely different spaces; in fact these can be called two separate rooms. The room occupied by the actors is called the stage; it is on one side. The rooms from which they come on to the stage in their costumes are hidden from the audience's view. On the other side is the room that the audience occupies; it is called the auditorium. This room has rows of seats, all facing in the same direction—the direction of the stage. As all the seats are on one side, the last row is quite far from the stage ... This is the first obstruction between the two groups—the distance. The next is the difference of levels—the floor of the stage is at a different level from the floor of the hall. And the third obstruction is the darkness. The stage is lighted, the hall is in darkness; the actors in light, the audience in darkness.

[5] Sircar, 'The Third Theatre', *On Theatre*, p. 12.
[6] Badal Sircar, 'Masks in Theatre', *On Theatre*, p. 67.
[7] Sircar, 'The Third Theatre', *On Theatre*, p. 14.
[8] Ibid.

> I think this factor creates the maximum distance between the two groups. The actors remain in light, they continue with their actions pretending that the audience is not present at all. The audience sits hiding under the cover of darkness pretending that they are not present, pretending that the actions on the stage are happening in real life, pretending that the incidents are actually happening in the room, street, or battlefield being shown. And since the presence of the audience infringes upon this attempted realism, the attempt is to behave as if the audience is not present at all.[9]

As this quote makes clear, Badal-da's discomfort with the proscenium was posited on its construction and maintenance of a 'distance' between the actor and the audience. As he describes it, the very architecture of the proscenium, with the audience on one side at a remove from the stage, was premised on this desired distance. The use of light and darkness was another distancing device, and the 'fourth wall' between the actors and the audience yet another. Sircar was interested in direct communication between the actor and the audience. This drove him to seek other ways of organising the theatre space to make the experience of theatre more participatory—more, as he termed it, 'free'.

As he began to question the structures and conventions of urban theatre in India, and to see how avant-garde groups in other parts of the world worked, he began to formulate the principles of his Third Theatre philosophy. If two groups of equals, the performers and the spectators, were to communicate in a meaningful way, the actor had to be close to the spectator and speak directly to him or her. There should be no masking devices between the two sets of people:

> Will the actor wear a mask even here? What use is direct communication then? If I am unable to rip off the mask and bring out the real person, then it will just amount to the costumes eyeing each other, the masks sniffing each other, the armours clanging against each other.[10]

This called for a whole different training and preparatory process for the actor, as we have already seen, and which we discuss further in the following chapter on the workshop process.

After doing more and more free theatre at Curzon Park and elsewhere, Badal-da says:

> *Free theatre* attracted us, not only for the fact that our countrymen are poor and can ill-afford the price of admission, but also because we came

[9] Quoted in Anjum Katyal, 'Distance, Access, Control', pp. 139–50.
[10] Sircar, 'Masks in Theatre', *On Theatre*, pp. 67–68.

> to the belief that in theatre, both the performers and the spectators should have equal status. Theatre is a human act, hence, all the human beings involved—whether as performers or as spectators—should be free in their relationship with one another; no external factor should affect the relationship. When admission is charged, the spectators automatically assume the role of *buyers* and the performers, of *sellers*, even though the receipts may not be for private profit. The buyer–seller relationship is more accentuated when the tickets have different prices depending on the location of the seats in the auditorium—as is done in almost all cases. This is not a condition conducive for a human act; and so free theatre, where people come and stay at will and donate voluntarily (or not at all) after the performance, became our choice.[11]

Hereafter, there was no entry fee for a Satabdi performance; instead, after the show, group members would approach the audience for any amount of contribution they felt like making—'passing the hat around' in the age-old tradition of street artistes and buskers. People gave what they could afford to or felt moved to.

The word 'free' is, thus, tremendously important to Badal-da's philosophy of Third Theatre. It is free because the audience has free access to the performance space; because the theatre can travel freely to the people, using any public area or venue, thereby proving that any space can be turned into a performance space; and because the actor is freed from certain restrictions inherent to proscenium theatre and can approach the audience freely.

For Badal-da, in theatre 'communication can occur in four ways: performer to spectator, performer to performer, spectator to performer and spectator to spectator.'[12]

With regard to the first kind of communication, the Third Theatre worker wants to see and talk to his audience, touch them and stir them, draw them close to him. To do this, access is essential. Space is organised so that there is no distance between actor and audience, no barriers or divides, not even props or make-up. Indoors, audience seating consists of light, movable benches which can be arranged in different configurations: a central island of benches on which people sit facing outwards or clusters of seating, with pathways winding through for the actors. This theatre involves being within and experiencing, not viewing from a safe distance. It involves communicating individually to another human being and receiving her response immediately, not projecting to a dark mass of anonymous bodies whom

[11] Sircar, 'The Third Theatre', *On Theatre*, p. 49.

[12] Badal Sircar, 'The Changing Language of Theatre', *On Theatre*, p. 81.

you try to forget are human beings. The actors use their bodies to indicate machines, forests, rocks, storms, factories, trains and buses. They crawl through the audience, growl, hum, chant, sing, make eye contact, ask questions and speak directly to them. At the end of a play, they often invite the audience to join them in solidarity or hope. In outdoor performances, the people who form a ring around the performance space are very accessible to the actors, who often make their way through the crowd while performing. Once again it is clear that this is a shared space.

The communication between performers must be as direct and open as that with the audience. Ideally, the Third Theatre co-workers should know each other well and develop a mutual closeness. The workshop process with its stress on building trust and breaking down inhibition emphasises this ideological principle; and the bare rehearsal and performance space, offering no place to hide nor anything to hide behind, not even the usual devices of scripted lines, costumes or make up, further promotes it. Moreover, this is ensemble theatre; the entire team of performers works in unison. Together, their bodies form trees, arches, a railway compartment, a bus and machines—whatever the narrative demands.

The third and fourth kinds of communication—spectator to performer, spectator to spectator—are linked to the logic of the theatre space. When an actor is in front of you, speaking directly to you, it is hard not to respond, in alarm, empathy or agreement. Spectators communicate with the actors more intimately and directly because of the shared space. Similarly, in the performance hall where they mingle as equals, or outdoors where they stand beside each other, they can see and are aware of each other's responses; and this enhances communication between members of the audience. Also, the plays often demand their participation, and this too causes them to communicate with each other. In *Michhil*, for example, members of the audience who join the procession share a bond by virtue of their common response:

> This theatre does not involve only a change in the inter-relationship of the spaces occupied by the performers and the spectators; it involves a basic change in the relation between the performer and the spectator as two human beings ... the performer comes down, comes close, appears as the human being he is to the human being the spectator is. He has to take off his own mask and be himself ... one of the most difficult tasks today ... But the new theatre demands a different language of performance altogether ... It is also a great risk to take, for he is vulnerable without his mask, without his protective armour. But the risk has to be taken, because that is the only way to appeal to

> the spectator to take off his own mask. When that happens, theatre becomes a real meeting of human beings.[13]

However, Badal-da insists, despite this emphasis on feelings and communicating emotion, that the importance of intellect is not being belittled:

> Knowledge without feelings makes one pedantic, as feelings without knowledge can put one in an ivory tower or send one to the mountains to meditate. The integration of knowledge and feelings is what can be called consciousness, and it is consciousness that can induce and guide any meaningful action that can in turn change the world for the better. We know that people in this world die of starvation, that people are tortured behind prison walls, that the planet earth can be destroyed totally by a minute fraction of the stockpile of nuclear weapons: all this is knowledge. But unless we feel the full import of that knowledge, we do not take action.[14]

This, then, is the core of the politics of his theatre: to create an emotional impact strong enough to be translated into action, into taking a stance. Not intellect alone, not ideas and information alone, but experience, feeling, alongside.

To sum up the salient features of his Third Theatre, it is a 'way of communicating directly in theatre, thereby utilising the strength of this live art form'; it is 'flexible, portable and inexpensive theatre—a free theatre' no longer dependent on the money required for the 'costly inessentials of the proscenium theatre'. It can be both an intimate theatre, where 'intense emotional communication' is possible, and an outdoor theatre that travels to the people.

> Both these theatres can be free in principle as well as in effect, for they can function on the basis of voluntary donation ... principally, because a *human act* like theatre should let people meet freely on the basis of equal status so that their relationship can be *human*.[15]

It is a theatre concerned with impacting social change, making people think and feel deeply about the injustices and inequities in the society they are part of, so that perhaps they will be moved to act for change. Badal-da insists that this new theatre is not just a matter of form but a

[13] Sircar, 'The Changing Language of Theatre', *On Theatre*, pp. 84–85.
[14] Ibid., pp. 85–86.
[15] Ibid., p. 89.

philosophy; the starting point is the content, what they have to say, and not how they say it.

Let us now take a look at some of the milestone productions of the Third Theatre, each important in a different way. We have already discussed *Spartacus* in detail. Another landmark production of this period is *Prastab* (Proposal).

This play came about because Badal-da needed a production that could be presented without too much preparation and practice. The message of the play grew out of his deep belief that vested interests had brought mankind to the edge of disaster ('we have been brought to the position where the total destruction of the planet is physically possible by using a minute fraction of the atomic weapons in stock')[16] and turned money into a monster which, instead of serving Man as it was supposed to do, has enslaved him.

Prastab is a proposition—to abolish money, the indecent symbol. In the theatre, he presents the same arguments as he was doing at the time in private discussions. 'It was nothing but an improvised speech delivered by one person and I ventured to put it forth as such in theatre because I *had to* at that time. I am glad that it was so,' says Badal-da.[17]

A first-hand account by Rustom Bharucha, combined with Badal-da's own description, allows us to reconstruct this production.[18] First, there is no entry fee charged—it would contradict the whole message of the show. The audience is let in one by one. They see platforms laid on the floor in the shape of a T, with Badal-da spread-eagled, lying still, blindfolded, stripped to the waist, his arms and legs bound with rope that is fastened to the four corners. Three sentries stand around him, unmoving, holding a knife, a whip and a gun, respectively. One corner of the room is blocked off by a screen.

Unsettled, the audience does not quite know what to do. Casually, the lights are switched off. A powerful beam of light falls onto the immobile sprawled and tied figure, focusing all attention on him. He begins to speak. First, he requests the audience to go behind the screen one by one and take a look at the obscene picture there. Slightly embarrassed, they do so and see a collage of bank notes and coins. They return to their seats. Then he makes his *prastab* (proposal) to abolish that obscene picture and the materialism it symbolises. It sounds rather naïve and trite, and the sentries, together with three other actors who have been planted in the audience, at once

[16] Sircar, 'The Third Theatre', *On Theatre*, p. 46

[17] Ibid., p. 47.

[18] Bharucha, *Rehearsals of Revolution*, pp. 154–56 and Sircar, 'The Third Theatre', *On Theatre*, pp. 46–48.

break out into loud laughter. After the laughter subsides, Badal-da begins his arguments, speaking for 40 to 50 minutes about the evils of money in today's society, expressing his own beliefs with conviction.

> If we can create a society where everyone works according to his ability and gets what he needs—a very sane arrangement but it can only be done when everyone agrees at the same time—then money will become redundant. Not only money, but other things like war, weapons, bank, insurance, police—and an enormous amount of energy will be released. I mean resources.[19]

A bell rings. The sentries now bring out the 'obscene' image from behind the screen and hold it up. The actors playing members of the public dart towards it, and then cavort and genuflect before it, their tongues hanging out in greed. They disperse, and there is silence in the room as the audience waits, uncertain if they should leave. Badal-da appeals to them to untie him. Some of them go up to do so. Badal-da sits up, then walks around looking into each one's eyes. Finally, he leaves the room and the show is over.

Badal-da says about *Prastab*:

> I know that most people will not accept this as theatre but to me it was the first experience of what I believe to be a genuine theatre—a theatre of feelings, a theatre of direct communication. Such theatre cannot have any script. One can only express what one really believes, feels and has an irrepressible urge to communicate.[20]

Rustom Bharucha is also confused: 'What are we to make of this event? How does one react to it? Is it theater?'[21] He finds that 'it is difficult to speak of *Prastab* as a theatrical event because it defies all notions and conventions of entertainment. One can speak of it more accurately as a *human* act that incorporates a deeply personal statement by Sircar.'[22] However, today we have no difficulty at all in placing this event in the tradition of Performance Art, or even the Happenings of the 1960s, in which an artist expresses a vision or a message in artistic or theatrical form. Even in the absence of a storyline, it is definitely a performance, crafted for maximum effect, with the use of supporting actors, lights, props and a set.

[19] Sircar, 'Voyages in the Theatre', *On Theatre*, p. 132.
[20] Sircar, 'The Third Theatre', *On Theatre*, pp. 47–48.
[21] Bharucha, *Rehearsals of Revolution*, p. 156.
[22] Ibid., p. 154.

For one theatre-goer at least, *Prastab*, despite its rather Utopian and idyllic proposal, worked; Rustom Bharucha analyses his response to the experience:

> In many ways, its denunciation of money is so violent, so absolute, that one is almost tempted to reject it as an appallingly simplistic statement.... Sircar's reasoning is very simple, very uncompromising, but his speech in *Prastab* is expressed so clearly, and, above all, so sincerely, that one is compelled to listen to it ... He says what he has to say with a belief that is sometimes intimidating ... His integrity is what makes his theater so significant ... Instead of making any attempt to entertain the audience (in the traditional sense of the word), *Prastab* asks the spectators to change their lives by specifically changing their attitude to money. It is less a message than a plea.[23]

Bharucha also explicitly compares *Prastab* to other political theatre of the time. He says that Badal-da uses none of the

> gimmicks and strategies one associates with the political playwrights in Bengal. It might be argued that the politics of *Prastab* is too personal to be taken seriously. One must emphasize, however, that it is not egotistic. Sircar does not exhibit his martyrdom as an artist. Nor does he at any point indulge in the kind of self-congratulatory righteousness to which representatives of the 'poor theatre' succumb in their most rapturous moments ... the most affecting moment in *Prastab* occurs when Sircar asks the spectators to release him. At that moment, Sircar does not stand apart from them like an enlightened guru. He is one with them.[24]

Taking the experience of *Prastab* further, Badal-da and Satabdi decided to mount *Muktamela* (lit., an open fair). It was apparently Badal-da's suggestion that they devise a show directed exclusively at a middle-class audience, done in an enclosed space.[25] The aim was to challenge comfortable middle-class assumptions; for example, that they lived a free existence unmarked by indignities and restrictions such as faced by the lower classes.

> Our idea was to put the spectators in a situation which would remind them of those indignities of life through a direct theatrical experience. We imposed a condition that once a spectator entered, he or she could not leave before

[23] Bharucha, *Rehearsals of Revolution*, pp. 154–56.
[24] Ibid., p. 156.
[25] Sircar, 'Voyages in the Theatre', *On Theatre*, p. 108.

the show was over for it was imperative to place them in a claustrophobic atmosphere.[26]

Badal-da describes the layout:

> Our small room on the second floor had two entrances. One was directly from the staircase landing but the other could be reached only by passing successively through a terrace, a small dressing room and another patch of terrace. The show was to begin at 7 p.m.; from 6.45 p.m. onwards we let the spectators in, one or two persons at a time, to the first terrace area.[27]

From the moment the spectator enters the first terrace area, the play begins for her. As she enters she finds that two sentries have mounted guard and are watching from an upper terrace. They have flashlights and revolvers. She is taken to a table where she faces an interrogation. Along with standard queries regarding name, age, profession and marital status, there are more intrusive questions, about salary, conjugal life and so on. If she tries to protest or jest in response, her entrance card is briskly stamped with terms such as 'antisocial', 'suspicious character', 'seditious' and so on. She then enters the dressing room. Here, she is frisked, as at the airport. Ladies are frisked behind a curtain by a woman 'official'. Emerging on to the semi-dark terrace on the other side, she is startled by a stentorian order to 'halt' and is brusquely told to produce her permit. Before she realises what that is, her entrance card is snatched from her hand, checked and the door is opened to let her in. And the first thing she sees in front of her is a barrier-like wooden frame with barbed wire.

Immediately one of the two 'hosts' comes up to greet and welcome her effusively. Both hosts are formally dressed. One is in a suit and tie, the other in a typical Bengali outfit of dhoti, kurta and shawl. A tea stall and some competitive games have been set up in the room, and there is a group of people with musical instruments; every so often they break into song. In one corner, there is a curtained-off area, which has 'No Admission' stamped on it in three languages. An actor playing a dog guards it. There are a lot of assorted activities going on. Someone brings in tea, someone plays a game, someone does magic card tricks. There is an auction at which one of the lots for sale is a blood-spattered shirt which is described in gruesome detail as having belonged to a man killed in police firing, how his eyes were shot

[26] Sircar, 'Voyages in the Theatre', *On Theatre*, p. 108.
[27] Ibid., pp. 108–09.

out, and so on. A young girl has her hands bound behind her back with the other end of the rope tied to a window grille. A dangerous-looking man in a lungi and vest is busy sharpening a threateningly large knife. A 'priest' invites her to pay a fee and take a look at the image of the deity in a hollow box. To do so she has to stoop as if paying obeisance. She sees a picture made up of currency notes and coins (like the 'obscene' image in *Prastab*). The butcher (the man with the knife) comes up and asks why she hasn't visited his meat-shop for such a long time. But the butcher sympathises—after all, mutton is so expensive. Now, if only the Hindus would eat more beef, the price would come down; or if the Calcuttan learnt to enjoy street dog or crow meat, not only would mutton be cheaper, but the city could also be rid of these pests. And, of course, the whole problem would be solved—as well as the great over-population issue—if we all learned to eat human flesh. When the spectator goes up to the young girl, she starts to narrate a schoolgirl's story about a picnic or a school function, speaking very rapidly and excitedly, then suddenly stops, looks around warily and whispers that she wants to be freed. She makes a move to untie the rope, but the 'dog' starts growling at her and one of the hosts comes up to say that the girl has been tied up at her own request. The girl confirms this and gives the spectator a stern look, as if her intentions had been dishonourable. A hawker enters. Just like the hawkers on the streets, he is selling 'lozenges' (boiled candy sweets), along with which pieces of paper containing the teachings of great men are being distributed free. The messages tell all men to be law abiding, while women are instructed to obey and respect their 'lords and masters' and keep busy in the kitchen. An actor furtively shows the spectator an obscene picture he is trying to sell: it is a photograph of the mutilated body of a war victim, or a victim of nuclear radiation.

After a series of such experiences, the spectator is led into a game of musical chairs. A prize is awarded to the winner in the first round. During the second round, suddenly there is the ear-splitting sound of crackers being burst outside. A group of uniformed men—soldiers, policemen, guards—rush in. They take control of the room, switch on extra lights. The host in a suit announces that an antisocial is hiding in the room. Has anybody seen anything suspicious? He or she must immediately make a report. No one comes forward. His tone grows increasingly intimidating, threatening to detain them overnight if the report is not made. Finally, the 'dog' is employed to sniff out the 'culprit'. As he begins sniffing, a young actor who had been behaving like one of the spectators throughout suddenly darts to the door. He is caught and dragged behind the curtain in the corner. The host declares that everything is now in order and the funfair can resume. But the officials are coming and going from the curtained area holding torture instruments and, every so often blood curdling shrieks of pain rise from behind the curtain only to be drowned out by the raucous pop songs and dancing that is part of the fair. The body of the young man is carried out, draped in a bloodstained sheet, through the second door. The first door is now opened to indicate the end of the show.

The entire environment is a strange fusion of the surreal, absurd, quotidian and the grimly realistic in terms of depiction of State terror. It is aimed at unsettling and disturbing the spectator, who cannot leave voluntarily and who is forced to bear witness to an act of violence. And the audience does respond, quite unpredictably at times:

> We could not anticipate even half of the reactions and we had to improvise to cope with them … once, lukewarm tea was thrown on the face of the 'dog'. Once, somebody tried to remove the curtain from the 'no admission' area and he was fighting the 'dog' to do it. The dog behaved like a dog; it bit his hand,' says Badal-da.[28]

The reference to the anti-Naxalite crackdown and the torture are all meant to make the spectator face up to the violent society he or she is part of. Several members of Satabdi at the time are young men and women who have been involved in the Naxalite movement, and their experiences permeate this production.

Badal-da says:

> The way we prepared it was to distribute the roles, fix up the props, decide upon the sequence and timing and then try to anticipate the reactions of the spectators … We had some benches and stools as part of our furniture. Normally, in all performances, we arrange these for people to sit on but in *Muktamela* the furniture lay scattered as in a godown, upside down and dumped here and there. When the game of 'musical chairs' began, we brought in some stools for the game. We thought, if the audience doesn't join, then all of us—a cast of 23 artistes—would play the game. Surprisingly, in all the six shows, the audience joined in … This production also did not have any script and involved conversations with the spectators for the most part. For this, we used not only the room of the theatre but also the dressing room and the attached terraces.[29]

[28] Sircar, 'Voyages in the Theatre', *On Theatre*, p. 112.
[29] Ibid.

This highly unusual production did not turn out to be very popular, according to Badal-da:

> We could do only six shows, and in the last of them there were more of us than the spectators; so it can be said that it was rejected by the audience. Only a handful of people said that it was our best so far; at least one young man joined our group after seeing it, and only a few months ago a lady told me that she had seen all the six performances when she was a first-year college student.[30]

It may not have been popular, but in terms of innovative ideas and a new approach to the whole theatrical experience, it was quite a milestone. Serious social commentary and the intention to hit hard without preaching or haranguing are very skilfully worked into this production. We see Badal-da and Satabdi riding a creative wave in terms of staging, and being able to integrate form and content in very unusual ways.

This creative wave continues with the next work. Perhaps Satabdi's most iconic production, *Michhil* remains one of the plays most often performed in several languages, both within India, across the borders and with the Indian diaspora on different continents. This play contains many typical features of Badal-da's Third Theatre style, such as: an intimacy with the audience, sharp satirical commentary on society and the status quo, the dream of a more just and equitable tomorrow, a collage-like juxtaposition of sequences, the actors' bodies forming a range of different sculptural images, and humour.

It seems that Badal-da had the germ of this play in mind from his very first workshop, as a sort of 'Calcutta collage'. In the introduction to a book of his plays, theatre critic Ella Dutta writes, 'For a long time, he had had the idea of making a kind of montage on Calcutta made up of scenes of Calcutta streets, chatting in teashops, conversations in the coffee houses, different scenes in the offices … And then suddenly the idea that Calcutta was a city of processions came vividly upon him.'[31] Badal-da says, 'It is one of the very few plays where I had the idea of the production even before I began writing it, particularly the procession idea.'[32] An actor from the first workshop recalls how the theme of the procession—all sorts of processions, religious, political, civic—cropped up from the very beginning.

[30] Sircar, 'Voyages in the Theatre', *On Theatre*, p. 107.

[31] Badal Sircar, *Three Plays* (Calcutta: Seagull Books, 1985), Introduction by Ella Dutta, p. viii.

[32] Sircar, *Three Plays*, Introduction by Ella Dutta, p. viii.

Badal-da explains the thinking behind the play:

I have always had a love–hate relationship with Calcutta. In the early 1970s, I had this idea of making a play on Calcutta in the form of a collage. As Calcutta is known as a city of processions, *Michhil* seemed to be an appropriate name as well as a suitable way of making the play. In the immediately preceding years, so many young people and adolescents were killed by the police, brutally and cruelly, secretly and openly, that the image of the man who is being killed every day was very strong in my mind, and I had a vague idea of a clownish old man, probably visualizing myself in the role. There were some loose notes, even some detached scenes, but there was no shape or direction.

We had our Anganmancha room on the second floor of the Academy of Fine Arts for three days a week, and we had our own benches and stools there. One afternoon I was there alone and I began arranging the benches in various ways to create a winding passage, twisting and turning, as in a maze. It was laborious work and I was panting with the effort, but various imaginary processions went on moving along the winding passage, passing the imaginary spectators sitting on both sides. The young man went on being killed and the old man lost his way in the streets. The boss-cum-guru and his stooges took shape, gradually. The chorus forming various processions already existed in the loose notes and scenes. That maze of benches actually seen with my own eyes made me bring the play to its final shape soon after.[33]

Rustom Bharucha describes this as:

[O]ne of Sircar's most intricately structured plays, with innumerable transitions and juxtapositions. The relentless flow of events in the text is most skillfully concretized in the swirling movement of the mise en scene. The actors are constantly on the move—walking, running, dancing, and jogging through the room's L-shaped passages.... A number of benches are placed against one another so that some spectators sit with their backs to one another. Sircar creates a most bewildering environment with the bodies, backs, faces and profiles of the spectators. When the actors begin to move between and around the environment created by the spectators, the effect is startling: one can almost see a procession winding its way around the streets of Calcutta.[34]

[33] Sircar, 'Voyages in the Theatre', *On Theatre*, pp. 115–16.
[34] Bharucha, *Rehearsals of Revolution*, p. 157.

Michhil begins with a ringing bell.[35] The Chorus enters the space like members of the audience and appears to look for places to sit. The bell stops. At once all the lights go out. Voices in the dark break into questions and comments, offering reasons for the blackout, warning each other to watch out. Suddenly a 'piercing death scream'[36] is heard. The Chorus exclaims in alarm, speculating that there has been a murder or accident and calling out for a torch, matches, lighter, any form of light. Matchsticks flicker into flame. There is a silent search for a few seconds, then darkness again. The Chorus is confused. No one can see a victim or a body, yet they heard the scream.... Suddenly the stentorian voice of an Officer roars out, asking what the matter is. Voices answer—someone screamed, someone was killed, someone fell into a hole, someone was stabbed—till he bawls 'Stop it!' Immediately the lights come on. The members of the Chorus shield their eyes in the sudden glare. At one end stands an Officer in full military regalia. He barks, 'Who was killed?' There is a futile search for a corpse. He declares, 'No one was killed', and cuts through the ensuing hubbub of protests with a command to stop spreading false rumours and go home. At this moment, Khoka, a young actor who has been sitting unnoticed in the audience, suddenly falls to the floor.[37]

From the very start of the play, there is no demarcation of the performance area as distinct from the audience space. Actors perform from amidst the audience, light and darkness are shared equally, and it is hard to tell who is an actor and who a spectator. A note in the play text explains that when performed in the open, the play starts with Khoka dropping dead with a scream, followed immediately by the Chorus bursting in with their exclamations and spreading out all over the performance area.

The young man, Khoka (indicating 'boy' in Bengali), dies over and over in the play. He tries desperately to get the Officer to notice him but his efforts are in vain. He speaks to the audience, 'I was killed. I. Me. Here I am. I've been killed... I was killed today. I was killed yesterday. I was killed the day before yesterday... Last week. Last month. Last year. I am killed every day.'[38] As he remains lost and unrecognised, scenes from Calcutta life unfold in a fluid montage all around him, some tongue in cheek, some violent, some farcical. The actors are continuously transforming the performance space by using

[35] The play text being followed is from Sircar, *Three Plays* (Calcutta: Seagull Books, 1985), pp. 1–42.

[36] Sircar, *Three Plays*, p. 4.

[37] Ibid., pp. 4–6.

[38] Sircar, *Three Plays*, p. 17.

their bodies to indicate a street, a funeral procession, a train or a bus (as well as the hawkers and passengers on them), a factory with machines, a telephone exchange with operators, a band of musicians, etc. The play spans the various evils that plague society—from communal clashes to profiteering to military transgressions. A broad sweep of space and time is contained in this one space, controlled and shaped by the actors' bodies. Just as they would on the streets, the audience lines both sides of the path of the *michhil* as actors pass before them. Actors speak to the audience from close quarters throughout the play as they urgently search for the missing Khoka or offer items for sale.

Only the Old Man bonds with the lost boy, the Old Man who, early in the play exhorts the audience:

> Take your seats on both sides of the road, choose a convenient spot and sit yourself down. Come along, come along quickly, take your seats—it's the Michhil, Michhil, Michhils for food and clothes, Michhils for salvation, Michhils for the revolution, military Michhils, Michhils of refugees, Michhils for flood relief, mourning Michhils, protest Michhils, festive Michhils, star-studded Michhils.[39]

Indian audiences, and Calcutta audiences in particular, are all familiar with processions of different kinds, from the protest procession against some perceived wrong, or the political procession flaunting banners and slogans, especially the typical 'Cholbe na!' (This won't do! Down with!) or 'Zindabad!' (Long live!), to the dead body carried in procession accompanied by cries of 'Hari bol!' (Call on Hari!), or the celebratory wedding procession with dancing and the music of brass bands, to the religious procession chanting *kirtans*, or the immersion of idols with hypnotic drumming and cheering crowds. The powerful motif of the procession is used throughout the play as a symbol of a community journey, a quest. The false processions that lead nowhere are contrasted with the search for the true *michhil*.

The Old Man has a memory of a road he walked down as a child with his father, a road that offered hope just around the corner, a road he is always seeking, a new road, not the same old tired road of promises betrayed. Hand in hand with Khoka, he sets out to find a new home, a new road—and to join a true procession, one that will show them the way.

> Khoka—What procession?
> Old Man—The procession to show us a way. The way home.

[39] Sircar, *Three Plays*, p. 18.

> Khoka (*tired*)—I've seen many processions. They never show you the way. It's always the same road, the same ...[40]

At the end, the Chorus enters in a procession, winding their way through the audience, singing a song:

> A song of hope. A song for the future. It is a procession of dreams. A song of dreams. Dreams that Old Man and Khoka have dreamt. The people in the procession are holding hands. Old Man holds Khoka's hand and leads him up to the procession and finally they become part of it, part of their song. The audience is invited to join. The procession continues.[41]

Rustom Bharucha provides a moving description of the emotional effect of this on the audience:

> The spectators and actors intermingle and the entire space of the room becomes a swirling mass of humanity. It is one of those moments in the theater when one becomes acutely aware of the possibilities of life and the essential brotherhood of man. Transcending the immediate issues of the play, it lingers long after the play ceases, compelling the spectators to reexamine their affinities and responsibilities as members of a society.[42]

One hears in this play echoes of *Ebong Indrajit*, almost as if this later work is in conversation with that earlier one. Is the Old Man an aged Indrajit, or perhaps the Writer? There is, of course, the symbol of the road down which he walks, endlessly seeking:

> Old Man: I'll keep searching, just a little further, that bend ...
> Khoka: Been searching so long now you're lost?
> Old Man: Lost and lost and lost again ...
> Khoka: But never gone back?
> Old Man: But never gone back. There's no going back, once you're lost you can't go back ...
> Khoka: Why didn't you die?
> Old Man: One can't die, one can't search once one is dead ...
> Khoka: Why do you search?
> Old Man: So that I may find, one can't find if one is dead.[43]

[40] Sircar, *Three Plays*, p. 52.
[41] Ibid., p. 53.
[42] Bharucha, *Rehearsals of Revolution*, p. 163.
[43] Sircar, *Three Plays*, p. 50.

Here again is the age-old question, raised by Badal-da over and over again, of why one continues to live at all. The ending of *Michhil* offers an answer—because there is hope of a better tomorrow.

According to Badal-da, 'the old home that the old man refuses to return to is nothing but the present society, and the new home he is seeking is a place where there will be no hunger, no privation, no injustice.'[44]

According to Sumanta Banerjee:

> As for his political message in the contemporary Indian context, *Michhil* (1974) was one of his first plays of the Third Theatre phase to express it. Sircar here picks up the all-too-familiar trait for which Calcutta is famous (or notorious?)—as a 'city of processions' … to show how this once radical demonstration of genuine popular urges has degenerated today into a ritual that is used by the ruling classes to confuse and exploit the masses. The play ends with all the people—the performers as well as the audience—forming a human chain, thus emphasizing the need for collective effort to form a new *michhil* or procession, that would translate into reality their dream of freedom from exploitation.[45]

Rustom Bharucha observes that *Michhil* 'is not a conventional political play.'[46] Yet it is a deeply political play. *Michhil* highlights the violence inherent in the social situation which the middle class Calcuttan refuses to see, the State terror which has been killing young men every day. The play builds a collage of everyday life in Calcutta—newspaper headlines about rising prices, black marketeering, postponement of examinations, crowded buses, communal clashes between different religious communities—and uses satire to savagely expose the hollowness of religious hypocrisy (a 'guru' figure blesses fawning, genuflecting believers), patriotism (a caricature of a typical 'neta' or leader perches imperiously on the back of crouching, subjugated, sycophantic subjects and spews platitudes about being a 'good' Indian); electioneering (preparations for an election campaign are made; the candidate is obese 'fat cat' hoarder-merchant Kaloram Bajaria; actors swagger around chanting the names of all the essential commodities one associates with such a figure: rice, lentils, coal, oil, sugar and flour; meanwhile, a destitute woman begs from the audience).

According to Rustom Bharucha, it becomes clear in the course of the play that 'the chorus represents that mass of people in Calcutta who continue

[44] Sircar, 'Voyages in the Theatre', *On Theatre*, p. 116.
[45] Banerjee, 'The Theatre of Badal Sircar', pp. 111–12.
[46] Bharucha, *Rehearsals of Revolution*, p. 158.

passively to accept the corruption that pervades their lives.'[47] They are supplicants to the ruling class figure who offers false blessings, empty words that don't change their lives for the better; hopeless, they end up turning to liquor to drown their sorrows. Later, the chorus 'voices a litany of middle-class prejudices, complaints, and demands. It is Sircar's most direct condemnation of the values and assumptions shared by his bourgeois spectators. Instead of attacking their ennui and selfishness directly, he lets his chorus reveal their shortcomings in a matter-of-fact manner.'[48]

> One: This country needs military dictatorship. They should all be thrashed into order.
> Two: In the park, pairs of young boys and girls sitting close. What's the country come to?
> Three: Strikes and gheraos all the time. No wonder prices soar…
> Four: At the temple yesterday I heard Sri Vishnu Maharaj's sermon. Oh, sublime.
> […]
> One: Will we remain a weak nation forever? Just about begun making atom bombs!
> Two: A Brahman boy marrying a low-caste sadgope girl?! That's why they say: When it's love, one doesn't care whether it's this low-caste or that!
> Three: The lower classes are getting so impertinent. Even the rickshaw-wallahs put on airs.[49]

Meanwhile, says Rustom Bharucha, 'the Boy continues to be "murdered" by the daily pressures, the political hypocrisies, and the everyday calamities of life in Calcutta.'[50]

However, to my mind, the Chorus is not just the insular and insulated bourgeoisie; they are more multi-faceted and flexible than that. They are also the concerned citizens who express anxiety about the murder in their midst, who search for the missing Khoka, and who, in the end, form the *michhil* of redemption and hope.

Despite its very urban imagery, this play has worked well in non-urban settings as well. Badal-da has an evocative account of how he performed it for a rural audience:

> Kapastikuri, a Santhal village in West Bengal.… The occasion was a conference of a village development organization. We were to perform *Michhil*

[47] Bharucha, *Rehearsals of Revolution*, pp. 160–61.
[48] Ibid., p. 161.
[49] Sircar, *Three Plays*, pp. 42–43.
[50] Bharucha, *Rehearsals of Revolution*, p. 158.

> in the afternoon. Of the 300 people sitting on the grass around the acting area, nearly 250 were bare-foot, bare-bodied Santhals. They knew Bengali, that was all.
>
> 'How can we get across?'—Was our thought. The play has no story, no character and it is full of city images. And then, suddenly, I had the realization that there is nothing in the play that could be difficult for them to understand. Rather, they would probably understand it better, for the young man getting killed every day is a concrete experience for them, not abstract as in our case. It was as simple as that and I found myself explaining this to them in my three-minute talk before the performance.
>
> There was pin-drop silence and rapt attention during the whole one-hour performance. At the end of the play, we sing a wordless melody, holding hands, and invite the audience to join us. An old Santhal came up with tears in his eyes and, instead of holding hands, he embraced the actor.[51]

Michhil was first performed on 14 April 1974 at village Ramchandrapur in West Bengal[52] and has since had more than 250 shows all over the country, in both Anganmancha and Muktamancha modes. It has been translated and performed by different groups and directors in several Indian languages, even internationally. Sircar felt that it remained relevant even in the twenty-first century, and said that it continued to communicate powerfully whenever performed.[53]

As Satabdi and Badal-da continue to hone their Third Theatre methodology and expertise, as the group coheres into a close unit—almost a repertory, an ensemble—a more collective way of creating plays begins to develop. We shall take a look at this phase of Badal-da's play making in the next chapter.

[51] Sircar, 'Voyages in the Theatre', *On Theatre*, p. 116.

[52] The production notes in the *Three Plays* give this as the date and place of the first performance (p. 12); however, Badal-da in 'Voyages in the Theatre' first gives the date as 13 April 1974 and later says, 'I finished writing in January 1974; its first performance was in a village in November of the same year' (p. 115).

[53] Interview with the author at Badal Sircar's residence, 11 January 2009.

CHAPTER TEN

DEVISED THEATRE

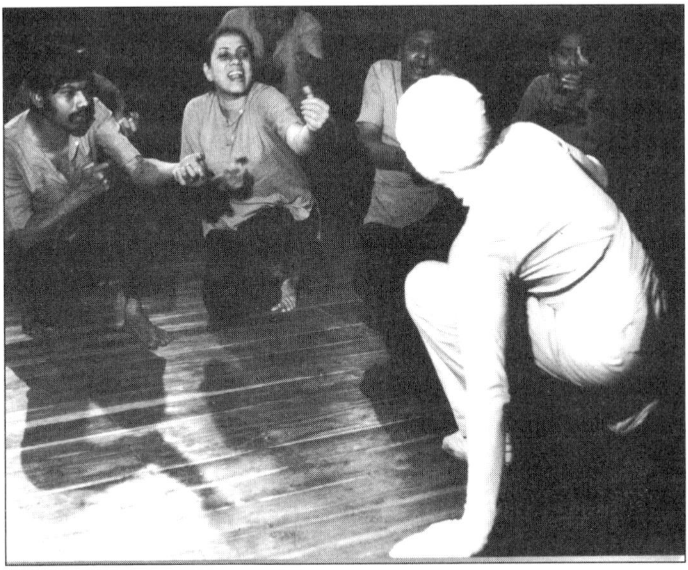

A scene from *Basi Khabar*
Courtesy: Satabdi

By 1975, Badal-da and Satabdi had begun to move into a new phase of collective play making. The current term for this kind of production is 'devised' theatre, indicating a performance text that emerges out of a joint creative process, such as a workshop, or is developed collaboratively in the course of rehearsal.

Improvisation had been an integral part of their workshop and rehearsal process from the start of the Third Theatre. Exercises included spontaneous creation of short sequences, tableaus and images, which inevitably came out of the personal experience of the participants. Inner expression was always encouraged. Badal-da would instigate the actors to 'confront' the script, to

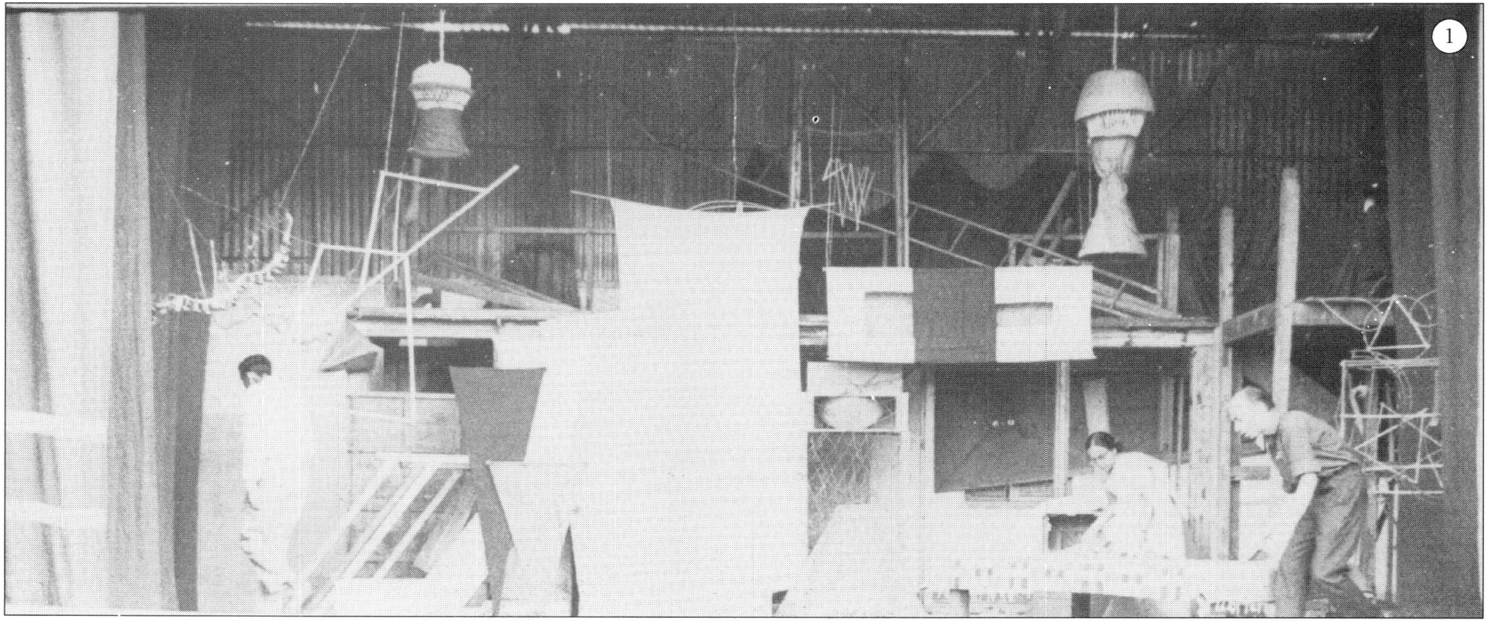

1. *Sara Rattir*: This was written after the path-breaking *Ebong Indrajit* in the span of one week, during which the playwright said that something was driving him to write this play. Although sets are not a prominent feature of his plays, in *Sara Rattir* the room in which the entire action unfolds is central to the narrative. However, it is much more than a setting or background; it is a character in the play. *Courtesy*: Satabdi

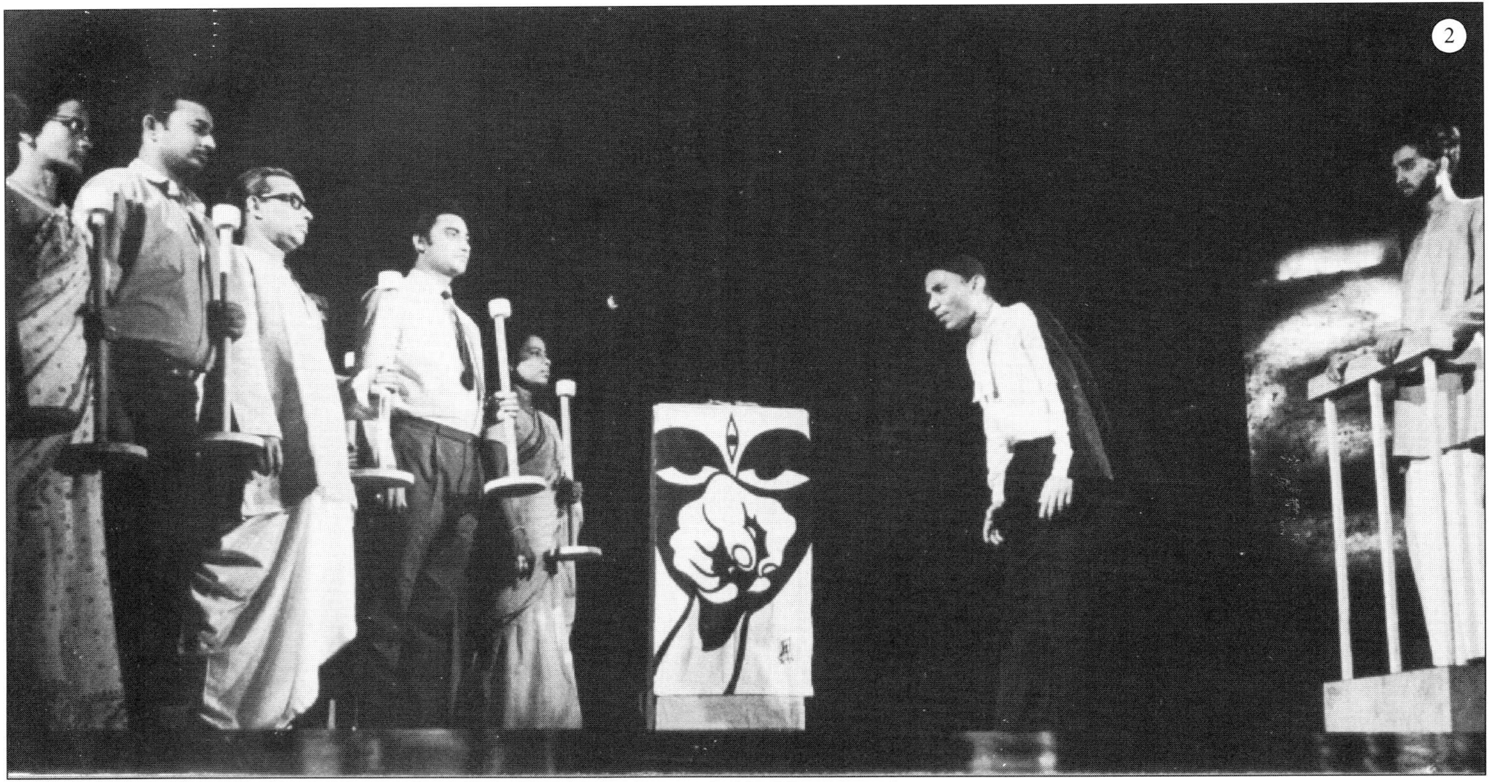

2. *Shesh Nei*: Written in 1970, *Shesh Nei* circles around the theme of guilt and responsibility, the individual conscience versus the expectations of the middle class with the protagonist on trial as characters from his own life accuse him on various grounds. *Courtesy*: Satabdi

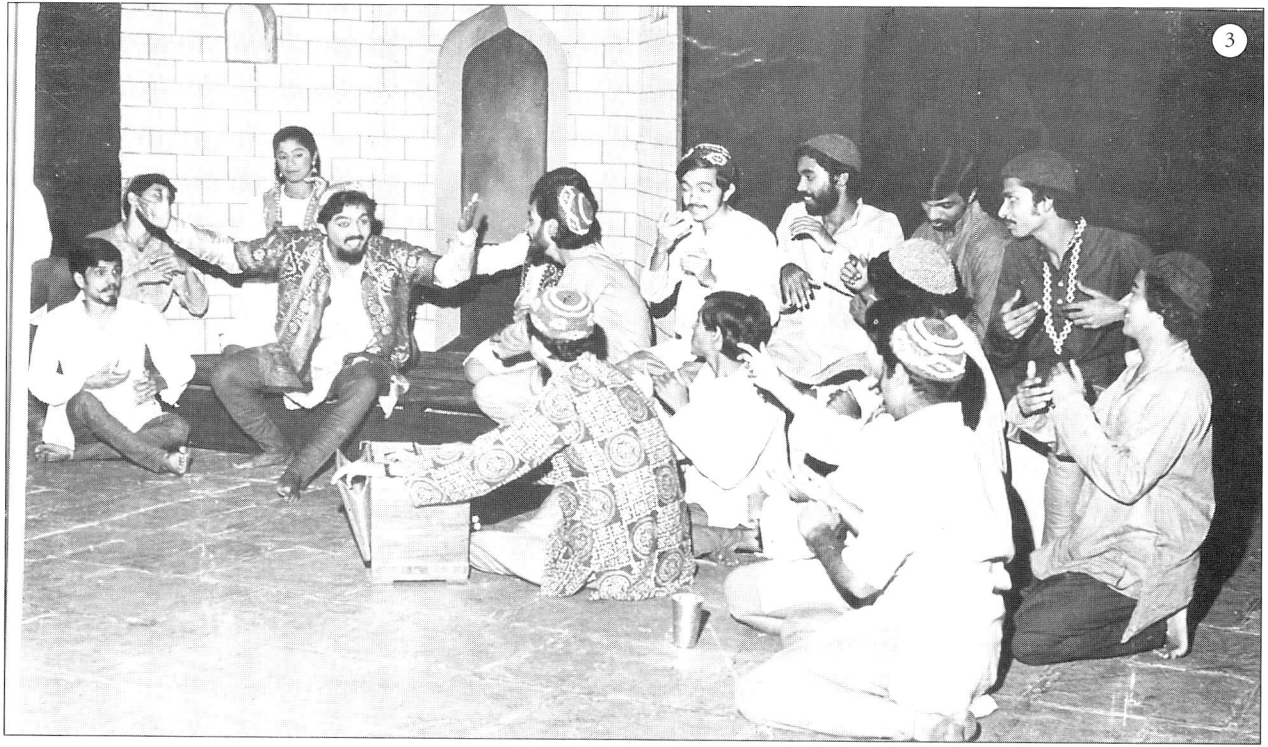

3. *Abu Hossain*: A musical farce by Girish Chandra Ghosh, Badal Sircar said of his production of *Abu Hossain* that 'although it was first produced on the conventional proscenium stage, it contained many elements that reflected my ideas about the Third Theatre.' He also said that they spent less than ₹100 on the sets for the play, an exercise in moving towards a 'poor theatre'. 'We learnt to use our imagination and the imagination of the audience.' *Courtesy*: Satabdi

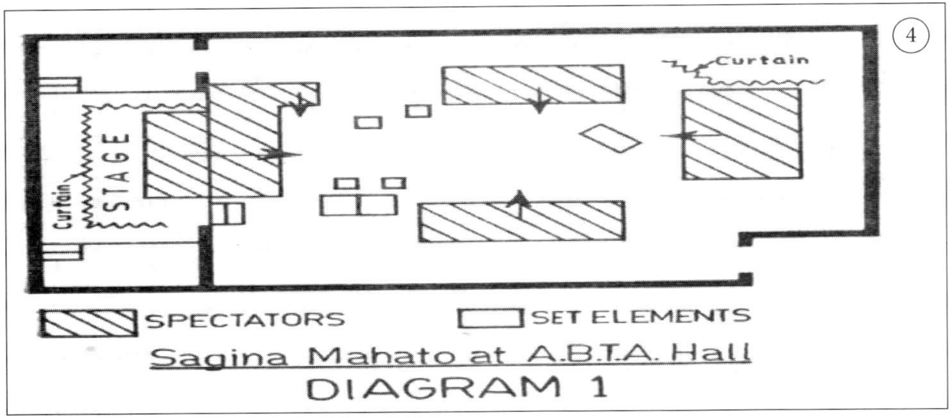

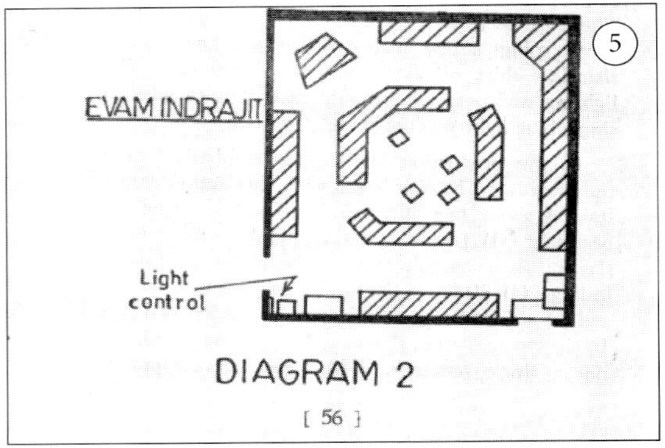

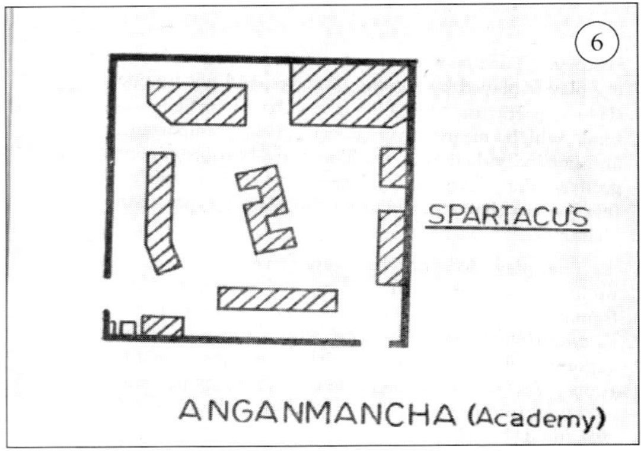

4, **5** and **6**. Reconfiguring space: With the shift out of the proscenium, Badal Sircar was seeking a different, more equal and interactive relationship between the performer and audience. This was directly connected with the approach to space. These three diagrams prepared by him show how he configured the use of space for three productions—with the audience placed within and around the action. *Courtesy*: Natya Shodh Sansthan

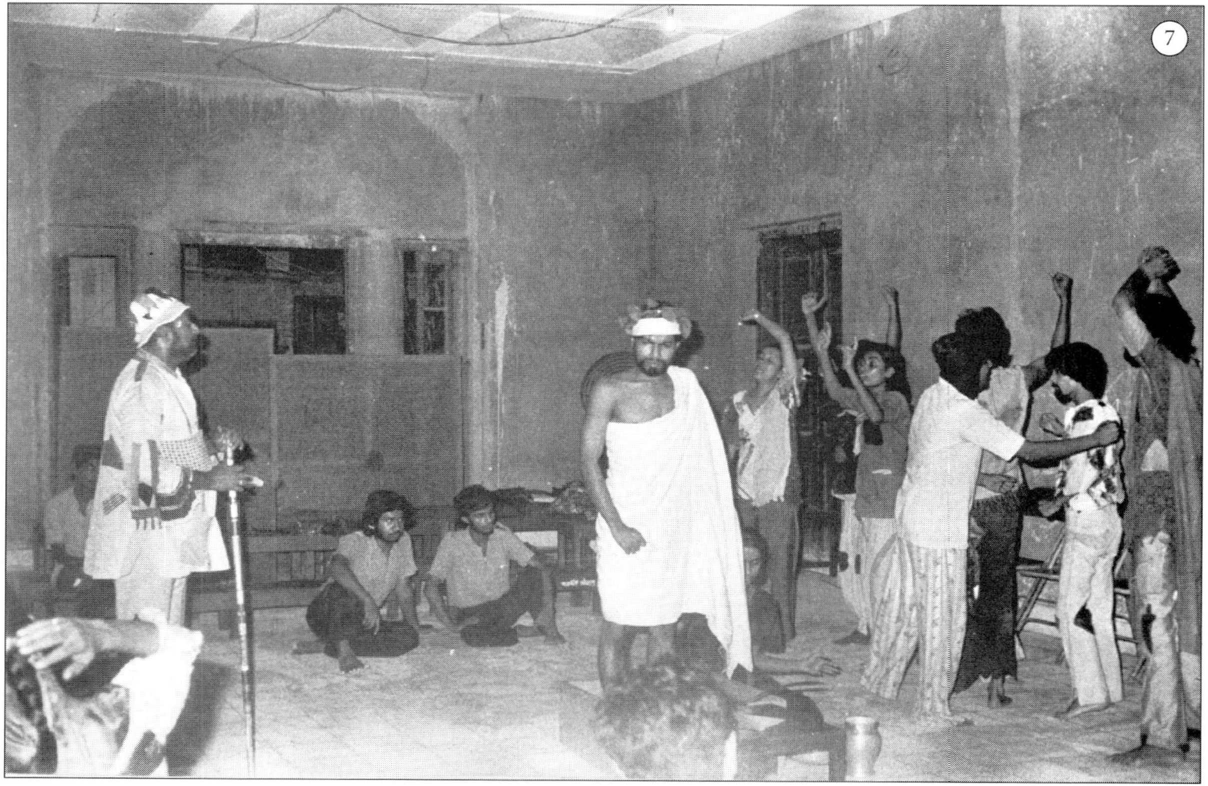

Ekti Hatyar Natak

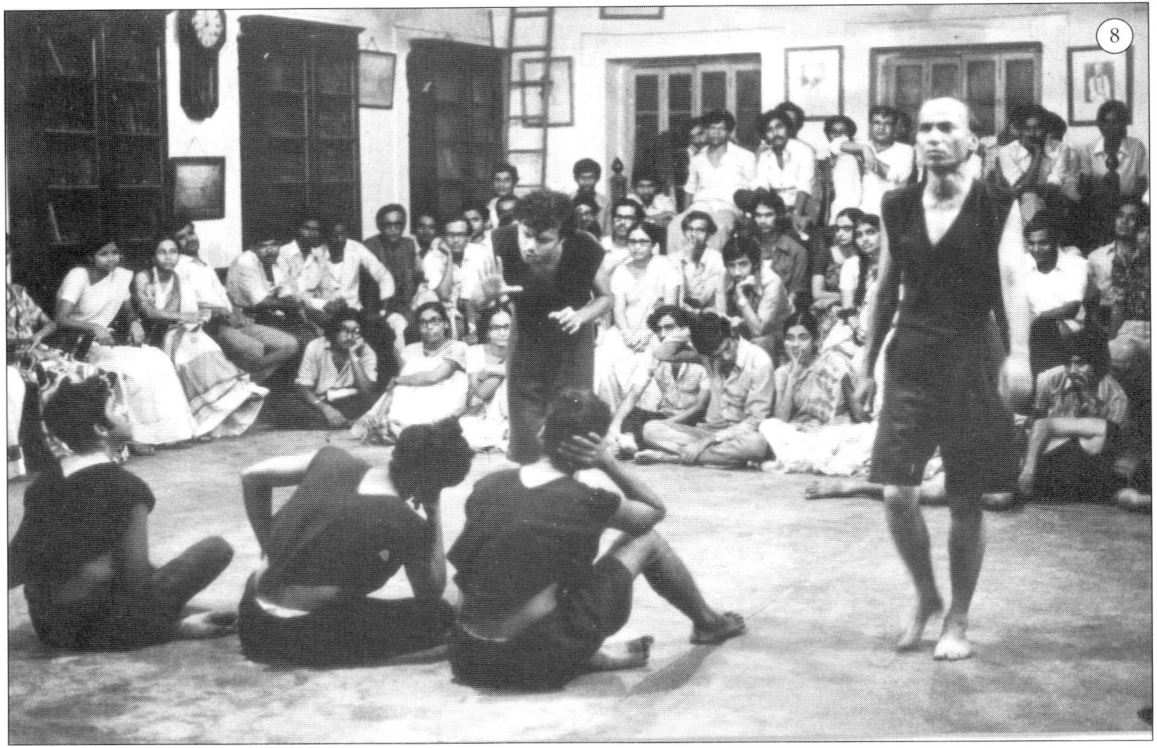

Bhoma

7 and **8**. The intimate space: These stills capture the atmosphere of the intimate indoor space, referred to as the Anganmancha space, of his early Third Theatre productions. Simplicity of sets, props, costume, lighting and proximity to the audience are amongst the main features of this form. *Courtesy*: Satabdi

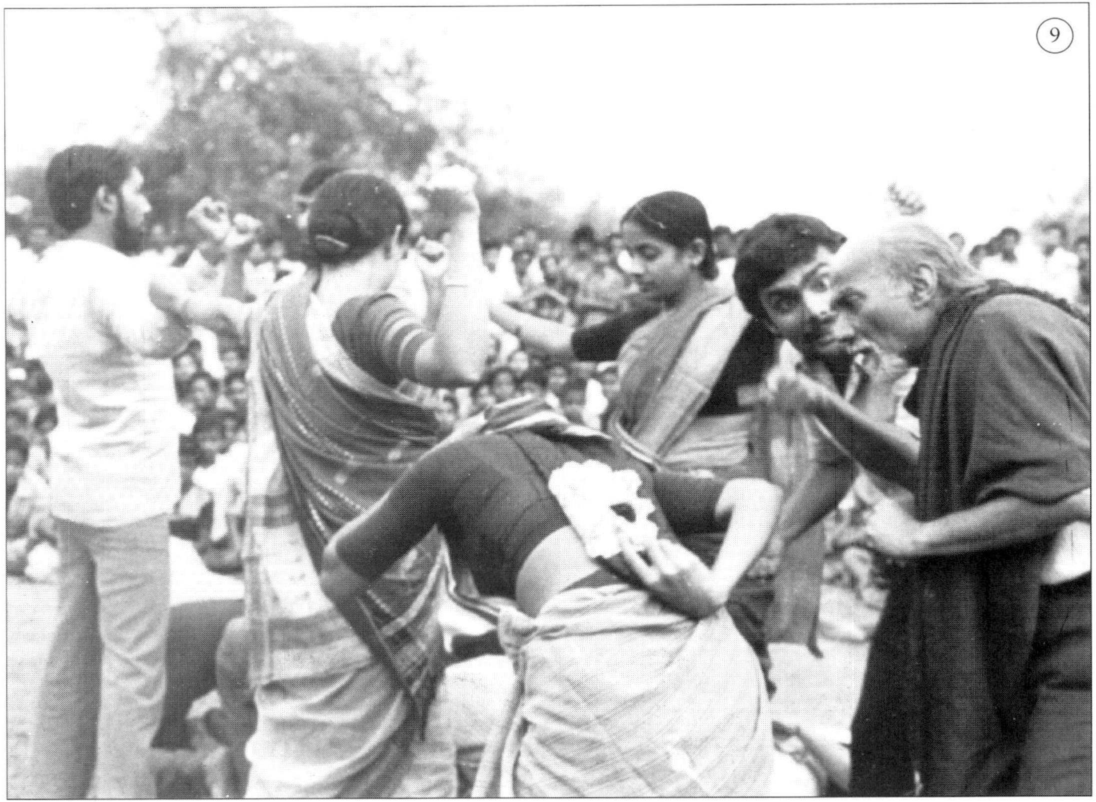

Gondi

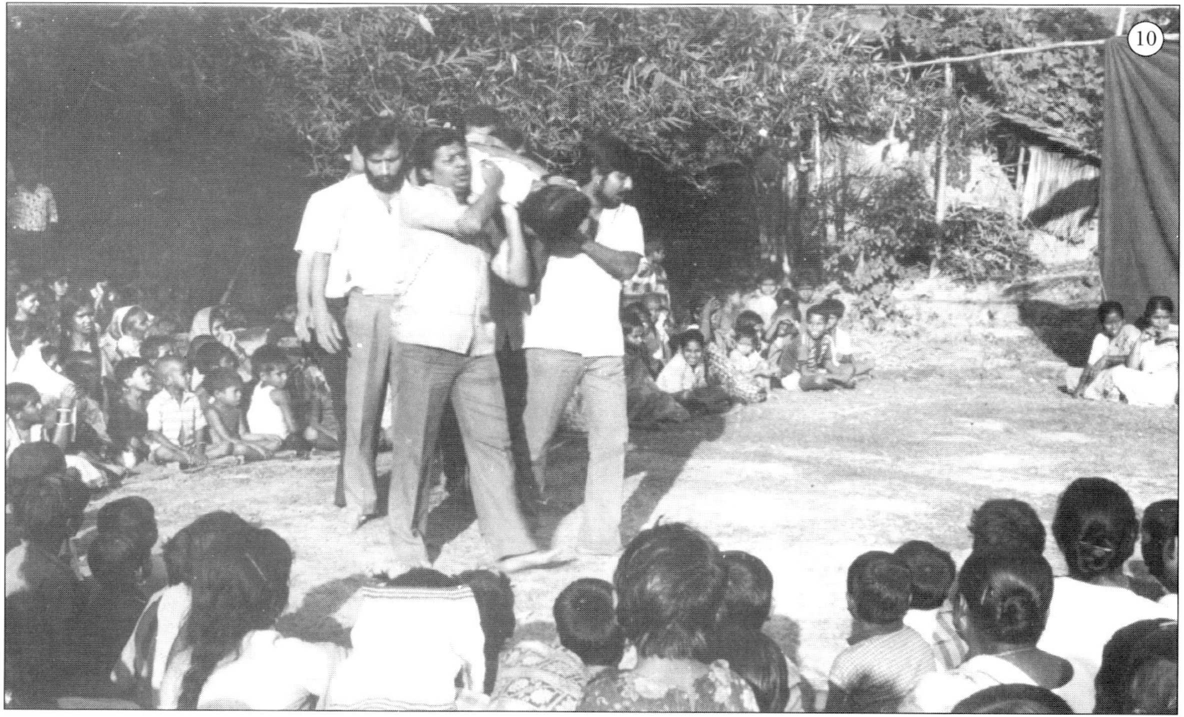

Michhil

9 and **10**. Physical theatre: Third Theatre was premised on the actor's body and direct human communication. These stills show the ways in which communication occurred through physical action—through the body of the actor. *Courtesy*: Satabdi

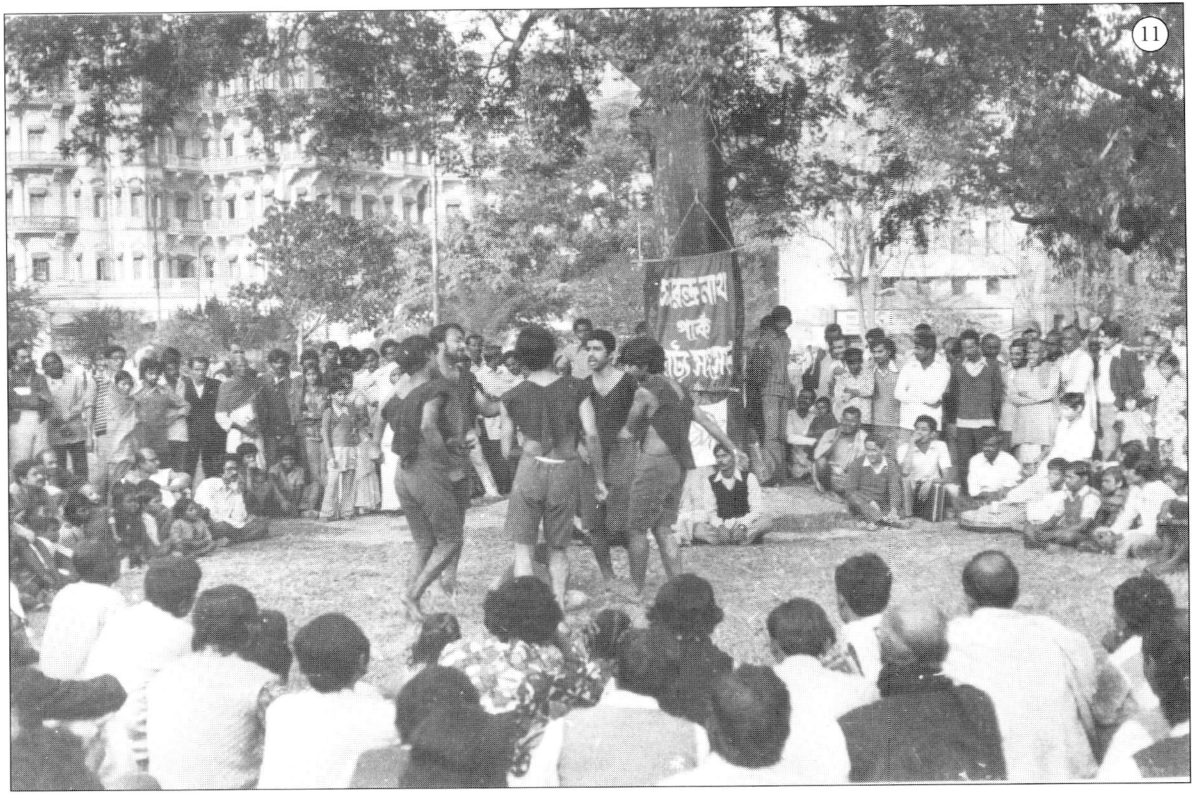

Bhoma

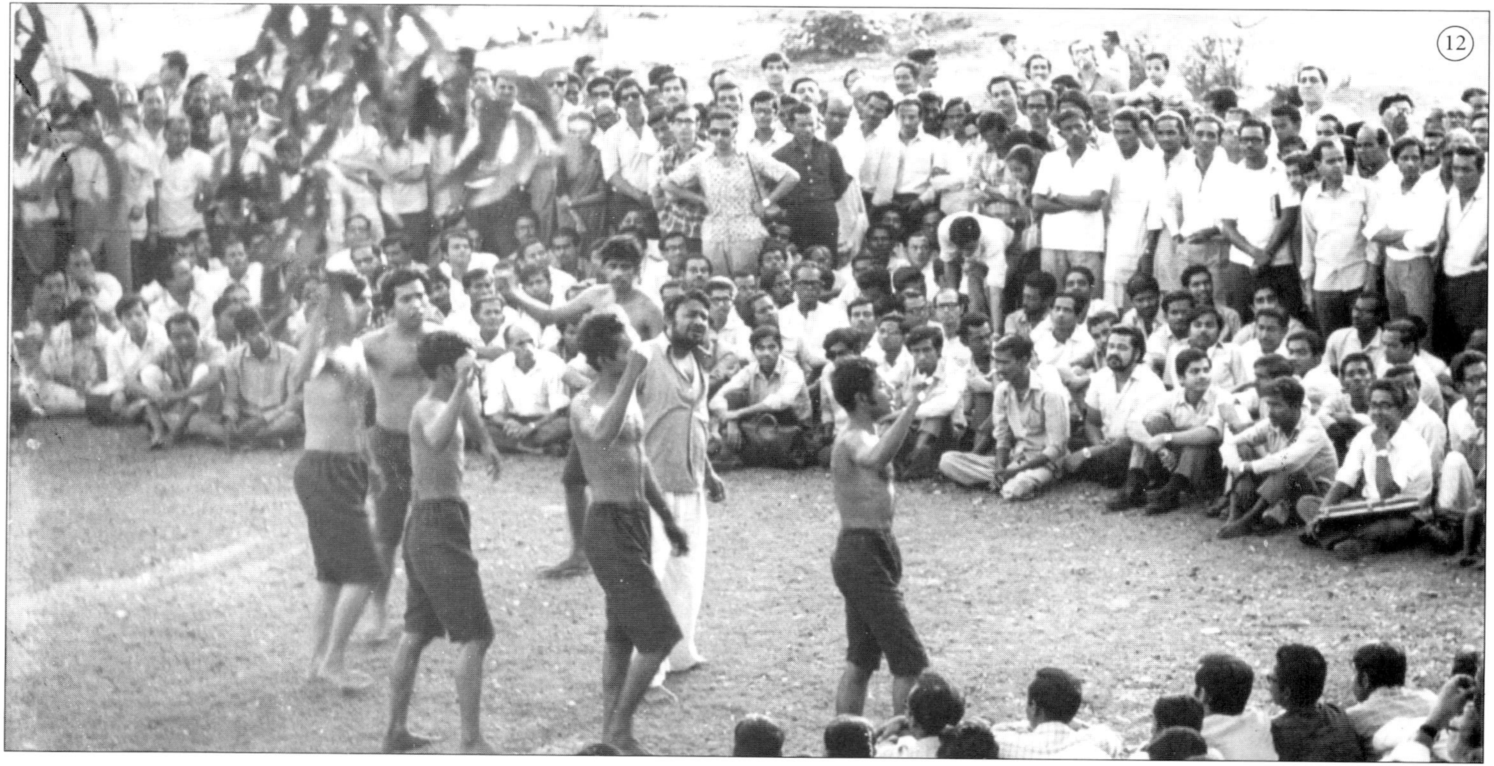

Spartacus

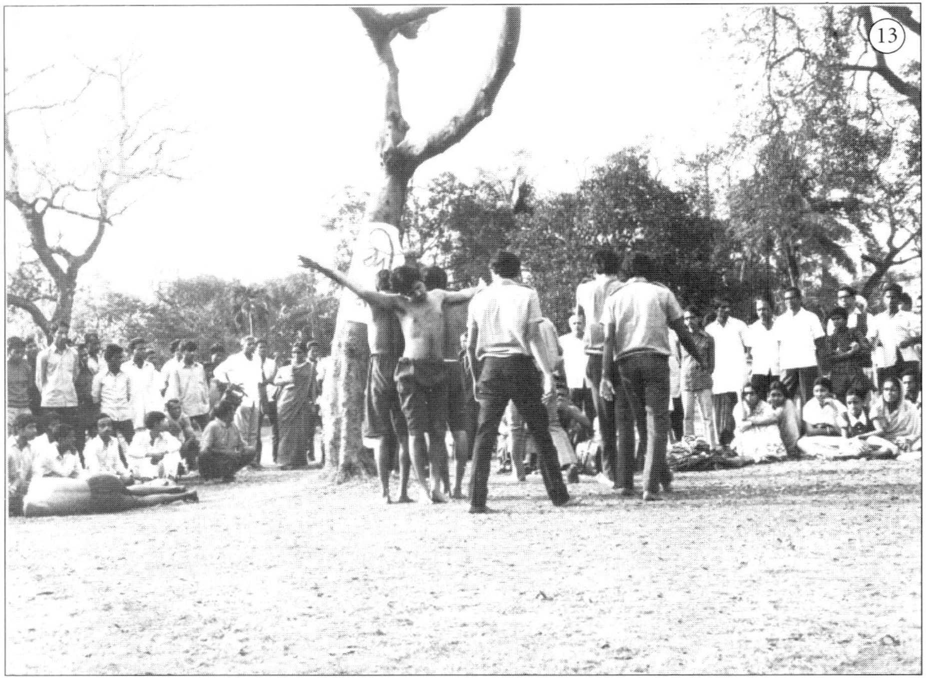

Spartacus

11, **12** and **13**. Curzon Park: When Satabdi became a regular at Curzon (or Surendranath) Park, the intimacy of the closed space was replaced by the ability to communicate with a much larger and mixed crowd. As these stills indicate, the audience was a combination of dedicated theatregoers and a variety of passers-by from different socio-economic strata who were drawn towards the drama unfolding before them. *Courtesy*: Satabdi

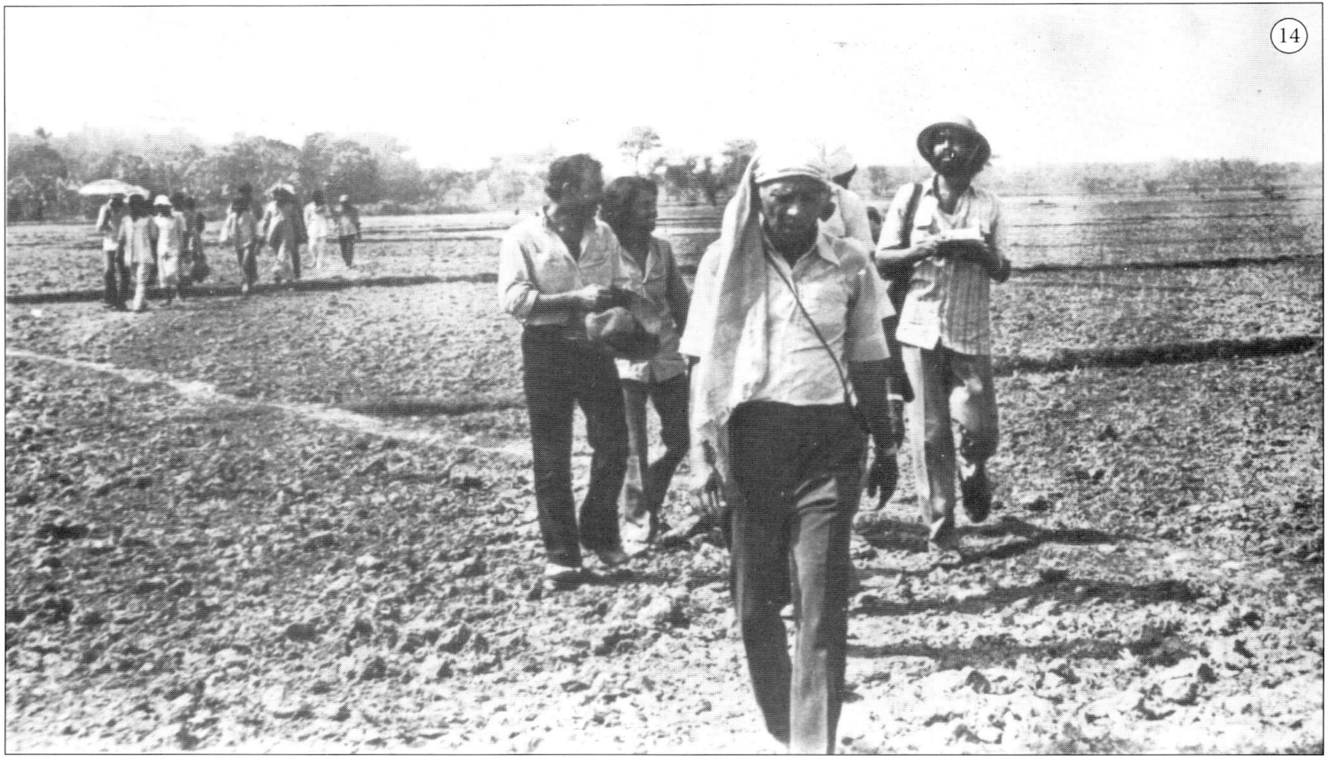

On the Way

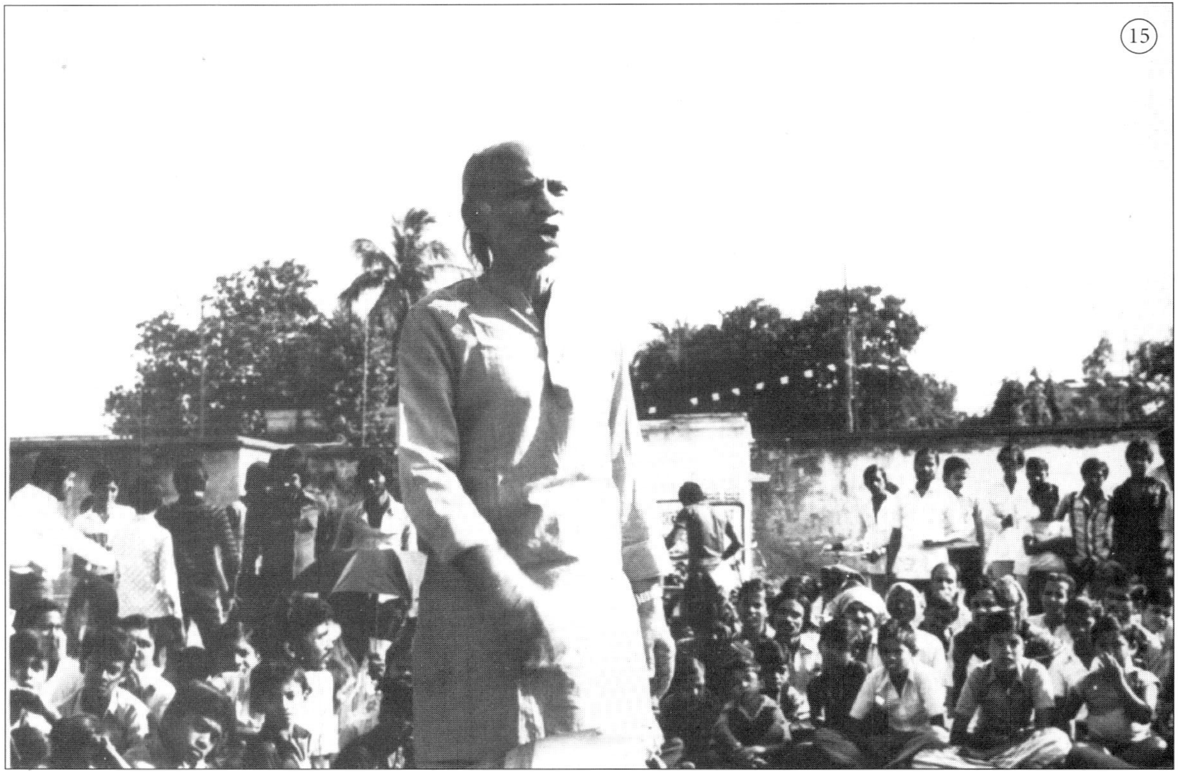

Michhil

16

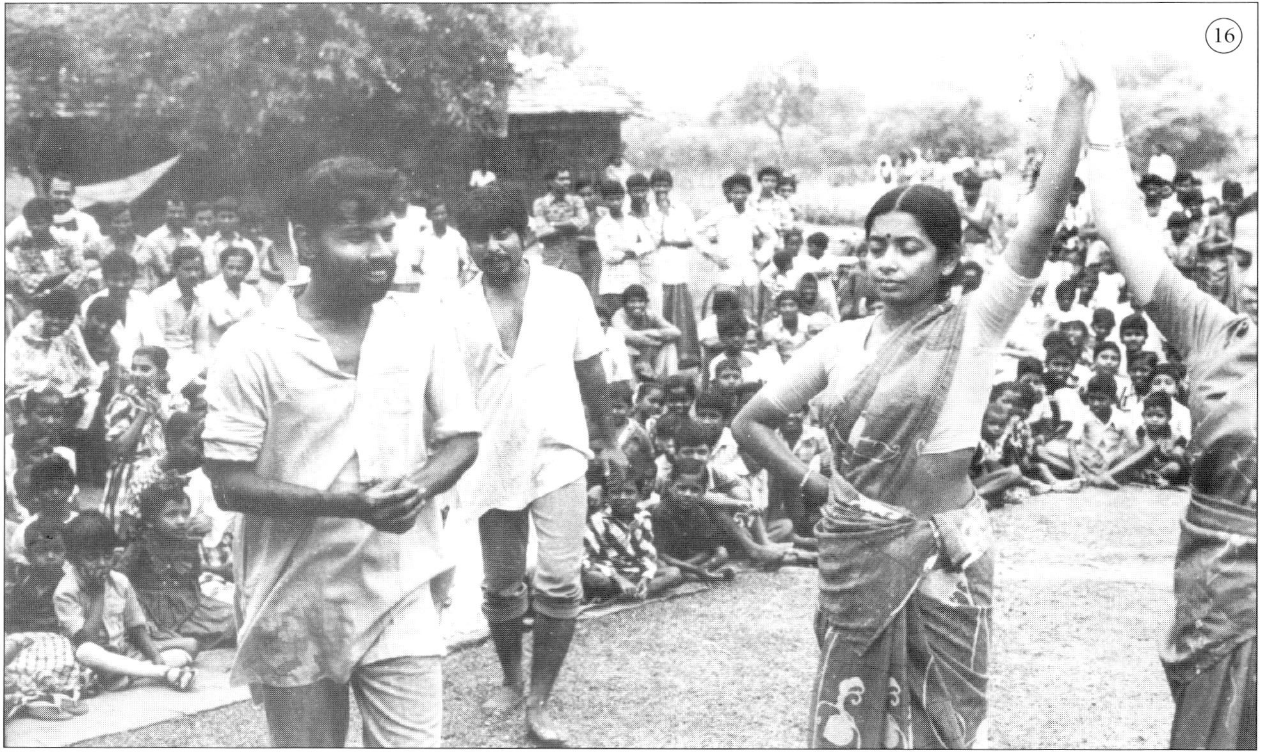

Hattamalar Oparey

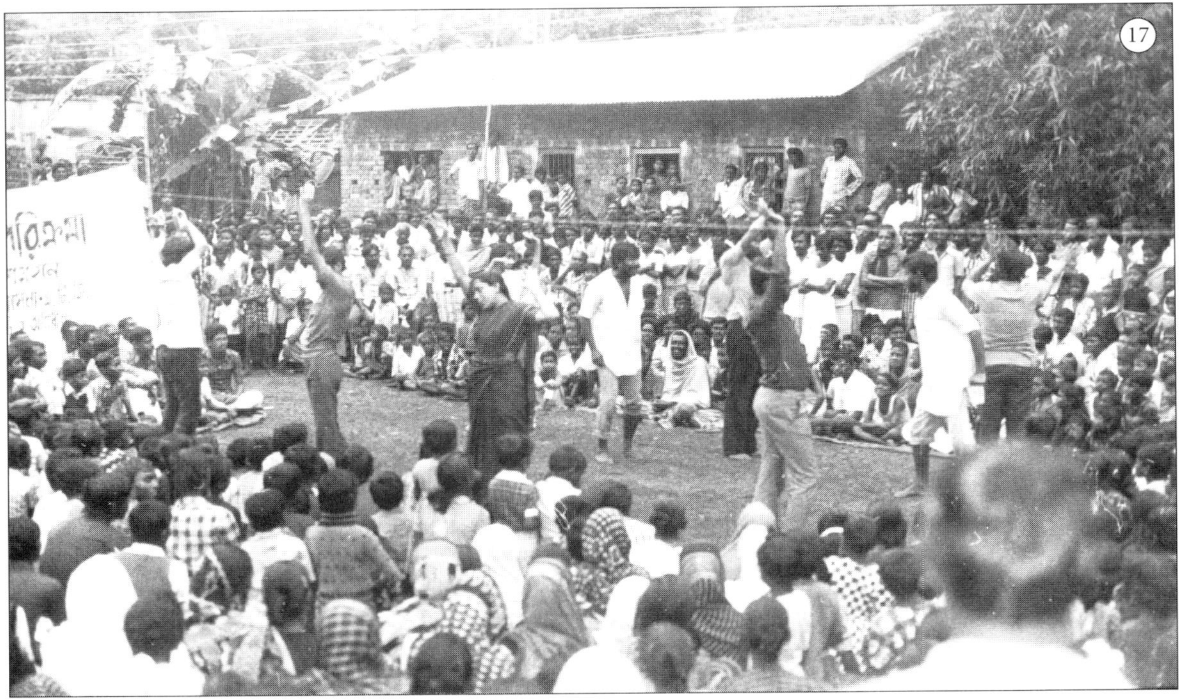

Hattamalar Oparey

14, **15**, **16** and **17**. *Gram Parikrama*: Badal Sircar's *Gram Parikrama* was an excursion to the interiors, during which the group went from village to village, stopping to perform and interact with the audience before moving on. This experience convinced him that the so-called 'uneducated' rural audience was as capable of following complex and layered texts as an urban audience, particularly since the themes and issues were of direct relevance to their lives. *Courtesy*: Satabdi

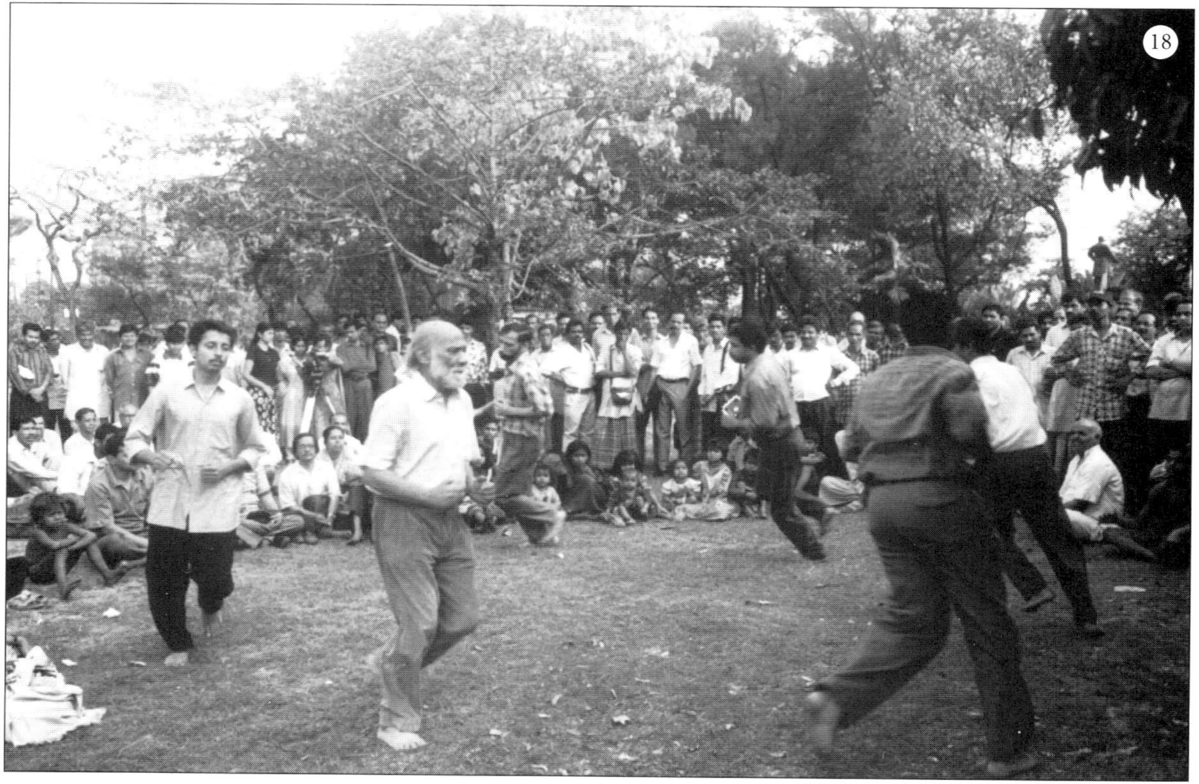

Michhil

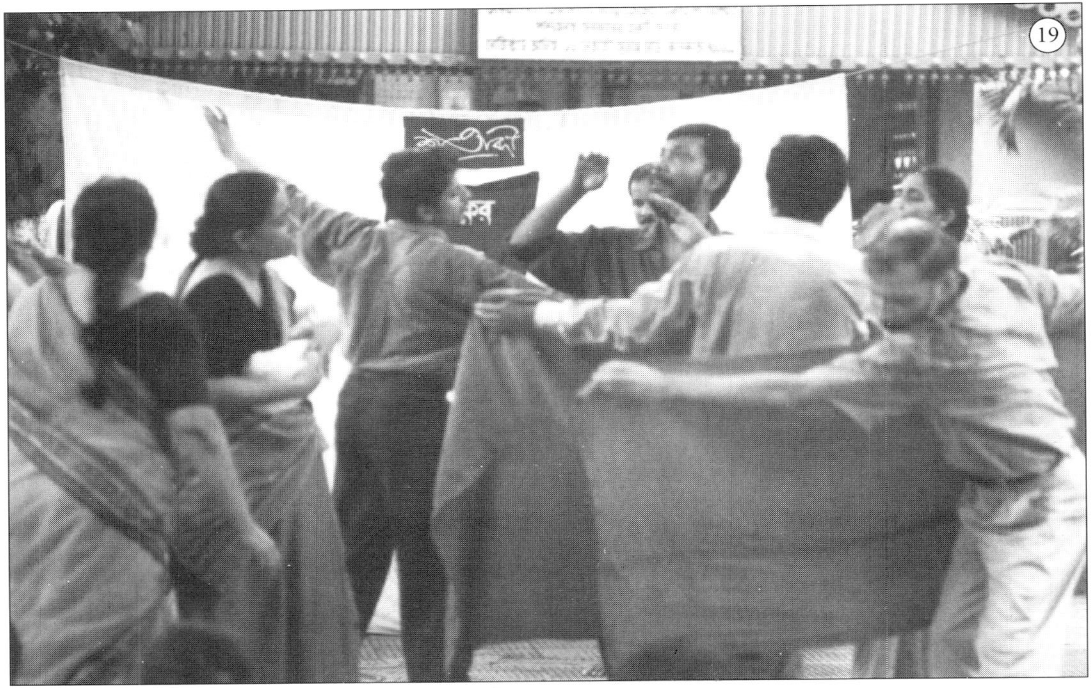

Naditey

18 and **19**. Later years: From the late 1990s till the 2000s, Badal Sircar continued to perform with Satabdi without much change in material or approach. In 18, a performance of *Michhil* in Curzon Park, dated 1999, features a much older Badal-da and in 19 (*Naditey*), in the Nandan complex, which continues to be a public space for weekend performances for groups such as Satabdi. *Courtesy*: Satabdi

Badal Sircar
1/A, PEARY ROW, CALCUTTA-6
PHONE: 55-2350

Dated 28.11.69.

Dear Rajindra Nathji –

Your letter reached my home some time back, but as I was in Trivandrum at that time, I saw it only the other day. I therefore plead guilty of being only ~~f~~ four days late, which you must admit is quite unusual as per my standards.

I'm glad you liked the "Thirtieth Century". Mr. Bajaj talked about translating it when I was in Delhi, but he didn't follow it up by any letter. He also promised to send me royalties in respect of Evam Indrajit which they produced. Their continued silence led me to believe that they are no longer interested. I therefore got into an agreement with Dr. Mrs. Prativa Agarwal giving her the first option of translating all my plays in Hindi. So Bajaj will have to take up the matter with Prativaji immediately. Her new address is:

233/5, Acharya J.C. Bose Road
Calcutta-20.

The same applies to the question of translating "Saranatha" in Hindi. You should write to Prativaji.

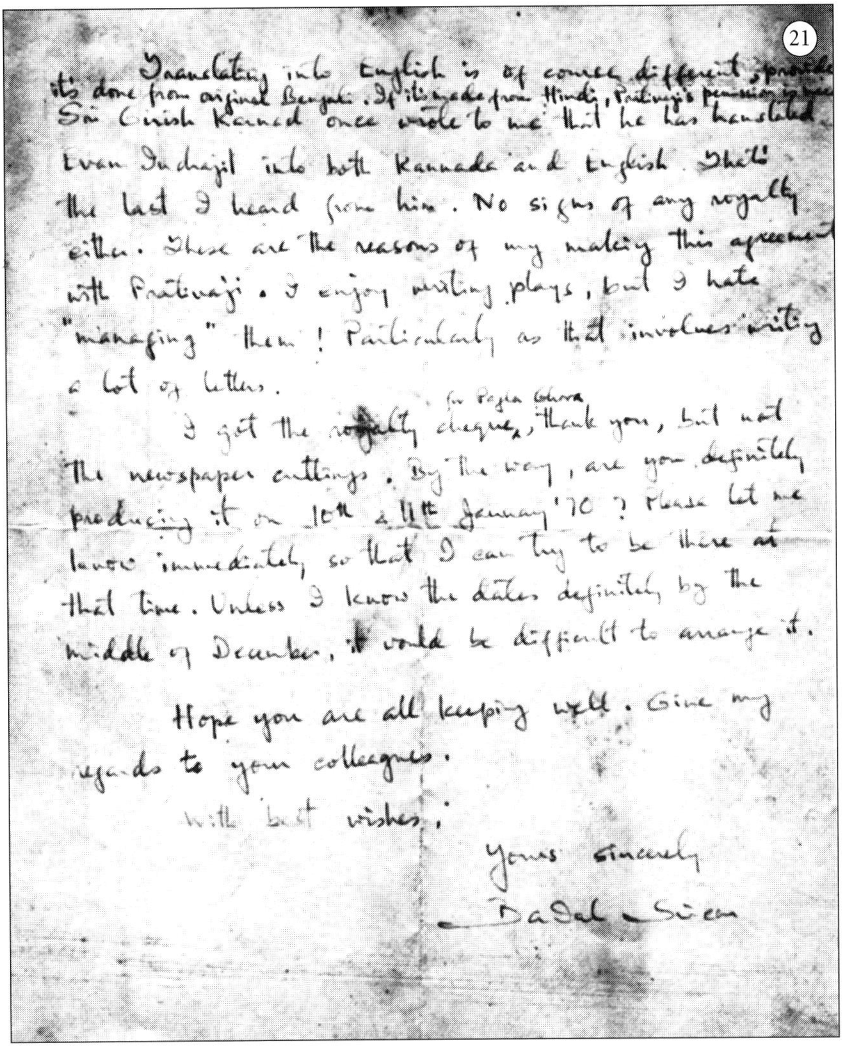

21

Translating into English is of course different, provided it's done from original Bengali. If it is made from Hindi, Pratibhaji's permission is needed. Sri Girish Karnad once wrote to me that he has translated Evam Indrajit into both Kannada and English. That's the last I heard from him. No signs of any royalty either. These are the reasons of my making this agreement with Pratibhaji. I enjoy writing plays, but I hate "managing" them! Particularly as that involves writing a lot of letters.

I got the royalty cheque, for Pagla Ghora, thank you, but not the newspaper cuttings. By the way, are you definitely producing it on 10th & 11th January '70? Please let me know immediately, so that I can try to be there at that time. Unless I know the dates definitely by the middle of December, it would be difficult to arrange it.

Hope you are all keeping well. Give my regards to your colleagues.

With best wishes,

Yours sincerely

Badal Sircar

20 and **21**. This letter was written during Badal-da's proscenium days. His opinion of play texts, translations and royalties indicates that he was very much part of the national theatre and playwriting scene at the time, with his texts being both produced and published in several languages by leading theatre personalities. His move away from the proscenium and the formal play script was from this position of recognition and respect. *Courtesy*: Natya Shodh Sansthan

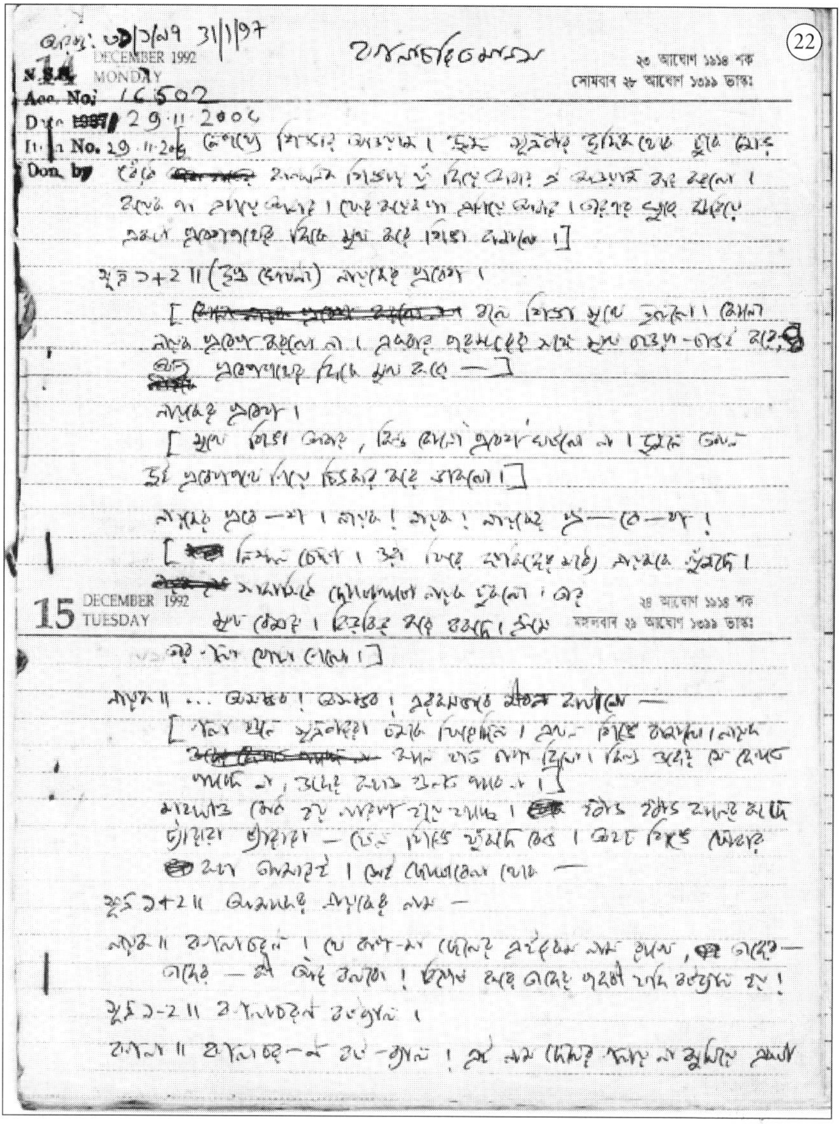

22. From the Natya Shodh Sansthan archives, a manuscript of *Bagalacharitmanas*, one of Badal-da's late plays produced in 1998 by Pathasena. *Courtesy*: Natya Shodh Sansthan

engage with it, bring their own personal experience to the interpretation of it and improvise sequences to enhance it. This was an approach inspired by his American study tour and the experimental theatre he observed there. Now the group takes this a step further. Each of them is invited to contribute experiences and ideas to jointly create a text. Badal-da's role morphs into that of eventually putting these contributions into a theatrically effective structure, but he is in no way the sole playwright of these texts, nor does he claim to be. In fact he says, of *Bhoma*, that, 'We took about a year to prepare the play and the workshop process was the basis of its preparation.'[1] In the preface to the play, he specifically mentions, 'When the pieces were being put together as a play, there were others in Satabdi who had also created images out of their experience (and feelings) which have been incorporated in the play. In that way, *Bhoma* is not entirely my creation.'[2]

Third Theatre practitioners I have spoken to, such as Sumit Biswas of Pathasena and Bisakha (Meera) Ray, earlier of Satabdi, made a point of mentioning that Badal-da never referred to himself as an 'artist'; rather, he always said he was a theatre 'worker' (*karmi*). In other words, he preferred not to privilege his role in the collective creative process. This was an expression of his politics, and no doubt underlies his discomfort with his earlier playwriting laurels and his expressed rejection of his earlier plays, all too bourgeois for him at this phase of his life.

However sincere his claim may be, one cannot gainsay that his inputs as an extremely talented playwright with a strong sense of what makes effective theatre, an innate feel for dialogue, a sardonic sense of humour that lifts scathing denunciations from rant and polemic to a more intellectual plane, and his uncanny ability to weave poetry, myth and beauty into otherwise savage or banal situations, have contributed to making these devised plays powerful and lasting works to which groups continue to return even after his demise.

Bhoma (1976) came out of this mode of play making. In her introduction to *Three Plays*, Ella Dutta writes:

> Describing the process of writing *Bhoma*, Sircar says that it was quite unique and not applicable to any of his other plays. It was not written at a stretch, nor was it written as a play. Different scenes—each centred around a particular theme, without any particular character or structure in mind—were written down over a period of three years. 'The different scenes were born

[1] Sircar, 'Voyages in the Theatre', *On Theatre*, p. 118.
[2] Preface to 'Bhoma' in Sircar, *Three Plays*, p. 57.

> of our reactions to different impulses that had come from our readings, our observations, our experiences at the time,' Sircar says. Then Sircar read out the scenes to some of Satabdi's members and found that they too had written down similar scenes. For example, Meera,[3] who did family planning work in the worst slums of Topsia, Tangra, had acquired an intimate picture of the problems of these people which she had then written down and described.[4]

Another major contribution to the script came from Tushar Kanjilal, headmaster of the Rangbelia Village School in the Sunderbans:

> I had heard Bhoma's story from him.... Seeing, feeling and learning about our surroundings shock us, hurt us, anger us—these have come out in disjointed, dramatic pictures. Bhoma's picture was then part of these pieces. But when those pictures were strung together into a play, then somehow it was Bhoma's image which started to become the link; in the end, the play could not be called anything but *Bhoma*.[5]

Badal-da describes the process of creating this play:

> *Bhoma* is a composition of many detached scenes that were written over a three-year period. Whenever I reacted strongly to a fact or a phenomenon I came across—in reality, in the newspapers, in a book, in a discussion—something emerged in the shape of a scene in a play. That is to say, there were speeches for actors but nothing on the left side of the colon to indicate the identity of the speaker of the lines. There were no dialogues as such, but connected speeches projected straight to the audience. When I wrote those scenes, I had no idea that I was creating a play—it was more like writing a diary. When we were searching for a new play sometime in early 1975, these scenes were read out to the group members. It was decided that everybody would henceforth write down the facts or phenomena he or she reacts to together with the reactions. Such a notebook we called the 'book of feelings'. The group began to deal with the scenes I wrote and with the contributions they made, and the play *Bhoma* gradually emerged.
>
> .... Bhoma gradually became more and more important in the play, to the extent of lending it his name, but he did not appear as a character in the play, nor did his life-story figure in it. The play speaks not of Bhoma but of the Bhomas who constitute a phenomenon, a social reality. In the collection of

[3] Dr Bisakha Ray, who became Badal Sircar's second wife and who was at that time an active member of Satabdi.

[4] Ella Dutta, Introduction to Sircar, *Three Plays*, p. 6

[5] Preface to 'Bhoma' in Sircar, *Three Plays*, p. 57.

loose and detached scenes dealing with subjects as diverse as the problem of ground water, the hazards of nuclear tests, the criminal Metro Rail project of Calcutta, dollar aid and so on, the connecting link is a city man in search of Bhoma, the only person who is capable of clearing the jungle of poison trees that our society has become, to make it habitable.[6]

The cast consists of six actors, identically dressed, with assigned numbers rather than names. A supporting chorus of four or five helps supply sound and melodies. There is no linear narrative and no characters in the accepted sense of the term. Actors speak directly to the audience using physical acting, words and sounds. Topu, one of the oldest members of Satabdi, in a recent interview reaffirmed this when she recalled how they all contributed news items and other ideas to *Bhoma*; she recounts how they discussed and decided that the point of view from which these events are being seen would be that of an ordinary middle-class person just like themselves.[7]

Bhoma, the poor villager from Rangabelia village in the Sunderbans is never seen in the course of the play, but is present throughout, as the cause, the motivation, the victim and the symbol. 'Unless Bhoma lives, unless Bhoma sustains us, I can't live, nobody lives!'[8] Who is Bhoma? is the question that is asked over and over again through the play. We are told that Bhoma is:

the jungle. Bhoma is the cornfield. Bhoma is the village. Three quarters of India's population live in villages. Millions and millions of Bhomas. In the cities we live on the blood of Bhomas ... if the Bhomas had rice, we would not have anything left to eat. Bhoma's blood, red blood, blossoms into white jasmines of rice on our plates.[9]

We are told,

When Bhoma was 16 he came to clear the forest. Father, mother and two kid brothers. The jungle of the Sunderbans ... when Bhoma was 20, the tree that he could fell alone in three hours two men couldn't working a whole day through ... Bhoma's mother died of snakebite. His father was dragged away by a crocodile before his very eyes. The younger brother ... died of diarrhoea.[10]

[6] Sircar, 'Voyages in the Theatre', *On Theatre*, pp. 117–18.
[7] Topu (Shanta Dutta) joined Satabdi in end 1973. Interview with the author, 6 July 2014.
[8] Sircar, 'Bhoma', *Three Plays*, p. 82.
[9] Ibid., pp. 94–95.
[10] Ibid., pp. 99–100.

Bhoma is the ugly story of the degradation of India's rural populace, reduced to destitution and hunger, desperately seeking to survive. Bhoma is the conscience of the privileged urban Indian. The play relentlessly juxtaposes the struggle for survival in the rural areas with the self-indulgently trivial concerns of a middle-class city dweller who is irritated or resentful when this other reality intrudes into his or her comfortable daily rhythm. While urban India spouts statistics and platitudes of prosperity and growth, the Sunderbans' villagers battle to save precious land from being swallowed by the waters. There is a caustic black humour to the interspersing of sequences which underscores the shallowness of the middle-class mindset, preoccupied with climbing the social ladder and having a good time watching films, planning picnics and shopping for jewellery. The atom bomb, that leitmotif of Badal-da's theatre, makes its appearance as well: 'Ladies and gentlemen, it's here at last, the pride of India, the atom bomb...another feather in India's cap.'[11] There is the powerful archetypal imagery of red blood throughout. 'Man's blood is cold' (*thanda*) is the refrain that flows through the play.

For Rustom Bharucha, *Bhoma* is a powerful political play:

> *Bhoma* confronts the dichotomy between urban and rural life in India... When Sircar came in contact with the villagers of the Sunderbans, he was shocked by the dehumanized conditions of their life. But more than shocked, he was enraged by the fact that the urban community of West Bengal (despite its own problems of transportation, generation of electricity, distribution of food) could be so totally indifferent to the impoverishment of the villagers in the Sunderbans. Anger is the driving force of *Bhoma*—a relentless, though rigorously controlled anger directed against the well-fed, easy-going bourgeoisie of Calcutta. It is this anger that makes the play more than a lament for Bhoma himself as an individual or for the thousands of Bhomas who continue to survive from day to day in Bengal.[12]

In his study of political theatre in Calcutta during the 1970s and early 1980s, Bharucha provides a valuable comparison between this play and other plays on similar themes. Characters like Bhoma have provided Bengali theatre with plenty of material and been much written about, so much so that the figure of the 'oppressed peasant' is as ubiquitous as that of the maharaja or politician. The actors playing such peasant characters always try hard to

[11] Sircar, 'Bhoma' in Badal Sircar, *Three Plays*, p. 69.

[12] Bharucha, *Rehearsals of Revolution*, p. 174.

identify with their suffering and state of exploitation. However, this causes a problem:

> My own experience as a spectator of this 'identification process' has been somewhat disturbing. It seems to me that the more an actor from the city attempts to give an authentic performance of a villager, the more distant he seems from the realities of rural life. The more accomplished his mastery of rural dialects, the more destitute his appearance, the more tattered his costume, the more remote he seems from the life of the oppressed peasant. The distance between a *bhadralok* actor and the oppression of the villagers he attempts to depict is often an embarrassment.[13]

Compared to this, he says, Satabdi actors, though no doubt as middle-class and bhadralok as their counterparts, are far more successful in their dramatisation of the life of the downtrodden peasant precisely because this attempt at identification is missing. There is a matter-of-fact, spare, down-to-earth 'impersonal' mode of acting favoured by the group that is much more powerful than sentimental gestures or melodrama.[14] He concludes by stating: 'I can think of no other play in the Bengali theater that makes an audience question its relation to the oppressed people with such emotional power and clarity.'[15]

The play abounds with sharp observations and telling juxtapositions that create a layered, complex analysis of contemporary socio-economic and political issues relating to development, progress and the rural–urban divide which is much more detailed and informed than we see, for example, in the earlier *Spartacus*. Politically, this is a far more evolved text. Nor has it sacrificed as a consequence its emotional appeal—its sheer theatricality and visual imagery ensures that.

Badal-da's comments throw light on the political moorings of this play:

> *Bhoma* was the first product of my direct personal experience of the reality of rural India. The first few lines of *Bhoma* explain why and how it came to be written. *Bhoma* is written for people like us, aimed at our kind of people, not meant to be performed in the villages. But when we took *Bhoma* to the village audiences, they found a point of identification in the issues it touched.[16]

[13] Bharucha, *Rehearsals of Revolution*, p. 175.

[14] Ibid.

[15] For a detailed and evocative description of *Bhoma*, see Bharucha, *Rehearsals of Revolution*, pp. 174–81.

[16] Quoted in Badal Utsav pamphlet, p. 9.

To Badal-da's great satisfaction, the very first performance of *Bhoma* could be held in Rangabelia village, Bhoma's home where, according to Rustom Bharucha, Bhoma's younger brother, and the only surviving member of his family, was present in the audience. Although no documentation of the performance exists, Badal-da told him that the villagers had no problem following the play although the form and style was so different from the *jatra*, the form of theatre they were most familiar with; in fact they watched with deep concentration.[17] After three performances in the rural areas, *Bhoma* was finally performed in Calcutta.

At this time, the political situation was tense. The Emergency was in place.[18] Satabdi had no indoor performance space. When the Academy of Fine Arts tenancy, which was for two years, came up for renewal, there was an increase in the rent amount. Satabdi had decided to let the space go and do only open-air performances at Curzon Park, a park opposite the Academy and other public spaces in and around the city. Saturday performances at these venues continued till the state of Emergency was declared, whereupon they were banned by the police.

Satabdi was then in the process of preparing *Bhoma*. They realised that at such a time, a political play like *Bhoma* would never be allowed. So, for the Calcutta shows, they hired a lecture hall and organised 'underground' shows of the play:

> In this hall, we could not make use of our special seats of different levels nor the lighting system we had at *Anganmancha*. There was no publicity whatsoever through newspapers, posters or leaflets. We approached our friends and well-wishers and accepted a donation of ₹1 only to cover costs.[19]

This was for six consecutive Sunday evenings. The hall could accommodate about 100 people, and so great was the support that once word got around, all the shows were totally booked. Badal-da says, 'We know that the response of our audience was not principally due to the play or the production, but because of such a play being presented in that way during such a time. In a way the response could clearly be termed a political action on the part of

[17] Bharucha, *Rehearsals of Revolution*, p. 181.

[18] The Emergency refers to a 21-month period from 25 June 1975 to 21 March 1977 when Prime Minister Indira Gandhi unilaterally had a state of emergency declared across the country, allowing elections to be suspended and civil liberties to be curbed.

[19] Sircar, 'The Third Theatre,' *On Theatre*, p. 51.

the audience.'[20] Although their request for an extension was denied, they managed to find another space, the Theosophical Society Hall near Calcutta University. Badal-da describes it as: 'An old building in the congested College Square area occupied by the Theosophical Society of India for more than ninety years. The lecture hall on the second story, 58 feet long and 24 feet wide, with its old dusty cupboards full of books on Theosophy and faded oil paintings of potentates of Theosophy given to Satabdi on hire every Friday after much persuasion.'[21] Here, their Anganmancha performances, which, during the period of the Emergency could be deemed underground shows, were held every Friday till the Emergency was lifted. In addition to *Bhoma,* they performed *Spartacus, Michhil, Tringsha Shatabdi* and *Prastab*. These Friday shows continued till 1986, and featured other theatre groups who believed in free theatre, constituting a minor theatre movement. A nominal donation of ₹1 was requested, but entry was never denied if someone was unable to pay.

Another devised work like *Bhoma* was *Basi Khabar*. Again, this was the culmination of a year's collective workshop, research and creative improvisation. Badal-da describes how this particular journey began:

> June 1978. The beginning of the third year of our weekly performances at the Theosophical Society Hall. There was no play at hand, so we were having workshops relating to various themes but not really hoping that something would come out of the workshops.
>
> I sometimes indulge in a hobby of making paper collages. At that time I made a collage depicting different aspects of Man: Man as genius, as cruel, as stupid, as callous, and so on . . . somebody suggested that we do workshops on the theme of that collage and that we collect materials that showed any of those aspects of the human being. In other words, we decided to revive our 'book of feelings'.
>
> So we found ourselves doing workshops relating to the cruel absurdities we live in. Enormous wealth and immeasurable poverty existing side by side. A devastating flood ruining hundreds of thousands in the villages, and a huge crowd of fans gathering to see the film stars raising donations in Calcutta for flood-relief. Construction of the underground railway in Calcutta, and 90 per cent of the underground water remaining untapped, rendering most of the arable land mono-crop ... Riots and war. Democracy and

[20] Sircar, 'Voyages in the Theatre,' *On Theatre*, p. 120.

[21] Sircar, 'A Letter from Badal Sircar'. 23 November 1981.' *The Drama Review*, Vol. 26, No. 2, Summer 1982, p. 51.

police brutality. The stupidity of man, the cruelty of man, the achievements of man, the indifference and callousness of man—not just in this country but in the whole world.

But what about the courage of man?—somebody asked. What about his protest, his fighting spirit? What about Spartacus, about whose struggles we made a play six years ago? What about all those who dream of and die for the creation of a new and better society? That aspect was not in the collage. So we decided to include it and, very soon, that became the most important aspect.[22]

Discussions and workshops were held, and a process of questioning started. They discussed issues of structure and form. If struggle was to be the central theme, should they show protest and rebellion in general terms, or should they base it on a specific instance from history, like the slave revolt led by Spartacus, which became a way of talking about exploitation, repression and revolt down the ages? It was decided, after discussion, to accept the suggestion that one specific revolt, the Santhal rebellion of the nineteenth century, be selected as the particular focus. Research on this historical subject began. Badal-da comments:

The aboriginals. Always subjected to the worst kind of exploitation, oppression and injustice. Pushed beyond limits, they have often burst out in spontaneous and unorganized revolts; revolts that were invariably suppressed in the most inhuman way. These accounts did not find any place in the history textbooks. We had to depend on the work of some rare researchers and some obscure sources. I shall not try to describe here the inhuman extortion, oppression and torture that the Santhals and other aboriginals were subjected to by the British colonists and their Indian collaborators and stooges—usurers, traders, native princes and landlords, tax-collectors, petty officials and policemen. One can imagine the extremes to which they were pushed when one finds that 50,000 hungry, half-naked Santhals of the region at the borders of Bengal, Bihar and Orissa took up their primitive arms—spears, axes, bows and arrows—fought against the trained, well-fed troops equipped with guns and cannons, horses and elephants, and liberated district after district. And they did not give up until 25,000 were killed, not counting the women, children and old folks in the villages razed to the ground, until after nine months of heroic struggle that shook the very base of the British imperialist rule in eastern India.[23]

[22] Sircar, 'Voyages in the Theatre,' *On Theatre*, pp. 125–26.
[23] Ibid., pp. 126–27.

Meanwhile, workshops around the general subject of revolts continued. Contemporary relevance was something that had to be kept in mind. The point of view from which the play is to be presented had to be decided:

> But should we make a play on the Santhal revolt of 1855–56, taking roles of Santhals and the oppressors? The answer was—no. Then what? We shall show it from our point of view, that is, the point of view of a contemporary person belonging to the city-bred, educated, middle-class community. Why? Because we want to link that revolt to present-day reality. And how? In the same way that our own experiences in life do.[24]

Badal-da may reject middle-class values as too bourgeois, hypocritical and limited, but he locates his theatre firmly in the urban middle-class milieu. He speaks to his own class, whose strengths, world view and weaknesses he knows perceptively and intimately. His rural audience is a delight, a surprise and a thrill, particularly when they respond positively to his plays, but it is the middle-class who remains his chief concern. His project is to challenge them, provoke them, conscientise them, move them. He strives to open their minds, make them think, feel, react, act and make choices. And he knows their mindset well because they are him and he is them:

> I accept the present conditions of middle-class life—education, examinations, jobs, promotions—all in a fiercely competitive situation. I also read the newspapers, and some accounts of cruelty and brutality, injustice and blind prejudice, ruthless exploitation and senseless killing, disturb my breakfast. But the defence mechanism I have within me makes me forget those accounts within hours, and I go on with my usual way of life. But maybe a disturbing element remains at the back of my mind, insignificant at first, but growing gradually, clashing with my day-to-day activities, with my self-centred aims and goals. At a certain point in my life, I happen to come across the history of the Santhal revolt, and that disturbing element within me gets strengthened, threatening to affect my so-called 'sane' choices. That is the way we should link the Santhal revolt of the last century to our present-day experiences, through the experience of a protagonist of our kind.[25]

The discussions around form and structure continue. The concept of a protagonist, for example: Who or what is he? He is certainly not the hero of the play, in the accepted meaning of that word. He could be one of the

[24] Sircar, 'Voyages in the Theatre,' *On Theatre*, p. 127.
[25] Ibid.

chorus, but move in and out. It is decided not to create roles, but to project the theme directly as was done in *Bhoma*. Badal-da describes how the central figure of the Dead or Slain man came about:

> At one point in the process, the suggestion of having a dead man or, rather, a slain man, was put forth and was accepted. His whole body would be dressed in white and his head and face, including his eyes, would be covered with bandages, and he would not utter a single word. He would enter and exit from time to time, all the others would remain in the arena throughout. The fact that he has been killed should be established right at the beginning, and we decided on the way to do it. The killed man was to be the visual representation of that disturbing element in the mind of the protagonist, thus he would be generally invisible to all except him, or the others would treat him as an ordinary person.
>
> As we went on working, the role of the non-speaking dead man acquired more and more importance, and ultimately it ... was decided that the dead man would hold his palm in front of the eyes of the protagonist at reading distance, and the latter would follow the hand, reading out, like a hypnotized person. The right palm would be used for contemporary newspaper items, and the left for the accounts of the Santhal revolt. Once this was established, we could easily use other devices to project the lines related to both the periods. And towards the end of the play, the dead man would go on holding his palms alternately in front of the eyes of the spectators one by one, when the two periods would be finally linked up.[26]

Like the other documentary dramas, *Bhoma* and *Tringsha Satabdi*, this play too presents the audience with a heavy dose of information and reality. This ranges from Santhal history to more contemporary items about the government, corporates, sports, cinema and even the weather. There is one witty sequence where a courting couple has a whole conversation in advertisement slogans and jingles. Meanwhile, the Santhal story ominously gathers momentum as the record of injustice and exploitation grows. Bengal cultural icons Rammohun, Bankimchandra, Vivekananda, spout arguments in support of British rule. News items about bonded labour, landless agricultural labourers, floods and flood relief, infant mortality, refugees and political prisoners are intercut with the increasingly intense narrative of the Santhal rebellion. Finally, like quick cuts in cinema, as the Dead Man holds up his palm before the eyes of the audience, there is a barrage of information about current-day atrocities against the poor juxtaposed with comments on the plight of the

[26] Sircar, 'Voyages in the Theatre', *On Theatre*, p. 128.

Santhals. The play closes with an actor directly questioning the audience: 'Death, blood and fear rule over this land. Everyone knows what happens and what will happen behind the prison walls. Why don't you scream? Is it still not time? Not time?'[27] Essentially, the question has not changed, from *Tringsha Satabdi* to *Basi Khabar*. What will it take for the middle class to join the protest against an unjust social system?

Basi Khabar was first performed by Satabdi on 6 July 1979 at Theosophical Society Hall.[28] A review dated 12 July tells us how this play was received:

> ...
> [T]he group acts out in a violent, virile, poetic choreography the experience of the tribe from its early way of life to its encounter with the British...In an almost breathtaking transition the group becomes a forest with all the forest sounds, and then the secret movements of men within the forests. The Shatabdi style that depends on the group's ability to create a locale with its physical properties and sounds and the enactment of a dramatic situation within that setting has now reached a richness that can tempt a director to play with it for its own sake.[29]

For Rustom Bharucha, however, this is not a successful production:

> Part of the problem with this production was its overtly abstract treatment of historical material.... Apart from obfuscating history, the production was also indiscriminately physicalized. There was no coherence in the transitions of the mise en scene. Many of the sections, which seemed to be deliberately tacked onto the production, were sensational in effect.... There were too many conflicting perspectives on the subject matter, which itself was never clarified in the course of the production. After a point, it seemed as if the Sanyasi rebellion was incidental to the diverse action of the play.[30]

It is significant that both these 'devised theatre' works deal with rural reality and emphasise the link between rural destitution and urban indifference. They re-introduce the documentary element which we first see in *Tringsha Satabdi*, barraging the audience with statistics, hard facts and data. In these plays, the metropolitan centre, Calcutta, dreams of its new bridges and underground railway, its signposts of development and progress, while

[27] Sircar, 'Stale News', *Three Plays*, p. 163.
[28] Ibid., p. 114.
[29] A Drama Critic, 'Badal Sircar's Latest Experiment', Hindustan Standard, 12 July 1979.
[30] Bharucha, *Rehearsals of Revolution*, pp. 187–88.

the rural poor struggles for mere subsistence levels of food and water. Badal-da's plays, as we have seen over the years, have increasingly dealt with issues of violence and injustice, of the nuclear threat holding us to ransom, of State terror; but these two texts bring in a new dimension, that of rural India's harsh reality. The cause is not far to find: devised theatre will inevitably reflect the interest and concerns of the participating collaborators, and the political convictions of the young Satabdi members, their dedication to cultural action as part of their left ideology, the Naxalite belief that revolution will begin in the rural areas, and that the village and the city must be linked, informs these two works in particular.

Before we move on from the devised theatre, let us spend a few moments thinking about Badal-da's journey from 'lauded playwright', praised as one of the four new 'modern' playwrights of contemporary India, to 'theatre worker' who prefers to be part of a collective making plays with no formal authorship. Tripurari Sharma, veteran director and women's activist says, 'It takes a lot of courage for someone who has established himself as a playwright to then say it's not about playwriting, it's about the actor, it's about energy, it's about communication.'[31] Today, when the issue of the playwright's text as opposed to either the director's text, or devised theatre, is once again being discussed, it is interesting to think about someone who walks away from his own plays in favour of a collaborative process.

Of *Basi Khabar,* Badal-da says:

> This play has been made by the group collectively. At a later stage, I made a script on the basis of the materials collected and the decisions made. Whatever I contributed, I did during the process like any other member, and not when I made the script. As such, I am not the author of the play, at best the editor.[32]

However, it is hard, when one looks back over the body of Badal-da's plays, both proscenium and non-proscenium, to ignore certain stylistic continuities. The use of satire, juxtapositions creating a montage effect, fluid movement between scenes without formal divisions, the presence of a powerful symbolic motif or image which lifts a play from the level of agitprop or propaganda to a more complex text, the introduction of 'found material' like commercial advertisements, newspaper headlines, reports, popular songs—these are all common elements of his playwriting. We recognise them even in the devised or more collaboratively constructed works. His hand is

[31] Tripurari Sharma, interview with the author, New Delhi, 30 May 2014.
[32] Sircar, 'Voyages in the Theatre,' *On Theatre*, p. 129.

clearly in evidence, a sort of signature style. So, although one respects the ideological stance that leads him to disavow any authorship, one reserves the right to assume that his contribution has been a major factor in the overall work. At the very least, he is responsible for the establishment of a recognisable 'Satabdi aesthetic'. And one can only honour and admire a personality who turns his back on a readymade reputation and refuses to rest on his laurels, preferring the risk and challenge of new experiments.

CHAPTER ELEVEN

THE WORKSHOP WAY

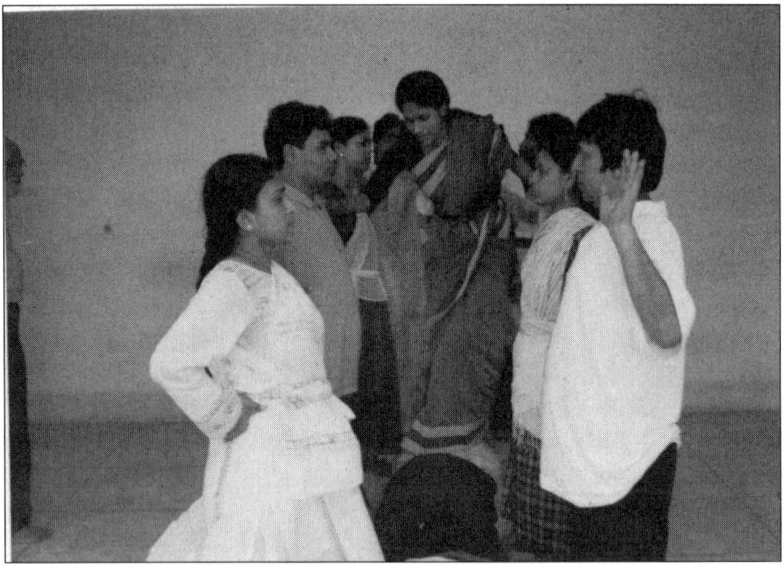

A scene from *Basi Khabar*
Courtesy: Satabdi

We now come to an aspect of Badal-da's theatre which is arguably as significant a part of his oeuvre as his playwriting and his Third Theatre work: his workshops. Badal-da's workshops have had a major impact on theatre practitioners as well as non-theatre participants, and have been held across the length and breadth of India as well as in Pakistan, Bangladesh and England. No study of his theatre would be complete without a discussion of the influence of his theatre workshops.

The theatre workshop is a widespread practice with directors and actors. Different from a rehearsal, a workshop is an open-ended space for developing a text, an actor or an idea. This is done through exploration, improvisation, exercises to develop different aspects and skills from vocal to physical to mental, the deepening of teamwork and trust, and the discussion of themes and interpretations. Any kind of theatre that encourages inputs and participation from actors rather than mere obedience to a director's instruction would find a workshop useful, as would any kind of experimental theatre that is trying out new ideas.

Badal-da's workshops can be considered as belonging to three different categories, each with its own objectives, although he says, 'My workshop is related to the theatre I believe in and practise. I cannot teach all kinds of theatre.'[1] First, there were the workshops with his own group, Satabdi, which had begun when he started to think of doing non-proscenium theatre. Second, there were the numerous workshops he held with theatre workers and actors of other groups, across the country as well as abroad. And third, there were the workshops he held with non-actors, with groups of people outside the world of theatre and performance, from all sections of society: social activists and the people they worked with and for, students, individuals who wanted to undergo the experience, and so on.

Let us begin with the workshops with his own group. Workshops are integral to Grotowski's theatre practice, as well as to the theatre of the American practitioners Badal-da admired, as we have already read. As he developed his idea of the Third Theatre, Badal-da also developed his workshop methodology with Satabdi. Badal-da explains:

> As I have mentioned before, initially I learnt the workshop process from theatre people of the West but through its application in our group as well as in workshops conducted outside, a methodology began to evolve. In the development of the methodology, I have had, and still have, two great teachers. First, our own theatre practice; and second, the feedback I get from the participants in different workshops.[2]

As Satabdi moved from the proscenium to non-proscenium theatre, in order to prepare the actors for this new theatre language, with its different relationship to space and to the audience, workshops were essential. One actor, who was present at the switchover from proscenium to the Third Theatre, emphasised how challenging it was to suddenly find oneself face to face with a viewer. There was no safe distance any more. So much depended on the person's response to you; you were in direct communication with

[1] Quoted in Badal Utsav pamphlet, p. 11.

[2] Sircar, 'Voyages in the Theatre', *On Theatre*, p. 148.

a stranger and it could be embarrassing. To prepare the actor for this and other differences—the physical acting, the ensemble approach—intense closed-door workshops were held, initially along the lines Sircar had seen in the US, but soon, inevitably, with adaptations that grew out of the specifics of experience.

Badal-da asserts that his Third Theatre worked only because of this workshop approach, which prepared the group for the special demands of this kind of theatre. In a nutshell:

> The basic workshop exercises help one, among other things, to get rid of inhibition which is a deadly enemy of theatrical expression. To be aware of one's own body; to discover the hidden potentials of the body; to develop mutual trust, both physical and psychological; to learn to relate to the space and to others in one's movements; to explore sound, movement and rhythm individually and in a group; to bring out and channelize one's creative faculties and to establish a strong sense of community and team spirit—these we categorize as the 'external' workshop exercises and they are carried out through games with definite rules. The next step is to take up themes, thus bringing the mind into play or, in other words, to establish the mind–body relationship which distinguishes the theatre from the circus. From that point onwards, the workshop exercises become 'internal' and, through this process, one explores ways of relating one's feeling about the theme to the expression through the body, through movement, sound, rhythm, energy and the totality of linguistic expression. The internal workshop exercises with the theme—the lines of the play do not by themselves create the choreography, but they do help the content of the play seep into our bloodstream and bring out the energy, the intensity, the mood and the necessary pattern of inter-relationship between the participants in the production. And that helps the group to determine the final choreography which is not imposed from outside and above but emerges from within and from the collective contribution of the whole group.[3]

Theatre director Probir Guha, who was part of Badal-da's group for a while in the early 1970s, recalls the exciting newness of the whole workshop experience.[4] 'We would play trust games, imagine that one's body was a leaf falling from a tree, feel how it touched the earth: working with feelings was something totally new to me, as was the workshop concept. I found it all deeply interesting.'[5]

[3] Sircar, 'Voyages in the Theatre', *On Theatre*, pp. 103–04.
[4] Probir Guha, interview with the author, Kolkata, 28 February 2015.
[5] Interview with the author, trans. Anjum Katyal, 28 February 2015.

Of first importance are trust exercises to break down the distance between actors and develop a strong team spirit, as important as the exercises to dissolve inhibitions, physical and emotional. Both men and women had to be equally comfortable with touching, entwining, being held and supported; this meant that they had to be equally comfortable with each other as human beings. In the early 1970s, when these workshops began, many of the actors came from a cultural background that discouraged such physical intimacy, especially between the sexes. One woman actor talked about how the women would sometimes express discomfort with some new member's attitude to them. These were awkward and delicate issues, but they were dealt with in the group in as sensitive a way as possible. Exercises encouraged individual actors to loosen up and lose their inhibitions in expression, bodily movement and improvisation. Mirroring was another common exercise to build concentration and create a connection. One actor recalled how these workshops threw up surprises: actors who had never shone on the proscenium suddenly flowered as physical actors, demonstrating creativity and imagination the others did not know they had. On the other hand, there were actors who were comfortable in the more conventional form of acting but could not make the transition to this physical, ensemble acting.

'As participants come closer to each other we gradually go nearer theatre—like movement in space, creating sound, movement rhythm, learning rhythm, setting sound movement in rhythm …' explains Badal-da.[6]

Improvisation was another important workshop focus. With his shift to the Third Theatre, Badal-da, the playwright, was also moving to another method of developing texts out of the workshop process. The actors often had no set dialogue; they would have to improvise within a sequence or situation. Improvisation had to be a well-developed skill because of the nature of the space and the theatre language, which demanded flexibility and a quick responsiveness. An actor from the very first workshop recalled how they were asked, working in groups, to come up with a 10-minute Ramayana. Preparatory to *Michhil*, they were asked to form processions of different kinds and improvise their actions, interactions and dialogue. Another exercise was to just keep talking, improvising as they went along.

Badal-da was very clear that the workshop was for more than building skills and technique:

> The 'human being' is the basic factor in these workshops. First the human being and then the theatre person—this is almost the motto of the workshop

[6] Quoted in Badal Utsav pamphlet, p. 11.

> process. I hope I have made it clear that in the kind of content-based theatre we practice, the thoughts and feelings of the performers are of basic and vital importance. Each performer must be involved in the content and make use of his or her emotional response to the content, not perform on the basis of skills and techniques alone. That is what we call acting by 'state of being', and not by 'enactment'. The self-awareness and the realization of one's potential, the coming in touch with one's depths and making contact with others at that level—all this can be something very much needed by any person, whether in the theatre or out of it.[7]

This is borne out by a young Satabdi member who joined the group only after Badal-da passed away, but who was drawn to it after participating in a workshop conducted by Satabdi stalwarts. Souvik Burai says:

> I come here straight from my job as a teacher, running to catch the train, it's hot and crowded, I'm drenched in sweat, exhausted—but the moment we begin, take the first step in the workshop, all my tiredness vanishes. As a teacher my work is to give positive energy to my students—and I can tell you that these workshops are a great source of positive energy. They can help a person lead a healthy, positive life, help him deal with conflict and tension.[8]

Sumit Biswas of Pathasena[9] speaks of several workshop experiences with Badal-da.[10] He is careful to explain that although the workshop would consist of some games and exercises which were 'external', which it is possible to describe, those that were 'internal' could only be experienced. These were more psychological and wrought an inner change in the participants. The circle was very important to the workshop, establishing that everyone was equal and that everyone was facing everyone else. Participants would sit with their knees touching, hand in hand. Eyes shut, an 'energy' would be passed along the circle, from one to the other, with a squeeze of the hand. Each one in turn would receive it, and then pass it on. Sumit said that this would create a 'miraculous' atmosphere that set the tone for the workshop to follow. Badal-da would then tell them that they were now a family in which everyone was equal. In this space, it didn't matter if you were rich or poor, what your caste, education or religious background was: you were

[7] Sircar, 'Voyages in the Theatre', *On Theatre*, p. 147.

[8] Interview with Satabdi actors, Kolkata 13 July 2014.

[9] Pathasena, formed in 1979, theatre group based in Kanchrapara, on the outskirts of Calcutta, part of the Third Theatre movement.

[10] Interview with the author, 18 April 2014 and 3 May 2014.

all the same. The outside world was a competitive place; here, there was no competition, only cooperation. This is the philosophy with which he would begin the workshop.

As Sumit explained, this approach played a big role in strengthening the theatre group, whether Satabdi or Pathasena. Even now, the circle is formed when there is something to discuss, debate or even quarrel over. And they consider their theatre work to be collective; an individual may be vested with the responsibility for a particular production, but he proceeds with the agreement and the support of the whole group. He recalls how, at a particular time of deep crisis within the group, Badal-da called everyone together and then told each of them to look the others in the eye; no speaking was permitted, but you could touch the other person. Sumit says that it was very difficult, almost impossible, to look each other in the eye, but Badal-da insisted that they persist, saying that eyes never lied. And eventually there was a great sense of healing, with everyone in tears, holding hands.

Malini Mukherjee, who participated in several workshops with Badal-da in Santiniketan in the mid-1990s, and later joined Satabdi,[11] summarises the main thrust and themes of his process:

> Workshops would begin and end with the passing of energy [described above], connecting all participants. There were Mirror games to break the ice, as well as to explore movement and develop leadership. There were games exploring different sounds, exploring movements, connecting sound with movement, and then with a theme. A particularly interesting one was where we explored several sounds and movements until it all culminated in a tribal uprising. Sense organ games helped us become aware of various sense organs. This was part of exploring the self. He had several games to understand theatrical space, and this later helped us understand Third Theatre space, which is quite different from proscenium space. Communication games and group building exercises were a focal point of Badal-da's exercises. Different forms of communication—verbal and non verbal—were explored. Group dynamics—how leadership is divided in a group, how even without speaking, the group thinks and acts together; the joy of being together. The 'Internal' games included trust games, blind games and very physical ones where you have to trust your partner/group completely, and where a lack of trust could cause physical injury. Only once did I see it fail. Working on

[11] Badal Sircar was a visiting professor at Viswa-Bharati University, Santiniketan, in 1994. He held a series of workshops in which Malini participated, leading to the founding of a theatre group, Saanko, which performed several plays in the Third Theatre style. Badal Sircar covers this phase of his life in *Purano Kasundi*, Vol. 4 (Kolkata: no pub, 2009), pp. 85–92.

> themes like violence, indifference, trust, love, bondage etc. For example, in the 'indifference' workshop participants would have to continue dancing and singing as they were fed with extremely disturbing news items (this was part of *Basi Khabar* and *Manushey Manushey*). In every workshop I saw people break down. Advanced workshops included making your own plays.[12]

Some workshops were specific to certain plays, like Pathasena's *Raktakarabi*, for example, where Badal-da would work on particular characters, sequences or scenes. Badal-da also held sessions on the text of this drama by Tagore to help the cast understand it better. Sumit Biswas gives an example of how he helped an actor to communicate with body language when he had no dialogue in a particular scene; or how he helped the character Nandini to react to the news of Ranjan's death.

To Badal-da, schooling or training in theatre was important, and the workshop was the medium through which this could be done:

> No art is possible without education. It is only in theatre that one comes across people who think they are born artistes. This is so perhaps because acting is supposed to be nothing but a more lucid demonstration of the masked condition of one's daily life.
>
> Learning to rip off the mask is not that easy. The first step in this learning process is getting to know oneself, learning to recognize one's inner human sensibilities. The next step is to learn how to express these sensibilities and to express the truth honestly. Art cannot be separated from an artist's life. Hence, in this mode of learning, there is no room for any kind of shortcuts or tricks; neither is there any room for facile imitation.
>
> The actor's body is to theatre what paint and paintbrush are to the artist, and vocal ability and musical instruments to the musician. Artistic sensibility is an imperative in all these cases but, in the case of an artiste, there must be a harmonious union of the body with the mind. Doing theatre bereft of masks actually amounts to the actor expressing his innermost sensibilities through his body (and through his voice, since voice is very much a part of the body). Just as a sitarist creates music through his fingers moving on the strings of the sitar, so also an actor uses words from man's innermost concerns to express through the body. Education is necessary for him.
>
> Acting has only one definition—expressing the innermost thoughts of man. If I do not empathize with the play that I am doing, then the purpose of doing theatre is lost.[13]

[12] Email communication, 7 August 2014.
[13] Badal Sircar, 'Masks in Theatre', *On Theatre*, pp. 70–71.

When working with his group, Badal-da also uses the workshop process as rehearsal: 'Our rehearsal process is really the workshop process, through which we aim to come to a position whereby each performer begins to believe that "this line" has been written by me, and not by any other person. "I am speaking my line".'[14]

Since the actor's body is the main vehicle of expression in Third Theatre, Badal-da's actors were trained to take on and form different entities such as trees, forests, bridges, machines, trains and buses—almost anything the scene demanded. This amazing flexibility and inventiveness was one of the most visually striking aspects of the Third Theatre. As a theatre scholar and critic who has followed the Third Theatre with interest, Samik Bandopadhyay does point out, however, that over time there was not enough exploration of a truly original performative language in Badal Sircar's productions. The actors fell into stock gestures and displayed a limited vocabulary of physical performance. He feels that since this is a theatre in which the actor's body is central to the form, more emphasis should have been placed on this aspect of training.[15] Alternative theatre director Probir Guha comments that the 'physicality' Badal-da's theatre was known for was rather limited, restricted as it was to using actors' bodies to depict furniture and natural or inanimate objects; it wasn't abstract or physical in a deeper sense.[16]

Turning to the next category, one of the first actors' workshops Badal-da held outside his own group Satabdi was in Imphal, Manipur, in April 1973. He was invited to conduct the workshop by the Manipur State Kala Akademi (MSKA). 'I was ... very happy ... as it gave me the scope of trying out the Third Theatre in a different setting and in a different language.'[17]

There were 44 participants in all, approximately one from each of the 40-odd theatre groups across Manipur, of which five were women. Badal-da says:

> I was very apprehensive about it, firstly because the number was nearly double of what is suitable for a workshop of this kind and secondly, because it meant a very heterogeneous group where teamwork would be very difficult to achieve within the short time available. But within the first two or three days, my apprehensions vanished. And what the workshop attained in three weeks was far beyond my most optimistic expectations'.[18]

[14] Quoted in Badal Utsav pamphlet, p. 13.

[15] In Anjum Katyal, 'Distance, Access, Control', pp. 139–50.

[16] Probir Guha, interview with the author, Kolkata, 28 February 2015.

[17] Sircar, 'The Third Theatre', *On Theatre*, p. 39.

[18] Ibid.

The work space was a rectangular room (41 ft × 23 ft) with an annexe for dressing, a metal roof, beaten-earth floor and *kutcha* walls. The participants spoke only Manipuri; so communication had to be through an interpreter.

The actual process of the workshop is best described in Badal-da's own words:

> I began by establishing the circle. Everybody sits in a circle whenever something is described or discussed. In the circle, nobody can sit behind another, so there are no back-benchers and no difference in status. Also, the closed circle brings about a sense of unity and team-spirit, the extent of which can hardly be imagined until the circle is actually tried out. I did not allow any observers, as that would have made the participants self-conscious. It is absolutely necessary for the participants to remove the psychological blocks from which the civilized person usually suffers, and that is possible in an atmosphere where everybody participates and nobody sits observing.[19]

The next morning, he begins with a series of psycho-physical exercises, not so much for muscle-building as for developing the strength and flexibility of the spinal system. These relax the muscles rather than tense them as in body-building exercises.

> Normally, we quite often use our muscles unnecessarily, thereby dissipating energy. The idea of these exercises is to teach the performer to stop such dissipation and to utilize the energy in theatrical projection; and I found out, by actual practice, how much energy the human body can generate through proper training and exercise.[20]

They also include voice exercises which help to project the voice without straining the larynx and facial muscle exercises which help voice projection and diction. Badal-da explains:

> The exercises not only help to relax the muscles but also to remove psychological blocks. Suppression of sound is one of the blocks and, in these exercises, it is advised that any sound can be or, rather, should be made freely whenever the participant is advised to (and the system also helps him to) let his mind go, not barring any thought that comes to his mind. After a period, various associations and images begin to form freely in the mind of the participant during the exercises, and a voyage to the inner self begins. It is a process of removing masks, of revelation and, to my mind, that is the process of genuine theatre,

[19] Sircar, 'The Third Theatre', *On Theatre*, pp. 40–42.
[20] Ibid.

> of direct communication as opposed to applying acting tricks and clichés and thereby cheating the audience by faking and pretending.[21]

Badal-da feels that exercising together helps develop teamwork and trust, relaxing inhibitions and allowing the participant to feel that she can do anything in front of others without the fear of ridicule or criticism:

> Some exercises involve direct trust. In one such exercise, a person is lifted high up by six persons supporting him in a lying position upon their palms; then, he is dropped suddenly and caught by their extended forearms. Another exercise involves a person diving from a high place (4–6 ft high) and being caught by six persons, standing face to face in two groups of three, on their extended forearms. Another person can lie below, and the first person then dives straight upon him and the arms of the people waiting to catch him are extended only after the dive is made. Very soon, every single member of the workshop, including the girls, did these exercises and enjoyed them; mutual trust, as well as self-confidence, developed rapidly.[22]

The workshop schedule consisted of a two-part day: from 8.30–11.30 AM, and again from 2–5 PM. During the first three days, in addition to the exercises and games, there were a few explanatory talks.

> As a principle, I kept talks and lectures to a minimum; I tried to raise questions in the minds of the trainees and talked only to answer those questions. I also tried to bring out their individual talents and qualities, such as singing, dancing, miming and physical agility.[23]

Another activity of the workshop was the creation of impromptu or 'instant' plays. A team of participants would prepare and rehearse a short play, about five minutes long, and present it to the others, with only 10 minutes' preparation time. The plays were to be as nonverbal as possible, but they could not be mere pantomime. They had to be theatre. 'This game generated tremendous enthusiasm and demonstrated the development of the trainees' imagination, creative faculties and self-confidence through the workshop.'[24]

Heisnam Kanhailal, who went on to become one of the most respected playwright-directors of Manipur, was the assistant director and interpreter

[21] Sircar, 'The Third Theatre', *On Theatre*, pp. 40–42.
[22] Ibid.
[23] Ibid.
[24] Ibid., p. 43.

to Badal-da at this workshop, which, as he has widely acknowledged, had a tremendous impact on the future direction of his own theatre. Indeed, Badal-da's workshops seeded a crop of theatre activists across the country and impacted many already engaged in theatre.

We know that Kanhailal was first exposed to non-verbal physical theatre at Badal-da's workshop, as was the Kannada left-wing theatre group Samudaya later.

> Samudaya invited Badal Sircar and Satabdi for a performance; Badal Sircar later also conducted a two-week workshop in Kumbulgod for Samudaya actors. Samudaya's street theatre was directly inspired by the Third Theatre. Pani, in fact, writing in 1979, never uses the term "street theatre"; he calls it "the technique of Third Theatre".[25]

Tripurari Sharma, Delhi-based theatre director and women's theatre activist, says that she was so impressed by the very different language of the Third Theatre that she began using aspects of it in her own work with various groups. She says, 'At that time we never realised that it was going to have such a wide influence on theatre in India over the next two decades.'[26] In the course of her own travels to hold workshops across the country, almost everywhere she would encounter people who had done a workshop with Badal Sircar and counted it as one of their most precious experiences—transformative and memorable. For some, the most important learning was that you don't need a stage to do theatre. For others, it was about working with the body, using the actor as the centre of the theatre. Not just theatre people, even those who didn't carry on with theatre later said that the workshop broke down their inhibitions, freed them and helped them connect with their psyche and their emotions. She felt that in terms of his workshops alone, Badal-da was a major influence across the country. Subodh Patnaik,[27] theatre activist, says that a meeting with Badal Sircar changed the course of his career forever. '"He was known as the father of street theatre in India and I got involved in it passionately after being trained under him," he acknowledges.'[28] Badal-da encouraged and

[25] Sudhanva Deshpande, 'The Inexhaustible Work of Criticism in Action: Street Theatre of the Left'. *Seagull Theatre Quarterly*, 16 December 1997, p. 14.

[26] Tripurari Sharma, interview with the author, New Delhi 30 May 2014.

[27] Subodh Patnaik founded and headed the Bhubaneswar-based Natya Chetana theatre group and its Natyagram (theatre village) nearby.

[28] Shyamhari Chakra, 'A Pioneer in Theatre', 30 August 2012, http://www.thehindu.com/arts/theatre/article3839107.ece (accessed 29 January 2015).

supported theatre groups doing like-minded theatre, such as Ayna (founded in 1978) and Pathasena (founded in 1979), taking an active part in training and also directing plays for them. This was an educative and nurturing role that went beyond his individual achievements as a playwright and theatre theorist. In fact, theatre artist Mangai draws a clear distinction between Badal-da's workshop methodology and his productions: 'At least in the case of Tamil Nadu, most groups that evolved out of Badal da's workshops chose to do what we would call street theatre rather than any of his texts or anything close to them' and she sees this as 'evidence of the disjuncture in the workshop process and production process of Badal Sircar's school of training.'[29] Engaging critically with Badal-da's texts and even aspects of his theatre form and practice, particularly in the context of his influence on activist theatre in Tamil Nadu, she nonetheless concludes:

> It is as a teacher of theatre, a person who introduced the workshop process for actors' training and theatre production that I find Badal-da inimitable. His workshops are indeed spaces for rehearsing revolution, however ephemeral they are! And it is that fervor that we have to carry forward as his legacy.[30]

Santanu Bose, theatre director, found Badal-da's theatre workshop particularly valuable because, he said, there was no such training programme available in theatre groups at the time.[31] He had undergone Bohurupee-style standard training, which consisted of learning a little singing, mime and dance from teachers, but the theatre-making, the interaction, was always text based. In Badal-da's workshop, as we have seen, they did several exercises for sound and voice, several to do with mirroring or watching someone else very closely. He particularly recalls one exercise where they were asked to talk about a recent life experience. This was followed by the listeners presenting it back to them: so something very personal that you had gone through was then enacted for you, changing the perspective. He feels this workshop really opened him up and gave him the courage not to privilege text or give it the primary position. He learnt how to use experience as material, how to look at it objectively or distance oneself from it, and how to take a very emotional personal moment and present it to the audience, a very important learning for him.

[29] A. Mangai, 'Badal Sircar—Playwright, Theorist and Teacher of Theatre' (unpublished mss)
[30] Ibid.
[31] The following account is from an interview with the author, New Delhi, 28 April 2014.

Let us hear from a theatre activist in Tamil Nadu about the impact of Badal-da's work there:

> Badal Sircar conducted quite a few workshops in Tamilnadu from the late seventies through to the late nineties. Over this period, the concept of the Third Theatre had gone 'viral' in Tamilnadu. From Gnani's theatre group Pareeksha in Chennai to Fr. Vincent and Sr. Chandra's Kalari theatre group in Nagercoil, very many 'activist' theatre groups and their splinter groups formed and worked all over the state, and continue to do so. They all wore the badge of the Third Theatre with pride, upholders of Sircar's vision.
>
> Theatre directors Dr K. A. Gunasekaran (group Tanane), Prof Mu. Ramaswamy (Nija Nataka Iyakkam), Mangai (Mauna Kuram/Voicing Silence) and filmmaker Amshan Kumar are some luminaries who count themselves as Sircar's pupils. They had continued contact with him in the eighties and nineties, and he occasionally watched their plays and rehearsals with his usual enthusiasm. Mu. Ramaswamy's *Spartacus*, Gnani's *Bhoma* and Mangai's *Theeni Por* (*Food Fight*) are amongst the plays he watched.[32]

In an essay which meticulously tries to trace Badal-da's legacy in the left-oriented, activist theatre world of Tamil Nadu, A. Mangai discusses the workshops he held there between 1980 and the early 2000s, at the invitation of various groups involved with socially aware theatre, the tours he and his group undertook in which they presented their plays and the surge of local 'street theatre' activity that flowed out of these encounters. As she points out, not all of them presented his texts or even adopted his form and style; yet there was a pervasive engagement with his approach and the underlying principles of the Third or Free Theatre that informed the theatre scene in the long term. And she separates out his workshops as a learning and training experience that had a wholly independent value of their own.[33]

Not just within India, Badal-da's influence, through his productions and his workshops, travelled across the border to Pakistan and Bangladesh as well.[34] Two prominent theatre activists of Pakistan speak about their encounter with Badal-da's theatre and its influence on their own work—Madeeha Gauhar of Ajoka Theatre and Mohammed Waseem, earlier of Lok Rehas. Mahmood Hasan and Nishat Jahan of Bangladesh recorded their experience with Badal-da as well.

[32] E-Rang newsletter, 'Remembering Badal Sircar', No. 24, 1 July 2011. http://theatre-forum.in/m/e-rang/?tab=issues&object_id=17 K. P. Pravin is an artist and theatre director based in Chennai.

[33] See A. Mangai, 'Badal Sircar'.

[34] See Sircar, *Purano Kasundi*, Vol. 4, pp. 93–100 (Pakistan), pp. 111–24 (Bangladesh).

Madeeha Gauhar set up the Ajoka Theatre in Lahore in 1983, along with her husband Shahid Nadeem. By that time, she had already met Badal-da on a trip to Delhi in 1980 and was impressed by him.[35] Later, in 1985, as a theatre student in London, she participated in a workshop led by Badal-da at Riverside Studio.[36] She was surprised by the very intense exercises, and as a woman found some of them, which involved a degree of physical intimacy, too challenging. But his concern with social issues, which made his work political, and his Third Theatre approach, which allowed theatre to be done effectively at minimum cost, was an eye opener and indicated a new direction for her. In May 1984, Ajoka chose Badal-da's *Michhil* or *Juloos* as its very first play. They did an Urdu translation from the Hindi version which Madeeha had acquired on a trip to India, adapting some references and details to make it more relevant to their immediate situation. There was censorship, then, and the play was political and anti-establishment, so they performed it, in the Third Theatre style, in the garden of a residence belonging to Madeeha's mother rather than in a public space. It was performed in almost underground conditions, amidst fears of an imminent police raid. It made an impact. The audience hadn't seen anything like this unconventional non-proscenium form before. In the repressive conditions prevalent at the time in Pakistan, this approach to theatre had instant appeal both for its political nature, and its form which was not just innovative but inexpensive, an important consideration for a fledgling alternative theatre movement. Ajoka's first production set the tone for their later theatre, not just stylistically but in terms of content, which remained political and also socially engaged.

Madeeha stayed in touch with Badal-da, who was a source of inspiration and a mentor, visiting him and seeing his plays at the Theosophical Society hall in 1985 when she went to Calcutta. She saw his open air shows in Calcutta and was amazed because this was not typical street theatre fare, which usually consisted of short, simple plays of about 10 minutes duration. These were long, complex plays with a lot of dialogue, quite philosophical. For her graduation directorial project at the theatre department of Royal Holloway, University of London, she selected *Basi Khabar*. Once again, it was the political nature of the work, and the innovative form, that spoke to her. Due, particularly, to the Union Carbide scandal of the Bhopal Gas Tragedy, the play's stance on colonialism and neo-colonialism had a particular resonance at that place and time.

[35] The account is based on an interview with the author, Lahore, 25 February 2014.

[36] See Sircar, *Purano Kasundi*, Vol. 4, p. 94.

Ajoka's third production was based on Badal-da's script of *Gondi* (1977), his adaptation of Brecht's *Caucasian Chalk Circle*; and soon after, Shahid Nadeem wrote an original play *It* (Brick) on bonded labour, influenced by Badal-da and very much in his style, which they produced in 1988. Thereafter, however, Madeeha found herself moving away from the Third Theatre style, diversifying and experimenting, introducing the richness of local forms with their colour, song and music into her plays, although Badal-da's influence remained as strong as ever in the workshops she held to train actors, as well as workshops with community-based organisations, encouraging them to form their own groups. She used the techniques learnt from him, and these in turn were passed on to others.

Madeeha remembers that Badal Sircar came to Pakistan in 1988, along with fellow theatre persons Safdar Hashmi, Rati Bartholomew and Anuradha Kapur, for a workshop and to interact with the local theatre people, on a visit organized by social activists Nighat Said Khan and Kamla Bhasin.[37] His visit led to further connections, and he came back again the following year to hold a workshop with another alternative political theatre group, Lok Rehas, spreading his theatre practice more widely.

According to Madeeha, Badal-da was a major influence on alternative and activist theatre in Pakistan. His commitment to socially engaged, politically subversive theatre, his thought-provoking content, his flexible, inexpensive and theatrically effective form without any need for sets, lights or costumes were liberating and inspiring. His workshop techniques helped train many groups.

Madeeha feels that despite having moved away from the Third Theatre form, Ajoka has kept the basic philosophy—performing for people without charging or charging a nominal amount, taking up issues that are relevant and of importance to their society, retaining the political element in their theatre. All these have come from Badal Sircar. Personally she is also very influenced by his total commitment to his theatre, which grew out of his ideological convictions and his progressive leftist outlook:

> That we can use theatre to try and bring about a change in society—my work is still grounded in that principle, and a lot of that has to do with the fact that I interacted with Badal-ji, worked with him and was inspired by his work, and his whole approach. If I had not met Badal-ji at that point of time, I don't know if I would have been on this path.[38]

[37] See Sircar, *Purano Kasundi*, Vol. 4, p. 93.

[38] Madeeha Gauhar of Ajoka, interview with the author, Lahore, 25 February 2014.

Another Pakistani theatre activist and director who claims Badal-da as a guru or mentor is Mohammed Waseem, who worked with Badal-da in the late 1980s, when he was with alternative theatre group Lok Rehas, a Punjabi theatre group which was at the time doing issue-based, socially meaningful theatre.[39] Waseem is now with Interactive Resource Centre, Lahore, where he is applying Augusto Boal's concepts and theories to his activist work.[40] He was a volunteer during the production of *Juloos* by Madeeha in 1984. A student at the time, with no previous experience of theatre, he was deeply influenced by the production, both in terms of content and form. He found it very relevant to the situation in Pakistan with its oppression, Islamisation, censorship and the ongoing struggle for democracy. This is the first time he had seen, as he put it a 'circle play' (theatre in the round). This created an interest in Badal-da's work and soon after, he had the opportunity to participate in the 1988 seminar, which also featured, as we know, other theatre persons from India including Safdar Hashmi. Of these, it was Badal-da who caught their imagination enough for them, now organised into a theatre group called Lok Rehas, to initiate a longer workshop with Badal-da. This was a 10-day workshop held in the Goethe-Institut later the same year.[41] Other students, theatre volunteers and activists, some of them studying and working in remote areas of Pakistan, were also invited. There were about 40 participants in all. Asked about what they learned that was valuable, he said:

> Badal-da was a great trainer. He really engaged with the participants, it was very physical, he challenged them to use the body in different positions, situations and images. The "situations" on which we were asked to improvise had to do with the plight of brick kiln workers, domestic violence, social and political issues. Most of his workshop was focused on acting skill and techniques. How, in a bare space, actors can create images of different locales, which are convincing for the audience.[42]

Apart from the exercises, Badal-da would also talk to them about his philosophy of theatre—his ideas of equality, justice, why we do theatre, his

[39] The following account is based on an interview with the author, Lahore, 25 February 2014.

[40] Augusto Boal (b. 1931), Brazilian theatre director, activist and theoretician, founder of Theatre of the Oppressed, a theatrical form originally used in radical popular education movements. Boal's concepts are being practised by activist performance groups on the Indian subcontinent.

[41] See Sircar, *Purano Kasundi*, Vol. 4, pp. 95–96.

[42] Mohammed Waseem, interview with the author, 25 February 2014, Lahore, Pakistan. All views expressed here are part of that interview.

work in the villages, trying to take theatre to the farmers and so on. As a role model, Waseem found Badal-da very democratic in his attitude. He spent time with them outside workshop hours, sharing meals with them in low-cost eateries, engaging in discussion. 'He was very humble, listened very carefully, tried to answer carefully, was honest with people, and developed bonds and links and support which continued even after the workshop, in fact till his death. He didn't mind being challenged, and we were young and very ready to criticize and challenge! He gave very logical answers, and would say, "In my opinion this is true, but you're welcome to think differently."'

Applying what he had learned through the workshop, Waseem directed a few plays with Lok Rehas, written by Lakhat Pasha: these were all in the Third Theatre style. They were *Kurlat* (Cry of Pain) on rape; *Ayaanie* (Children), on child labour and child abuse; and *Saar* (Consciousness) on women's issues and the political situation. He had noticed Badal-da's use of geometrical forms like pyramids, circles within circles, hexagons, which he felt were essential for a bare stage, making it visually pleasing. Lok Rehas adopted the principle of no tickets, offering free access to anyone who wished to attend. Also, he himself did workshops along the lines of Badal-da's, and after seeing their plays and participating in such workshops, there has been a spreading ripple effect of Badal-da's ideas. According to Waseem, other participants of Badal-da's 1988 workshop are doing his kind of theatre in remote areas of interior Punjab and other rural areas.

Waseem has now left Lok Rehas and does more directly activist work with his Interactive Resource Centre. He found himself moving away from Badal-da's kind of theatre to a more dialogue-based model inspired by Augusto Boal and his Forum theatre. And yet, he says:

> I use a lot of Badal-da in my theatre. He challenged the audience, like Brecht. But at the same time it was all propagative—you want to tell people what is what. Whatever aesthetic you may use, propaganda is very much part of it. It is prescriptive. I've always felt that there is very little difference between the priest and the communist, because they both believe that they have the truth and people should follow them, and they never doubt their own ideology—this is a negative element, to my mind. That's why they can't grow much. With Badal-da, the enemy is still outside—one is faced with inevitable situations and people have to make decisions. With Boal it is more about the enemy within, urge and desire.

Waseem feels that 'street theatre in our countries should be thankful to Badal-da for his contribution; taking the play out of the proscenium, performing in public areas, in a circle, asking the audience a lot of questions . . .' Badal-da remained an inspiration to him because, even as a much older man,

> He always asked and tried to answer questions; although in his plays he is prescribing a solution he is also very open; he has spaces in his script for people to reflect and think. His is not agit-prop theatre. From my point of view he is one of the greatest twentieth century theatre activists of India, one step ahead of all his contemporaries.

It is safe to conclude that the alternative, activist, socially and politically-engaged theatre being done in Pakistan today owes a great deal to Badal-da, a claim no other Indian theatre practitioner can really make.

In Bangladesh, too, Badal-da's workshops have facilitated the spread of activist theatre, as Nishat Jahan Rana, Bangladesh activist,[43] writes:

> Badal Sircar visited Bangladesh several times in order to hold workshops for theatre workers here. Those who took part in his workshops can testify to what an extraordinary teacher he was. His method of teaching was very participatory and scientific; it combined the objective and the subjective, being both intellectual and emotional at the same time.[44]

Badal-da also rehearsed and prepared *Gondi* with the theatre activists.[45]

In 1998, he participated in a street theatre festival organised by Gana Shahajya Sanstha (GSS) and Bangladesh Shilpakala Academy, along with three theatre groups he was associated with—Satabdi, Ayna and Pathasena. Nishat recalls how they mesmerised the 1,000-strong audience in the stadium without the use of any microphones.[46] Apparently, they did close to 10 plays directed by him. He too acted, with energy and elan, although he was already 72 years old at the time. They presented Rabindranath's *Raktakarabi* under his guidance, in a completely new form.

Nishat recalls:

> We took him to Rajshahi University, where he spent time with the students. He thoroughly enjoyed being with them. He was a man of strong personal

[43] Nishat Jahan (Rana) is a writer, publisher and documentary film-maker involved with the development sector in Bangladesh.

[44] Nishat Jahan (Rana), 'Ebong Badal Sircar' (And Badal Sircar), tribute to Badal Sircar printed immediately after his passing away on 13 May 2011, in Bangladesh daily *Doinik Samakal*. Trans. by Anjum Katyal.

[45] See Sircar, *Purano Kasundi*, Vol. 4, pp. 123–24.

[46] For an account of this, see Sircar, *Purano Kasundi*, Vol. 4, pp. 119–22.

> values and principles, which he never compromised. He got on well with young people, and vice versa. He had a youthful vision, a clear, transparent and young mind. That's why he constantly challenged all that was stagnant and rigid, all that went against his principles of humanity and humaneness.[47]

Mahmood Hasan of Bangladesh testifies to the successful contribution of Badal-da to development initiatives there:

> Badal da visited Bangladesh as our guest on two occasions probably during 1997 and 1998. Each time he spent little over a month mainly running workshops. GSS[48] was a fairly large organisation at the time with 6,500 staff and was best known for its unique programming. We focused on the quality of primary education, and civil society, rights and governance. Under the latter we facilitated over 700 theatre groups in the rural areas of Bangladesh and organised a month-long 'Bangali Sangskriti Utshob' in 10 districts each year for a decade. We retained a central team of some 40 performing artists who facilitated theatre groups across the country. Many of these artists are celebrities today. Badal Da loved working with them, building their capacity, and the young boys and girls adored him.... The 700 groups I mentioned above organised plays based mainly on what had happened in their own or in a neighbouring community mainly between them and the vested interest groups. These were predominantly stories of oppression and torture. They didn't use any script. But what was unique, we managed to put across the message that human species is always performing. We don't see this because we don't notice. Therefore, anybody could perform. All they need is a little bit of encouragement and appreciation.[49]

Badal Sircar's legacy lives on in Bangladesh. A dramatised reading of *Raktakarabi* in his voice was brought out as a CD by Media Centre in Bangladesh. A collection of four of his plays was published in 2008, consisting of *Ebong Indrajit, Sara Rattir, Pagla Ghora* and *Bhoma*. His *Hattamalar Oparey, Michhil* and others have been produced by various theatre groups across the years.[50]

Let us now turn to the innumerable workshops that Badal-da conducted with and for non-theatre persons. Speaking in 1992, he said:

> I have so far conducted over 80 workshops of three full days (i.e. 18 hours) or more, and about 50 of shorter duration, in India, Bangladesh, Pakistan

[47] Nishat Jahan Rana, 'Ebong Badal Sircar' (And Badal Sircar), trans. Anjum Katyal.
[48] Gana Sahajjya Sanstha.
[49] Email communication with the author, 23 April 2014.
[50] Rana, 'Ebong Badal Sircar' (And Badal Sircar).

> and Britain. Of these, probably more than half have been either with wholly non-theatre people or with mixed batches. The non-theatre people mainly comprised college students, and grassroot-level workers of voluntary agencies engaged in social development work in villages and city slums.... I have been fortunate in having people from different walks of life in the workshops I have conducted.[51]

Badal-da recalls doing workshops with the poorest of the poor, as in Vishrampura village in Gujarat, where the participants were all landless workers. It was a three-day workshop. Hoping to retain their interest and their presence on day two, he decided to try them out on 'playmaking' (described earlier in this chapter). This exercise is usually introduced towards the end of a five-day workshop by which time the participants are relaxed and confident with the workshop process. But he decided to take the risk much earlier in the workshop process:

> In the latter part of the second day, I narrated to them the Aesop's fable about 'cry wolf' and the 'bunch of sticks'. Some of them knew the stories, but not all. Then, cautiously and timidly, I asked if anybody would volunteer to make a five-minute play out of any of these two stories in 10 minutes. There was a long pause, and I could hear my heart thumping in my chest. Then one young man, about 18, volunteered to try the first story. Immediately after, there was another volunteer for the second one.... From then on it was plain sailing. Each of the 22 participants made plays of their own either on that afternoon or the next day. Many of them were based on their own problems in life. There was great excitement and enthusiasm. They loved props, and on the next day they brought the props and their ideas with them.[52]

This experience gave him the courage to try a similar experiment at a two-day workshop in Rangabelia village in the Sunderbans. Here too the participants were poor, mostly illiterate villagers of peasant stock. He expected that they would draw heavily from the Jatra, the form of theatre they were most familiar with, but was pleasantly surprised when they came up with scenes from daily life. Another surprise was with regard to the women participants:

> Bengali women are rather conservative about their dress, and at that time an adult woman even in Calcutta could hardly think of going out in public clad in anything but a sari. Although loose garments like sari, dhoti or

[51] Sircar, 'Voyages in the Theatre', *On Theatre*, p. 147.
[52] Ibid., p. 149.

lungi are restrictive in the workshop, I insisted on this point only in the case of men in Rangabelia, not daring to suggest it to the women. But in the second session of the first day, I found all the women wearing ill-fitting pyjamas and shirts or kurtas borrowed from the male relatives at home. It was a decision they took. It must have been the first time since the age of 12 or 13 that any of them was wearing anything but a sari, and that too in the presence of men.[53]

Rustom Bharucha describes one such workshop in Rangabelia, consisting of about 25 participants, half of them unable to even sign their own name, some who had done a few years of school before poverty forced them to discontinue and one or two who had completed their matriculation. 'Within two days he had established a relationship with them based on trust and mutual respect,' he says.[54] Badal-da's aim was, as we know, the removal of psychological blocks and inhibitions:

In order to make his participants realize the strength of their interrelations as people, Sircar improvised situations and games that compelled them to respond instinctively and as members of a community. Like all significant workshops, the one in Rangabelia was generated by the participants themselves. Sircar functioned less as a leader and more as a catalyst who enabled the participants to discover themselves as people by confronting their inner resources, tensions and moments of communion.[55]

The short plays they created as part of the workshop were all on 'their everyday activities with a telling use of detail.'[56] Experiences in the forest, the constant fear of tigers, poachers and dacoits; exploitation and abuse by police and moneylenders; the loss of lives, including a man dying of overwork; everyday activities, such as cutting wood or gathering honey; these were the subjects they chose to work on. A constant running theme was the economic exploitation they faced from all quarters.

These workshops left a lasting impact: some of those who had participated decided to continue with more such workshops on their own, thereby ensuring that Badal-da's inputs continued to bear fruit. They made two half-hour plays based on their own problems in the village.[57]

[53] Sircar, 'Voyages in the Theatre', *On Theatre*, p. 150.
[54] Bharucha, *Rehearsals of Revolution*, p. 182.
[55] Ibid., p. 182.
[56] Ibid.
[57] Sircar, 'Voyages in the Theatre', *On Theatre*, p. 150.

Some of the workshops Badal-da took were in urban situations, and consisted of mixed groups of people from varied backgrounds. Badal-da says:

> The most heterogeneous batch I have had in a workshop was in a seven-day one in Calcutta. There were theatre people, non-theatre people, activists in rural areas or in city slums, university students and people in service, one Roman Catholic priest and two nuns, illiterate or semi-literate women from villages and slums, a young man and a young girl from Britain, and so on. The youngest participant was 15 and the oldest was 59.[58]

Of all of them, the one participant who interested—and rewarded—him the most, according to him, was Savitri. She was a slum dweller from the sweeper caste, around 30 years old, a single mother with two children, abandoned by her husband: a very common tale. Badal-da noticed that she was very inhibited and tense as can be expected from someone who had never been close to such a mixed group before:

> I did not have any hope of getting her out of her inhibitions in the short span of seven days. On the fifth day or so, while some of us were sitting in the room during lunch break, we suddenly saw Savitri singing and dancing across the room, without the slightest concern about who was European or who was educated. And when one of the participants was taking photographs after the workshop had ended, Savitri literally fought her way victoriously to sit next to me. I can say that it was Savitri who made that voyage a very remarkable one for me.[59]

Shikar, organised in Calcutta from 24 May to 6 June 1982 by production group Seagull Empire, was held in the grounds of St James' school and consisted of another mixed group of urban men and women. One of the participants, a media professional with an interest in social communication, looks back on it as one of the most rewarding experiences of her life, liberating and transformative. Another woman, academic and activist, talks of a workshop organised in the early 1980s by a development NGO working with teenage girls on the outskirts of Calcutta. With no reason to extol Badal-da unduly, she remembers that workshop with appreciation and respect for his sincerity and ability to communicate, and to break through emotional and psychological barriers. Again, it remained a rewarding and valuable experience even years later.

[58] Sircar, 'Voyages in the Theatre', *On Theatre*, p. 150.
[59] Ibid., p. 151.

Speaking of his workshops in the UK, Badal-da says:

> When in 1985 I was first invited to conduct workshops in different places in Britain, I felt apprehensive and diffident. (I was invited by these persons in their early 20s who were jobless and lived on unemployment dole, but that again is another story!) I was thinking that there would be trained theatre workers in my workshops who must be familiar with the workshop process, and, anyway, what works here may not work there, and so on. In reality, I found that many human problems are the same everywhere, and the workshop process that got evolved in India with the human being as its base works as well in a European country.... I have made two more visits to Britain in 1986 and 1989, and all the three have been good voyages of a different kind for me.[60]

He elaborates on these experiences in the fourth and final volume of his autobiographical *Purano Kasundi*.[61] In particular, he notes that in the excessively competitive climate of the west, these workshops allowed participants the freedom and relaxation of a space totally devoid of competitiveness, one that develops instead a sense of cooperation and bonding. He mentions several letters from his workshop participants which contained detailed responses. One, in particular, is from a woman who says how, on day two, when she realised that she did not have to think of how anyone was doing better than her, or how she herself was outdoing others, she began to find the workshop truly meaningful, and thereafter was able to immerse herself in the experience fully and completely.[62]

Clearly, Badal-da was able to reach people of varied age groups, educational levels and socio-economic backgrounds, a rare ability that no doubt came from his honesty and sincerity of approach. This ability to communicate successfully is indeed remarkable, given the very personal nature of the workshop process and the hierarchies and stratification that exist in our society between people of different educational and class backgrounds. To achieve something personally and individually meaningful in the course of a few days during the fixed hours of a workshop indicates that the process and the approach ring true.

This is further borne out by the testimony of two participants who took part in his workshops at Santiniketan, during his time as a visiting professor

[60] Sircar, 'Voyages in the Theatre', *On Theatre*, p. 151.
[61] Sircar, *Purano Kasundi*, Vol. 4.
[62] Ibid., pp. 61–62.

at the Visva-Bharati University theatre department.[63] Malini Mukherjee heard about Badal-da's workshop and joined out of curiosity, with no fixed intention of doing theatre thereafter. She insists that his workshops are about forming the human being, of liberating and empowering the person, rather than about theatre per se, which bears out what Badal-da himself claimed. Enthralled, she enrolled in a series of his workshops and went on to form a group, Saanko, along with fellow students. They did a few plays. After Saanko dissolved, she came to Kolkata and joined Satabdi. Currently, she is an educator who uses Badal-da's process and approach in her own work with disadvantaged children and other marginalised groups. Anshuman Das, too, found meaning in the workshops he did with Badal-da, which led him to form Saanko, and then become a part of Satabdi for some years. He is a development professional who says that the values and philosophy he learned through Badal-da infuse his choice of work and his approach even today. To them both, Third Theatre is a way of life rather than just a theatre form.

One demographic Badal-da was apprehensive about was children. He felt that he did not understand them well enough to do workshops with them. Also, with his instinctive desire to engage as an equal on the human level, which was fundamental to his whole approach to theatre, he was concerned that he may begin to talk down to them, somehow take on the role of a 'teacher' which is something most adults do without even realising it, and which immediately creates a distance that mitigates against the loosening up that is the objective of such a workshop. Despite these reservations, however, Badal-da did a workshop with children, and it is instructive to hear what he says about it:

> In 1985... I found myself in Namaldiha village in West Bengal charged with the task of doing a two-day workshop with 20 children between eight to 12, eight of them girls. They belonged to a community of palanquin-bearers and . . . belonged to the poorest section of the village.
>
> That was another time when I had an almost sleepless night in between the two days. The first day we had only four hours or so in the afternoon, and nothing I tried seemed to work. They played the games out of duty, never letting themselves go, whereas I had made a firm resolution of not imposing anything on them, even if the workshop got absolutely frustrating.

[63] Malini Mukherjee and Anshuman Das spoke of their interaction with Badal-da during this period, around 1995. Interview with the author, Kolkata, 4 August 2014. An account of his Santiniketan experiences can be found in Sircar, *Purano Kasundi*, Vol. 4, pp. 85–92.

> Well, on the second day, although we could not come to playmaking, they made a play jointly, with me staying away from them. They also mimed and created many other things. What made the voyage particularly exciting for me is the fact that two records were created on that second day which have not been broken in any workshop till today. First, it was the longest workshop session—they worked and made me work for 10 hours on that day. They simply refused to go home. Secondly, at the fag end of the day, I was unable to sit in the circle with them—a thing which I always do. A fight was growing between the two sides on the issue of who would sit next to me. At first I tried to resolve the problem by making them take turns, but they insisted on fighting it out. So ultimately I stood in the centre while they sat in a circle. That however was unanimously accepted. One might criticize this as 'competitive', but I do not think so. I think it expressed their love for the workshop and for the person who had brought it to them.[64]

A documentary film titled *Ebong Badal Sircar* (*And Badal Sircar*)[65] captures him interacting with a group of neighbourhood children around 10–12 years of age. He is telling them stories, chatting and answering questions. Since the camera is present, it is hard to tell how genuine the children's interest or engagement is—they may well have been prompted, or put on their best behaviour. However, it is interesting to see Badal-da with them: a little shy to begin with, diffident, never acting the 'authority' although they call him Dadu and look to him for answers, very natural and honest, never talking down to them or putting on the 'let me make this simple for you' voice which so many adults use to children and which puts one's teeth on edge. By the second day, he was talking to them about war and injustice, and other such serious matters. One never sensed any condescension or artifice in his manner. This was not a workshop, certainly, but it was a 'study session' of a kind. It would be fitting to recall a quote about his evolving workshop methodology in this context:

> Each workshop presents some unique problems, demanding unique solutions on the spot. This is bound to happen in a situation where the 'human being' is the basic factor. A fixed and finalized methodology is possible only when the participants are not taken as subjects but are objectified into a passive body of 'students' at the receiving end, which unfortunately is in general the situation in our educational system.[66]

[64] Sircar, 'Voyages in the Theatre', *On Theatre*, pp. 151–52.
[65] *Ebong Badal Sircar* (2008, 47 mins), directed by Swapna Dutta.
[66] Sircar, 'Voyages in the Theatre', *On Theatre*, p. 148.

Perhaps, but it is not the situation with him.

In a recent interview, years after his important study of Badal-da's theatre, Rustom Bharucha recognises the significant seeding role Badal-da has played in the alternative, activist theatre scene on our subcontinent:

> I think he's probably one of the most influential theatre personalities in contemporary India. His model of theatre actually has influenced more people than anybody else. We have to acknowledge that. Nobody has had this kind of outreach. It really travelled, and without trying to be 'national'. Even people who later dissociated themselves began with him; he really was the forerunner of another way of doing theatre and that cannot be taken away from him...he gave Indian theatre workers, in a very concrete way, a new way of doing theatre where you didn't have to work on a stage, you could create your own script, you didn't need the paraphernalia of theatre—and that is very liberating.[67]

And a major factor of this 'outreach' was the extensive number of workshops Badal-da conducted, in all sorts of locations and contexts, with a wide range of people, leading to a ripple effect across the entire subcontinent. As I worked on this book, I was taken aback by the number of people in different cities and locales, who, when they heard I was researching Badal Sircar, would spontaneously say that they had done a workshop with him, or with someone trained by him. And this is not just in metros, but small towns across the country. It gave me a rough idea of just how widespread Badal-da's influence really was. If we add to that the number of people who have, through their interaction with his process and his philosophy, been empowered to carry his ideas further in their work outside the theatre, or simply been changed fundamentally, then the influence is even more extensive. This is one aspect of his legacy which should get its due.

[67] Interview with the author, Kolkata, 5 May 2014.

CHAPTER TWELVE

THE WOMAN QUESTION

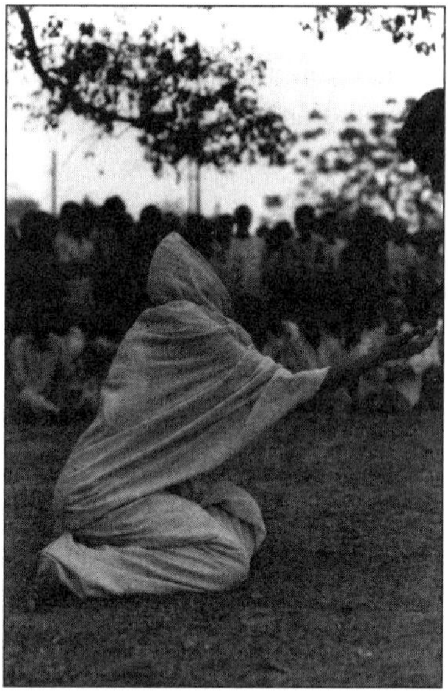

A scene from *Basi Khabar*
Courtesy: Satabdi

Since Badal-da's theatre is so much about equality and justice, about challenging restrictive middle-class conventions and propagating parity between human beings, it is only natural to wonder how progressive it is in terms of gender as well. An essay on women in Badal-da's theatre expresses a similar argument:

> Badal Sircar's views of theatre as a form of social work are well-known and it is of interest to see what issues his plays have raised, whether and how they have approached the position and the possibilities for women in the society of the times. That his theatre should stand up to this scrutiny is underlined by

> the fact that Sircar defines his theatre as being 'a human act' ... his theatre is founded on this belief that it is about human relationship, unmediated at least in certain ways. If this be the case it would be interesting to explore whether Sircar creates newer patterns of relationships or explodes older ones, whether he creates a different space for women or even different kinds of women.[1]

In this chapter, we set out to look at Badal-da's theatre through the lens of gender, to gain an understanding of how it fares in this regard.

Badal-da can be read in conjunction with his contemporaries Mohan Rakesh, Vijay Tendulkar and Girish Karnad, since all four were producing path-breaking new work around the same time, in the 1960s and 1970s. It is interesting to note that each of these three playwrights' major plays grapple with the questions of women's role in society, women's desire and the relationship between men and women, within and without the family. At this time, when much is changing in the social fabric of middle-class India with rapid urbanisation, women going out to work, and changes in family structure, traditional mores regarding women are under attack, but there is ambiguity over what the desirable alternative may be, even in women themselves. And these playwrights are part of the same bind. If one tries to depict a woman who is liberated enough to exercise choice in her relationships with men, one may end up portraying her as too dependent on men and the need for romance in her life. In trying to showcase man's insensitivity towards or exploitation of a woman, one may end up portraying the woman as a hapless victim. Attempting to show a confident, assertive woman, one may end up stereotyping her as a harridan. However, despite this turmoil and confusion, there is no doubt that at this time women characters and women's issues are becoming part of the discourse in these plays. Is this true of Badal-da's plays as well? How significant are concerns about women and gender parity in his oeuvre?

It is important to keep historical considerations in mind while we study his texts from a gender perspective. By that I simply mean that the ideas of what constitutes progressive thinking regarding gender have gone through several shifts over the decades, and one must remember what a particular action would have signified at the time, whatever it may look like to us today. Today, for example, when women proudly claim their bodies and dressing up is a factor of personal pleasure and choice, it may be hard to appreciate why

[1] G.J.V. Prasad, 'The Third Gaze: The Theatre of Badal Sircar' in Lakshmi Subramanyam (ed.), *Muffled Voices: Women in Modern Indian Theatre* (New Delhi: Har-Anand Publications Pvt Ltd, revised edition, 2013), p. 61.

feminists of decades ago chose to eschew makeup and pretty clothes, while to them it was an expression of their freedom from the imposed standards of femininity and grooming that a patriarchal society expected of them.

A young woman director, Abanti Chakravarty, although admiring of Badal-da as an artist, states, while discussing the gender aspect of Badal-da's plays, that she feels he is 'a male playwright.'[2] She says:

> I read Badal Sircar's women in three phases. The first phase consists of his comedies—very stereotyped and clichéd. I sometimes feel—how strange that Badal Sircar has written these plays! Such an intellectual person, such a political person! In the second phase—which includes *Ebong Indrajit, Pagla Ghora, Baki Itihas*—there is a modernity to the women, but it is men-centric. They are conditioned by men. I also feel that the women sort of belong to a dream world, not real. And then, in the third phase, women vanish. There is no woman.[3]

Let us see how far her views are supported by a closer look at the material.

The first cluster of plays Badal-da wrote were, as we know, domestic situational comedies set in a middle-class milieu. All of them have stock, and rather stereotypical characters in them, and the women are no exception. They exist only to advance the storyline. There are no surprises in the characters, only in the plot. Nothing challenges or subverts the standard social attitudes towards the young girls, wives and matrons we see in these plays. Mostly, in these initial comedies, the women are sweet young things or supportive wives or mothers and aunts who seem to spend all their time worrying about whether the boys and men have eaten or not, or scolding them for not coming for their meals on time.

Boro Pishima draws directly on Badal-da's own experience of doing theatre as part of a neighbourhood club, particularly his insistence that women play women's roles in his plays. It was not socially acceptable for bhadralok women to appear on the public stage. This was a social taboo he was proud to help break in Maithon. In his play, it is the aunt, of whom everyone is petrified due to her overbearing personality, who disapproves of theatre as an activity, let alone young girls like her niece taking part in it. All the men run scared of her, particularly her henpecked husband, but in the end she is appeased by the desirable happy ending—a marriage between her niece and the young lad who tries hardest to outwit her. One could say that in its

[2] Abanti Chakravarty, interview with the author, 3 July 2014.

[3] Ibid.

own none-too-serious way, this play does take up a serious issue—that of making a space for women in theatre. However, this was no longer a radical stance for its time and audience, and, moreover, nothing in the play—not the characters nor the denouement—challenges preconceived notions in any way. The characters are all too recognisable.

What one can get from these plays, though, is an idea of social norms and accepted custom. Wives are concerned with household issues like serving tea and food, offering hospitality to guests and supporting husbands in their demanding jobs and careers, with the license to bully them for their own good. Men pretend to be under their domestic thumb while doing exactly as they please. Interacting with the outside world is their domain. Young girls are sweet, naïve and selfless. There is no sexuality or transgression of these demarcated identities. Clearly these were well-entrenched roles, unquestioned neither by the audience who found them all too familiar nor the playwright who used them to construct amusing situations.

Is it not possible for feel-good comedies of this sort, full of laughs and with the inevitable happy ending, to also introduce some fresh perspective regarding gender roles? There are comedies that do so—in which the characters are daring, or different, or push the envelope in some way. However, these plays, enjoyable as they are, are not of their number. The laughter they evoke is comfortable, with no hint of discomfort or unease.

With *Ebong Indrajit,* we pass on to Badal-da's serious plays. Given its landmark status in Indian playwriting, admired for breaking new ground in terms of content and form, discussed as a work that captured the emotions and psychology of the time, particularly for the young urban middle-class male, it becomes all the more important to see what this play says about women.

Let us begin with the opening stage directions. A man sits at a table, surrounded by discarded sheets of paper. He is absorbed in writing. 'Mashima enters. She is designated "aunt" but she could just as easily be Mother. Pishima, Kakima, Mamima, older sister-in-law—any one of these will do. Mashima is upset. She can't understand what's going on. Not being able to understand is the *dharma* of Mashimas,'[4] writes the playwright. She immediately launches into a tirade—what is going on, why aren't you coming to eat, I'm tired of waiting, tired of calling you. All the man says in return is, 'Coming'. 'That's the third time you've said that,' she grumbles. 'And that's the third time *you've* said *that*,' he counters, still writing. 'Do as you please.

[4] Sircar, 'Ebong Indrajit', *Natak Samagra,* Vol. 1, trans. Anjum Katyal, p. 263.

Writing, writing, writing, no eating, no sleeping, only writing—God knows what you'll do with all that writing…' Muttering, she leaves.[5]

With these opening moments, a few things are established. First, the author's stage directions: this woman is the archetypal 'mother' figure: maternal, nurturing, looking after one's bodily needs. She is also conditioned to 'not understand' anything outside this domestic domain. This comes directly from the author, this is what he thinks about such Mashimas. She stands for the domestic, the quotidian, routine and order. All is well with the world if one has one's meals on time. This figure is set up in direct opposition to the Writer who is oblivious of this world, transgressive of it, immersed in abstract tasks of the mind which are unfathomable and mysterious to persons of the domestic world. The sequence is meant to be mildly humorous—one is meant to recognise the mother figure with affection and dismiss her with condescension; one is meant to empathise with the solitary striving artist who struggles alone and needs his privacy and mental space. Mashimas, of course, don't need mental space. It would take a feminist reading to say that just as she is seen to be intruding into and disrupting his 'artistic' space, he can be said to be disrupting her 'domestic' space—the space she has been given charge of to order and control—by refusing to respect its routines, and perhaps eating into her personal time while she waits for him. But we aren't meant to see Mashima as a real person, unlike the Writer. She stands in for not just a type, but a whole value system and worldview: that of the domestic bourgeois routine. She stands in for everything the Writer and Indrajit are in conflict with. She is Ma for Indrajit, whom she continues to chide for not eating, as the play progresses.

There is a sequence in which the Writer attempts to have a philosophical conversation with Mashima. This follows on from a poem spoken by the Writer which begins 'I. Sit and think. Just think.'[6]

> Mashima: You're here?! I've been looking all over for you. What are you doing, sitting here all alone?
> Writer: Thinking. Sitting and thinking.
> Mashima: And what are you thinking about so gloomily?
> Writer: Thinking—who are we?
> Mashima: What's there to think about? You are—you! Who else?
> Writer: Of course. We are—we. I didn't think of that! But—*what* are we?
> Mashima: Listen to you! What are we indeed! You are all great kids—diamond chips, all. Look at how you've all passed your exams so well, got good jobs…

[5] Sircar, 'Ebong Indrajit', *Natak Samagra*, Vol. 1, trans. Anjum Katyal, p. 263.
[6] Ibid., transl. Anjum Katyal, p. 289.

Writer: You're right. Diamond chips. I got as far as the chips; somehow the diamond part escaped me.
Mashima: Really, always speaking in riddles!
Writer: Indeed. You've got two right—now let's see if you get this one. It won't be as easy.
Mashima: What?
Writer: *Why* are we?
Mashima: What d'you mean?
Writer: I mean—why do we exist?
Mashima: God forbid! Why shouldn't you exist?! Who are you harming by being alive?
Writer: Uh Uh—didn't work. That logic didn't work.[7]

Throughout, the Writer is humouring her with his sarcastic (albeit affectionate) responses, indicating that he knows that such a philosophical discussion is way above her head. And sure enough, Mashima acts true to type and dismisses all this philosophical talk as silly nonsense, blaming it on his bachelor status. Why won't he get married, she demands. Asked why he *should* get married she counters: 'Because everyone does. Why can't you do the same?' And he crows with delight at having elicited exactly the response he was expecting from this representative of bourgeois respectability: 'That's it! "Everyone does it"!' He immediately launches into a jingle about conformity, with the refrain—'Coz everybody does it, yes, everybody, bhai!' Exasperated and amused, she hurries away, reiterating her belief that he's crazy but marriage would sort him out.[8] This sequence is meant to reaffirm beyond a doubt that Mashima stands for everything the Writer rejects, or is in resistance to.

Then we have Manasi. Whose very name means 'creation of the mind': the playwright's mind, clearly, and also the Writer's and perhaps also Indrajit's. She is set in opposition to the maternal presence as the other female role—the helpmeet, the muse, the soulmate and romantic partner. Mashima and Manasi are the only two female presences in the play; but Manasi is, in a sense, everywoman. Since she is a creature of the male imagination, it is interesting to see what the contours of her identity are.

She enters on the heels of the intrusive Mashima at the start of the play, but hers is a totally different feminine presence. She is not aggressive. She understands the Writer's emotional state; she is supportive, unthreatening

[7] Sircar, 'Ebong Indrajit', *Natak Samagra*, Vol. 1, trans. Anjum Katyal, p. 290.
[8] Ibid., trans. Anjum Katyal, pp. 290–91.

and warm. She is his muse. This Manasi is sympathetic to the Writer's creative struggle, enquires after his progress and gently questions him when he confesses that he has nothing meaningful to write about. She also facilitates his creative process at various points through the play by suggesting ideas and directions. At the start, she says that despite his pessimism, it may be worth his while to try and write about the people all around them—indicating the audience. And then she melts away. He immediately calls up four men from the audience who are Amal, Vimal, Kamal and Indrajit. And the play proper begins. Later, she tells the Writer that it will be better if Indrajit gives up his incessant dreaming and finds his true self. And that's how the play resolves in an understanding that real life consists in persisting with the road, with no falsely romantic dreams, just the reality of the road.

Indrajit's Manasi is his soulmate. We first see them together as a romantic pair, seated on green grass under a sheltering tree: a pastoral idyll. It is a long conversation. She is sweet and undemanding. She insists that she is dumber than he is; that she needs him to explain intellectual things to her. The very first conversation establishes that she feels obliged, being a woman, to respect the norms (*niyam*) of society, unlike him who, being male, can challenge them. (This point is re-iterated later in the play: women have to conform, they do not have the social leeway to rebel.) He is full of inchoate anger against the whole system, the way things are, the way one is expected to accept 'the norm' without question, despite the blatant injustices all around them. She says that she too feels disturbed, but not angry; she feels scared by his anger. But she doesn't want him to change; his presence in her life makes her own existence bearable, it gives her strength. He wants them to get married; she demurs because they are cousins and it is taboo. She is uncomfortable with public displays of affection and moves away when he puts his arm around her.

This Manasi affirms the social rules and conventions they all live by. She will suffer, but she will acquiesce. In that way, she is strong, but it is the strength of resignation rather than positive choice. She is the one who rebukes Indrajit, saying that life is not a children's game. At one point, she asks if marriage to her would have quelled his restlessness. She is not a rebel.

She is his closest confidante. He says he can speak to her about things his male friends won't understand or be interested in. She is the recipient of his confession that he feels he is walking on a railway line, a key metaphor of the play. He can see the parallel tracks come together far into the distance ahead and behind him; yet, as he walks, that point keeps receding—both in the future and the past. And he realises that there is no use in walking any more. He will never reach that point. He should just lie down on the tracks and wait for a train. Manasi disagrees:

Manasi: You can't do that, Indrajit.
Indrajit: Why not?
Manasi: You have to keep walking. On the road.
Indrajit: I've walked and walked.
Manasi: You have to keep walking.
Indrajit: I'm weary.
Manasi: Still you have to keep walking.
Indrajit: But why? Why? The same old road. I keep walking and walking and walking. And still there's no release?
Manasi: No, there's no release.[9]

She is the one to whom he confesses that he has given up. He has nothing to believe in, no hope, nothing to plan for. He is now one of them. He is no longer Indrajit, but Nirmal, just like Amal Vimal Kamal. And this is the point at which the Writer appears, to persuade him that he is different and to accompany him on the road. Manasi joins them. And the play ends.

So what are we to make of Manasi in her several incarnations through the play? (Manasi is also the wife who appears in vignettes of a typical marriage to Bimal, from new bride to neglected wife to harried mother; and again, the woman Indrajit marries when he succumbs to what society expects of him.) The Writer's Manasi is muse and creative facilitator. Despite her romantic lineaments, Indrajit's Manasi stands for conformity. She has a certain inner strength that keeps her from being a victim figure: she is not afraid to speak her mind; she advises him when she feels he is wrong; she chooses a life alone rather than go against societal norms; and she remains a friend and confidante till the end. And yet her quiet resigned acceptance of a woman's lot is as old as the Ramayana. This is an image, a construct, of woman that has persisted in the popular imagination: the long-suffering, self-sacrificing figure who never rebels against an unfair society but resolutely fulfils the role expected of her. She is meant to be a figure of admiration.

Overall, it is true that Manasi is a major presence in the play. She influences the direction of the action. She is a moral force. But, like Mashima, and indeed like Amal Kamal Vimal, she is a symbol. She represents something, rather than being someone. In a play that is about the individual who cannot accept what is expected of him, who questions societal norms, Manasi

[9] Sircar, 'Ebong Indrajit', *Natak Samagra*, Vol. 1, p. 308.

is a set of ideas. The idea of a woman who completes the man, who fills in all the gaps, as it were, and matches what the man needs. She does not have her own story. She appears in response to the male's needs. She is a sort of dream of the male mind—as her name suggests. Manasi is not a restless female version of Indrajit, though she could have been.

In his analysis of Badal-da's treatment of women, Sibaji Bandypadhyay says:

> In *Ebong Indrajit* and also in later plays [women] are mostly portrayed as *Manasi*, a construct of men who are themselves pre-fabricated. At best they signify some elusive Telos. They are there to remind the men how closed-in they are... Manasi, for example, is ephemeral; she is not a character; she is not there for herself. She is there to show the limits within which the masculine psyche moves. It is a signifier of the closure of the masculine characters. As a result she does not have a claim to autonomy. She is some sense Utopic. The woman signifies a lack which is constituted by the male.[10]

Yet in his very next play, *Sara Rattir*, Badal-da makes the woman character central to the narrative. This play once again takes up the question of conformity to middle-class norms—with bourgeois marriage being shown as paradigmatic of this—in contrast with a much bigger world out there, waiting to be discovered. Unlike its predecessor, however, this play delves into the emotional and psychological world rather than focus on the social system. Although the woman is just called Stree (woman) and her husband Purush (man), they are individuals from the moment they enter, squabbling in the way of much-married couples, arguing and provoking each other out of irritation. There are indications of a deeper communication gap amidst the superficial quarrelling—signs that the woman doesn't express everything she feels—but with mutual caring evident under it all: she worries that he will catch a cold, he is concerned about her wet clothes, and so on. Their banal conversational exchange is pierced by hints of something ominous and inexplicable in the setting: eerie stirrings in the gloom, an oddly selective echo that only repeats certain words and phrases. And the presence of a strange Old Man who materialises out of the dark reaches, welcoming them into his home. The figure of the Old Man is other-worldly and mysterious; he speaks of the mystical number seven, does magic card tricks, and seems to know more about them—how long they've been married, for example, or how old each of them is—than is logically possible. He also seems to

[10] Bandyopadhyay, interview with the author, Kolkata 17 May 2014.

understand that Stree is more than she appears to be. He ricochets her question back at her—'Why do *you* live all alone?'—and something about her reaction indicates that he has hit home, although her husband quickly intervenes saying, 'But she doesn't live alone!' As the play progresses, Stree grows increasingly and noticeably disturbed, unsettled. We learn from a conversation between the Old Man and the Purush that they are a childless couple, that she is often moody and withdrawn, and behaves unpredictably. Purush, a practical man with his feet firmly on the ground, fears this unpredictability which excludes him, which he can neither control nor understand. When he points out that the Old Man puts a poetic spin on everything he says, Old Man replies that poetry is often truer than prosaic language, but no one wants to admit that. Poetry is not Purush's element. Purush thinks that having a child would ground his wife, bring her back to him and her domestic world. He asserts, as if convincing himself, that their mutual love is so strong that nothing can come between them; he knows everything about her and she knows everything about him.

Old Man and Stree talk in a register far removed from the prosaic exchange with the husband. Their words evoke a different world, of something ineffable and intangible. He knows that she wakes up at night to sit by the window, brooding; her husband doesn't know this about her. We learn more about Stree: that she is not eager to have a child, unlike her husband, that she works and her job is important to her. It seems that she is reluctant to be defined totally by her domestic duties of housewife, mother.

As they talk she says to herself, 'It's as if I understand a bit more about Ranjan.' This is the first time this name is brought into the play. Old Man's reply is terse, stern: 'Don't bring up Ranjan now.' Ranjan is the pivot around which the plot turns. Ranjan represents a spiritual mode of being, an all-consuming passion, something which is the complete Other of the prescribed, limited domestic routine in which Stree is bound. Stree yearns for Ranjan, but the Old Man warns her that to unite with Ranjan one must be eternally awake, all night long, night after night. Awakening, consciousness—these cannot be assumed lightly.

As the couple prepares to wait out the storm that night, Stree suddenly recalls that a window was left open in her room—she is concerned that the house will be flooded; her domestic sureties are being threatened, destabilised. But Old Man states that homes do not get washed away easily; they endure. Stree is soon going to be torn between the security of home and the unpredictability of everything Ranjan stands for. The unravelling has already begun as she tells Old Man that she feels as if he is unearthing something deep within her she barely recognises—something so strange it has no name. She flings an accusation at her husband—that he does not understand her at all. That he has never tried or wanted to really know her. Whenever she tries to express herself, he dismisses it as craziness or childishness. She challenges the Old Man, taking a hard, aggressive tone that amazes her husband. He has never seen his wife like this. She is emerging from the contours that both defined and confined her.

That night Stree approaches Old Man who keeps vigil, ever watchful, as is his practice. She tells him she is ready for Ranjan. He questions her. This is an initiation process of a kind. Does she know how much pain lies ahead? Yes, she is prepared for that—because before that there is Bliss. Ecstasy. *Ananda*. However fleeting. Does she realise the price she has to pay? Yes, she does. She will have to give up peace and contentment. But she has lived her whole life within the limits of peace and contentment. She wants more. Does she realise that once she has the knowledge she is seeking, there will be no turning back, no returning to the way things were before? Yes, she realises, and she still wants to know. Does she know Ranjan? Yes, a little. Does she love Ranjan? She replies—do I have the courage? Does Ranjan love her? She replies—do the stars in the sky love the flowers of the soil? Is Ranjan then so remote? To her, yes—she is, after all just an ordinary creature. And is Ranjan then extraordinary? Yes, in her eyes he is. Old Man tells her—You have created a Ranjan of your imagination, your dreams. That is not Ranjan. But she says—That is Ranjan, the Ranjan I see. Ranjan is the sky, and cannot be bound by the earth. Ranjan is the wind one can feel but never hold. Ranjan's eyes hold the whole world.

Still the testing persists. Does she know how those eyes burn, how they are lidless, unclosing, all night, every night? How consciousness is a responsibility that never ends, never sleeps? How it destroys you? She says—I want that. For years she has been restlessly seeking meaning, value, sitting sleepless at her window, unable to bear the emptiness, the nothingness. Tonight, in this wakeful room, she has come to understand—she wants Ranjan. At all cost. She does not want to think about her husband, her earlier life. She does not expect Ranjan to want her. How does it matter? 'My desire—is mine. My desire—is me. All this time I didn't understand, and I was nothing. Now I know, and I am complete. Today I have a meaning. Today I exist. From today onwards I will live.' She insists, 'This single desire is enough for me.'

This entire segment of question and answer serves to establish that here is a woman who has agency, who assumes responsibility for her own choices, who asserts her own desire. This woman is no Manasi. Nor is she just a marker of a certain kind of consciousness that could be male or female. She has been constructed as a gendered character, and her assertion of desire is linked to her gendered role in society. It is the emptiness of that life that has led to her quest for fulfilment.

It seems that she has passed the test. Old Man begins to talk about Ranjan—how his all-seeing eyes are in conflict with his dreaming mind that cannot accept what the eyes insist on showing him; how he weaves a vast net of dreams which is destroyed over and over and yet he persists in weaving the same dream over and over (note the echoes of Sisyphus' boulder in *Ebong Indrajit*). A dream of a woman. A woman who will offer unconditional love, commit her all, asking nothing in return. But his dream is betrayed by woman after woman who makes the pledge only to find that she cannot after all give up everything. Her worldly life tugs at her, and she falters.

This image of the ideal female devotee—a Radha figure from popular Bhakti poetry?—who will somehow, through her total submission, complete Ranjan, give him/it meaning, is an example of Woman as trope, standing in for pure devotion and sacrifice, for worship, in this case.

Stree makes the commitment. She pledges her total devotion, asking nothing in return but that Ranjan acknowledge her in his dream. And Old Man admits: she was in the dream. She casts herself on his breast with a cry of ecstasy. It is a moment of union. The lights go off.

None of this is meant to be taken as 'realistic', clearly. This is not a love scene between an older man and a younger woman. The language used throughout is that of spiritual devotion, a mystic desire for union and completion, very reminiscent of the language of Sufi and Bhakti poetry. It is indicative of a deep longing in Stree for something deeper, more meaningful than her current existence. But the playwright does not spell out what that goal is, what exactly Ranjan or the Old Man signifies. I have already commented on the Rabindranath reference in an earlier chapter—suffice it to say that even the heightened poetic and metaphoric language used here echoes the symbolic vocabulary of Rabindranath's dramas.

This is not the climax of the play. The lights come on again, and Purush is in the room. From spiritual ecstasy, the discourse moves to the reality of the here and now. He has witnessed the embrace. Predictably, he accuses his wife of *paap*—sin. She denies it. He says she was all he had. She says that nothing has changed. She still cares about him as she always did. However, she has a lot more within her which he never cared to know about. They launch into an argument about love. He says he loves her as much as he did when he married her. She says so does she, but all he really expected from her was to provide companionship, the comfort of daily habit, to run his household well, to create a harmonious life for him; and she had done all that. He never asked anything more of her. She is prepared to continue as before, because this other need of hers has nothing to do with their domestic life or their relationship. Ultimately he begs her not to leave him; she agrees only once he promises that he will not bring this up again.[11]

This exchange between them shows her as strong, unbowed, outspoken. She is free of the restrictions that kept her quiet all these years. She expresses her needs and desires frankly. She insists on her right to her own space. She is a liberated woman, sure of herself and in control of the situation. And the memory of her epiphany will stay with her as a precious memory, a source of strength, as she continues with her life. Her husband will not take her for granted easily either—for him too, this has been a night of self-discovery. He has come a long way from the man who described her as a childish creature about whom he knew all there was to know. He has realised that he needs her; that without her he has nothing.

Sara Rattir stands out in the list of Badal-da's plays for its focus on a woman's needs and self-expression, although the central problematic is his constant preoccupation—the conflict between bourgeois limitations (in this case symbolised in a married couple) and a larger consciousness that embraces the world (conveyed through Ranjan, and the Old Man). The gendered particularities of a woman's life are very much part of the discourse of the play, rendered visible as it were, and that too by the woman herself as she articulates her concerns and her desires. It would not be possible to say of this play that the woman character 'lacks autonomy'. It is interesting to see the progression, in gender terms, between *Ebong Indrajit* and *Sara Rattir*, written within a few months of each other. Even though both plays share the same core theme of dissatisfaction with the limits of the middle-class life and a search for meaning beyond it, in the earlier play the woman plays a supporting role (literally) and speaks for stability, continuity and custom, no matter how unhappy it may make her. In the later play, it is the woman who takes the lead (again, literally!) and brings about change.

Baki Itihas is the next 'serious' play Badal-da writes, after three outright comedies in between. The characters are completely of his milieu: Saradindu is a college lecturer and his wife Basanti has just begun to write short stories. Cultured, middle–middle class people. They spend a Sunday exploring their creativity by each crafting a story to explain the possible reasons why a mutual acquaintance, Sitanath, committed suicide.

[11] Sircar, 'Sara Rattir', *Natak Samagra*, Vol. 1, trans. Anjum Katyal, pp. 315–56.

The character of Basanti is realistically etched, as is that of Saradindu. She displays all the attributes of a capable and content housewife, welcoming a guest with offers of tea, joining easily in the banter and teasing, fussing mildly about completing her cooking and chores. Her identity as a creative writer is worn lightly: her husband teases her about it but she underplays her success and insists that she is stuck for a new story idea and that he must help her find one. He is supportive and encouraging, although he comes across as the more knowledgeable one, giving her advice on how to develop a story; but then he is the literature professor who writes essays on Modernism in Theatre, and she is just a fledgling writer.

Her story explaining Sitanath's suicide takes the wife, Kona, as the pivot of the tale. Kona initiates the action, her husband only reacts. Let us see what else we glean from the narrative Basanti weaves. Kona is obsessed with security, a safe home. She comes from a destitute family where her mother and the eldest of three daughters died due to dire poverty; her middle sister has accepted a proposition from a moneyed man to live under his protection; Kona herself has escaped into marriage with a decent provider. She mourns the fact that her father died in a hospital fire; had he been alive, they would all have been safe. When she finds out that her husband too has no money in the bank and has mortgaged their piece of land, she decides that her dream of security through marriage is false. She chooses to follow her middle sister's path and seeks the protection of a rich friend of Sitanath. He finds himself completely betrayed because he had been protecting her all along from knowing the disturbing truth about her father—that he is alive and is a complete criminal and no-good, who has bankrupted them through blackmail. And now she leaves him for his friend. He hangs himself.

There is a sharp-eyed comprehension here of how financial security underpins much of the sentimental propaganda around the concept of marriage and household. A woman is shown single-mindedly doing what she feels is in her best interest; also, there is an assertion that living with a man out of matrimony is not wrong. The man is the victim, the woman the survivor. A reversal of what is to be, in a few years, the theme of *Pagla Ghora*.

Saradindu's explanation of the suicide is that Sitanath was a paedophile; he hanged himself when he realised he was unable to control his sickness. In his story, the wife is like a child to be protected from the ugly truth about her husband, who is a much admired, much loved Principal of a school. There are no strong women characters in his story.

We know, of course, that the third and final act explodes all such 'individualistic' and bourgeois explanations for Sitanath's suicide, which is a result of guilt and responsibility all right, not for personal tragedies, but over the 'baki itihas' or 'other history' of the world.

Written immediately after this play comes *Bagh*. The essential theme of this play is friendship, says Badal-da in his preface to the play[12]: friendship between a man and a woman. This is a two-character play. It has a surreal feel in that the dialogue and the tone are very realistic but the characters consist of a Tiger ('Bagh, Royal Bengal Tiger, Sher Khan the Tiger') and a young woman. The Tiger has abducted her and brought her to his 'den', which is crammed with books of history, philosophy, economics, literature and poetry. Clearly the Tiger is a metaphor. He is a misfit, a loner who is too straightforward and honest to fit into society, like a jungle animal trapped in the city. He has retreated into his lair, shutting himself off from the empty talk (the *bak bak bak bak*) of the outside world. The play starts with the Tiger putting on a show of power for his captive, threatening her with his anger and his brute strength, but it slowly becomes clear that this is all empty bluster. It is unclear why he has resorted to this violent act of abduction. It seems that he has been stalking her for some time, and he appears to harbour a rage against women like her. But she takes him by surprise as she refuses to be cowed by him. The two start a conversation, then begin to share confidences and find that they think alike on many issues. At one point he tells her she can leave, but she hesitates when she senses his loneliness and chooses to stay. He confesses that he could not pass his matriculation because of his weakness with numbers and mathematics, and she offers to teach him. Eventually she leaves with the promise that she will return every week to tutor him. There is nothing sexual about the relationship; that would make it too obvious and predictable. It is simply a friendship between two lonely people who have made a human connection.

When the play begins, the girl seems destined to be a sweet, young helpless victim figure; but the tables are turned as she gains control of the situation, and we end up seeing that it is her abductor who is the more vulnerable and helpless of the two. She is confident, she can fit into the real world and she has figured out how to negotiate a lonely marriage, a husband with whom she has little in common, and a job she doesn't seem to think much of. She has found an outlet for her interests in the *mahila samiti*. And she walks out of the Tiger's den on her own terms, having made a friend and added

[12] Sircar, 'Bagh', *Natak Samagra*, Vol. 2, p. 100.

another interest to her life. From the gender perspective, she is a refreshing addition to Badal-da's cast of women characters.

Pagla Ghora has often been seen as a progressive play in support of women. It establishes that men are essentially exploitative and calculating in their relationships with women, that they allow themselves to be constrained by social mores and norms rather than follow their hearts and desires; that they are ready to sacrifice the woman they love rather than take a risk that may cause scandal and outrage, or result in them losing their reputations and their jobs. This play is populated by several women characters, and we will see how they are constructed and what they say to us.

Once again in this play, there is the introduction of a surreal element: the setting, which is a cremation ground at night. Four men play cards as they wait out the cremation of the corpse of a young woman who has killed herself. As the night deepens, they share their tales of love and dishonour with us, revisiting their shame and acknowledging guilt. The spirit of the young, nameless girl exhorts them to tell their stories while she mourns the total lack of any passion or love in her life—a barrenness that has led to her suicide.

Almost schematically, Badal-da sets out four different relationships from four different socio-economic segments of society, as if to prove that regardless of education and background, men are the same in this one aspect of their lives—their handling of passion, love and women.

Shashi is a middle-class gentleman, the love of whose life, Malti, is supposed to be marrying his childhood friend Pradip. She pleads with him to marry her, saying the man is a brute whom she can never care for, even showing him evidence of physical abuse. Shashi cannot face either the social scandal or the rift with his friend and sends her back to her hell. During their showdown, she asks, 'You reject me just for this—for Pradip?'[13] Is their love, then, not as important to him as the older relationship between the two men—the brotherhood? 'Just because you will lose face with him?' she goads. But his response defeats her: 'Not with Pradip, Malti. Myself. I will lose respect for myself. If I lose to myself like this and marry you, I will never be able to be happy myself and neither will I be able to make you happy.' Even if she refuses to marry Pradip, he insists that the knowledge that he came between her and his best friend will haunt him forever. Unable to strip him of his self-esteem and his future peace of mind, she gives up.

[13] This and all other references to the play are from Badal Sircar, 'Pagla Ghora', *Natak Samagra*, Vol. 2, trans. Anjum Katyal, pp. 379–438.

She returns to her abusive, loveless situation, but kills herself soon after. He lives with the guilt and remorse. His high-sounding moral stance now seems hollow and hypocritical.

Himadri, the youngest of the four men, was a tutor to the brother of the girl he fell in love with, and who in turn fell in love with him. In his case, it is the class barrier, with its ensuing cultural differences, that keeps him from committing fully to her. Milli comes from a wealthy, Westernised family; hers is a life of 'tennis, swimming, driving, party-picnics.' He cannot accept her habits and her drinking in particular. When she pleads with him not to be angry she turns into a little girl, using childish terms to make her point: 'God promise I will never touch a drink again.' Eventually, in their final showdown, it comes down to the unbridgeable gap between their worlds. She accuses him of valuing his 'world' above her; she has tried to fit into his world, but she feels constantly judged by him. His pride does not allow him to see beyond her father's wealth and status to the vulnerable girl beyond. She childishly threatens to start drinking if he leaves her. He scoffs, 'Congratulations, Miss Ray! So your world is victorious after all.' He walks out on her. Later he hears that she has died—the car she was driving too fast while 'under the influence' crashed into a tree: once again, guilt and remorse, and a distrust of alcohol and its influence on human beings.

Satu is the street-smart one amongst them—plying them with liquor, always ready with a risqué comment, amused by Himadri's earnest 'good boy' persona. He is a contractor, a job that keeps him on the road. He boasts, 'Why bother getting married when I can get the benefits without it?' There is a raffish air about him, which he makes no attempt to disguise. It is all the more surprising, therefore, when his sad story emerges. Lachmi is the woman he rescued from trafficking, who is shown as slavishly adoring—she wants nothing better than to serve and look after him. Yet, when she comes to him for protection one night, clearly petrified, and begs him to take her in, he refuses. He has found her a job in someone's home—she has to adjust—he cannot possibly have her live with him. She even offers to be his maid servant, but he is scared of 'what people will say'. Is it fear of commitment that holds him back or fear of scandal? Whatever the reason, he tells her to forget about him. She says, brokenly, 'Why did you rescue me, Babuji? You should have left me there to die.' He sends her away. The next time he sees her, she is a corpse. She has died destitute, sick, alone. He is left with questions—was it wrong to rescue her in the first place and raise her expectations? Was it wrong to entrust her to others? Again, guilt and responsibility, and the failure to love.

The last story to be unfolded is Kartik's. He is a chemist, a compounder by profession. Early in the play, he relates an anecdote about a man who spent his whole life loving someone from afar, single mindedly devoted to her as he observes her grow from a young girl to a woman, but never summoning up the courage to declare his love. We later come to know that the devoted lover is himself, and the object of his devotion none other than the unnamed girl who is being cremated. We learn that she had gone to him to say that she wanted to kill herself and to ask if he would give her some poison for a quick death. He asked her why she wanted to end her life. Her reason was that she had nothing to live for. No one had ever loved her, and she herself had never known passion or desire. Rather than persist with her empty life, she had decided to finish it. Shaken, he extracts a promise from her that she will wait a week and visit him again. Why, what will change in a week, she asks. You will find out something, he offers. However, within the week, he hears that she has hanged herself. He has lost forever not just his chance at love but a chance to make her feel loved because of his inability to take a risk and declare his feelings. And she dies without knowing that she had inspired passion in at least one human heart. Guilt and responsibility, along with grief, have brought him to the cremation ground tonight. Left alone, he uncaps the vial of poison and considers drinking it. Finally, he upturns the poison and pours it carefully into the earth. He has chosen to continue living. The play ends.

So, all four men have betrayed the women in their lives, while the women, on the other hand, have offered themselves unconditionally, daring to love uninhibitedly and willing to risk the consequences. Each of the women dies for love. We see the men as idiosyncratic individuals with their distinct characters, as they banter with and tease each other, playing cards and drinking together, sharing stories and experiences. There is a bonhomie and brotherhood between them, despite each one harbouring a secret sorrow. Let us see how the women are portrayed.

Malti, Milli and Lachmi, except for age and social background, could be interchangeable. This is because all we see of them is the tearful supplicant, the hurt woman begging her lover to accept her, but being spurned in return. Each of the women's only identity in the play is that of a victim. The young Milli is the only one who shows a hint of defiance; her death too is achieved in a flourish of defiance. The other two accept their lovers' dismissal quietly. The overwhelming impression created is that love, and a relationship with a man, is the only thing that gives value to a woman's life. She is incomplete, empty, of no value, unless a man ascribes her value by claiming her. Moreover, the image of a woman as the custodian of pure, selfless and sacrificial love feeds right into the traditional construct of a woman. 'Badal Sircar's treatment of Woman is a repetition of a very old paradigm which is part and parcel of Bengal's modernity. The entire scheme of modernity of Bengal was articulated through the figure of the woman. So the woman is in most cases a kind of storehouse of various desires—an empty signifier,'[14] says Sibaji Bandyopadhyay. In this play, women are 'modern' enough to aspire to romantic love, and to express their desire to their men, but they remained defined by what the men are not—they are indicative of a lack in the male.

The fourth woman—who remains unnamed—is a prominent presence in the play. As the spirit of the girl who is being cremated, she goads the men into revisiting their memories, provoking, challenging, commenting and questioning throughout. She also repeatedly invokes the *pagla ghora* metaphor—the wild horse of untamed passion which has never visited her. She longs to know true passion, with all its promise of pain and deep emotion. At the end, when she realises that she is the object of Kartik's unrequited longing, she cries to be taken off the funeral pyre. She would never have killed herself if she had known there was some love in her life after all. This just makes her victimhood all the more pathetic.

Although the depiction of women in the play is one-dimensional and weak, the play does show us the social discrimination against women, the double standards that prevail, and the restrictions women have to accept. Marriage against their will to men who have the license to mistreat them, financial dependency leading to exploitation, a paucity of options if they wish to change or better their lives—these are the causes that lie behind the women's situations in the play. In this sense, *Pagla Ghora* does showcase women's issues. As G.J.V. Prasad says, 'In *Pagla Ghora* you don't have a play about what men do to men, which is vintage Sircar, but what men do to women. Thus it has a unique place in Sircar's oeuvre.'[15] Feminist director Tripurari Sharma referred to *Pagla Ghora* as a play that showed how insensitively men treated women across social strata, as a play that showcased the double standards that prevailed: at the time it was considered a progressive play with an important message.[16]

[14] Bandyopadhyay, interview with the author, Kolkata 17 May 2014.

[15] Prasad, 'The Third Gaze: The Theatre of Badal Sircar' in Lakshmi Subramanyam (ed.), *Muffled Voices*, p. 75.

[16] Interview with the author, New Delhi, 30 May 2014.

In the early 1970s, after Badal-da wrote *Spartacus*, his first play for the Anganmancha space, he returned to tried and tested ground with *Suitcase*, another serious play set squarely in the now familiar middle-class Bengali home. In the Preface to this play, Badal-da says he planned to write three short pieces set in three distinct political situations, linked by the common motif of the suitcase. He ended up writing just the first in the trilogy. It is a short play, in which Parul, a housewife, is the central character.[17] It is the year 1942. The anti-British nationalist movement is at its peak. Parul's husband Abani is a successful officer in a British company. One day, Shyamal, an old friend of theirs from their college days, comes to see him on urgent business. He is involved with the nationalist movement, and he is being hunted by the authorities. He needs a place to hide; failing that, he has to leave a suitcase in safe keeping overnight. It contains compromising material. He believes that due to their common history of political activism during their younger days, Parul and Abani are bound to help him and will not betray him to the police. Since Abani is not home, Parul reluctantly takes custody of the suitcase just for that night. In conversation with him, she begins to recall their idealist days, when they stood up for their nationalist beliefs. All that anti-British sentiment is now kept firmly under wraps, given Abani's professional life. When Abani returns, there is a confrontation between the husband and the wife. He wants her to accompany him to an official party; she is uneasy at such affairs and tries to avoid them. Finally, she agrees to go since it is important for his career. Then he notices the suitcase and at first she tries to lie to avoid admitting that she is harbouring potentially damning evidence in their home. However, the story is soon out, and immediately all the buried tensions over his changed political beliefs surface. He accuses her of nursing a soft spot for Shyamal ('If he had agreed to marry you, you would never have accepted me.'), and threatens to inform the police about the suitcase. She reminds him that he was once an idealist like Shyamal, not the self-serving sycophant he has now become. She warns him—if he calls the police, she will indict him, hold him culpable, and that will be the end of his promising future. He is stunned.

Abani: You're blackmailing me?
Parul: Yes.
Abani: Your own husband?
Parul: Yes.

[17] Badal Sircar, 'Suitcase', *Natak Samagra*, Vol. 3 (Kolkata: Mitra and Ghosh, 2012), pp. 182–98.

Abani: Shyamal Dasgupta means that much to you?
Parul: No, Shyamal Dasgupta doesn't. But the young Abani Sen I once knew does.[18]

He backs down. But he realises that the suitcase will always be a silent presence between them, a watershed moment in their relationship.

In this play, we see a full-fledged woman character who evolves from an unremarkable, conventional housewife to a voice of conscience, who stands up to a husband she feels has abandoned his principles. This is no meek biddable creature like the women in *Pagla Ghora*. This woman is capable of criticising and threatening her husband, of taking decisions like keeping the suitcase to help the cause and an old friend, even though she suspects that her husband will disapprove.

We have looked at those plays by Badal-da in which women characters have a substantial presence, even if not always a significant role, and seen that there is sufficient variety in his depiction of women to discourage any easy summarising on the subject. Tripurari Sharma said, looking back, that for those of them who followed his theatre closely from the early 1980s onwards, there was an overall sense that the plays were generally progressive with regard to women—'A step forward, at least. Certainly not negative.'[19]

After this stage in his work, as Sibaji Bandyopadhyay points out, 'Badal Sircar gives up on "character" itself. Every character in his [later] plays literally shrivels up to become mere datum. And what he then seeks to dramatize is the structure itself; to be precise, "structure without subject".'[20] In such plays, attempting to analyse representation of a character is irrelevant. They are there as so many signifiers, as symbols and metaphors and ideas. The plays themselves take up societal and political issues which affect both men and women equally. It is fair to say, as several people have, that after a point, in Badal-da's plays, the women disappear.[21] But that is because they become, like and alongside the men, part of general humanity.

We know that Badal-da's Third Theatre is premised on direct human communication based on equality between the actors and the audience; it is premised on politically and socially meaningful content, with equality being fundamental to the ethics of the theatre. Let us see how these ideals

[18] Sircar, 'Suitcase', *Natak Samagra*, Vol. 3, trans. Anjum Katyal, p. 198.

[19] Interview with the author, New Delhi, 30 May 2014.

[20] Interview with the author, Kolkata, 17 May 2014.

[21] These comments were made by Rustom Bharucha and Abanti Chakravarty during their interviews.

translate into the treatment of men and women within the group and in the Third Theatre, as well as in his workshops with non-Satabdi participants.

In the area of alternative, political or socially activist theatre, where women participate alongside men, it is a sad reality that they are often not accepted or treated as equal. In this space which is supposed to be progressive, they often face all the same forms of discrimination that exist in the society around them. They usually end up playing a supportive role both in the group and in performance. This was all the more true of the period in which Badal-da was most active, the 1970s to 1990s. Was this situation reflected in Satabdi as well?

Bharati Chatterjee (nee Sircar), Bisakha (Meera) Ray and Topu were part of Satabdi in the early 1970s. They are amongst the earliest women members of the group. Of them, Topu is still part of Satabdi. Each of them, in their interviews with me, spoke of a gender-neutral atmosphere in their group workshops. In this space, everyone was treated as an equal human being, regardless of sex, age, background or creed. Exercises were for all, and the trust building games which involved physical proximity were practised without inhibition; that was the point of these exercises, to break through the inbuilt barriers and inhibitions we are socialised to internalise. For the women, there was an added layer of discomfort, in that from childhood girls are taught to guard their bodies and hold themselves apart from the bodies of all males, and after puberty this self-consciousness is even more developed. Madeeha Gauhar questioned Badal-da about this when she felt physically uncomfortable being in such close proximity to men's bodies, and his response was that it was about loosening inhibitions.[22] At the time when Badal-da started these workshops, they were not common theatrical practice in our society. It required a high comfort level for women to relax in the workshop space.

Another factor that acquired an additional gendered dimension was that of leaving your 'daily' identity and stresses behind once the workshop began. Many of the regular Satabdi actors talked about how this space and process allowed them the joy of such an unmooring.[23] For young middle-class women, there was even less permitted space into which they could escape from the selves they formed to cope with familial and societal expectations. The workshop allowed them this free space. This benefit was felt not just within Satabdi but by female participants in outside workshops as

[22] Madeeha Gauhar, interview with the author, Lahore, 25 February 2014.
[23] Interview with Satabdi actors, 13 July 2014.

well. One development NGO organised a workshop for teenage girls from the Panchannagram/VIP Nagar area on the outskirts of Calcutta. These were the daughters of women with whom they worked, and the aim was to help them build confidence and also to develop a spirit of collectivity and teamwork amongst them. The adolescents, who started off withdrawn and awkward, were visibly enjoying themselves on day two and three, much more relaxed and forthcoming than when they began. Badal-da was approachable, encouraging, but firm about pushing them to express themselves freely, and it was liberating for them.[24] Topu said the same thing about Badal-da.

> When I joined I had no idea of doing theatre; I didn't join to perform. I just wanted to be associated with Badal-da's work. But he wouldn't take no for an answer, he just insisted and wouldn't let up till I started participating—and I've been a performer ever since.[25]

The fundamental premise of a workshop—that everyone is a human being, everyone is equal, and all other identities are to be shed at the door—is deeply liberating for men as well as women, but given that women are usually treated as less than equal in our society, additionally so for them.

Another goal of the workshop was creative self-expression and improvisation. This naturally called on inner experience, and it allowed women to draw on their own lives legitimately as relevant subject material. It was also liberating given that women's voices did not have too many opportunities to speak or be heard. This was one route for women's experience and concerns to enter the discourse of theatre.

Then, Badal-da's workshops with his group were about content—socially and politically relevant subject matter—discussion and learning. Not only did this keep the women intellectually engaged in terms of developing opinions and points of view, it also encouraged them to contribute information, news and material to the common discussion pool, as for example, Bisakha's experiences of family planning work in Topsia.[26]

What was the position of women within Satabdi? Bisakha talked about the degree of autonomy Badal-da allowed her, as a core member of the group, to conduct workshops on her own. Topu mentioned how she along with others, contributed content and ideas to plays they devised together.

[24] First-hand account by Kavita Panjabi, who participated alongside them (Badal-da did not permit observers in his workshop; he felt it was inhibiting for the participants.). This was around 1983.

[25] Topu, during Satabdi actors' interview, 13 July 2014.

[26] Ella Dutta, Introduction, Badal Sircar, *Three Plays*, p. 6.

Bharati said that if the women members felt uncomfortable about the attitude of the men in the group (for whom, too, the whole experience of such free interaction with women was unfamiliar), they would address it as sensitively as possible through internal discussion. None of the women group members indicated that there was unaddressed sexual friction, harassment or exploitation that they were aware of. None of them said that they felt less equal than the male members of the group.[27] Mangai confirms this with her own observation after interacting with Satabdi: 'Meeting Shanta Dutta and Krishna Ghosh along with a few other younger women in the team helped me understand that they were taking crucial decisions within the group. They were not frills attached to the group. And they have earned their place.'[28]

There is little doubt that Badal-da tried to promote a democratic atmosphere within the group. One heard even from those outside Satabdi (such as Mohammed Waseem) about how he was always open, accessible and a good listener. Satabdi members talked of how he communicated with them at their level, made complex things simple and easy to understand and never let them feel that he was above them in any way. And yet it is clear that they all looked up to him. He was, of course, much older than they were, and they saw him as a mentor figure rather than a peer.[29] This caused an inevitable hierarchy with him as the 'head' but at least within the other members of Satabdi there was equality. There were no lead actors, stars or divas.

The Third Theatre approach did not privilege men over women, nor did it permit a distinction between the two. Both dressed almost the same, and sans makeup, the overall effect was that of a homogenous group. Women played male roles at will. In the chorus, women and men were indistinguishable in terms of movement, action, behaviour and roles. Together their bodies formed forests, streams, bridges, factories and trains. There was no femininisation of the women in the group. This was refreshing for the activist women who joined the group, given that conventional theatre was still an area where women were a relatively recent entry, and that they were expected to play up and emphasise their feminine qualities. Tripurari Sharma speaks of the significance of this:

> At that time, it was a step forward to have women as part of the chorus, seen as equal and not as different from men. At the time, women were trying not

[27] Interviews with: Bharati Chatterjee, Kolkata, January 2009; Bisakha Ray, Kolkata, 14 May 2014; and Topu, Kolkata, 13 July 2014.

[28] A. Mangai, 'Badal Sircar'.

[29] Interview with Satabdi actors, 13 July 2014.

> to be seen just as objects of beauty, sex objects, as 'feminine' creatures. It was a period when women were just beginning to go out to work; they were probably more comfortable not being singled out in terms of clothes, makeup etc. It was also part of showing that theatre is not just decorative or entertaining, but a serious form of communication. And they felt more comfortable that way. From today's perspective, one could ask—did you make them invisible as a result? But no, they were all actors, that's how they thought of it.[30]

Bisakha emphasised that the Third Theatre required a commitment to social engagement, a political awareness, rather than just an interest in performance. If you were looking for recognition, fame or a far more lucrative career in film or television—common motivations for actors joining theatre—the Third Theatre was not for you. So, it followed that the actors, both male and female, who joined the Third Theatre were more interested in the message of the work, in the cultural action that it embodied, than in showcasing themselves as individuals or earning a good living. This was meant to be a cooperative rather than competitive environment, as Sumit Biswas pointed out in his interview, so individuals were not on a one-upmanship course. This was an added facet to the gender neutrality of the group's appearance. The plays addressed society as a whole, attacked injustice for all, preached equality for everyone. Women and women's issues were considered part of this overall social fabric.

As a theatre activist focusing on women's issues, Tripurari Sharma has travelled quite extensively all over the country to do workshops and projects with a wide range of people, many of whom had experienced workshops with Badal-da. When asked if she had picked up any negative comments about the treatment of women in his workshops she said no. No one had ever even hinted at anything derogatory to women.[31]

Tripurari mentioned that like her, Badal-da was interested in working with non-actors, human beings who were not part of the theatre world, but who had something to say, who needed a voice. Since she too was interested in the same thing, they both did many workshops with marginalised peoples, NGOs and their target groups. Perhaps these people would never become theatre workers, but they emerged more empowered and confident. Nishat Jahan of Bangladesh too testifies to the impact of his workshops on their rural constituency of agricultural workers.[32] Again, women benefited

[30] Tripurari Sharma, interview with the author, New Delhi, 30 May 2014.
[31] Ibid.
[32] Nishat Jahan, email interview, 6 July 2014.

hugely from the exercise since it was so much more unusual for them to be granted a space for public self-expression. Talking about his workshops, Badal-da himself mentions how women participants found it enabling and liberating (see Chapter 11).

In terms of her own work as a feminist director, Tripurari said that she learned from Badal-da how any space can be turned into a performance space. Working with women, as she often did, this was useful. It could be a room, a hall, a courtyard, a library in a college, almost any space. She also learned from him how to design in relation to the audience, not the set; to think of the actor and the performance in relation with the spectator.

One should mention here too that Badal-da was capable of developing very close relationships in terms of equality with strong women who were rebels and nonconformists in their own way. His letters to Monu, published in *Prabasher Hijibiji*, testify to one such relationship. In the third volume of *Purano Kasundi*, he tells us about his respect for and close friendship with Chandralekha whom he admiringly describes as much more than a dancer.[33] Along with praise for her various accomplishments—her pioneering work in 'breaking through the walls' of tradition to forge a new dance style, her excellent writing and drawing—he points admiringly to her free and liberated lifestyle and behaviour: 'No rules or limitations of social convention could restrain her. She was uninhibited in the way she spoke, uninhibited in the way she behaved.'[34] Bisakha, who became his second wife, came to Satabdi from a political background. She was part of the Naxalite Movement and had chosen a far from conventional life in pursuance of her emotional and political commitment to social revolution. She saw Satabdi's work as cultural action, as an extension of political activity. She describes a relationship of mutual respect in the early years, in which, despite the considerable age difference between her and Badal-da (over 20 years), they discussed and argued freely and during which she contributed conceptually to the Third Theatre repertoire.[35]

One often sees, in theatre, a contradiction between the progressive ideals professed in the plays (in terms of representation of women on stage, female characters or taking up women's issues) and the day-to-day reality of how

[33] Chandralekha Prabhudas Patel (1928–2006), commonly known as Chandralekha, pioneering Indian dancer, and innovative, influential choreographer.

[34] Sircar, *Purano Kasundi*, Vol. 3, trans. Anjum Katyal, p. 76.

[35] Bisakha (Meera) Ray, interview with the author, Kolkata, 14 May 2014. By 1990, the relationship had soured, but the 1970s and 1980s were years of 'Badal-Meera chemistry', in her words.

women are treated within the group. Theatre is a collective activity, as much about process as output, and if the progressive thinking is not practised on the ground, then one cannot claim to be either politically or socially evolved. Even group theatre, conceived as an alternative to the market-driven, commercial theatre, and a supposedly forward-thinking and liberated space, has a disappointing track record as far as treating women as equals goes. It has remained a rather patriarchal space. From the Third Theatre, then, with its commitment to being 'free' in all senses of the word, one expects a lot more. I specifically mention women here since we are looking at gender, but this would apply equally to caste, religion, class or any other divisive stratification that exists in society. That is why I felt it important to explore this side of Badal-da's theatre: not just the representation of women, but the relationship with women as well.

We are left with the question—did Badal-da's theatre remain a patriarchal space, despite the ideological commitment to human equality? The answer is complicated and may not have a single correct answer. From all accounts and conversations, one gleans that Badal-da certainly was a mentor figure. His group, Satabdi, consisted of much younger people; none of them were peers. But does that make him a patriarch? I think not. By temperament and behaviour he was democratic, open and, from all accounts, never pulled rank. He was clearly the one in charge, but, it seems, more like a guide than an autocrat. Satabdi members have talked about how troublesome issues were resolved through discussion as a group rather than diktats or orders from above. The telling example provided by Sumit Biswas of how Badal-da got them to work through a major internal crisis by using a workshop exercise is a case in point (see Chapter 11).

And yet there are ambiguities and confusions which emerge in his plays in terms of how women are represented. Sibaji Bandyopadhyay says,

> The chief weakness of Badal Sircar's plays, to my mind, is that even when women are imagined to be not wholly engulfed by stifling structure, the political significance of this "exceptionalism" is not probed with sufficient alacrity. What his plays lack is a sustained feminist scrutiny.[36]

This is certainly true if we go by our reading of the gender aspect in his plays. With his move to the Third Theatre, women disappear from the discourse, but that is because the discourse is about humanity on the whole, of which women are an equal part. If we turn to Satabdi, evidence seems

[36] Bandyopadhyay, interview with the author, Kolkata, 17 May 2014.

to indicate that women and men were given equal treatment, and if there were discrepancies they were not on account of gender. It is also important to note that women theatre activists and feminist directors have embraced the Third Theatre concepts and methodology as much as the men—it offers a liberatory and enabling alternative for them.

Taking all this into account, it seems reductionist and far too simplistic to assess his theatre within the paradigm of patriarchy. It would be more useful to assess it in terms of how it has helped empower or enable women—and there, I feel, it has been successful for all the reasons discussed above. His methodology and approach have tremendous potential to be even more so in the future.

CHAPTER THIRTEEN

TALKING POLITICS

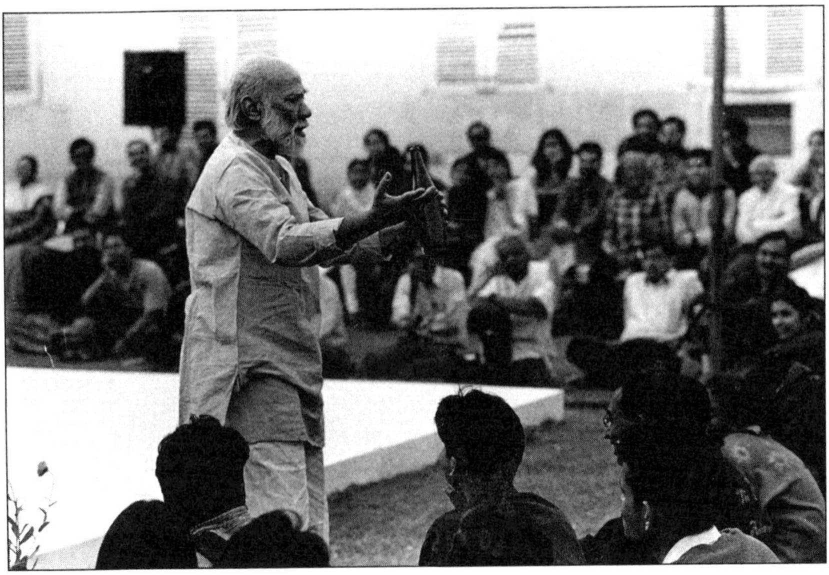

Badal Sircar performs
Courtesy: Satabdi

How would one assess the politics of Badal-*da*'s theatre? There seems to be a wide range of answers to this question, which makes it all the more interesting. No one doubts that he was doing political theatre, but no one quite agrees on the degree, type or efficacy of its politics. Let us try and understand the nuances—and contradictions—of the politics of his theatre.

As we have traced the trajectory of Badal-da's theatre, I have pointed out a pattern of steadily growing politicisation of his plays, and also a deepening concern with questions that can be seen as moral, ethical or political, depending on one's point of view—questions of socio-economic inequality, the injustice prevailing in the status quo, man's violence against man, nuclear annihilation. Before Badal—the young man—came to Marxism, there was Sunday School and the very Christian feelings of guilt and responsibility have been an urgent consideration in his plays, a fundamental imperative that runs like a strong current through his theatre from its early manifestation in *Ebong Indrajit* to his Third Theatre work.

We know from the first volume of his autobiography, *Purano Kasundi*, that Badal-da was a member of the Communist Party as a young man in the early 1940s. He also mentions it in an interview he gave in his 80s:

> I had been a member since 1943... I left the party in 1951. Before that, I had been suspended for a year for criticising the party's role in the railway strike... I didn't join the party under the influence of some *dada*. I—and many others like me at that time—came to the party from a feeling that this world has to be changed. Even after leaving the party, I feel I am still doing its work—I mean the work I was there for, in the first place. The work of changing the world. That is not finished and I am still doing it. Through theatre.[1]

The impulse to work for change, for the betterment of the world, predated his coming to theatre. And yet, despite examples all around him of socially and politically conscious theatre—IPTA, for example, of which he even mentions seeing a performance[2])—he spent more than a decade after he left the Party engaging in purely entertainment theatre. It was only with *Ebong Indrajit* that the first hints of questioning the status quo, of critiquing the middle-class bourgeois worldview, began. Thereafter, we can trace the steadily growing rejection of middle-class complacency and self-interest, the recognition of a history of injustice in the world, and an assumption of guilt and responsibility, leading eventually to action.

Badal-da reiterates—both in his plays and in his writings and interviews—that despite the lack of hope and the loss of belief, one must keep on keeping on. Rolling that boulder up the hill. Walking the unending road. Looking for hope around the next bend. Re-weaving the net of dreams. Surviving so that one can continue to search for the meaning, the value, of life. In this

[1] Nilanjan Dutta, 'Badal Sircar: Ideology has not failed me', http://currentnews.in/2011/01/03/ideology-has-not-failed-me/ (accessed 10 October 2013). It should be noted that there is some discrepancy in estimates of the length of Badal-da's association with the party.

[2] Sircar, *Purano Kasundi*, Vol. 1, p. 60.

lies the heroism of the educated, urban middle-class subject Badal-da writes about and for. Sibaji Bandyopadhyay says:

> The conclusion is a kind of optimistic note—to 'keep trying'. Now what is this 'keep trying'? This is his politics: to remain a political animal even when you know that your very notion of action is not going to be fulfilled. This applies not just to dramatic texts but also to revolutionary practice.[3]

His experience of Europe after the Second World War made Badal-da ruminate on the unpredictability and absurdity (in the sense of being illogical, irrational) of death by war. It changed his perspective on the ordered existence of middle-class living, with its prescribed narrative of birth, education, career, marriage, procreation, death, in an unbroken loop. Death by war ruptures this narrative so definitively that a new, a different meaning has to be found to replace it. In Nigeria Badal-da had a life-altering encounter with Fernand Gigon's book *Formula for Death, e = mc2*, which he worked into a play (*Tringsha Satabdi*). The significance of the nuclear attack on Hiroshima changed forever Badal-da's thinking about death, and therefore life and living. He was already thinking about it in *Ebong Indrajit*; thereafter there is hardly a play which does not make mention of the atom bomb. As Sibaji Bandopadhyay says:

> The book left an indelible mark on him.... The book made him aware of an awesome truth—which was, that following the technological application of Einstein's formula *e* = mc2, the animal euphemistically called the *homo sapien* had it in its power to destroy the earth at one go. Moving from the domain of myth, absolute destruction or *pralaya* had become a concrete possibility... over and above individualistic *diachronic* death global *synchronic* death was both realistically and radically affecting the human psyche.[4]

This nuclear horror became a defining factor of Badal-da's politics, avers Sibaji Bandopadhyay:

> The recognition that from 6 August 1945, i.e., from Hiroshima Day, the pairing of individualistic *Thanatos* with globalized *Thanatos* would be inexorable gave birth to a set of discursive projects collectively termed *Nuclear Criticism*. In my opinion the only Bengali author whose imagination was gripped by the new regime of death was Badal Sircar.[5]

[3] Bandyopadhyay, interview with the author, Kolkata, 17 May 2014.
[4] Ibid.
[5] Ibid.

According to Bandopadhyay:

> [Badal-da's] *Baki Itihas* (1965), *Porey Konodin* (1966), *Tringsha Satabdi* (1966) are three full-fledged instances of mature Nuclear Criticism. The memory of Hiroshima Day and the terrifying apocalypse which would 'not only be the final and fullest extension of every cruelty and viciousness but also the annihilation of every possibility of justification or condemnation' haunts many of Badal Sircar's plays—e.g., *Bagh* (1965), *Pralaap* (1966).[6]

Badal-da himself says:

> Nowadays many of my plays, one after the other, have mentioned the atom bomb. *Ebong Indrajit, Baki Itihas, Porey Konodin, Pralaap*. And of course that's totally true of *Hiroshima Chhariye*. I'm not at all concerned about it. The more mentions about this issue the better, is how I feel.[7]

This is upon completing his first full play on the nuclear issue, which he later called *Tringsha Satabdi*. He has forgotten to add *Bagh* to this list, and later there will be more. But it shows how this particular subject was important to him.

Sadanand Menon, theatre critic, recognises the centrality of the nuclear threat in Badal-da's work. 'Sircar took a more affirmative direction in 1966–67 in his "anti-nuclear" trilogy *Baki Itihaas* (Remaining History), *Tringsha Shatabdi* (Thirtieth Century) and *Shesh Nei* (No End). To date, these remain the only critique in Indian theatre of the country's demented nuclear pursuits.'[8]

In fact, Sibaji Bandopadhyay sees a direct connection between nuclear criticism and Badal-da's adoption of the Third Theatre, saying:

> I strongly feel that Badal Sircar's move towards the Third Theatre—the title for dramatic practices devoted to the study of 'structure without subject'—would not have taken place if his reflections on death and disaster had not widened. Hiroshima Day holds the key for the dramatic elaborations brought on by Badal Sircar during the Third Theatre phase.[9]

[6] Bandyopadhyay, interview with the author, Kolkata, 17 May 2014.

[7] Sircar, *Prabasher Hijibiji*, trans. Anjum Katyal, p. 279.

[8] Sadanand Menon, 'Badal Sircar (1925–2011): A Curtain Call for Political Theatre', *Economic and Political Weekly*, Vol. xlvi, No. 22, 28 May 2011, p. 17.

[9] Bandyopadhyay, interview with the author, Kolkata, 17 May 2014.

Elaborating on his assertion that Badal-da's output should be seen through the framework of Nuclear Criticism, Sibaji Bandopadhyay proffers evidence in support of his theory:

> The Hiroshima moment is constantly invoked by referring to Bengali middle-class life. How they are not concerned. This lack of concern of the individual vis-à-vis a general collapse is the message of the structure. Many left-wing dramatists have also tried to depict structure, class-struggle etc. What stands out in the case of Badal Sircar is that this depiction of class-struggle, class-contradiction, etc, is done under the shadow of total death. I don't think Utpal Dutt or any other such dramatist ever thought about it. That's what gives a special psychic charge to his plays.
>
> I will just read out lines from some of his plays of the 60s, when he is not even talking about nuclear devastation. Even then this theme constantly returns.
>
> *Bagh*
>
> —Atom bombs! Making atom bombs!
>
> *Baki Itihas*
>
> I keep cuttings, not of news items but of images, of news images . . . this is an image from the Second World War, and of course, you are right, Hiroshima.
>
> *Porey Konodin*
>
> —Japan. Hiroshima. 6 August 1945. The end of creation because of something man created. We are the past.
>
> So the point is, his basic complaint is—is writing possible? And *Ebong Indrajit* says that writing is not possible. The second phase is—what is the meaning of writing? At any moment the entire thing can vanish. So therefore writing becomes for him a site of contest. Like in *Baki Itihas*—The history of death cannot be the history of life. So the first is a positive statement. Then he says—Perhaps. But when the past, present and future came together, why didn't you commit suicide?
>
> You can just translate this question back to *Ebong Indrajit*. Why do you write? Why didn't you write? Why didn't you commit suicide? Writing and living both become very important, but they also become inconsequential. So, how do you make that consequential, is the politics of his writing.
>
> *Tringsha Satabdi*
>
> —The 20th Century is indicted. On 6 August 1945 a man-made atomic bomb destroyed Hiroshima. I am the 20th Century.
>
> So 'I am Indrajit' becomes 'I am the 20th Century'. But the utterance has now changed in quality . . . because he has now actually hit upon the theme of death. But not of individual death . . . I say he is a dramatist of *thanatos*—not the Freudian individual *thanatos* but total, complete *thanatos*.[10]

[10] Bandyopadhyay, interview with the author, Kolkata, 17 May 2014.

Guilt and responsibility, the need to challenge the status quo, the courage to continue in the face of futility—not to give up: till the early 1970s, the plays circle around this central cluster of ideas, informed with the knowledge of imminent annihilation. With his exposure to serious, avant-garde, socially and politically committed theatre internationally, almost all of it in the round, the shortcomings of the proscenium begin to gnaw at Badal-da. Direct, human communication becomes primary to him and he forsakes the proscenium for what he at first terms the Third Theatre, then the Free Theatre: portable, flexible and inexpensive. This is a political choice to dedicate himself and his group to socially meaningful theatre, which can play a role in bringing about a positive change in society. He has written widely on his ideas about this, so we need not elaborate on it here.[11]

What is important to note is that this shift to the Anganmancha, with its corresponding shift of subject matter and material aimed at shaking up middle-class complacency and creating awareness about the prevailing oppression and inequity in society, also corresponded with the introduction of group members who were young, committed, and who brought with them a strong political ideology. Several of them were Naxalites. Bisakha Ray was one of them:

> I came to theatre directly from the political field. I had been part of the Naxalite movement. I joined Satabdi officially in 1973, and was there till 1989. The people who joined along with me were all from a political background. Not all Naxalites, some were CPM,[12] but we were serious about doing socially meaningful theatre. We didn't do party line theatre, nor did we always take up current issues and do issue-based theatre. But we seriously studied the roots of our economy, trying to understand why the dichotomy exists in our society. Our Naxalbari political slogan, raised by Charu Mazumdar, was 'gram diye shahar ghera, Mao Tse Tung-er chinta dhara'.[13] At the time we believed in it. We felt that we had to reach the villages, that unless there was emancipation in the villages there would be no real transformation. That would be real revolution. We wanted to bring these values, part of our Naxalite beliefs, into theatre. Our group members would sit and discuss issues—is it socially relevant, should we bring this up?[14]

[11] See Sircar, *On Theatre* (Calcutta: Seagull Books, 2009), for important essays and lectures.
[12] CPI(M): Communist Party of India (Marxist).
[13] A rough translation: 'Villages will seize the city, Mao Tse Tung's philosophy'.
[14] Bisakha Ray, interview with the author, Kolkata, 14 May 2014.

Samik Bandyopadhyay analyses this development:

> An alternative Left, as residue of the Naxalite protest of the late 60s, broke into a variant of the street theatre, spatially differentiating itself from the street theatre by locating itself in a park, a surrounded space, a room, and by divesting itself of the authoritarian raised platform to allow for a greater closeness and sharing with the audience.[15]

There is a direct correlation between this infusion of political energy into the group, and the plays that Satabdi began to do, indeed, the whole methodology of how the plays were created. Badal-da may remain the one who ultimately gave shape and form to the play, but the entire group's improvisations, ideas and viewpoints went into making it. The presence of State terror, repression, exploitation and corruption began to be vividly felt in works of the 1970s and 1980s. The village outreach through *gram parikramas* (village tours) also reflects the political thinking of the group at the time. Impromptu performances in outlying districts of Calcutta, open-air performances at various city sites, workshops with theatre and non-theatre groups, all these were part of their ideology.

Badal-da reconfirms what Bisakha says:

> It is not a theatre one can perform by 'enacting'. It can only be performed by 'state of being'. The performer acts out his own feelings, his own concerns and questions and contradictions and guilt. Through the play, our protagonist changed a little, we changed a little, and we hoped that our spectators, some of them, would change a little. The sum-total of all these little, almost imperceptible changes, all these little positive choices we take, can one day bring about the change we are all waiting for. Yes, our theatre has become a theatre of change. A long voyage—*Spartacus, Michhil, Bhoma, Bhanga Manush*, many other plays. We came out of the proscenium stage in 1972, five years after the inception of Satabdi, twenty years after the beginning of my involvement in theatre.... Obviously, such a theatre takes the character of a movement, and cannot be taken as a profession ... Only those who feel the urge to change, and want to use theatre to contribute to the forces of change, can be in this theatre.[16]

As we can tell from this quote, change is the goal not just for the audience but for the actors as well; this is part of the politics of this theatre, that

[15] Bandyopadhyay, 'Theatrescapes', *Seagull Theatre Quarterly*, No. 16, December 1997, p. 28.

[16] Badal Sircar, 'A Letter from Badal Sircar', pp. 55–57.

it promotes self-evolution in addition to trying to change the attitudes of others. This is linked to the workshops as well as the productions. K.V. Akshara, the activist theatre director who heads the institution Ninasam in Heggodu, Karnataka, had the opportunity to work with Badal-da as a second year student at the National School of Drama on a production of *Basi Khabar* in 1982. He picks up on this aspect of the political in Badal-da:

> Badalda made us deeply aware of the political imperativeness at the personal level. Being political, as I learnt from him, was neither about wearing it on one's sleeve or about throwing oneself into the public sphere. It was a consciousness that took shape to negotiate the self as much as one had to negotiate the world. And true to his spirit, sometime after that production, many of us began questioning Badalda's method of work and doubted whether he really supported a 'thinking actor' who has no biases or an emotionally indulgent person who refuses to take political positions. But the deep regard for his intense personal commitment to the idea of the political remains with many of us, even to this day and it has helped me through times of ambivalent political contexts.[17]

Probir Guha, who continues to do alternative, socio-politically concerned theatre in semi-urban greater Kolkata, avers that if he had not encountered Badal Sircar when he did, and fallen under his spell, indeed, fallen in love with him in a way, he would not have been the theatre person he is today.[18] He broke away to form his own group in Khardah, in outlying Calcutta, when he began to feel that he was too influenced by Badal-da and admits that his first works were very much in the Badal Sircar mode; yet, despite the distance that subsequently grew between them, he acknowledges the formative influence of Badal Sircar on the evolution of his politically charged theatre, particularly in terms of theatre philosophy. This is another way in which Badal-da's theatre functioned politically.

Sadanand Menon finds a particular focus on colonial violence circulating through the plays of the 1970s to the 1990s:

> Badal Sircar's 50-odd productions, cumulatively performed over a thousand times by his own group and multiplied many more times by other theatre groups in other linguistic regions of India—setting up a sort of relay

[17] K.V. Akshara, 'Badal-da: A Personal Memoir', E-Rang newsletter, 'Remembering Badal Sircar'.

[18] Interview with the author, 28 February 2015.

> transmission from the 1970s through to the 1990s—almost all dealt with the continuing asphyxiation caused by 'colonial violence' in a free nation. Frantz Fanon, in his *The Wretched of the Earth* had described most artists and professors as *disorientateurs* (obfuscators) who continually propagated 'respect for the established order', thereby separating and insulating the exploiters from the exploited. Fanon had proposed that a true artist, rather than colluding with this order, could only contest it—turning theatre, for example, into a site for resistance. This was a strategy most consistently explored in postcolonial Indian theatre by Badal Sircar.[19]

If critiquing, questioning and challenging the 'established order' is resistance, this is certainly true of much of Badal-da's theatre.

However, his work went beyond mere resistance, to an alternative discourse. 'His plays, he says, are part of a counterculture, intending to expose media lies and Government untruths. Uncovering blatant lies and myths (such as "nuclear tests are safe and used for peaceful purposes") through intense research.'[20] By introducing the term 'counterculture' into a discussion of Badal-da's theatre, Hemangini Gupta invokes the concept of the 'public sphere', a space where a counterculture can mobilise and take shape.[21] Whether Badal-da was conscious of it or not, his Anganmancha and Muktamancha theatre practices are very much in line with this theory. He saw his theatre as being accessible to everyone and also as a stimulant for provoking response, discussion and, hopefully, action. Inviting participation and engaging the audience in discussion after the performance played an important role in his theatre activity.

With the shift to Third Theatre, Badal-da and Satabdi became part of the alternative, political theatre activity of the city. They performed regularly on Saturdays at Sudhindranath (or Curzon) Park, along with other alternative groups like Silhouette. Badal-da was involved in one of the most significant political moments of alternative culture in the city—the protest around the death of Prabir Datta. As a part of urban folklore and

[19] Sadanand Menon, 'Badal Sircar (1925–2011): A Curtain Call for Political Theatre', *Economic and Political Weekly*, Vol. xlvi, No. 22, 28 May 2011, p. 16.

[20] Hemangini Gupta, 'Plays of Purpose: Badal Sircar Friday Review Article, http://hemanginigupta.blogspot.com/2004/12/plays-of-purpose-badal-sircar-friday.html (accessed 18 Apr 2014).

[21] A sociological concept, the short Wikipedia definition is 'an area in social life where individuals can come together to freely discuss and identify societal problems, and through that discussion influence political action.' Associated with Jurgen Habermaas, with modifications by other commentators.

the cultural history of the city, this tale deserves to be related in some detail, in Badal-da's own words:

> July 1974, before the imposition of Emergency. The authorities were trying in various ways to stop the Saturday performances at Surendranath Park, without much success. Ultimately, in a brutal attack by the police one Saturday afternoon, an innocent young spectator called Prabir Datta was killed. Moreover, some members of the theatre group which was to perform on that day (it happened to be the group that had initiated Saturday performances at that park) were arrested. They were identified by police informers even though they were at a bus terminus at quite a distance from the park. However, a massive protest rally was mobilized by the citizens and artistes of Calcutta. I doubt whether such a protest will ever occur again in Calcutta for a similar occasion. One Saturday, five weeks after the incident, the right to perform at Surendranath Park was re-established by a rally of 10,000 in which almost all the famous personalities in the fields of theatre and film participated. Apart from addresses, recitation of poems and songs, a symbolic performance of *Michhil* was held in which representatives of various theatre groups participated.
>
> But at the end of the programme, people were asking us . . . whether the Saturday shows would continue. We . . . said that it was not likely for we did not know what would happen when the protection of numbers and names was missing. Later we discussed amongst ourselves and ventured out on the performance next Saturday. We laid out a detailed plan and when, according to the plan, we entered simultaneously in bands of twos and threes from different sides of the park, we were greatly astonished to find a gathering of about 3,000 people patiently waiting for us, although we had told them that there was hardly any likelihood of our coming to perform. From then on, the Saturday performances continued till the promulgation of the state of Emergency; and they began again on the Saturday after the Emergency was withdrawn.[22]

Sadanand Menon also finds a lasting value in the pedagogic contribution made by Badal-da to alternative theatre in India:

> Badal Sircar was no politician; neither was he a teacher. However when he set out on the second phase of his theatre-making in 1972 with his group Satabdi in Calcutta, he was to inaugurate the most historic artistic programme in contemporary India of educating and "conscientising" theatre audiences on

[22] Sircar, 'Voyages in the Theatre', *On Theatre*, pp. 120–21.

> the travesty—nay absurdity—of their contemporary postcolonial deprivation. A significant section of his audiences came from the urban middle or working classes. But he also made unforgettable interventions with the rural poor, like in the Sundarbans and in the Santhal villages. His was a theatre that relentlessly and self-consciously chose to operate as a Paulo Freirean kind of 'pedagogy for the oppressed'.[23]

True, Badal-da was no politician: his political beliefs were too heartfelt and uncompromising to sit comfortably with the hypocrisies expected of one. He was, however, an excellent teacher, even if not by profession. Testimonies from a range of people who have benefited from his workshops, or learned from him, like members of theatre groups, testify to this. The preceding chapters offer plenty of examples.

Badal-da spoke often of the need to build a Third Theatre movement. His extensive workshops were part of this commitment, and he encouraged like-minded groups whenever possible, offering them performance space and nurturing them in other ways. Veteran theatre activist and actor Sumit Biswas talks of how he and his group discovered Badal-da, and how he helped them develop their theatre skills.[24] Pathasena is a suburban theatre group which has long formed a team, with Ayna as a third, with Satabdi, performing together and collaborating closely over the years. Pathasena was formed in 1979; they did street and 'slogan' plays. One day a friend told them that Satabdi performed every Friday evening at Theosophical Society Hall on College Street. The play that was on then was *Gondi*.[25] They arrived around 5 PM on a Friday, all the way across the city from Kanchrapara, only to be told that all the limited seats were pre-booked. However, given that they had travelled such a distance, if they cared to check closer to the time of the show, perhaps something could be arranged. So they did, and seats were found for them on a bench at the back. 'We were totally spellbound by *Gondi*. We could never have imagined that theatre could be done like this. To take such a text, and to do it so simply, in such a space, was an eye opener for us. I saw a river, a waterfall, a bridge—no cardboard anywhere, just human bodies. And then voice, songs—the whole thing was amazing.' They began to attend every Friday. When Badal-da came to know that they did *Spartacus*, he invited them to perform at Curzon Park. After the performance, he told them—'I'm going to be frank. That was not a play, that

[23] Sadanand Menon, 'Badal Sircar (1925–2011): A Curtain Call for Political Theatre', p. 16.

[24] The following account is from an interview with the author, 18 April 2014.

[25] Badal Sircar's version of Brecht's *Caucasian Chalk Circle*.

was third-rate jatra. But I like your energy. Are you prepared to work hard?' Of course they said they were. He told them how important training was to theatre, and he despatched a Satabdi group member to do a preliminary workshop with them in Kanchrapara. Then he himself worked on *Spartacus* with them. Even today, Sumit recalls the tips and guidance he gave them. And Pathasena has been associated with the Third Theatre ever since.

From 1971, when he formulated his project for the Nehru Fellowship, entitled 'Workshop for a Theatre of Synthesis as a Rural–Urban Link,' Badal-da was thinking about a rural audience. After moving out of the proscenium, and then out of the Anganmancha into the open air, he realised that his new theatre language, the language of the Third Theatre, contrary to expectations and the received wisdom of the educated middle classes, was accepted and enjoyed by the village spectator, or even the poor, lower-class audience in the public spaces of the city. In The Third Theatre, he says, 'We learned from our performances in villages, slum areas and public parks that it is not true that the common people are only capable of grasping the crude and over-simplified themes and dialogue of Jatra,'[26] which was the most popular and widespread performance form in the Bengal countryside. 'We realized that when we say that Jatra is the only popular theatre for the village people, we forget that no alternative has so far been made available to them.'[27]

He says that when he did *Spartacus* in Manipur and saw the genuine involvement of the local people gathered around to watch, he realised that village and rural folk would respond to his theatre, even though the subject matter may seem to the 'civilized' urban bourgeois to be too alien or sophisticated for them. 'In fact, I am inclined to believe that the common people quite often understood the main points and the spirit of the play more than the so-called urban intelligentsia. Our experience with the other plays was similar.'[28] In Manipur, the uninvited onlookers who crowded around the performance space clapped spontaneously when the slaves revolted, while the well-heeled invitees showed no reaction. Clearly, they had grasped the basic message of the play. When *Spartacus* was performed for other poor and rural audiences, Satabdi received a similar response:

> After our very first visit to a village with this play, we became absolutely convinced that we would get a response to it in every village, despite its sophistication. Villagers in Bengal, familiar with the folk form Jatra, are used

[26] Sircar, 'The Third Theatre' *On Theatre*, p. 50.
[27] Ibid.
[28] Ibid.

> to applauding when the speech of an actor or an actress builds up gradually to a crescendo, usually before an exit. In *Spartacus*, there was no speech at all: the outbreak of the first revolt in the gladiatorial school of Capua was communicated only with a burst of energy in sound and movement. The villagers invariably applauded at that point. This never happened with the exclusive middle-class audience in urban areas. It only meant that the toil and the sufferings of the slaves was successfully conveyed and the villagers wanted the slaves to revolt.[29]

Badal-da began familiarising himself with the harsh realities of the rural countryside by making regular visits to the villages from the mid-1970s. This was 'both in connection with our theatre and with the rural development work of the organization I served in for nearly three years from January 1975, which made me more aware of the problems of the real India. The experiences are reflected in my work in theatre.'[30] Both *Bhoma* and *Basi Khabar* highlight the exploitation and destitution of rural West Bengal. Here, the journey is in reverse: the docu-dramas bring back to the city, especially for the middle-class audience, the silenced and marginalised history and reality of the villages.

The attraction of the village performances was great. First, it felt ideologically right. The bridging of the rural–urban divide was an important part of the political beliefs of the young, committed members of Satabdi who had been part of the Naxalite Movement, and it resonated with Badal-da's own convictions. Second, the rural audience grasped the content of the play perfectly:

> In *Spartacus* as well as in several other plays, we found that the illiterates got the essence of the play better than the city folk who often praised the form, style and techniques of the production, hardly mentioning the content. In our case however, the content is the starting point.[31]

Third, there was a tremendous emotional satisfaction in the encounters they had on these forays into the villages. Badal-da recounts with deep feeling the stories of the penurious old woman who insisted on contributing a precious five-paise coin to their post-performance collection; the old villager who unheedingly walked miles with them on a village tour because he got 'high' seeing their play; the elderly Muslim peasant who began explaining

[29] Sircar, 'Voyages in the Theatre', *On Theatre*, pp. 105–06.
[30] Sircar, 'The Third Theatre' *On Theatre*, p. 52.
[31] Sircar, 'Voyages in the Theatre', *On Theatre*, p. 106.

Bhoma to him; the Santhal labourer who coolly replied, when probed about *Bhoma*, that the rich may need it explained to them but the poor understood it perfectly. 'These are the people we try to think about when our voyages tend to become hazardous and frustrating,' says Badal-da.[32]

In 1986, Satabdi began their gram parikramas, the name given to the 'walks undertaken by several theatre and choir groups, performing and singing from morning to night in various villages.'[33] The travelling troupe consisted of about 70 people. Badal-da describes their first foray:

> In March 1986, when we planned our first *parikrama* in the villages, we were in the process of preparing this poetry montage. Ten persons were participating in it and we were about half-way through. One of us suggested that we try out whatever we had prepared so far in the villages. My objections to the seemingly absurd proposition were the strongest. . . . The proposer countered with the argument that . . . we would be getting a captive audience of 70, those participating in the walk, even if no villager came to our performances, whereas some of our Friday shows in Calcutta were being attended by less than 30 . . . we had to perform that half-prepared piece at four villages, though the normal average was supposed to be only two. Two of those four performances were at places close to a bus route or railway station, but the other two were at remote interior villages.... It really surprised us when we found that the production got a much greater response in those interior villages, although the poems were written by city people for city people. We realized that the feelings in the poems about hunger and poverty were what really mattered in those villages, not the form of the poems. I cannot resist the temptation of translating one six-line poem of Birendra Chattopadhyay, which would probably explain what I mean, even though much would be lost in translation.
>
> The marvellous smell of rice in the night sky!
> Even in these days there must be some who cook rice,
> Serve rice, eat rice!
> And we remain awake the whole night
> With the marvellous smell of rice,
> With longing—the whole night.[34]

The *parikrama* was an elaborate enterprise, involving much planning, and Satabdi did only one a year, in the winter. According to Satabdi members I interviewed, they undertook about 10 in all, with some years' gap in

[32] Sircar, 'Voyages in the Theatre', *On Theatre*, p. 117.
[33] Ibid., p. 100.
[34] Sircar, 'Voyages in the Theatre', *On Theatre*, pp. 142–43.

between.[35] At first they planned trips of three days and two nights, but logistical difficulties reduced it to two days and one night. There were other difficulties—the rising cost of train fares, the inability to recoup their expenses from a rural audience, the lack of an audience during the day when the population was hard at work. 'In fact in one village, where we had performed successfully earlier, the women scolded us, saying, "What makes you come in the daytime, depriving us of seeing your theatre?"'[36]

One participant records his purpose in joining the gram parikrama:

> From village to village we journey. With our message, our language. With all we wish to say to the village dweller. Through the medium of theatre. And song. Or sometimes through face to face contact. We want to say, the town culture that usually comes to the villages, that the villager normally gets to see, is not the only culture there is. It is not the culture of all city people. It does not include all we want to say, a lot gets left out. And all that is left unsaid forms an alternative culture—with different plays, different songs. This parikrama is our attempt to familiarize them with this alternative culture. From village to village we travel. We want to listen, to see—how the eighty percent live, talk, sing. How they express themselves outside the daily grind of earning a living.[37]

He speaks here not only of a one-way process in which the urban troupe delivers culture to the villager who receives it passively, but of a two-way communication through which the city folk and the villagers both give and take, share and receive. This is an idealistic goal, but how far does the structure of the *parikrama*, where the troupe arrives, performs, and moves on after a brief interaction at best, allow for true learning and growth on both sides? Surely, at best it can be a mere glimpse, a window.

Bisakha Ray, who joined Satabdi formally in 1973, and whose background in Naxalite politics made the rural connect an important aspect of the group's work, spoke of impromptu day trips into the countryside. They would simply hop on to a local train and travel, getting off to perform anywhere, at a station, in a local bazaar. 'We didn't wait to get invited, we just went. We felt that what we had to say needed to reach the people.'[38] When asked about the plays they performed, she said they did everything

[35] Interview with Satabdi actors, 13 July 2014.

[36] Sircar, 'Voyages in the Theatre', *On Theatre*, p. 153.

[37] Apu Chattopadhyay, in Samik Bandyopadhyay (ed.), *Parikrama 1986* (Calcutta, 1986), p. 6. No publisher mentioned (joint publication), trans. Anjum Katyal.

[38] Bisakha Ray, interview with the author, 14 May 2014.

in their repertoire, from *Michhil* to *Bhoma* to *Hattamalar Oparey*. Ashu of Satabdi talked enthusiastically of such forays to outlying suburbs like Kanchrapara and Kalyanpur where they gathered large crowds and got a positive response to their plays.[39]

Apart from performing in the villages, Badal-da also held workshops, as we have seen in Chapter 12. Between these two practices, the Third Theatre's reach beyond the city grew quite substantial. However, Rustom Bharucha, who had watched with interest to see how Badal-da would develop this relationship with the non-urban audience, was disappointed to find that, as he put it, the momentum slackened in the late 1980s:

> With Bhoma he was going to find that link between the rural and the urban, activate that link. By going on a more regular basis to the villages. For me going to the rural areas meant long, sustained, intense interactions. But this was weekend theatre. And it made me realize that this is not really going anywhere. He was still going to remain that middle class person, displaced, guilt ridden, all of that, with humanist values, taking his angst to the rural areas, and not really engaging with their problems the way *Bhoma* had represented the rural poor.[40]

Badal-da and his group travelled to rural areas in other parts of the country as well. An account by Sister Clare, veteran theatre activist, captures the impact of their performance on a rural audience deep within Tamil Nadu:

> In 1993, the first performance of *Sada Kalo* [Black and White, 1986]...was held in a remote village in Karur District. The performance started, and it was drizzling! Badalda suggested that we stop, as it began to drizzle heavily, but the people wanted the play to continue. With my brief translation in Tamil, the villagers kept watching with wonder, not minding the rain. That was a great success, to keep a non-Bengali audience spellbound. The power and energy vibrating through the body language was the secret.[41]

Badal-da too writes about how well their plays were received by the villagers.

Without detracting from either the sincerity or the degree of achievement Satabdi and Badal-da did attain in their mission to do theatre for the villages, there are still some questions that come to mind regarding the rural

[39] Interview with Satabdi actors, 13 July 2014.

[40] Rustom Bharucha, interview with the author, 5 May 2014.

[41] Sr Clare, 'Dipankar, Who said you are gone? You are alive in us!' *Dipankar*, Kolkata, 1998.

outreach Badal-da undertook with his performances. Plays like *Spartacus*, *Michhil*, *Bhoma* and *Basi Khabar* were written for the urban middle class, to raise awareness and jog consciences. Certainly, they were understood, even appreciated, by the lower-class and rural audience, as Badal-da records: but what was their message for such audiences? Were they not preaching to the converted? Yes, that audience certainly identified with the content, recognised the conditions, the problems, the exploitation, violence and injustice portrayed—after all, it was their life. But their consciences did not need awakening in the same way, surely. So, what did these plays offer them, apart, perhaps, from a reassurance that their histories were not forgotten? Was there an agenda for social change beyond that? When Badal-da speaks about theatre being a useful part of the whole process of social change, one can clearly see how this works in terms of his theatre for the urban audience, but how exactly does it work in the rural context? Beyond showing solidarity? Which is also important, sure—but is it enough?

His workshops, on the other hand, are a whole different activity. Through this form of activism he truly did empower, enable and initiate a long-term change. He helped build self-confidence, teamwork and powers of self-expression. He became a catalyst for change, as participants continued to spread his methodology and his form of theatre, which being content-based, flexible, portable and inexpensive, was eminently suited to rural conditions. With his workshops, one can see a viable agenda of social activism through theatre.

In my last interview with him in 2009, when he was well into his 80s, with decades of Third Theatre behind him, Badal-da reiterated the ideal of a truly democratic space for theatre—a non-commercial space where human beings meet voluntarily as equals; a space with no distance or barriers between the two sets of people, facilitating direct communication between the actor and the spectator, and enabling freedom. He stood by what he had said earlier,

> When afterwards we spread our cloth for contributions, they don't have to pay. If they do pay, it is neither a gift nor a price—it is participation, in some way. They are indicating that they liked what they saw, that they want this kind of theatre to go on. *That* is a human relationship.[42]

Theatre as a democratic space of equal communication between human beings: if that is his goal, then one can see some validation in the attempt to reach out to the rural audiences through his performances.

[42] Quoted in Anjum Katyal, 'Distance, Access, Control', pp. 139–50.

Through the 1970s and 1980s Badal-da's plays were at their most politically direct, and yet different from other political theatre of the time. Rustom Bharucha analyses how:

> This theater is not explicitly political. It avoids all the stereotypes associated with bourgeois theater groups who propagate revolution with lectures on dialectical materialism, quotations from Mao, glorified accounts of the Communist movement, and exhortations for the good of the people. The Third Theater asserts its political independence by resisting party politics. Though its plays frequently deal with the false promises, hypocrisies, and the corruption of politicians, there are no specific references to the misdeeds of the Congress party or the CPI(M) party. The Third Theater does not side with one party against another. It is less interested in featuring controversial personalities and topical events than in dramatizing the contradictions of politics and their effect on the lives of the people.... His theater does not pretend to be militant. It does not incite its audience to think in terms of necessary violence. Instead of advocating strikes, lockouts and the destruction of governmental property, it is content with merely disturbing the consciousness of its spectators.
>
> One leaves a play by Satabdi acutely aware of the exploitation and injustices that pervade life in Calcutta and rural Bengal. Sircar makes his audience confront their indifference to the chaos and corruption that characterize urban life. He never fails to emphasize that his spectators are responsible for the world they live in ... Sircar focuses on the callousness of the middle class and their capacity to watch the suffering of the people without doing anything about it.[43]

Stating that 'there are as many ways to do political theatre as there are directors with visions and political beliefs,'[44] Rustom Bharucha concludes that Badal-da is more a humanist than a Marxist.

> Despite his attack on the bourgeois values and innate selfishness of his spectators, Sircar never fails to appeal to their humanity ... he urges them to feel more compassion for the underprivileged, who have been denied the basic necessities of life. In this respect Sircar represents a kind of radical humanism one associates with William Blake, who believed that no revolution was possible in the social and political structure until men were prepared to break 'the mind forged manacles' which governed their lives.[45]

[43] Bharucha, *Rehearsals of Revolution*, pp. 131–32.
[44] Ibid., p. xiv.
[45] Ibid., p. 132.

The adjectives 'humanist' and 'middle-class' surface in Sudhanva Deshpande's assessment of Badal-da as well. Sudhanva is part of Jana Natya Mancha (JANAM), a left-wing street theatre group founded in 1973. His perspective is informed both by his political theatre experience and his Communist ideology. He writes:

> His theatre was, variously, angry, nihilist, hopeful and deeply humanist. I am not being pejorative when I say that Badal Sircar's theatre reflected a certain 'middle class' view of life. In fact, it could be argued that this was the result of his deep honesty and self-reflexivity. He didn't delude himself that he could, in some magical way, transcend his class roots simply by mouthing radical slogans ... Sircar made a tremendous contribution by taking quality theatre to non-formal spaces. He was a key figure in what Safdar Hashmi called the 'democratisation of Indian theatre'.[46]

Sudhanva recognises the important contribution made by Badal-da in training practitioners and spreading his practice of theatre through workshops, which he considers a major part of Badal-da's legacy.

Mihir Bhattacharya maps Badal-da's route to the political through modernism. To him:

> [Badal Sircar] was the complete modernist in Indian theatre, carefully treading through the huge repertoire of devices realism brought to the 20th century stage and emerging on the other side and, at the same time, skirting the seductive richness of a vibrant people's culture, which the urban intelligentsia was gradually discovering. Internationally speaking, the modernist had by then ceased to be the elegant flaneur, a slightly decadent stroller through the angst-ridden cityscape, celebrated by Walter Benjamin in his account of Baudelaire's Paris. After the two World Wars of the 20th century, he turned into a stalker in the 1950s, grimly moving through the aimless scuttle of unheroic creatures, all waiting for a whimpering end...Sircar discovered this new inflection of modernism in the mature phase of his career, starting with *Ebong Indrajit*... and then going on to develop both performance and stagecraft indices that would sustain this discursive sensibility...He knew very well that modernist work in a poor, vast, multilingual, post-colonial country under oppressive ruling classes meant a great deal more than catching the winds of change among the intelligentsia. His commitment, therefore, was far more political than that of many of his European and Indian contemporaries.[47]

[46] Sudhanva Deshpande, 'The Outsider: Badal Sircar (1925–2011)', *Newsclick*, May 16, 2011. http://newsclick.in/india/outsider-badal-sircar-1925-2011.

[47] Mihir Bhattacharya, 'Obituary: Radical Modernist', Frontline, Vol. 28, Issue 12, Jun 04–17, 2011. http://www.frontlineonnet.com/fl2812/stories/20110617281209000.htm

Mangai feels that 'though his theatre has political critique, it is skeptical about organised struggles of any kind'.[48] Sadanand Menon finds Badal-da's work in identifying concerns and issues of the dispossessed poor in our country invaluable, much more so than the blinkered thinking of the official or organised Left:

> How much the humiliated Left Front in Bengal might have benefited if only they had watched and listened and paid attention to half the things on rural poverty, deprivation and the brutalisation of the poor in the state that Sircar had dealt with in his plays through the 1970s and 1980s ... Instead, they conveniently dismissed him as a 'middle class messiah'. They ranted and raved against him, called him names, briefly restrained him from performing outdoors and dubbed him an agent of the decadent American avant-garde ... What they refused to acknowledge was that Sircar and his Satabdi group represented the cleanest example within modern Indian theatre of a group relentlessly questioning its own politics and, in the process, persuading its audiences also into intense self-reflexivity.[49]

Marathi playwright and scholar G.P. Deshpande makes a perceptive comment: 'for Sircar, theatre had to be—and indeed was—a celebration of the political.'[50] In fact, Badal-da insisted that what he wanted to say dictated the form; in other words, politically driven content led to a politically equitable form of free and direct communication, collectively presented by the group. In addition, there was his rejection of money and commerce in his theatre, his workshops with developmental NGOs, his support of other political activist theatre groups, his writings and lectures on how theatre could be an instrument of social change: a whole range of activities and processes which celebrated the political. And yet, he did not exaggerate the overall impact of his efforts. He was clear that theatre was just one of the tools in the movement for social change and said so in several essays. Shayoni Mitra writes that when asked how much change has resulted from Satabdi's work

> Sircar is characteristically self-effacing in his reply. 'Infinitesimal. The actual change our theatre has helped bring about is infinitesimal. But my question to you is what else should we do? We are people of the theatre. That is the only thing I know how to do.'[51]

[48] A. Mangai, 'Badal Sircar'.

[49] Menon, 'Badal Sircar (1925–2011): A Curtain Call for Political Theatre', pp. 18–19.

[50] G.P. Deshpande (1938–2013), wrote after Badal's passing in 'Remembering Badal Sircar or Thinking of a Phenomenon', E-Rang newsletter, 'Remembering Badal Sircar'.

[51] Shayoni Mitra, 'Badal Sircar: Scripting a Movement', *The Drama Review*, Vol. 48, No. 3 (Autumn, 2004). Interview with Badal Sircar, Kolkata 27, 29 December 2003.

Shades of *Ebong Indrajit*: to keep on keeping on, although the outcome may look hopeless. Again, a political stance, although not of the flag-waving kind.

Sumanta Banerjee, while appreciative of much of Badal-da's oeuvre, criticises some of the more 'political' Third Theatre plays:

> Even though his plays might not have come up with any original ideas, his passionate commitment to the cause of social justice and his excellent skill in translating it into theatrical terms—helped by his penchant for witty dialogues—have remained undimmed all through the various stages of his experiments. But there seems to be a certain lack of focus in his choice of issues, and dearth of conciseness in handling them. He wants to explain too many problems within the framework of a single play—the economic plight of the poor, the capitalist system which causes this plight, the political options before the exploited poor and the middle-class intellectuals who sympathize with them, the militarist nature of the world capitalist order, the danger of a nuclear war threatened by this order, etc.etc. While all these dimensions are surely relevant for a political analysis of the situation in India, Badal Sircar somehow fails to bind together these various strands into a pithy theatrical statement. As a result, these plays seem to exist in an amorphous zone—moving between the world of sentimental self-flagellation by the guilt-stricken middle-classes on the one hand, and that of political self-affirmation by the oppressed poor on the other. The dialogues therefore vary from gushing emotional outbursts to didactic political arguments.[52]

Safdar Hashmi,[53] street theatre activist, echoed this criticism of a lack of focus in even harsher terms. For him, Badal-da's plays deserve to be castigated for 'cynicism':

> In one breath he goes from Marx, to Engels, to Freud, to Hitler, to Boris Becker. You equate everything. He does it constantly. There is anarchy in his thought. I think it is calculated. It is reflected in his style also. It is so fragmented. While it goes on you think there is lots of energy, but once it is over it leaves you only confused.[54]

[52] Banerjee, 'The Theatre of Badal Sircar', pp. 117–18.

[53] Safdar Hashmi (1954–89) was a Communist playwright, actor, director, lyricist, and theorist, who founded the street theatre group Jana Natya Manch (Janam). He died as the result of an attack by political hoodlums during a street performance.

[54] Sudhanva Deshpande (ed.). *Theatre of the Streets: The Jana Natya Manch Experience* (New Delhi: Janam, 2007), pp. 23–24.

Both these opinions reflect a certain expectation of left-oriented political theatre—that it would be fairly straightforward in its method of communication, if not actually social realist; that it would uphold a basic positive outlook on the way forward; that it would offer solutions or at least hope—which Badal-da's work never delivered (aside from his early comedies). With an expansion in the concept of what constitutes the political, it is possible to find a political engagement, which is far from anarchy, in his oeuvre.

Like Sudhanva Deshpande, Sumanta Banerjee concludes that it is Badal-da's 'ability to inspire and influence a new generation of young practitioners in the alternative theatre movement in India'[55] that will be remembered as his major contribution to Indian theatre.

Santanu Bose salutes the political conviction that made Badal-da reject funding, grants and other institutional sources of money on principle, concerned that it may compromise his freedom to say what he really wanted to say. With his status and national recognition, it would have been easy for him to get financial support for his theatre, but he chose to remain independent in this regard. Rustom Bharucha sees this differently. He feels that by rejecting money as evil, Badal-da took a moralistic position which was essentially untenable. He said in his recent interview:

> Some of the great political artists of our time have had no option but to engage with the contradictions of money. To rail against money is a privilege. Theatre demands cunning. It works through contamination, uneasy alliances, discomfort. There are no perfect solutions. It doesn't mean you lose your integrity in the process.[56]

However, he also qualifies this by conceding that today, when money, funding and sponsorship have got a real stranglehold on theatre, it is time to revisit Badal-da's ideas of keeping theatre inexpensive, using available spaces, and breaking free from the dependence on financial support.

After this wide spectrum of opinions on and readings of Badal-da's politics, and also of the political nature of his theatre, let us see what he himself, at the tail end of his life, has to say on the subject. This is from a late interview:

> When you talk of changing the world, what kind of world do you envision?
>
> I know I won't be able to see it in my lifetime, but it will be a world without domination. A world that I have portrayed in my play *Hattamalar Opare*. From each according to one's ability, to each according to one's needs.

[55] Banerjee, 'The Theatre of Badal Sircar', pp. 117–18.

[56] Interview with the author, 5 May 2014.

That's Marx again!
I said ideology hasn't failed me.[57]

It is due to the nature of our twenty-first century reality that this goal sounds merely Utopic to us, an idyll, a dream, with no basis in reality. To Sircar, on the other hand, it was 'a myth of possibility.'[58] He averred that this was one of the plays he was truly proud of, and said:

> At a time when defining Communism anew almost looks like a counter-revolutionary act, I have overheard people in a village discussing the play after a performance and saying, "Well, there's no reason why it can't be like that!" If we can set people thinking, isn't that the most we can achieve?[59]

[57] Nilanjan Dutt, 'Badal Sircar: Ideology has not failed me'.
[58] Samik Bandyopadhyay, Introduction, *Beyond the Land of Hattamala and Scandal in Fairyland* (Kolkata: Seagull Books, 2003/1992), p. ix.
[59] Quoted in Ibid.

CHAPTER FOURTEEN

THE FINAL YEARS

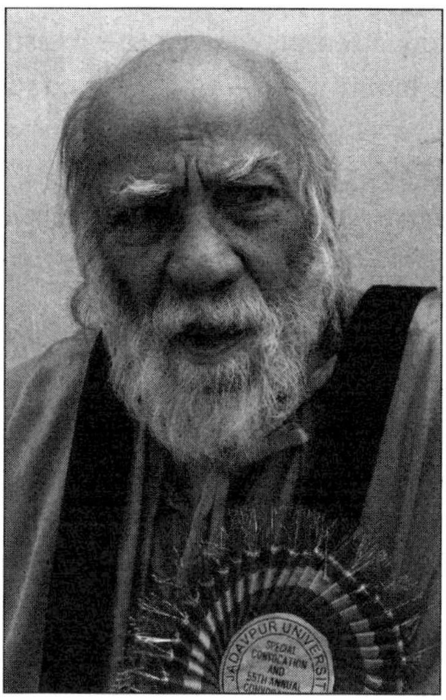

The Eternal Student
Courtesy: Satabdi

The early 1990s and the first decade of the 2000s saw an eclipsed Badal-da. The cutting edge and energy were missing from Satabdi's performances, which became repetitious and mannerist. New plays were written, but not at the pace they were earlier. Somehow Satabdi seemed to be stuck in a time warp. Despite Badal-da's hopes that the Third Theatre would turn into a full-fledged alternative theatre movement, this did not really happen, though for some time it looked as if it might. Let alone growing into a movement, Satabdi found that its audience was dwindling from the 1990s onwards.

And yet, Badal-da himself, delivering the Shriram Memorial Lectures in April 1992, sounds buoyant and full of plans about his theatre. He says:

> Doing one kind of thing over and over again year after year can bring boredom; but that has never happened to me. Particularly after we chose the new course in theatre about 20 years ago, almost every play and production has been a challenge, revealed new areas of exploration, sprung surprises and shown new possibilities.[1]

He speaks of how audience feedback from across socio-economic strata has been 'a great source of surprises and insights, realization of mistakes and inspiration for new attempts'.[2] Even the logistical and practical difficulties the group has had to face—'when somebody had fallen ill or had left the group, when a particular hall had kicked us out or when a production had not received the expected response'[3]—did not manage to defeat them; rather, 'the theatre went on renewing itself in our experience and our consciousness'.[4]

This optimistic picture is not borne out by discerning viewers. Theatre director Santanu Bose recalls going to their Anganmancha performances between 1990 and 1992.[5] Not only were there very few people attending—not more than 10 or 15, he says—but they were also more or less the same individuals each time. Moreover, by then slackness had set in amongst the actors. They didn't have the tightly trained efficient physicality for which Satabdi had been known. They were overweight, slower and not well coordinated. Altogether it seemed to be a theatre in decline, one that appeared to be merely going through the motions. 'A serious interest in the form and practice, in finding newer ways, somehow got lost.' Rustom Bharucha felt the same: 'I became increasingly disappointed by what I was seeing, the repetition of certain mechanisms and conventions, like any alienation effect that loses its effect when it gets repeated.'[6] He felt that by then, the Third Theatre had lost its conviction, its creativity and its momentum. Heisnam Kanhailal, who acknowledges his debt to Badal-da on several counts, nonetheless offers a critique: 'It seems me that he didn't emphasize enough on theatre as communication, expression; ultimately the focus was

[1] Sircar, 'Voyages in the Theatre', *On Theatre*, p. 136.
[2] Ibid.
[3] Ibid.
[4] Ibid.
[5] The following account is based on an interview with the author, New Delhi, 28 April 2014.
[6] Rustom Bharucha, interview with the author, Kolkata, 5 May 2014.

on propaganda. Could his later theatre truly disturb the spectators, affect the resilience of the human spirit?'[7]

A young woman director who recalls being fascinated, as a child, with *Muktamela*, never having seen anything like that in theatre before, eagerly attended a Satabdi performance at Loreto Sealdah in the 2000s, but was disappointed. She felt it was repetitious, lacked conviction and energy, and that the actors betrayed a lack of physical training. She had no interest in going back for any further shows.

There are many conjectures and theories around why Badal-da allowed this to happen. It is indeed difficult to understand. This is a man who enrolled as an M.A. student when he was over 60 years old, sharing bench space with 20-year olds—not the action of someone who is either convention-bound or close-minded about learning anything new.[8] In fact, Santanu Bose and Mohammed Waseem both commented on how they admired his keenness, as an older man, to engage in learning new things. It is true that he had both personal and health issues, but equally true that he remained mentally engaged and active right till the end, even though in his last few years, his physical mobility was restricted. Although he was still accessible to alternative theatre practitioners who sought him out and continued his mentoring role with Satabdi, Ayna and Pathasena as always, one does not hear of a forging of alliances with other activist groups with similar aims, nor was there any real induction of new ideas, approaches or material to revive or renew the energy of the group. There is some mention of Satabdi holding workshops in the 1990s, mostly with NGOs. The annual gram parikrama continued through most of the 1990s, but tapered off eventually. From the early 2000s, Loreto Day School Sealdah allowed Satabdi the use of its compound for regular weekly performances. The Principal, Sister Cyril, who took the initiative, said that the gates were kept open and anyone could enter; she was happy that the street children who sheltered and studied in the school could attend; they loved to sit and watch the plays. From all accounts, there was a small but loyal audience; but due to poor attendance, the weekly shows were reduced to one every three months.

Samik Bandyopadhyay, a close observer of Badal-da's theatre from the beginning, comments on the decline he saw in the last years.[9] He felt a loss

[7] Heisnam Kanhailal, email communication with the author, 9 August 2014.

[8] Badal Sircar enrolled as an MA student in the Comparative Literature department at Jadavpur University in 1989.

[9] Samik Bandyopadhyay, Foreword, to Badal Sircar's Last Interview with Bandikishore Mitra and Sabuj Mukhopadhyay, *Sabbcheye Sasta To Manusher Mangsha. Seta Kheley Damta Komto*—Human Flesh is Cheapest of All; Eating that would Bring Down Prices (Kolkata: Unjan/The Minority, 2011).

of vitality, stagnation and lack of new thinking or ideas. He says that Badal-babu's last published play *Naditey* (At the River, 1980), based on Edward Bond's *We Come to the River* was completely mediocre, with none of the daring and originality he had shown in *Gondi*, for example. He states:

> When I heard Badal-babu complaining that no one came to watch his plays any more, I asked myself, don't you and your fellow workers ever try and understand why that is? Is there really nothing to be done about it? Except just go on doing the same thing, like a blind routine? Badal-babu's last few years passed in this manner.[10]

It would be deeply sad and ironic if the very practice that Badal-da railed against in his earlier plays—that of mechanically following a routine or set pattern—was to be followed by him in his last years.

However, there is evidence that this may not be the whole picture. In December 2003, Shayoni Mitra visited Badal-da on a research trip. She interviewed him and met the Satabdi members as well. Badal-da was almost 80 years old at the time. She describes a very different scene:

> I encountered an indomitable spirit walking along his life path looking resolutely ahead. A kind old man who drew me a map to his house and saved tea for me in a thermos. A theatre person extraordinaire recounting his latest workshop in Laos, devising how to return as soon as possible. Sircar's criticisms of city life have not lost their edge with time, nor has his vision of social change dulled. It's true that he now operates on what he calls "a principle of conservation of energy", but that does not prevent him from being mentally and physically involved with the work of his group, Satabdi, at every juncture.[11]

She visited the group and watched the rehearsal of a new play, *Charuibhati* (Picnic, 1994) with Tapas Mukherjee guiding or coordinating the group (they don't use the term director). According to her, Satabdi was still doing about 40 shows a year, including weekly shows at a fixed venue, and the gram parikrama was still being held. She did not think that Satabdi had isolated itself. 'It consciously sees itself as part of a theatrical movement for social change. It has nurtured alliances with other groups that do Third Theatre in and around Kolkata.'[12] These are Ayna and Pathasena, who have been fellow-travellers

[10] Samik Bandyopadhyay, Foreword, to Badal Sircar's Last Interview, trans. Anjum Katyal.
[11] Shayoni Mitra, 'Badal Sircar: Scripting a Movement', p. 59.
[12] Ibid., p. 72.

for decades. They take turns to perform at the regular venues, which at the time were Loreto Sealdah and the Nandan complex.[13] Since they have a ready repertoire between them of Badal-da's plays, they can trade actors if needed.

She concludes:

> Badal Sircar is still very much the life force of each of these groups...With advancing age, Sircar's everyday interaction with Satabdi is diminishing. He has long since stopped writing plays. Of late his directorial intervention also has been minimal. He has stepped aside from all his acting roles except that of the old man in *Michhil*. Even that he is now willing to let go of ... but he does attend Satabdi rehearsals regularly. It is his presence that is important, for he takes on any and every function ... From refining the 'actors' accents to filling in for missing actors.[14]

This does not sound like someone who has given up on the Third Theatre. Six years later, in 2009, in a long interview subsequently published in the form of a book[15] two fans get him to talk about the past. He is now 84 years old. Not much in the interview is new, most of the information being already available in earlier published writings, but we get a rare glimpse of his activities at the time. An excerpt:

> Bandi: You are still writing ...
>
> Badal: Not plays.
>
> Bandi: No, you haven't written a play for a long time. But your memoirs, that kind of stuff. Won't you write something about workshops, Badal-da?
>
> Sabuj: The workshop is such a unique ...
>
> Badal: If I'm alive long enough, maybe ...
>
> Sabuj: And about your group?
>
> [...]
>
> Badal: Satabdi exists. It's not dead yet. It should've died, but it hasn't. Nor will it die.
>
> Sabuj: I'd like to share a point of view. Bandi feels that Pathasena and Ayna are both writing and performing their own plays. Pathasena is doing lots of shows. But with Satabdi we feel somehow that a stagnation has set in.
>
> Badal: I don't feel that. What they're doing at the moment is for the most part following the earlier direction. I was last able to direct them in

[13] Nandan is a government movie theatre complex which stands in a compound along with two other government cultural buildings, alongside the Academy of Fine Arts in Kolkata, creating a public space widely used for performance and other cultural events like exhibitions.

[14] Mitra, 'Badal Sircar: Scripting a Movement', p. 73.

[15] 'Badal Sircar's Last Interview' with Bandikishore Mitra and Sabuj Mukhopadhyay.

> *Naditey*—before my accident. After that I couldn't direct them anymore. I tried. A play called *Parashuram* (2003).[16]

One could say that he was tired (it's a long interview, and this comes right at the end), that he was on the defensive (he hasn't been particularly warm or encouraging so far), or that he doesn't see the need to be frank. However, his refusal to engage with the critique of Satabdi is telling. He goes on to talk about all the old plays that Satabdi is reviving, following his earlier direction—he mentions *Bhoma, Michhil,* among others—but doesn't address the question of why Satabdi is not being able to write and do their own plays, why they are still so dependent on his direction to develop new material. Surely this points to some sort of failure of his methodology, at least with regard to this group? After all, when so many theatre persons all across the country have been inspired and empowered to do their own theatre after much shorter interactions with him, why not Satabdi? The question haunts one.

Two subsequent interviews by journalists, done shortly before his passing away, speak of a man still busy with the life of the mind.

Nilanjan Dutt interviewed Badal-da at the age of 85, and Badal-da told him that he was working long hours at translations into Bengali of seminal texts, including Greek plays and Camus' *The Outsider*, translations into English of his own plays, other fiction and the fourth volume of his autobiography *Purano Kasundi*. He was looking forward to travelling abroad on workshops and attending the Esperanto Congress in Copenhagen. He had also initiated public play readings with Satabdi at Loreto Sealdah.[17] The term he uses is 'audio plays'—full circle back to his earliest induction into theatre, the audio plays he would listen to over the radio, as a child.

Madhusree Chatterjee did a telephonic interview with Badal-da in March 2011, some months before he passed away. He was 86 years old. He had just been awarded the Mahindra Excellence in Theatre Award for lifetime achievement. She quotes him as saying, 'I am reading plays, writing novels, plays and short stories in a frenzy. Currently, I am adapting William Shakespeare's *Macbeth* into a play, two of Graham Greene's stories and a novel, 'History of Love'. I am not in a position to direct or take part in active physical theatre any more. I spend my days writing, writing ... and writing.' As for theatre, he says, 'I concentrate on play readings. Every two months,

[16] Badal Sircar's Last Interview' with Bandikishore Mitra and Sabuj Mukhopadhyay, pp. 92–93, transl. Anjum Katyal.

[17] Nilanjan Dutta, 'Badal Sircar: Ideology has not failed me'.

45 members of my troupe assemble at Loreto Day School in Kolkata to read plays. The last play I read was *Pagla Ghoda*—an old hit.'[18]

Satabdi members mentioned the play reading of *Pagla Ghora* as the last time Badal-da performed with them.[19] Again, ironic that this play from his pre-Third Theatre phase, a phase he rejected vocally at one time, was to find a place in his repertoire in his last days. Apparently, Badal-da announced that he would regularly hold such dramatised readings—but it was not to be. Bharati Chatterjee, his daughter, speaking after his demise, said:

> Nothing could affect his mental vigour. Even in his illness, he ate, drank and slept theatre. The latter kept his spirit alive till death took him away from this world. He would ask me to read out a few plays to him while lying in bed or would urge me to translate a few of his plays into English. In fact, often he would himself translate and dictate to me several paragraphs.[20]

Although the above interviews do show us that Badal-da kept himself occupied and continued to write and translate, the other concerns we voiced earlier remain unexplained: the stagnancy in Satabdi's style, the inability to attract an audience, the sense of sameness and tiredness to the theatre. These issues were not being addressed.

It is also a paradox that although his theatre ideas have influenced protest and activist theatre groups widely, there is no unified Third Theatre movement, not even a forum or network, at least not to the knowledge of Satabdi, whom I asked about this during my interview.[21] They know of a few groups active in Bengal and Tamil Nadu, but profess to have no contact with them. This is in contrast to the Theatre of the Oppressed movement inspired by Augusto Boal, which began in India much later but has gained ground on the subcontinent to the extent that they have regular national and international get-togethers and a well-developed network.

Having said this, however, it is only fair that mention be made of the very different impression formed by Mangai when Satabdi performed in Tamil Nadu in early December 2011, six months after the demise of Badal-da. She says:

> The rigour found in the Shatabdi group during their recent tour in Tamil Nadu revealed the commitment and involvement of the group to whatever

[18] Madhusree Chatterjee, 'At 86, Badal Sircar frenziedly writes, reads plays', New Delhi, March 10 (IANS).

[19] Interview with Satabdi actors, 13 July 2014, Kolkata.

[20] Bharati Chatterjee, http://www.rediff.com/news/slide-show/slide-show-1-badal-sircars-daughter-speaks-up/20110530.htm#5 (accessed 30 January 2015).

[21] Interview with Satabdi actors, Kolkata 13 July 2014.

> Badal da stood for… It was moving to find the seriousness with which the group rehearsed each day in Chennai. One could feel the discipline that has gone into such a practice.[22]

Satabdi was in Chennai for a week, performing at different venues. They did *Michhil, Hattamalar Oparey, Picnic, Naditey* and *Bhool Rasta*. Mangai found that the plays shared an 'ideological fervor, a dream of a better world—a world where there is equality and justice.' She also noticed that the 'style of performance' was similar to *Michhil* in many ways, 'with minor changes in terms of a few visualizations, the establishment of the protagonist's view point and the handling of props in some cases.'[23] This in fact bears out the impression that Satabdi was stuck in a time warp, without the induction of new ideas.

However, this is not the point at which the Badal-da story ends. No matter that his theatre did not continue to evolve till his last days, that Satabdi has not been able to reinvent or rejuvenate itself. Badal-da is now much more than Satabdi and his own directorial work. Badal's legacy stands for politically committed theatre, for holding on to one's principles, for the centrality of the actor, for a theatre of human communication, for theatre as a democratic space. This has been reaffirmed over and over again by theatre practitioners of all ages, even those who are not dedicated to alternative theatre. His play texts—not just the 'classic' plays from his proscenium phase, but even those created for the Third Theatre—continue to be sought out. A recent example is a production of *Basi Khabar* as *Stale News* mounted by a Bengaluru group in November 2014. According to a review:

> A contemporised adaptation of Badal Sircar's Baasi Khabar … completed its maiden run on Sunday evening at Jagriti theatre. Directed by Ajith Hande, the play looks at the Santhal rebellion of 1855 and juxtaposes it with the state of affairs in the current sociopolitical scenario… The story of India as it is now, India shining, or is it?[24]

The review continues to talk of how the historic Santhal rebellion is interwoven with current headlines—a perfect example of how Badal-da's politically charged critiques remain relevant.

[22] A. Mangai, 'Badal Sircar'.

[23] Ibid.

[24] Shyama Krishna Kumar, 'A Fresh Look at Badal Sircar's Baasi Khabar', *New Indian Express*, 11 Nov 2014; http://www.newindianexpress.com/cities/bangalore/A-Fresh-Look-at-Badal-Sircar%E2%80%99s-Baasi-Khabar/2014/11/11/article2517159.ece (accessed 12 November 2014).

A younger generation is continuing to find meaning, value and direction in Badal-da's ideas and processes.

> I would definitely say that Badal Sircar is a great artist of our country. I didn't have the opportunity to meet him or interact with him, I only know him through his plays and his books. His political position was very clear—his plays belong to the left ideology. His politics is also about his life choices, his artistic process, his relationship with his company, creating the dynamics of the play, his aesthetics. I respect him as a playwright and a theatre artist.[25]

These are the words of Abanti Chakravarty, an NSD graduate, actor and theatre director in her 30s.

For me, possibly more than anything else, the primary legacy of a figure like Badal-da is his commitment, as an artist, to social engagement. Naseeruddin Shah, whose theatre may be at the other end of the spectrum from Badal-da's, still has this to say about him:

> I admire Badal Sircar deeply. I didn't know him, but I saw his plays, and I remember their impact. I saw *Spartacus*, and *Juloos*. Both were very different, cutting edge, very intense. I respect him for his immense courage in sticking to his own path, taking his theatre to the people. Right till the end of his life, he never changed his conviction that what he was doing was right. He could look back on a life lived by his principles. He could look at himself in the mirror and feel that he had lived life on his own terms, done what he believed in. Whether it was successful or not was not the issue—the issue was that he stuck to what he believed in.[26]

Badal-da has left behind a solid body of play texts, several theoretical writings, a whole methodology of theatre. Just as he donated his body as a resource for science, he has left us his theory and his practice as a resource for the future. It is now up to the practitioners of tomorrow to take this legacy further.

[25] Abanti Chakravarty, interview with the author, 3 July 2014.

[26] Naseeruddin Shah, interview with the author, Kolkata, 2 May 2014.

APPENDIX: LIST OF PLAYS

Key:
B = Published in book form
M = Published in a magazine named
Tr. = Translated into

Title	Year Created	Year of Publication	First Staged	Group/ Director	Translations
Solution X	1956	(M) Khapchara 1957 (B) 1962	1961	Chakra/ Badal Sircar	Tr. Hindi 'Yama X', 1979
Boro Pishima	1957	(B) 1961	1960	Chakra/ Badal Sircar	Tr. Hindi By Pratibha Agarwal, *Bari Buaji,* 1977
Shanibar	1959	(B) In *Nana Mukh,* ed. Anjali Basu 1962		Chakra/ Badal Sircar	
Ram Shyam Jadu	1961	(B) 1962		Chakra/ Badal Sircar	Tr. Hindi by Pratibha Agarwal
Samabritta	1961				
Ebong Indrajit	1963	(M) *Bohuroopee* July 1965 (B) 1968	16 September 1965	Souvanik/ Gobinda Ganguly	Tr. Hindi, Pratibha Agarwal 1969 Tr. Eng, Girish Karnad 1974 Tr. Marathi Shrikant Kulkarni 1977

(Appendix 1 contd.)

(Appendix 1 contd.)

Title	Year Created	Year of Publication	First Staged	Group/ Director	Translations
Sara Rattir	1963	1977	14 December 1969	Satabdi/ Badal Sircar	Tr. Hindi by Pratibha Agarwal, *Sari Raat*, 1991
Ballabh-purer Rupkatha	1963–64	(B) 1974	In Hindi 1968 In Beng 28 November 1970	Anamika (Hindi) Satabdi/ Badal Sircar	Tr. Hindi by Pratibha Agarwal 1976 Tr. Marathi by Amol Palekar
Kabikahini	1964	(B) 1971			
Bichitra-nushthan	1964				
Baki Itihas	1965	(M) *Bohuroopee*, Sep 1967 (B) 1976	7 May 1967	Bohuroopee/ Sombhu Mitra	
Bagh	1965	(M) *Bohuroopee*, Sep 1968 (B) in *Nana Mukh Sankalan Grantha* 1988 Pub. Anjali Basu	9 August 1968	Satabdi/ Badal Sircar	
Porey Konodin	1966	In *Bangla Natak O Natyakar 3* 1972 Pub. Opera	1968	Satabdi/ Badal Sircar	
Jodi Aar Ekbar	1966	*Badal Sircarer Swanirbachita Natya Sangraha* 1978 Pub. Opera	26 February 1976	Bohuroopee/ Tripti Mitra	
Pralaap	1966	*Natya Sanka-lan* 1967 Pub. Baulmon	3 October 1967	Bohuroopee/ Badal Sircar	

(Appendix 1 contd.)

(Appendix 1 contd.)

Title	Year Created	Year of Publication	First Staged	Group/ Director	Translations
Tringsha Satabdi	1966	(M) *Bohuroopee*, 1969 (B) in *Nana-mukh Sankalan Grantha* 1988 Pub. Anjali Basu	22 June 1969	Bohuroopee/ Himangshu Chattopad-hyay	
Bibar	1967				
Pagla Ghora	1967	*Badal Sircarer Swanirbachita Natya Sangraha* 1978 Pub. Opera	28 August 1971	Bohuroopee/ Sombhu Mitra	
Circus	1968	(M) *Angan Anyariti Natyapatra* 1988			
Shesh Nei	1970	*Badal Sircarer Swanirbachita Natya Sangraha* 1978. Pub. Opera	24 May 1970	Satabdi/ Badal Sircar	
Sagina Mahato 1	1970	(M) *Pratibhas* 1993 (B) in *Tinti Natak* 2007 Pub. Lekhani	8 August 1971	Satabdi/ Badal Sircar	
Sagina Mahato 2	1970		24 October 1971	Satabdi/ Badal Sircar	
Abu Hossain	1971	(B) 2007 Pub. Lekhani		Satabdi/ Badal Sircar	
Spartacus	1972	(B) 1976 Pub. Anjali Basu	28 January 1973	Satabdi/ Badal Sircar	
Suitcase	1972		1972	Satabdi/ Badal Sircar	
Beej	1973				
Michhil	1974	(B) 1978 Pub. Opera	14 April 1974	Satabdi/ Badal Sircar	
Bhanumati Ka Khel	1974		19 October 1974	Satabdi/ Badal Sircar	

(Appendix 1 contd.)

(Appendix 1 contd.)

Title	Year Created	Year of Publication	First Staged	Group/ Director	Translations
Laksh-micharar Panchali	1974	1975 Pub. Anjali Basu	19 October 1974	Satabdi/ Badal Sircar	
Natyakarer Sandhane Tinti Charitra		(M) *Angan Anyariti Natya-patra* 1998			
Rupkathar Kelankari	1974		18 January 1975	Satabdi/ Badal Sircar	
Bhoma	1975	(B) 1980 Pub. Opera	21 March 1976	Satabdi/ Badal Sircar	
Sukhapa-thhya Bharater Itihas	1976	(B) 1981 Pub. Opera	17 December 1976	Satabdi/ Badal Sircar	
Hattama-lar Oparey	1977	1984 Pub. Anjali Basu	22 July 1977	Satabdi/ Badal Sircar	
Manikan-chan	1977	(M) *Desh* 1988	22 July 1977	Satabdi/ Badal Sircar	
Gondi	1977	(B) 1985 Pub. Opera	12 May 1978	Satabdi/ Badal Sircar	
Padma Nadir Majhi	1978		22 May 1990	Satabdi/ Badal Sircar	
Basi Khabar	1978	(M) *Angan Anyariti Natya-patra* 1987	6 July 1979	Satabdi/ Badal Sircar	
Memoran-dum	1979				
Ekti Hatyar Natyaka-tha	1979	(M) *Angan Anyariti Natyapatra* 1987 (B) *Rupantarit Natak* 2003	1 August 1980	Joint production Satabdi/ Ritam and Cave/Badal Sircar	

(Appendix 1 contd.)

(Appendix 1 contd.)

Title	Year Created	Year of Publication	First Staged	Group/ Director	Translations
Naditey	1980				
Nagini Kanya	1981		6 August 1982	Joint production Satabdi/ Ritam and Pathasena/ Badal Sircar	
Dwoirath	1982				
Udyog Parba	1982	(M) *Angan Anyariti Natya-patra* 1987 (B) *Tritiya Dharar Natak* 1989 Pub. Anjali Basu	1983	Satabdi/ Badal Sircar	
Androcles O Singha	1982	(M) *Angan Anyariti Natya-patra* 1993	29 July 1991	Satabdi/ Badal Sircar	
Khat Mat Kring	1983	(B) in *Nana-mukh Sankalan Grantha* 1988 Pub. Anjali Basu	16 December 1983	Satabdi/ Badal Sircar	
Shiri	1984	(M) *Angan Anyariti Natya-patra* 1989	1 February 1985	Satabdi/ Badal Sircar	
Sada Kalo	1986		26 August 1987	Joint production Pathasena and Angan Theatre Group/ Dipankar Datta	
Churna Prithibi	1987	(M) *Syas* 10	12 May 1988	Joint production Pathasena and Satabdi/ Badal Sircar	

(Appendix 1 contd.)

(Appendix 1 contd.)

Title	Year Created	Year of Publication	First Staged	Group/ Director	Translations
Dampatya	1987/88	(B) in *Nanamukh Sankalan Grantha* 1988			
Bioscope	1988		6 January 1989	Satabdi/ Badal Sircar	
Bhool Rasta	1988		2 March 1989	Satabdi/ Badal Sircar	
Ka Cha Ta Ta Pa	1993	(M) *Angan Anyariti Natya-patra* 1997			
Charuib-hati	1994	(M) *Punaruth-than*, no 12 1995 (B) in *Rupan-tarita Natak* 2003	1994	Satabdi/ Badal Sircar	
Bagalacha-ritmanas	1997/98		1998	Pathasena	
Andhakar	1999				
Aeschy-luser Natak	2002				
Par-ashuram	2003				

Source: Compiled by Agniv Ghosh.

SELECT BIBLIOGRAPHY

Books by Badal Sircar

Sircar, Badal. *Evam Indrajit*. Introduction by Satyadev Dubey, translated into English by Girish Karnad. New Delhi: Oxford University Press, 1965/1974.

———. *Baki Itihas*. Edited by Chandrasekhar Kambar, translated into Hindi by Nemichandra Jain. New Delhi: Radhakrishna, 1969/2001.

———. *Bhoma*. Translated into Hindi by Theatre Workshop. New Delhi: Vidya Prakashan Mandir, 1979/2003.

———. *The Changing Language of the Theatre*. New Delhi: Indian Council for Cultural Relations, 1982.

———. *Three Plays: Procession, Bhoma, Stale News*. Introduction and translation into English by Samik Bandyopadhyay. Calcutta: Seagull Books, 1985.

———. *The Third Theatre*, New Delhi: Pioneer, 1992.

———. *Beyond the Land of Hattamala and Scandal in Fairyland*. Kolkata: Seagull Books, 2003.

———. *Prabasher Hijibiji*. Kolkata: Lekhani, 2006. In Bengali.

———. *Purano Kasundi*, Vol. 1. Kolkata: Lekhani, 2006. In Bengali.

———. *Purano Kasundi*, Vol. 2. Kolkata: Lekhani, 2007. In Bengali.

———. *Purano Kasundi*, Vol. 3. Kolkata: Lekhani, 2008. In Bengali.

———. *On Theatre*. Kolkata: Seagull Books, 2009 (The Third Theatre, Buying and Selling in the Theatre, Masks in Theatre, The Changing Language of Theatre, Voyages in the Theatre).

———. *Natak Samagra*, Vol. 1. Kolkata: Mitra and Ghosh, 2009. In Bengali.

———. *Natak Samagra*, Vol. 2. Kolkata: Mitra and Ghosh, 2010/2013. In Bengali.

———. *Two Plays: Indian History Made Easy/Life of Bagala*. Translated by Subhendu Sarkar. New York, USA: OUP, 2010.

Sircar, Badal. *Sabbcheye Sasta To Manusher Mangsha. Seta Kheley Damta Komto:* Human Flesh is Cheapest of All; Eating that would Bring Down Prices. Last Interview with Bandikishore Mitra and Sabuj Mukhopadhyay. Kolkata: Unjan/The Minority, 2011. In Bengali.

———. *Natak Samagra*, Vol. 3. Kolkata: Mitra and Ghosh, 2012. In Bengali.

———. 'Shesh Nei'. *Modern Indian Plays*, Vol. 1. Edited by Chandrasekhar Kambar, translated into English by Sarah K. Ensley. New Delhi: National School of Drama, pp. 317–97, 1969/2002.

———. 'A Letter from Badal Sircar. 23 November 1981.' *The Drama Review*, 26(2): 51–58, Intercultural Performance, (Summer, 1982).

———. 'Alternative Practitioners and "Theatre of Development"'. In Ralph Yarrow, *Indian Theatre: Theatre of Origin, Theatre of Freedom*. Surrey: Curzon Press, pp. 176–95, 2001.

Books on Badal Sircar

Bandyopadhyay, Samik, ed. *Parikrama 1986*. Kolkata: publisher unnamed, 1986.

Banfield, Chris and Brian Crow. 'Badal Sircar's Third Theatre of Kolkata'. In *An Introduction to Post-Colonial Theatre*. Cambridge: Cambridge University Press, 1996.

Bharucha, Rustom. *Rehearsals of Revolution: The Political Theatre of Bengal*. Calcutta: Seagull Books, 1983.

———. *Theatre and the World: Performance and the Politics of Culture*. London: Routledge, 1990/1993.

———. *The Theatre of Kanhailal: Pebet and Memoirs of Africa*. Calcutta: Seagull Books, 1992.

Bhatia, Nandi. *Acts of Authority/Acts of Resistance: Theater and Politics in Colonial and Postcolonial India*. New Delhi: Oxford University Press, 2004.

Chakraborty, Kaustav. *Indian Drama in English*. New Delhi: PHI Learning Pvt Ltd., 2011.

Chattopadhyay, Kuntal. *Third Theater*. Kolkata: Ratnabali, 2002.

Deshpande, Sudhanva, ed. *Theatre of the Streets: The Jana Natya Manch Experience*. New Delhi: Leftword Books, 2007.

Dharwadker, Aparna Bhargava. *Theatres of Independence: Drama, Theory, and Urban Performance in India since 1947*. Iowa City: University of Iowa Press, 2005.

Dipankar. Kolkata: publisher unnamed, 1998.

Gigon, Fernand. *Formula for Death: E = MC2: The Atom Bombs and After.* New York: Roy Publishers, 1958.

Iyer, Natesan Sharda. 'Badal Sircar: Evam Indrajit, An Overview'. In *Musings on Indian Writing in English Drama.* New Delhi: Sarup and Sons, pp. 138–53, 2007.

Kambar, Chandrasekhar, ed. *Modern Indian Plays,* Vol. 1. Translated into English by Sarah K. Ensley, New Delhi: National School of Drama, 1969/2002.

Pani, Narendar. *Staging a Change.* Bangalore: Samudaya, 1979.

Richmond, Farley P. 'Characteristics of the Modern Theatre'. In Farley P Richmond, Darrius L. Swann and Philip B. Zarrilli, ed. *Indian Theatre: Traditions of Performance,* Vol. 1. New Delhi: Motilal Banarasidass Publishers Private Limited, 387–461, 1993.

Sarkar, Pabitra. *Natyamancha Natyarup.* Kolkata: Dey's Publishing, 2002. In Bengali.

Schechner, Richard. *Performative Circumstances: From the Avant Garde to Ramlila.* Calcutta: Seagull Books, 1983.

Schechner, Richard. *Environmental Theatre.* New York: Applause Books, 1973/1994.

Subramanyam, Lakshmi, ed. *Muffled Voices: Women in Modern Indian Theatre.* New Delhi: Har Anand Publications, 2002.

Tandon, Neeru, ed. *Perspectives and Challenges in Indian-English Drama.* New Delhi: Atlantic Publishers, 2006.

Yarrow, Ralph. 'Alternative Practitioners and "Theatre of Development"'. In *Indian Theatre: Theatre of Origin, Theatre of Freedom.* Surrey: Curzon Press, 2001.

Articles and Essays

Babu, Sarat M. 'Theatre Log: A Retrospective of Badal Sircar's Plays'. *Seagull Theatre Quarterly,* 8 December 1995.

Bandhopadhyay, Sibaji. Introduction, Badal Sircar. *Natak Samagra,* Vol. 2. Kolkata: Mitra and Ghosh, 2010.

———. Introduction, Badal Sircar. *Natak Samagra,* Vol. 3. Kolkata: Mitra and Ghosh, 2012.

Bandyopadhyay, Samik. 'Middle-class Responsibilities'. *Sangeet Natak,* No 22 (October–December 1971).

———. 'Theatrescapes'. *Seagull Theatre Quarterly,* 16 December 1997.

Bandyopadhyay, Samik. 'Introduction'. In Badal Sircar, *Beyond the Land of Hattamala and Scandal in Fairyland*. Calcutta: Seagull Books, 1992/2003.

Banerjee, Arundhati. 'Brecht Adaptations in Modern Bengali Theatre: A Study in Reception'. *Asian Theatre Journal*, 7(1): 1–28, Spring, 1990.

Banerjee, Paramita. 'Street Theatre in Bengal: A Glimpse.' With Bulbuli Biswas. *Seagull Theatre Quarterly*, 16 December 1997.

———. '"Pagla Ghora": A Review'. *Seagull Theatre Quarterly*, 11, September 1996.

Banerjee, Sumanta. 'The Theatre of Badal Sircar'. *Theatre India*, No 2, November 1999: 102.

Bartholomew, Rati. 'Samudaya's Jatha, Karnataka', *How*, 6: 1–2, 1983.

Deshpande, G.P. 'The Literary Scene'. *India International Centre Quarterly*, 14(3), India: Forty Years: 155–61, Monsoon, 1987.

———. 'Theatre of Modernity: A Celebration of Modernity?' *Theatre India*, No. 5, May 2002: 8–14.

Gunawardana, A.J. 'Problems and Directions: Calcutta's New Theatre'. *The Drama Review*, 15(3), 1971.

Katyal, Anjum. 'Distance, Access, Control: The Philosophy of Space in Badal Sircar'. In Anmol Vellani (ed.), *Beyond the Proscenium: Reimagining the Space for Performance* (Bangalore: IFA Theatre Infrastructure Cell, 2010), pp. 139–50.

Kishore, Shrikant. 'Plight of a Playwright: Theatre in Hindi Belt'. *Indian Literature*, 49(4), (July–August, 2005): 49–53.

Lal, Ananda. 'Badal Sircar'. In *The Oxford Encyclopedia of Theatre and Performance*, Vol. 2, edited by Dennis Kennedy. Oxford: Oxford University Press, 2003.

M.B. '"Dramatic" Happenings'. *Economic and Political Weekly*, 9(41): 1727–28, 12 October 1974.

Menon, Sadanand. 'Badal Sircar (1925–2011): A Curtain Call for Political Theatre'. *Economic and Political Weekly*, xlvi(22): 20, 28 May 2011.

Mitra, Shayoni. 'Badal Sircar: Scripting a Movement'. *The Drama Review*, 48(3), Fall 2004.

Paranjape, Makarand. 'Post-Independence Indian English Literature: Towards a New Literary History'. *Economic and Political Weekly*, 33(18): 1049–56, May 2–8, 1998.

Prasad, G.J.V. 'The Third Gaze: The Theatre of Badal Sircar'. In Lakshmi Subramanyam (ed.), *Muffled Voices: Women in Modern Indian Theatre*, New Delhi: Har-Anand Publications Pvt Ltd, revised ed. 2013.

Raha, Kironmoy. 'Quest for Modernity'. *Theatre India*, No. 5, May 2002.

Raha, Kironmoy. 'The "Other Theatre"'. In *Bengali Theatre*. New Delhi: National Book Trust of India, 1978.

Salomon, Carol. *Bengali Literature*. By Dusan Zbavitel (Book Review), *The Journal of Asian Studies*, 37(2): 382–83, February 1978.

Sarkar, Pabitra. Introduction, Badal Sircar. *Natak Samagra*, Vol. 1, Kolkata: Mitra and Ghosh, 2009.

Sen, Aditya. 'The Bengali Literary Scene'. *Indian Literature*, 17(4): 20–29, October–December 1974.

Shiva Prakash, H.S. 'Here and Now: The Search for the New in Indian Drama and Theatre'. *Indian Literature*, Vol. 44, No. 1 (195) (January–February, 2000): 5–8.

Magazines

Jagannathan, N.S. 'Last Month in Delhi: Bengali Plays'; '"Baki Itihas": Which History?' *ENACT* 27, April 1969.

'Satabdi Plays,' 'Evam Indrajit.' *ENACT 72*, December 1972.

'The Savage God' by Iqbal Masud; "Juloos": Garlands around Chains; and "Pagla Ghora". *ENACT* 116–117, August–September 1976.

Gupta, Neena. 'Oh Kolkata!' *ENACT* 139–140, July–August 1978.

Kaushal, J.N. 'Kolkata: Anamika's "Intimate Seminar".' *ENACT* 207–208, March–April 1984.

Schechner, Richard. 'On Badal Sircar and Tripti Mitra.' ENACT 61–62, January–February 1972.

Online Sources

Shantanu Datta, http://www.indianexpress.com/oldStory/54083/, accessed on 24 June 2015.

Nilanjan Dutta, 'Badal Sircar: Ideology has not failed me', http://currentnews.in/2011/01/03/ideology-has-not-failed-me/, accessed on 10 October 2013.

Hemangini Gupta, 'Plays of Purpose: Badal Sircar Friday Review Article', http://hemanginigupta.blogspot.com/2004/12/plays-of-purpose-badal-sircar-friday.html, accessed on 18 April 2014.

Tribute/A life on the fringes Deepika Arwind/The Hindu Online Edition, Sunday, 22 May 2011, http://www.hindu.com/mag/2011/05/22/stories/2011052250130200.htm, accessed on 24 June 2015.

'Badal Sircar – Off Stage', http://www.indiaprofile.com/people/badalsircar.htm, accessed on 24 June 2015.

Sudhanva Deshpande, 'The Outsider: Badal Sircar (1925–2011)', *Newsclick*, 16 May 2011, http://newsclick.in/india/outsider-badal-sircar-1925-2011, accessed on 24 June 2015.

Neelima Talwar, 'Science-Drama in India: 1940 to 2000', https://helda.helsinki.fi/bitstream/handle/10138/15280/55_Talwar.pdf?sequence=1, accessed on 24 June 2015.

Mihir Bhattacharya, 'Obituary: Radical Modernist', *Frontline*, 28(12), 04–17 June 2011, http://www.frontlineonnet.com/fl2812/stories/20110617281209000.htm, accessed on 24 June 2015.

Frontier, 1(1): 16, 14 April 1968, http://frontierweekly.com/archive/vol-number/vol/vol-1/vol-1-issues/1_1_14april1968.pdf, accessed on 24 June 2015.

E-Rang newsletter, 'Remembering Badal Sircar', No 24, 1 July 2011. http://theatreforum.in/m/e-rang/?tab=issues&object_id=17, accessed on 24 June 2015.

Shyamhari Chakra, 'A pioneer in theatre', 30 August 2012, http://www.thehindu.com/arts/theatre/article3839107.ece, accessed on 24 June 2015.

Mihir Bhattacharya, 'Obituary: Radical Modernist', *Frontline*, 28(12), 4–17 June 2011, http://www.frontlineonnet.com/fl2812/stories/20110617281209000.htm, accessed on 24 June 2015.

The Telegraph, 10 June 2005, http://www.telegraphindia.com/1050610/asp/calcutta/story_4851102.asp, accessed on 24 June 2015.

Madhusree Chatterjee, 'At 86, Badal Sircar frenziedly writes, reads plays', New Delhi, 10 March (IANS), https://in.news.yahoo.com/86-badal-sircar-frenziedly-writes-reads-plays-20110309-193859-055.html, accessed on 24 June 2015.

Other Sources

'Plays in a National Perspective', Round Table–I, 28–30 November 1996, organised by Natya Shodh Sansthan (NSS), at the Bharatiya Bhasha Parishad Conference Room, Kolkata. From the NSS archives.

INDEX

ABOUT THE AUTHOR

Anjum Katyal has been the Chief Editor, Seagull Books, Calcutta (1987–2006) and Editor, *Seagull Theatre Quarterly* (1994–2004), as well as the Web Editor, Saregama-HMV (2006–11) and Editor, *Art and the City*, a web magazine on the contemporary arts in India (2010–13). As the editorial head of a specialist arts publisher, she was responsible for a broad range of books on art and culture between 1987 and 2006. She is the author of *Habib Tanvir: Towards an Inclusive Theatre* (SAGE, 2012). She has translated Habib Tanvir's *Charandas Chor* and *Hirma ki Amar Kahani* (*The Living Tale of Hirma*), as well as Usha Ganguli's *Rudali* and stories by Mahasweta Devi and Meera Mukherjee. She is translating Habib Tanvir's *Bahadur Kalarin*. She has been involved in organising several exhibitions of contemporary art, as well as writing catalogues for exhibitions by Chittrovanu Mazumdar, Somnath Hore, Manu Parekh, Madhvi Parekh, Reba Hore and Nasreen Moochhala. She has a background in education and teacher training. A published poet, she also sings the blues, and writes on theatre and the visual arts.